Tracks, Tires & Wires

PUBLIC TRANSPORTATION in California's Santa Clara Valley

Interurbans Special 78

By

Charles S. McCaleb

INTERURBAN PRESS

Glendale, California • 1981

DUST JACKET PAINTING

The light of a fine spring morning bathes downtown San Jose. It is 1914, and a Peninsular interurban arrives from Los Gatos, having all of Market Street nearly to itself. A city car waits to cross at right. Automobiles are still a rich man's toy; the electric cars are every man's transportation.

(By Mike Kotowski)

BACK COVER PHOTO

Peninsular 52, a 1903 American Car Co. product, lays over in San Jose before another dash to the blossom fields, circa 1929. This car has survived, and runs again today at the California Railway Museum, Rio Vista Junction, California. Even in 1929 the car was beginning to show its age. (J.C. Gordon Photo from Charles Smallwood and Henry E. Morse Jr. Collection)

FRONT ENDSHEET

A Peninsular 50-class car southbound on Market Street halts at San Fernando Street during a 1907 parade in San Jose. At right is St. Joseph's Church and a corner of the former Carnegie Library Building. Famed electric light tower looms in the background.

(J.C. Gordon Photo from Henry E. Morse Jr. Collection)

REAR ENDSHEET

Car 8 is eastbound on Santa Clara Street at First Street, San Jose, about 1908. Wooden streetcars of this type were discontinued by San Jose Railroads during the 1920s after introduction of the Birney Safety Cars. Long skirts, parasols, and horse-drawn ice cream wagon are the nostalgic stuff of yesteryear. (The Association of Metropolitan San Jose)

Tracks, Tires and Wires

Library of Congress Cataloguing in Publication Data

McCaleb, Charles S., 1927-
    Tracks, tires, and wires.

    (Interurbans special; no. 78)
    Bibliography: p.
    Includes index.
    1. Local transit—California—San Jose—History. 2. Local transit—California—Santa Clara Valley—History. I. Title. II. Series.
    HE4491.S4932M37   388.4′09794′74   81-13712
    ISBN 0-916374-48-3   AACR2

First printing: 1981

Dedicated to my father, Charles Albert McCaleb, and to
my dear friend, Fredrick William Schilla,
both of whom were extraordinary men.

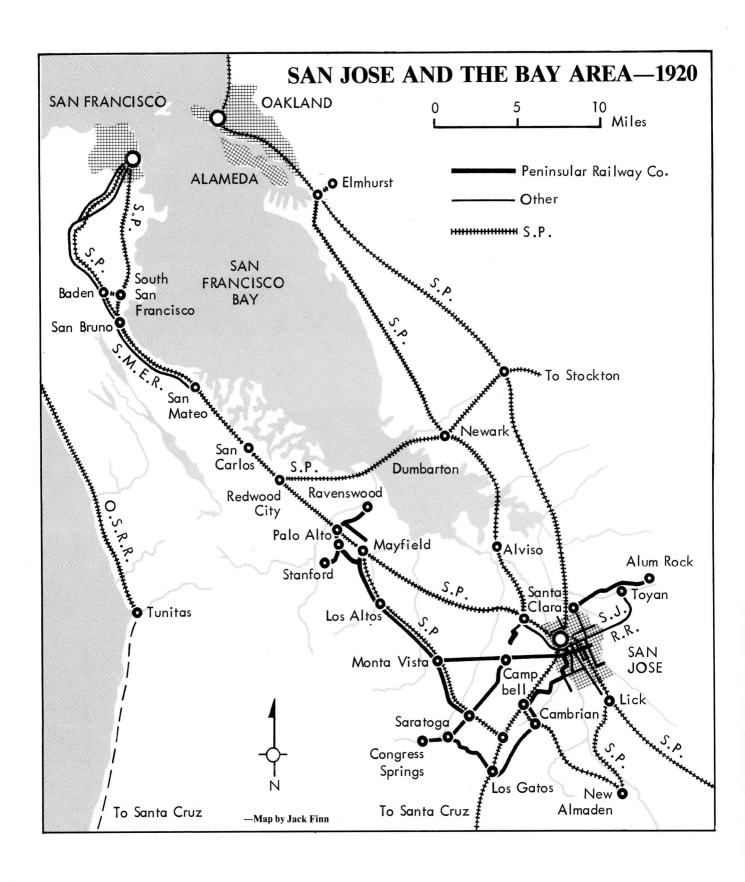

SAN JOSE AND THE BAY AREA—1920

0   5   10   Miles

━━━━━ Peninsular Railway Co.

───── Other

++++++++ S.P.

SAN FRANCISCO

OAKLAND

ALAMEDA

Elmhurst

SAN FRANCISCO BAY

S.P.

S.P.

S.P.

To Stockton

S.P.

Baden

South San Francisco

San Bruno

S.M.E.R.

San Mateo

Newark

San Carlos

S.P.

Dumbarton

Redwood City

Ravenswood

O.S.R.R.

Palo Alto

Mayfield

Alviso

Alum Rock

Stanford

Toyan

Santa Clara

S.J.

Tunitas

Los Altos

S.P

S.P

SAN JOSE

Monta Vista

Camp bell

Lick

Cambrian

Saratoga

S.P.

Congress Springs

Los Gatos

New Almaden

To Santa Cruz

To Santa Cruz

N

—Map by Jack Finn

Prologue

GEOGRAPHY has profoundly influenced the transit history of California's teeming Santa Clara County—or South Bay as it is called—now the nation's 20th largest urban area. A glance at the map shows why. Most of its residents, some 1.27 million at last count, live in a central valley cradling the lower end of San Francisco Bay. The principal city is San Jose (population 600,000). At one time the South Bay was mainly agricultural; now it is heavily industrialized, nicknamed "Silicon Valley" for its concentration of electronics manufacturing. Flanking the valley on two sides are mountain ranges: the Diablos on the east and the Santa Cruz Mountains on the west and southwest, both part of the Coast Ranges. The Diablos, extending southward from the Sacramento-San Joaquin delta northeast of Oakland, are broken locally only by Niles Canyon 25 miles north of San Jose and by Pacheco Pass, opposite Gilroy, 40 miles south. Otherwise there is no convenient rail access eastward to California's broad San Joaquin Valley. The Santa Cruz Mountains, running south from San Francisco, likewise afford no easy route for rail development although a railroad with two long tunnels once ran through San Jose to the coastal city of Santa Cruz.

To the southeast the county opens into a series of valleys cut off from the San Joaquin Valley and eventually pinched out by the Coast Ranges. Only to the north is it truly open, sweeping up the shores of San Francisco Bay to the cities of Oakland on the east (the East Bay) and San Francisco on the west (the Peninsula), some 50 miles above San Jose.

It was from this direction, then, that transportation first reached the South Bay: stages (1850) and bay steamers (1860s) from San Francisco; railroads from San Francisco (1864) and from Oakland (1869) with transcontinental service that year through Stockton and Niles Canyon. For about a decade some Eastern trains terminated at San Jose; ultimately they all went to Oakland when the Central Pacific Railroad (Southern Pacific) began direct service from Sacramento via Carquinez Strait (1880), a shorter route than through Stockton. The bay steamers stopped carrying passengers in 1875. The stages disappeared. Through rail service to Los Angeles did not commence for another 20 years. That left the South Bay with only regional rail—always looking northward for its transcontinental connections—but also free to explore its own transit future, which it did with a special flavor that lasts today.

The basic arrangement is this. Northward from San Jose, up the peninsula, runs the Southern Pacific's commute rail line to San Francisco, the spine of local transit. Despite many abortive attempts, the San Jose-Oakland (East Bay) route never really developed; once it offered train service, but for the past several decades it has been handled exclusively by buses. (Amtrak now operates north-south trains through San Jose and Oakland; local buses meet the Bay Area Rapid Transit District railhead at Fremont, in Alameda County.) Some South Bay transit lines— once streetcar and interurban routes, now bus routes—feed and support the S. P. commute line, meeting it at several places. Others provide a cross-grid extending throughout the central valley and running down as far as Gilroy. This structure developed during the horsecar days (1868-1901), lasted through the electric and corporate eras (1887-1939), and persists even today during the public era (since 1973) in which local bus service is provided by the Santa Clara County Transit District (County Transit).

Some of the stories told here relate to the birth and development of South Bay transit. Others tell of the many unsuccessful struggles to dislodge the mighty S. P. with schemes as provocative, in some instances, as they were unworkable. One returns to a time when horsecar companies battled for business in San Jose, trolleys rumbled through Palo Alto, and the Peninsular's big red cars whizzed down country lanes toward Los Gatos, Monta Vista, or the Blossom Festival at Saratoga. Told again are some of the most memorable stories from yesteryear: of the morning when a street railway was disabled by pinkeye, the afternoon when a horsecar nag chased two frightened little girls out of their kitchen into the barnyard, of high-jinks on the San Jose Birney cars and the Stanford Toonerville, and the day when San Jose residents could bring trolley operations to a halt

Looking east from Second and San Antonio streets in 1876. From left to right are the First Baptist Tabernacle, Temple Bickur Cholim, the State Normal School, and First Congregational Church.
(S.P. Saunders Photo from San Jose Historic Landmarks Commission)

Often their stories are told in the original words preserved in council and court documents, in county histories and contemporary newspaper accounts which contain many details never previously reported. Among these records are some examples of remarkably eloquent writing, such as author Mary Field's 1878 portrait of San Jose's historic Alameda: "...like sentinels arrayed/a triple line of willows cast a league of flickering shade." In 1871 Historian Frederic Hall saw the newly completed county courthouse through the eyes of an architect:

"The magnificent Court-house, the finest in the State, and next to the State house the most splended edifice, was commenced this summer (1866) and finished in 1868. From whatever direction chance brings the visitor to San Jose, the first object that greets his eye is the strong-ribbed and gracefully curved dome which surmounts this grand and spacious structure. The earliest light which comes streaming through the pearly gates of Morn smiles upon its noble facade, fashioned after the forms modeled by the artistic hand of Pericles, to adorn the Athenian city, to attract the Athenian gaze; and the last rays of the setting sun linger and play in rose and purple tints on its glassy dome. This splendid edifice of the Roman Corinthian Order is situated on the west side of First Street opposite St. James Square."

No less eloquent was Hall in behalf of the new California State Normal School, now San Jose State University, the cornerstone of which was laid October 20, 1870: "This edifice will stand facing westward, that the inmates of the palatial pile, whose sight may become wearied by the view of man's printed theory of nature, may, at the closing hour of study, be refreshed by a glance at Nature herself; in beholding the setting sun as he leads away the parting day, and leaves behind a gorgeous imagery, in rose, purpose, and golden tints arrayed in aweful majesty athwart the living sky; beneath which, the serrated mountains, azured in the dye of distance, seem the supporting columns of the heavenly dome."

merely by probing the rails with a metal umbrella handle "just to see the sparks fly." There are personal accounts and photographs of the great 1906 earthquake plus descriptions of other disasters such as runaway cars, the big carbarn fire of 1905, the floods of 1911, and the Coyote Bridge collapse of 1917.

Mostly this story is a testimonial to the people who built and operated the South Bay rail and bus systems, among them several of the most colorful personalities ever to parade across a local scene:

- Opera lover Sam Bishop, the 300-pound frontiersman who dropped a bundle trying to bring electric streetcars to San Jose
- Jacob Rich, the retired tailor who once turned down $325,000 for a trolley line that brought him to financial ruin
- Ex-banker Jim Henry, who wagered his trolley empire on a turn of the cards
- F. M. "Borax" Smith, whose turn-of-the-century ambitions included an Oakland-San Jose interurban road and a transbay tunnel to San Francisco
- Promoter Jim Rea, who built the South Bay's first interurban line
- John Parkinson, the "father of Palo Alto streetcars," who claimed to have made and lost a fortune in Palo Alto and, in retrospect, couldn't have picked a better place to do either
- John Martin, founder of a utility empire, who especially relished battling the S. P.
- Mining heir Lewis Hanchett, progenitor of the Los Angeles Union Station, who didn't relish a fray but never quit fighting.

In preparing this book I'm indebted to railfans Randolph (Rudy) Brandt, Francis Guido, Jim Harrison, Norman Holmes, Dave Mitchell, Henry Morse, Willys Peck, Jack Perry, Vernon Sappers, Charley Smallwood, Lorin Silleman, Paul Trimble, Will Whittaker, and Bill Wulf, several of whose photographs and brief biographies appear at the back. County Transit chief Jim Graebner not only reviewed the text but also opened his files and those of several colleagues. Jim Gibson checked data in State Public Utilities Commission files; Bob Burrowes provided information on early bus operations in the county. Dave Nelson and my son, Don McCaleb, helped with the research. Several people volunteered information and photographs, among them Lew Bohnett, Palo Alto architect George Cody, Stanford historian Rixford Snyder, and George C. Praisewater and Dorothy Keeler of the California Pioneers of Santa Clara County. Former county historian Clyde Arbuckle was ready at all times to verify data, supply background color, and provide anecdotes, several of which appear in the book.

I am indebted to the San Jose Public Library (especially George Aldrich, Lynn Vermillion, and George Kobayashi) and to the Palo Alto Public Library (especially Ruth Wilson) for their assistance in gathering information and also, in some cases, photographs. I acknowledge the help of the San Jose Historical Museum and the contributions not only of Dr. Walter Warren, who's done so much to promote local history in the Santa Clara Valley, but also of the many newspaper writers and historians who paid such careful attention to what people told them about the past.

April 1981   **Charles S. McCaleb**
                                              San Jose, California

Contents

This horsecar is broad-gauge No. 12, on Franklin Street, Santa Clara, about 1880. It is not self-propelled; the horse is on the other end, hidden from the cameraman.

(Charles Smallwood and Henry E. Morse Jr. Collections)

1. Horsecar Days

ON A SUNNY DAY in November, more than a century ago, San Jose's first horsecar set out from First and Santa Clara streets bound for the town of Santa Clara, three and a half miles away. Among dignitaries aboard the gaily painted little car were genial Samuel Addison Bishop, "father" of San Jose's local transit system, attorney John Hendley Moore, rancher Dwight Jay Burnett, Dr. James Clark Cobb, attorney Charles Silent, and others who had helped bring about this pioneering venture, the San Jose and Santa Clara Railroad.

It was a festive moment. Wine had been drunk and speeches given at an opening ceremony attended by civic leaders of both communities but, curiously enough, not by the local press. Editor James J. Owen of the *San Jose Mercury* was elsewhere reporting an earthquake. Editor William A. January of the rival *Santa Clara Argus* sent his regrets; he noted the event, however, congratulating Bishop and company for completing the line and bemoaning his ill fortune at being away when a "free lunch, free ride, or free wine" was to be had.

Westward along Santa Clara Street plodded the little car, past Notre Dame College and out across the wooden bridges spanning the Guadalupe River and Los Gatos Creek. Ahead lay the proud Alameda, its triple line of willows grown into a leafy double tunnel. The rails ran up the north center of this historic road

to the bend opposite Agricultural Park, where they swung onto higher ground at the east side, beneath the trees. Here the houses began to thin out. Onward clacked the horsecar in a northwesterly direction past the Fredericksburg Brewery and Cook's Pond, whose proximity to the car tracks later led to passage of an ordinance forbidding duck hunting from streetcars. On past Santa Clara College it rolled, finally turning westward along Franklin Street to reach its Santa Clara terminus at Franklin and Main.

The date of this first run was November 1, 1868. The trip took 45 minutes. On November 4, the San Jose and Santa Clara established regular service between the two communities, and the West had what has been claimed to be its first interurban horsecar line.

1. Early Days on The Alameda

If rail travel was new to The Alameda (which means tree-shaded way), not so was public transportation by stages and accommodation wagons. The avenue, laid out and planted in 1799 by Father Magin de Catala, had long been regarded as the safest road over the flatlands from San Jose to Mission Santa Clara, offering protection from wolves and other predators. It became the natural route for stage lines linking San Francisco with San Jose, commencing in the fall of 1849 when John W. Whisman, later proprietor of a prosperous flour mill in the canyon above McCartysville (now Saratoga), began operating a mule- and mustang-drawn coach down the peninsula. Reportedly this was California's first stage line. The next year he was running coaches to San Jose via Alviso, charging $35 for a one-way trip. Things were expensive those days, as now, but that fare must have seemed excessive even to Whisman; he slashed it to $32 or its equivalent—two ounces of gold—when he wiped Alviso off his schedule.

In April 1850 Ackley and Morrison began tri-weekly service to San Jose with a nine-hour run from San Francisco. Warren Hall and Jared Crandall bought out Whisman in late 1850 and, the following July, cut his San Jose fare in half, offering semi-weekly service. In 1853 they commenced daily service and announced another big reduction, advertised January 13 on the front page of the San Francisco *Daily Alta California*:

> "Stage Line for San Jose. Hall & Crandall, Proprietors.—Fare reduced. On and after the 15th inst., the price of passage to San Jose will be reduced to $10. The stage leaves Berford & Co.'s office (in the California Exchange, corner of Clay and Kearny Streets) every morning at 8 o'clock precisely; also, the Mansion House, in San Jose, daily at 7 o'clock A.M.
>
> "At considerable expense, two new and very superior coaches have been added to the line, thereby promoting the comfort of passengers. All the sandy part of the road is planked; the stages now make the trip in very quick time.
>
> "The Agent of the line will be happy to give passengers any information or advice that may be needed."

Even at reduced rates, the San Jose-San Francisco stage business was a moneymaker. It was safe to predict that local coaches would soon make their appearance, seeking to scalp off the lucrative short-haul trade between San Jose and Santa Clara. That happened in the late 1850s when one Captain Ham established a local omnibus line he sold in 1860 to Whisman, who in turn peddled it two years later to G. A. Seaver. Seaver also bought up a competing line started by Emil Train. Popular William (Billy) Fitts, one of Ham's drivers, founded his own line in 1861. Business was so good that Levi Millard in October 1863 started yet another line, a four-horse omnibus that ran to McCartysville via Santa Clara. The local stages, like their intercity counterparts, operated on The Alameda between San Jose and Santa Clara, their drivers usually preferring a three-mile trip through the avenue to a tortuous six-mile journey over the fields.

One must say "usually" because, despite its heavy use, The Alameda was in poor condition. The beautiful arching willows, protection though they were, shaded the roadway and kept it boggy long after the surrounding open lands dried out. The avenue was not paved or even graded. During winter months it was nearly impassable. Stage drivers trying to keep to their schedules steered around the ruts and mudholes, sometimes taking to the fields in frustration. Tales are told of discouraged passengers slogging knee-deep in their Sunday best, shoulders to the mired wheels, hoping to free the stage and continue their journey.

In 1862 a Santa Claran named Hiram Shartzer set out to improve conditions on the avenue, organizing his Alameda Turnpike Company and securing a county franchise to operate it as a toll road. The county guaranteed him an 18% annual return on his improvements and promised to repay his full investment in 1872 when the franchise expired. Shartzer graded and partly filled the road and erected toll gates, charging a dime for buggies, 25¢ for double teams, and a special $1 daily rate for stages. The stage drivers paid the dollar although the improve-

ments were modest; heavy shade still kept the road a quagmire, and coaches still got stuck in the mud.

With completion of the San Francisco and San Jose steam railroad to San Jose in January 1864—a celebration marked locally by wide acclaim—the city's population increased rapidly and so did business for the local stages. Competition among the omnibus lines was spirited. Patrons paid 25¢ for a one-way ride between San Jose and Santa Clara, the only public alternative being a hack costing much more. According to Gus England, $5 was the going rate for young blades intent on impressing their lady fair and enjoying her exclusive company on a trip up The Alameda. The stages were full most of the time.

By 1867 real estate values in San Jose had soared. The rich Santa Clara Valley lands around the city were planted in orchards that returned bountiful harvests. Trade was booming. Houses were scarce, commanding $4,000 or more. A half acre of good commercial land brought up to $18,000. Churches and schools were under construction. A $150,000 county courthouse, hailed locally as the "finest building of its kind in the United States," was nearing completion.

It was this scene that greeted Sam Bishop on his arrival in San Jose, $200,000 in his pocket and an interest in taking on almost any project of merit. He was destined to become one of the city's most colorful and respected leaders, both in vision and in avoirdupois.

2. Bishop Promotes Horsecar Line

Affable Samuel Addison Bishop—at 42 an accomplished politician, businessman, and soldier of fortune—had come to San Jose by a circuitous route from his native Virginia. From Missouri, in 1849, he emigrated to California by oxen team over the old Santa Fe Trail, hiking 700 miles across the deserts when the wagons broke down. For a time, hoping to uncover gold, he built dams on the Stanislaus and Merced Rivers, only to see the dams wash out in the floods of 1850.

The Mariposa Indian War of 1851 brought him command of a military company that ran down Chief Tenaya in the Yosemite Valley. Briefly an Indian trader, he was named State Superintendent of Indian Affairs by President Millard Fillmore. In this capacity he moved the Indian tribes of the San Joaquin Valley to Fort Tejon, in Southern California, where he located in 1853.

The government next asked Bishop to build a military road from the Colorado River across Arizona and New Mexico. This also he undertook, fighting off an attack by 1,500 Indians near the river. His party of 42 men with camels, pack-mules, and wagons fended off the Indians for 17 days until Federal troops arrived on the scene.

Bishop then bought up a large land grant in northern Los Angeles County—the Castaic grant, sometimes called Castic—and went heavily into cattle ranching, running herds to Inyo County in the early 1860s to market beef to the newly discovered Comstock Lode mines. That is how the town of Bishop got its name. He later helped to organize Kern County, serving as one of its first supervisors. Eventually he came to San Jose, admitting that he intended to escape the rigors of frontier life.

If this 300-pound trailblazer had come north to escape the frontier, he had not come to rest. Inactivity bored him. Among his interests were mining, lumbering, real estate, finance, and transportation, all of which he intended to pursue.

By year's end 1867 Bishop was deeply involved in his pursuits. He was buying real estate with an eye to the future and already had been instrumental in laying out plans for the new San Jose Savings Bank, of which he was to become vice president. Never one to hide his light, he moved as a familiar and esteemed figure in the city's business circles, to which he tuned a

In the 1880s The Alameda had a long line of trees and a horsecar line. Though heavy shadows make confirmation difficult, the car appears to be operated by a Franciscan friar.

(Harre Demoro Collection)

sensitive ear. Word soon reached him of a scheme that caught his fancy.

San Jose's politicians and businessmen had come to regard Shartzer's Alameda toll road with impatience. Not only were improvements slow to materialize, but the opening of free roads through the nearby fields cut deeply into the tollway's revenues, forcing the county to make good its 18% guarantee. In these days of prosperity, argued the businessmen, why put up with the mudholes and pay for the privilege? Proposals were afoot to buy back the franchise and improve the road at county expense. Of more interest to Bishop was talk of an alternative plan he heartedly endorsed—construction of a horse railroad or some other kind of all-weather transit line to Santa Clara.

Bishop must have viewed rights to the Santa Clara horse railroad as a rich plum ready for harvest. The Alameda's stage lines would prove no competition. The railroad would be a moneymaker and could easily become a springboard for promoting his real estate interests. Beyond this lay the possibility of yet another profitable venture: a rail line from San Jose to the nearby port of Alviso, where the bay steamers from San Francisco put in. This was lucrative trade involving the transport of Santa Clara Valley produce to San Francisco and manufactured goods to San Jose. Prospects for the seven-mile line to Alviso had been the subject of local speculation for many years. Bishop reasoned that the road's length made it impractical for horses. So perhaps another kind of locomotion could be devised for the Alviso run—a pneumatic or steam engine of some kind—which in turn could be used on the Santa Clara horsecar line.

Bishop cut short his speculations. Rumor had it that several groups were eyeing the Santa Clara franchise, and his first task was to enlist allies in a road of his own making. This he hastened to do, offering front money, expertise, and know-how around the state capital. His leadership was welcomed.

Plans soon emerged for a line that would pass through the heart of San Jose along its main artery, Santa Clara Street, extending from Coyote Creek on the east to the entrance of The Alameda turnpike on the northwest. There the horsecar road would take to the fields, arriving at Santa Clara by a route roughly parallel to The Alameda. Local franchises having been obtained, Bishop and associates submitted a bill to the state legislature asking permission to operate a railroad in the county, as was the custom of the day.

February 1868 brought news of a prospective competitor, a "wooden horse railroad" that would strike out for Santa Clara in a northwesterly direction through Stockton Avenue and Elm Street, passing by the campus of the University of the Pacific. This road, though never built, was also sanctioned locally and sent to the state legislature for ratification.

Negotiations by the county to buy out Shartzer's turnpike franchise had now begun in earnest, Shartzer asking $28,000 and county officials offering less. Hope was expressed that compromise might soon by reached. Bishop and his cronies watched the proceedings with special interest, the outcome affecting as it would the route of their horsecar line from the end of Santa Clara Street.

On March 24, 1868, action by the state legislature "formed

an association to run and maintain a horse railroad within Santa Clara County under franchises granted to Charles Silent, D. Murphy, D. B. Moody, S. A. Bishop and their associates." Reported the *Mercury:* "The company are to commence on Santa Clara Street at the Coyote bridge in San Jose and run up Santa Clara Street to near the toll gate, and thence on a line to the town of Santa Clara, and are to have the road finished in two years and the entire line in three years." The line thus contemplated was about 4½ miles long.

Bishop's association was incorporated July 9 as the *San Jose and Santa Clara Railroad Company,* to operate 40 years with a capital of $200,000. Less than $10,000 was actually raised or needed at this time. The chairman and principal shareholder was Bishop, with an investment of $4000. Moore and Burnett each contributed $1000, the other shareholders lesser amounts. In addition to Bishop, Moore, and Burnett, the incorporators were Silent, Lewis H. Van Schaick, Isaac Branham, Samuel Q. Broughton, John Trimble, Thomas Bodley, and Adolph Pfister, soon to be mayor of San Jose. Bishop became president of the fledgling company with Dr. Benjamin Bryant vice president, Dr. Cobb treasurer, and Silent secretary.

Close cooperation maintained between the company and the local governing bodies. The railroad, seeking to avoid buying a private right of way, committed itself to building on The Alameda when and if purchased by the county, promising to keep the avenue in good repair for 20 years. "We believe we express the wishes of a large majority," commented the *Merc-*

ury, "when we urge the County Board of Supervisors to take the company at their offer and immediately abate the toll-gate nuisance." The *Argus* concurred.

August brought welcome news that the county had succeeded in buying out Shartzer for $16,500, the railroad company contributing $500 toward the purchase. Down went the toll gate, and the railroad completed its survey for a line along the east side of The Alameda. The *Argus* took this occasion to commend the railroad promoters and offer a sincere if somewhat precocious editorial blessing:

> "We look upon the project as one of the most promising enterprises ever proposed to the people of this section. Wherever these roads have been established, they have been successful, and this system of cheap conveyance is now very generally established throughout all large cities of the United States. Here our proposed line will run on a road about three miles in length along the beautiful Alameda, sheltered by those fine old trees which were planted by the Mission fathers. When built, the road will immediately stimulate settlement along the route, and so rapid will this become that we venture to predict that San Jose and Santa Clara will, in less than two years thereafter, be but one continuous city."

The company now advertised for a contractor to supply materials and build the road. Specifications called for lightweight iron T-rail and standard gauge. Bids were opened August 15, the contract going to S. J. Davenport of San Francisco. Construc-

A San Jose landmark was the Fredericksburg Brewery between Cinnabar and Lenzen streets near The Alameda carbarn. The brewery was the dividing point for horsecar fares: 5¢ from downtown San Jose, 5¢ more to Santa Clara. A water tower with a Falstaff emblem marked the site in 1981.

(San Jose Historical Museum)

tion began with a formal ground-breaking ceremony August 31 in front of Charlie Youngworth's property opposite Crandall's grocery, reported in some detail by the *Mercury*:

> "At the request of Mr. Davenport, the contractor, Judge Peckham, in a neat and appropriate speech, presented the president of the company, Mr. Bishop, with a pick and shovel. The latter proceeded to excavate a bed for the first tie. Mr. Bishop performed his task skillfully, handling the pick with a dexterity creditable with his muscle.
>
> "The judge spoke of San Jose and Santa Clara as he saw them 23 years ago in contrast with their present citified appearance, paying a glowing tribute to the industry and enterprise which have made them what they are.
>
> "After the ceremonies, the crowd adjourned to Crandall's where they partook of a sumptuous lunch and cracked sundry and divers bottles of champagne.
>
> "The road will be completed and the cars running on or about the first of October. This road will add immensely to the value of property along The Alameda.
>
> "The track is to be laid on the north side of the carriage way within the avenue of trees, but it will not at all interfere with the road as a public drive."

What matter that the projected October 1 start date was optimistic: the work was now under way in earnest. That fall the avenue echoed with the rumble of construction wagons, the shouts of workers, and the clang of iron rails being laid in place on hardwood ties. The roadbed was finished by the end of October and, as we know, the line officially opened for business November 4 from downtown San Jose to Santa Clara.

3. Horsecars Prove Popular

From the beginning, the new horsecar line to Santa Clara enjoyed great popularity. The company established a 10¢ fare between the communities: 5¢ from downtown San Jose to the Fredericksburg Brewery, a nickel from the brewery to Santa Clara. The stages continued to charge 25¢. Though the stages, drawn by two mustangs, raced along much faster in dry weather, most patrons favored the cheaper rate and relative reliability of the bobtail cars. Bishop experimented briefly with two-horse cars, then settled for a smaller one-nag version with seats on top. Passengers wishing to embellish their summertime journey sometimes rode on the roof, ducking down when the branches of the overhanging trees scraped their heads. Martin Corcoran's Cameron House at the corner of Franklin and Main Streets, Santa Clara—claimed by its proprietor to be "one of the best family hotels outside of San Francisco, with a fine livery stable connected"—became a favored gathering place of local travelers, served both by horsecars and by stages.

A. C. Clevenger of Santa Clara later recalled that it took him about an hour and three quarters to drive his plodding horsecar back and forth to Santa Clara. "The one-track affair had switches at semi-convenient intervals," he related, "to allow cars to pass. Only six cars and six drivers were the whole show. You collected fares during the switch wait. Spring's store sold trolley tickets to the public. The conductors were forbidden to carry tickets although some used their own money to provide tickets for regular riders."

Dominic Higgins, another of the drivers, confirmed these recollections. "The company's working force was made up of 12 to 14 men consisting of six regular drivers, plus two stable hands," Higgins reported. "The pay was $40 to $55 per month. You could get board and room in back of the barns located near the halfway point, if you so desired, for about $12 a month. The horses were changed each round trip."

Stages ran spasmodically on The Alameda through 1876 (and again briefly in the late 1880s), but the 10¢ horsecar fare and the winter floods of 1868-69 effectively ended competition from the omnibus lines. Two went out of business in 1868. In August 1868 Fitts placed in service "another new and beautiful omnibus purchased about a year ago before the horse railroad assumed tangible shape and delayed for several months by an accident to the vessel on which it was shipped." Its arrival was inopportune. Fitts struggled along with his omnibus line another few months but capitulated in 1869, joining ranks with the horsecar company as a driver and eventually serving as superintendent (1883-90).

The floods of 1868-69 also took their toll on the horsecar line. Water from the Guadalupe River and Los Gatos Creek spilled over the banks, backing up behind the high grade of the horsecar line on West Santa Clara Street. The flood finally broke over the tracks, inundating the lowlands between the Guadalupe and Notre Dame College, sweeping away about 100 feet of track. The main portion of the city from Third to Seventh Streets was said to be under water to a depth of several inches.

Bishop repaired his line as soon as possible. In August 1869 he extended his horse railroad eastward along Santa Clara Street to Coyote Creek, completing in one year the terms of his franchise. His first objective was satisfied. Bishop was ready to move on toward further goals.

4. Experiment with Steam Cars

On July 6, 1870, Bishop obtained general permission from the County Board of Supervisors to devise means for "conducting cars by steam, pony, or pneumatic propelling power" as alternatives to the company's restrictive horsecar franchise. Bishop's chief interest at this time was steam propulsion, which seemed to offer promise. The 4½ mile run from the Coyote to Santa Clara was proving inconveniently long for his horses; steam-powered cars might solve this problem and also pave the way for his Alviso line.

Accordingly, he shopped among manufacturers and obtained a steam dummy which, in 1871, he proposed to test. San Jose's city fathers were reluctant to allow the experiment but agreed in July to let him proceed. The dummy was successfully tested July 11. Soon afterward, the Common Council (San Jose's governing board) decided that it did not have the right, after all, to upset the restrictions of Bishop's franchise. Horses said the franchise, so horses it had to be. Permission was withdrawn by the council and the experiment discontinued.

On October 17, however, the council made amends, granting Bishop rights to build, operate, and maintain a horse railroad southward on First Street from the San Pedro Street steam railroad depot (San Pedro and Dame Streets) to a terminus between Martha and Bestor Streets. Thus Bishop gained San Jose's second-most-valuable street railroad franchise, serving the railroad station and bisecting the city at right angles to his Santa Clara street route.

To build the new line he teamed up with attorney Peter O. Minor and Judge Augustus L. Rhodes, a wagon train captain of the 1850s, in an unincorporated partnership, the *First Street Railroad*. Construction contracts were let. Because of the narrow streets through which the new road would pass, Bishop chose a three-foot gauge which later became standardized throughout the city, requiring the entire system to be rebuilt after the turn of the century. Sixteen-pound T-rail was specified. Construction was delayed by severe flooding during the winter 1871-72, so the line was not completed for nearly six months. On April 5, 1872, with appropriate flourishes, horsecars made their debut on the First Street Railroad.

During the early 1870s Bishop made strenuous efforts to

build the narrow-gauge line to Alviso. Pending completion of the road, Captains A. Nelson and N. E. Anderson, proprietors of the only passenger ferry to serve the South Bay, put a fast boat on their San Francisco-Alviso run, skipping most of the customary stops. Then came the crash of 1873, ending Bishop's aspirations for an Alviso railroad. Nelson and Anderson threw in the sponge a couple of years later, turning their attention to San Francisco-Delta ferry service.

Failure of the Alviso plans in no way slowed Bishop in his other areas of endeavor. He bought an interest in the Sierra Lumber Company, of which he became a director. He invested heavily in and became president of the San Jose Homestead Association, organized to buy acreage in East San Jose and subdivide it into lots. With six others he purchased, in 1876, the Stayton quicksilver and antimony mines in the mountains separating San Benito and Fresno Counties.

The big man was now a celebrity on the San Jose streets, through which he reportedly drove in a tiny phaeton, lopsided from his weight, behind a skinny, rat-tailed mare. He was Grand Mogul of the 1876 Centennial Celebration, heading the July 4 parade in a little willow carriage drawn by a donkey. At the old California Theater he was an avid first-nighter, so popular that the gallery traditionally applauded when he entered. He turned and graciously acknowledged the applause with a bow.

5. Competitors Emerge

Thus far Sam Bishop had had no competitors in the horsecar business, but San Jose's leading citizens were watching and carefully evaluating his progress. By 1875 certain facts had become apparent: namely, that horsecar lines could be profitable (or at least break even) and that, as Bishop had earlier predicted, property values skyrocketed wherever horsecars ran. This latter fact was the key to the sudden scramble that began in 1875 to secure routes to all corners of the city.

The first competitor was the *North Side Horse Railroad Company* incorporated June 16, 1875, for 50 years. This company projected and built a three-foot-gauge line of 16-pound T-rail from First and St. John Streets to Fourteenth (now Seventeenth) Street near the northeast city limits. The incorporators were some of the city's most influential citizens: Judge Davis Divine, who in the 1860s had helped bring the steam railroad to San Jose; former State Senator William S. McMurtry and John Y. McMillan, partners in a sawmill venture on Los Gatos Creek above Lexington; mill owner Cornelius G. Harrison, now involved with Silent and others in several projects in Santa Cruz County; Stillman A. Moulton; DeWitt C. Vestal; and William P. Dougherty. McMurtry and Harrison, who were to play important roles in San Jose transit, each subscribed $1,000 of the $8,000 initial capital. Divine was the first president, stepping down in favor of McMurtry. McMillin became secretary and Harrison manager of the road.

Construction proceeded quickly, and the North Side line opened for business with two horsecars by the end of the year.

The next franchise went February 11, 1876, to developers of the Bird tract—"Hop Ranch," some called it—in southwestern San Jose. Their company, the *Market Street and Willow Glen Railroad,* planned a three-foot-gauge line of 20-pound T-rail from Market and Santa Clara Streets, near the city center, to open land in The Willows (Willow Glen). Rights were secured to strike out across the Bird tract by "the best available route" to the corner of Lincoln Avenue and Willow Street.

The Market Street and Willow Glen Railroad was formally incorporated February 23, 1876, with J. J. Denny, John Auzerais, Isaac Bird, Francois J. Sauffrignon, and Calvert T. Bird as directors. Calvert Bird was named president, Auzerais

treasurer, and importer Ferdinand Brassy secretary. Others sharing in the franchise were orchardist Sylvester Newhall, auctioneer John C. Bland, merchant Thaddeus W. Spring (one of San Jose's wealthiest men), Oliver Cottle, James R. Lowe, Rufus C. Swan, and Charles B. Hensley, owner of hacks, proprietor of the San Jose Music Hall, and heir to a family fortune.

Construction plans were somewhat more complicated than those for the North Side road, since the Willow Glen line required a bridge over the Guadalupe River at San Salvador Street (now Auzerais Avenue). This the city agreed to build if the horsecar company footed half the bill because, as the city council observed, the bridge was being built expressly for the company. Agreement was reached and the bridge completed by June 6. Rails were installed on the span during construction, the first time this had happened in San Jose. By August 4 the company had on hand 5,400 redwood ties from Watsonville, with another 1,000 to come. According to the *Mercury,* two horsecars (Nos. 1 and 2), manufactured by Faulkner, were stored in the Central Market: "perfect beauties, by the way."

Cars made their appearance on the Willow Glen line the evening of Saturday, January 6, 1877. Formal ceremonies a week later (January 13) marked the inauguration of regular service, the company setting fares at a nickel a ride or 25 tickets to the dollar.

Scarcely a month had passed (February 26) before the Common Council approved another franchise, this time from the budding *South East Side Horse Railroad, Company* proposed by McMurtry, McMillin, and Harrison of the North Side road. The northern terminus of this three-foot-gauge line would be Second and St. John streets, already served by the North Side road. The southern terminus would be Ninth and Reed streets, where the new company would build its car stables on the southwest corner. The 1½ mile line was intended to serve the State Normal School (San Carlos Street) and O'Donnell's famous Zoological Gardens and Park (Ninth and William streets). History records that the line did well until the gardens, which cost only a quarter to visit, closed, and the area was subdivided into residential tracts.

McMurtry, McMillin, and Harrison were joined in this request by Samuel W. Boring, realtor and later mayor of San Jose, and by a man named Jacob Rich, tailor and hatter by trade, who was to become the second of San Jose's giants of local transportation.

The South East Side company began calling in subscriptions March 5, 1877. On March 14 it filed articles of incorporation with the County Clerk's Office, establishing a term of 50 years and capital of $20,000 shared equally among its five directors. Two cars were ordered and a construction contract let locally to Henry Craven, who began laying track in March along San Carlos Street.

By April 8 a connection had been made at Second and St. John streets to tracks of the North Side Railroad, whose cars now ran south to Second and Santa Clara streets instead of terminating at First and St. John. Rumors circulated about an impending merger of the North Side and South East Side companies. Craven's crews finished their work April 14, and the line formally opened April 25 using a car borrowed from the North Side line; those ordered by the new company had not yet arrived. The *Mercury* commended both Craven and the new railroad on the excellence of the roadbed.

The rumors about consolidation proved well founded when, on May 19, the companies jointly announced end-to-end schedules from the northern terminus of the North Side road (Fourteenth Street at the city limits) to the southern terminus of the South East Side line (Ninth and Reed). The additional rolling stock arrived, and three cars were set on the run. John W. Morris, later ticket agent for the San Jose and Santa Clara, announced that he was now prepared to solicit advertising for the new company as well as for Bishop's road.

6. Battle of Julian Street

Meanwhile, San Jose's first horsecar feud was about to ignite and it involved Bishop, who until now had taken a more or less indulgent attitude toward the competition. Transfers were standard, for example, between Bishop's First Street Railroad and the Willow Glen line, although rails of the two companies didn't actually meet.

It was the Willow Glen company that touched a match to the controversy, petitioning the common council April 2, 1877, to extend its line from Market and Santa Clara Streets to the San Pedro Street railroad depot. Not only would this put Willow Glen in direct competition with Bishop's First Street line, but it also called for parallel trackage along Julian and San Pedro Streets, Bishop's route to the station. Bishop and the Julian Street property owners protested angrily, contending that the street was too narrow for two horsecar lines. On April 10, however, the council gave Willow Glen an unofficial go-ahead with its plans. The official ordinance presumably would be forthcoming.

Jacob Rich arrived on the scene in 1853 and soon became a traction force in San Jose to be reckoned with.

(San Jose Historic Landmarks Commission)

Willow Glen was not of a mind to wait. It hired Henry Craven, who, having completed the South East Side line, sent tracklayers into Julian Street April 16 in behalf of the Willow Glen company. Trouble emerged in the person of one Thomas McCloskey, irate property owner, who planted himself in the path of the crews and refused to budge. When the workmen tried to drive their plows forward, McCloskey took to clubbing the horses. A fight broke out, McCloskey decking Ferdinand Brassy of the Willow Glen company and landing in jail. From behind bars the property owner swore out complaints against Brassy, Craven, and Calvert Bird, president of the Willow Glen company, claiming they had no right to build the road without official approval. (On this point, agreed the *Mercury*, McCloskey was absolutely correct.)

All this commotion was to no avail. By candlelight Craven's crews proceeded uninterrupted with their work, before a large crowd that was loathe to disperse. The following morning (April 17), Willow Glen cars were on hand near the depot to meet all trains. Brassy and McCloskey dropped their charges that same day. Bishop was left with no more option than to summarily cancel his transfer arrangements with the Willow Glen company, which he did. Willow Glen reciprocated in kind May 2.

Bishop himself went to the city fathers May 16 asking permission to extend his First Street Railroad south from Reed Street to the city limits, to enter Oak Hill Cemetery (a city property), and to quarry rock from a large hill on the cemetery grounds. On June 6 he petitioned the County Board of Supervisors for a franchise along Monterey Road from the city limits to the cemetery. He got the necessary approvals, but his plan to enter the cemetery met such public opposition that Bishop voluntarily withdrew the idea.

Instead, he gained a much more valuable franchise: the right to extend his East Santa Clara Street line across Coyote Creek to the Homestead Association tracts in East San Jose, considerably enhancing their value. This extension required replacement of the existing Santa Clara Street bridge, which was down by mid-June 1877. The new bridge was accepted August 6, and Bishop ran his first cars to McLaughlin Avenue, in East San Jose, on November 6.

7. Rich Builds Santa Clara Line

Bishop, vexed by his brief fracas with the Willow Glen company, soon was to encounter the first direct threat to his horsecar dominance in the persistent attentions of Jacob Rich, shareholder in the South East Side road. As early as 1878 it must have been obvious to the big man that Rich had the determination and resourcefulness to give him a run for his money.

Rich, a Polish Jew just a year younger than Bishop, had learned tailoring and hat-making in Germany as a young man, putting his trades to work briefly in Manchester, England, before emigrating to New York in 1851 or 1852. With his partner and close friend Herman Levy, he came west to San Francisco, finally settling in San Jose in 1853. The partners built a prosperous tailoring business, Rich & Levy, which occupied quarters on Market Street. Rich, a frugal and industrious man, salted away his money, increasing it through banking and real estate. He served as director of several local banks and organized Temple Bickur Cholim, the first Jewish synagogue in San Jose, of which he was for years president and a main supporter.

Rich had practically retired from business when, in the mid-1870s, he got involved in the South East Side road and decided that streetcars were a likely place to invest his life savings. He attacked the challenge with a vengeance.

Here was a man quite unlike Bishop in most respects. Bishop, a flambouyant and gregarious soul, built by instinct and was sensitive to the shifting winds of public opinion. He liked speculative ventures and ran his horsecar lines in trusting fashion with an open hand. Rich was by nature a retiring man whose chief recreation was playing chess, who built with precision and stood firm as a rock on his personal convictions. Rich liked the intricacies of banking and ran his horsecar operations at tight rein, meticulously checking and cross-checking the books. It was said that Rich knew each car's receipts almost to the penny and summarily dealt with any conductor he suspected of pocketing fares: "There are two kinds of people I can't stand to work for me—hoodoos and cheats. You are a hoodoo, so out you must go."

As regards personal principles, Rich brooked no compromise. What was right, to him, was right. For years it was a familiar sight at the old Auzerais House to see him sitting among his cronies enjoying a game of chess, which he dearly loved. Yet in 1876, on learning of his father's death in Europe, he gave up the game completely, honoring in this fashion the memory of his father. When bad times in later years forced Rich into bankruptcy, he gave his health trying to repay his creditors and struggled to live long enough to win one of his most important battles—clearing his name of all debts.

Always Rich's principles were tempered by mercy and reason. As a bank director he often raised his voice against foreclosure: "For heaven's sake, give the man another show." It is an irony of this story that this upright and honorable man had no "second show" himself when the going got rough.

8. Contest in the Courts

Rich made the first move, in 1878, when the two men squared off to battle over Bishop's exclusive right to the Santa Clara run. On April 1 he and McMurtry won approval from the city council to build a narrow-gauge line on Santa Clara Street from Second Street to the west city limits, paralleling Bishop's San Jose and Santa Clara Railroad every foot of the way. Next they got a county franchise to extend their line westward on Santa Clara Street from the city limits to Stockton Avenue, then northward on Stockton to the University of the Pacific and west on University Avenue to The Alameda, where the line was to terminate. This route was nearly identical with that of the "wooden horse railroad" of the late 1860s, which never came into being.

Failing to block Rich in the city council, Bishop turned to the courts, obtaining on June 28 a temporary injunction to halt construction of the new line. At question was only that portion of Rich's railroad that paralleled Bishop's tracks within the corporate limits of San Jose (Santa Clara Street from Second Street to the west city limits). Bishop's lawyers had dug up a provision of the state civil code—Section 499—forbidding competing lines from running more than five blocks side by side on the same street in a city.

The local court subsequently found against Bishop, frankly admitting it couldn't decide whether the parallel trackage exceeded five blocks. It dissolved the injunction. Bishop rushed an appeal to the California Supreme Court, and Rich rushed to complete his line. Rich won. Service commenced over part of the new line in the fall of 1878.

Cars were procured from a local source, Fitzgerald Brothers, on Santa Clara Street. Frames were ash and the sides white poplar. The seats were cut to shape in three pieces from a log, then glued together. The new cars, which according to the *Mercury* "could hardly be excelled for excellence of workmanship or beauty of finish," were pressed into service as soon as delivered.

While Bishop was awaiting decision on his appeal to the Supreme Court, Rich made the final moves to complete his Santa Clara line. On December 4 the county granted him and McMurtry rights to extend their tracks on University Avenue across The Alameda to Union Avenue, then northward through the Chapman and Davis tract to the Santa Clara town line. Five days later, Santa Clara's trustees extended them a franchise to Main and Franklin Streets contingent on their establishing a stable in Santa Clara for cars and horses. Rich and McMurtry willingly complied.

By mid-January 1879, construction of the Santa Clara extension was well under way. Service was inaugurated the evening of Saturday, February 22, for the benefit of patrons attending a play at the University of the Pacific. Regular service began February 26 with 15-minute headway, Rich's cars alternating with those of the San Jose and Santa Clara so that a horsecar set out for Santa Clara every 7½ minutes. "Those who aren't satisfied with this service," gloated the *Mercury*, "can walk."

On March 8 Rich and associates incorporated the *Peoples Horse Railroad Company* for 50 years, based on the new franchises and construction. Capital was set at $100,000, trustees Rich, McMurtry, McMillin, Harrison, and Boring each subscribing $20,000. Rich became president of the new company and Harrison treasurer. Oliver Habadere was named superintendent. Intent to buy the South East Side Horse Railroad Company's franchises, track, and equipment was spelled out in the corporate documents and soon accomplished, the South East Side road disappearing as a legal entity.

9. Horsecar Feud Continues

One who was not gloating over the new service was Bishop. As feared, Rich's newer equipment and faster operating schedules cut into his business. The bright blue cars of the Peoples line handled most of the college traffic, a good share of the intercity traffic to Santa Clara, and even some of Bishop's Agricultural Park trade. Rich had won the first round. However, round two was about to begin.

Late in 1879 the California Supreme Court handed down its decision on Bishop's appeal. The parallel trackage on Santa Clara Street, it said, was in fact illegal as defined by the civil code. Bishop promptly went to Superior Court for judgment pursuant to the Supreme Court decision. A temporary injunction was served January 7, 1880, halting traffic on Rich's Santa Clara Street route between Second Street and the bridge over Los Gatos Creek. Accommodation wagons were hurriedly pressed into service. Rich promised to restore regular service shortly. It was a rash promise.

The case was heard in Superior Court February 16, and to Judge David Belden, one of San Jose's most distinguished jurists, the proceedings evidently bordered on the ridiculous. Though the general intent of the law was clear, the code referred only to streets within a city's corporate limits. What about roads and streets outside the city? Also, Belden asked, where was the word "block" defined? How long was a block? Did the law mean existing blocks or those that might be created? But the law was the law. After taking the legislators to task for fuzzy definition, Judge Belden made the injunction permanent.

Rich had not been idle in the meantime. With the practiced skill of a chessmaster he had flooded the city council January 26 with petitions that would lop two blocks off his Santa Clara Street run and allow him to reconnect his severed lines. He asked reaffirmation of his right to run on Santa Clara Street, and put in for alternative franchises if that right were denied him.

The councilmen, apparently in general sympathy with Rich, deferred action on his proposals pending final word from Judge Belden. His decision once rendered, they gave Rich permission February 23 to reconnect his lines via St. John and Market streets if he wished. On February 26 they franchised an alternate route via San Fernando and Market Streets and affirmed his right to run parallel with the San Jose and Santa Clara on Santa Clara Street from Market Street to Los Gatos Creek—a lawful distance, opined the city attorney.

Thus Rich untied the legal knot that for almost two months had blocked him from restoring through service to Santa Clara, but not before a matter of personal principle almost did him in.

Whichever route he chose (St. John Street or San Fernando Street), Rich had to run his cars on Market Street, long the exclusive domain of the Willow Glen company. The councilmen, perhaps fearing a repetition of the Santa Clara Street court case, insisted as a condition of the franchise that Rich use rails of the Willow Glen road "and none other" on Market Street.

A Santa Clara Street horsecar beneath the Electric Tower being erected at the corner of Market Street, 1881. *San Jose Mercury* editor **J.J. Owen** **was a prime mover in the project to light San Jose from overhead.**
(San Jose Historic Landmarks Commission)

Rich at once rose in indignation: how could the council be party to such a precedent, forcing competing companies to use the same tracks? Who would pay the maintenance costs? What about conflicts in schedules? If these were the franchise conditions, well, then....

The threat went unvoiced. Rich's associate, Samuel Boring, quickly interceded and agreed to the terms. General law dictated under such circumstances that the new company would pay half the original cost and running expenses, Boring said. The Peoples Horse Railroad would gladly comply. The franchises went through without a hitch.

Rich chose to restore service via San Fernando Street, past the old Chinatown that stood across from St. Joseph's Church at San Fernando and Market. Connections were made in short order, and Rich's cars resumed their downtown run to Santa Clara.

In short order, also, Bishop's lawyers were back in court, again enjoining Rich and claiming this time that the city attorney was wrong in his February 26 opinion. Judge Belden summarily disagreed in a September 16 decision: "In the present case the road of the defendant (Rich) is not upon the street of the San Jose and Santa Clara Company for a distance of over five blocks...and the plaintiff's writ is dismissed."

Predictably, Bishop filed an appeal to Judge Belden's verdict. Pending decision on this appeal, the Bishop-Rich feud persisted throughout 1881 as a stalemate.

10. Rich Extends Empire

As the 1870s drew to a close, two of the city's pioneering horsecar companies—Bishop's First Street line and Calvert Bird's Market Street and Willow Glen road—began a series of ownership changes that eventually put both in the hands of Jacob Rich and Rich into partnership with Sam Bishop.

The First Street company was the first to go. Perhaps frustrated by the Santa Clara Street legal shenanigans and disappointed over his failure to extend the First Street line, Bishop sold it to Major Franklin C. Bethel, a retired merchant of 10 years' local residence. Bethel hired Dominick Higgins, a jolly Irishman and veteran conductor from Bishop's Santa Clara line, as his conductor and unofficial section boss, superintendent, and general manager. Reportedly Higgins consulted his employer only when facing a deficit.

Bethel sought to extend the road at both ends and obtained a franchise to build northward along First Street from Julian to Hobson Street. He sold the road early in 1881, however, before the plans could materialize. The new owner was George F. Baker, former county superintendent of schools and, at 31, president pro-tem of the California State Senate. A lawyer, he had been elected to the senate in 1879 as one of California's youngest legislators.

Baker also planned to extend the First Street road, gaining rights in August 1881 to build southward along Monterey Road to the gates of Oak Hill Cemetery (one of Bishop's 1877 targets). But the senator sickened late in 1881 and died the following March. Control of the First Street Railroad had now passed to Rich.

Calvert Bird wrestled with the financial ills of the Willow Glen company until the spring of 1880, when he decided to pursue a law career and stepped down as company president in favor of merchant Felix Gambert, a Frenchman who had emigrated to San Jose in the mid-1860's. From the beginning this road had been built mainly to stimulate property values in The Willows and to that end had been successful; land selling for $10 an acre in 1854-55 now brought as much as $300 an acre. But there weren't enough people in southwestern San Jose to support the horsecar line, which had become a financial drain on the developers.

Various schemes were put forth to save the road, but it tumbled into bankruptcy before they bore fruit. On March 10, 1881, the railroad "together with the franchise, road-bed, equipments and real estate belonging thereto" were sold at public auction to Gambert for $6500. Presiding over the sale was auctioneer John C. Bland, an unusual experience indeed for an original incorporator of the company.

Gambert struggled with the line into 1882, leasing it to the industrious Higgins in an effort to rid himself of the burdens. Higgins tried to make a go of it, hiring two other drivers. But the little cars, traversing fields of mustard so high they were sometimes hidden from view, often made the run nearly empty. Service was finally suspended south of William and Lincoln (now Bird) avenues.

Rich had now associated himself with the Market Street and Willow Glen as a stockholder. Soon it, too, would be his company.

11. Trials of Horsecar Conductors

To the delight and sometimes consternation of San Joseans, horsecars by the early 1880s were well woven into the fabric of community life. To ride the cars was to invite adventure. To depend on them regularly was to court frustration. How could one depend on streetcars that had a mind of their own and set out for home when nobody was looking? How could one anticipate the day when pinkeye would incapacitate an entire railroad?

The conductors who kept the cars running despite all tribulations deserved a special place of honor in the community and often were accorded it. For the equivalent of $200 a month or less (in today's buying power), men such as Higgins, Billy Fitts, William J. Tran, and Wallace J. Malone drove, collected fares and, if necessary, repaired the track. They were obliged always to look after the horses, sometimes working from 5 a.m. to midnight or even later. On dance and theater nights they took personal responsibility for hauling out the cars and making sure their patrons got home safely, whatever the hour.

Troublesome to the conductors were the schoolboys who traveled between San Jose and Santa Clara. Most cars, as noted, were equipped with a ladder for the convenience of passengers who wanted to sun themselves on the roof during summer months. The boys soon learned to climb upstairs and station themselves at the back of the car, teetering it so that the front rose and fell. When the conductor stopped the car and clambered up to investigate, innocence reigned. Sometimes the students became unmanageable, wresting the reins away from the conductor and telling him to go inside while they drove to Santa Clara. For the boys this was a supreme adventure.

Handling the bobtail cars, behind unpredictable horses, occasionally involved the conductors in bizarre accidents. Few were so spectacular as the "Carnival of Collisions" reported by the *Mercury* December 12, 1878:

"Yesterday afternoon about a quarter past 2 o'clock while Archie McGinnes, the driver of one of Charlie Hensley's hacks, was standing against the walls of the Auzerais House watching his team, some person from the upper stories threw out a roll of paper, which in its descent struck one of the horses, causing them to spring away without a single premonitory movement. Archie at once sprang toward them but was kept from their heads by an intervening buggy. As they reached the center of the street they were almost in contact with a horse and light wagon, driven by William Berringer. Seeing his danger, Mr. Berringer struck the runaway horses with his whip over their heads, caus-

ing them to swerve to the right, but not sufficient to clear the vehicles, which collided with a crash, and Mr. Berringer was landed in the street upon his head after a brief aerial voyage.

"This interruption delayed the runaways but a moment, and they sprang forward at renewed speed. About ten steps from the scene of the first collision there stood a devoted wagon loaded with tin roofing, long sections of water spout, tools, and one fated man. In a second there was another crash and the air was filled with humming plates of tin, sections of new shaped water spout, and in the midst, and fully ten feet high, was the vision of a man, whose arms and legs resembled in their motions the fans of a windmill in a storm.

"But the wild team paused not to ponder on its conquests, for right in front of it was a streetcar belonging to the First Street line, and though the hope seemed a forlorn one it hesitated not. Sweeping by the rear end of the car so close as to brush the body of the 'off' horse (both seemed a little off), the wheels of the hack struck the rear platform with tremendous force, throwing it from the track, turning it almost at right angles across the road and rolling it completely over amid the crash of rending wood and jingling glass much to the apparent discomfort and danger of a single occupant, a lady, who was made a part of the debris, which for a few moments performed rapid revolutions around the bottom, sides and ceiling of the car as it rapidly changed the position thereof. Here, at the supreme moment of victory, the victors fell entangled with their victim and their harness.

"An immense crowd at once assembled, and the imprisoned lady, Miss Clarkson, was liberated serene and smiling, replying to the question, 'Are you injured, Madam' with a placid, 'No, I thank you; neither frightened nor hurt.'

"Of the other collisions no more serious results are to be recorded. Mr. Berringer was unhurt, as was also the driver of the tin wagon, and none of horses or vehicles, except the streetcar, was much injured. That chariot was pretty thoroughly wrecked. Strange to state, the hack was utterly uninjured, save for a single paint scratch. During the excitement a dozen other horses attempted to run away, but were caught and held, and thus prevented."

Most vexatious to the conductors were the firecrackers thrown beneath their cars during Fourth of July week to scare the horses. The conductors finally attached brooms to the fronts of their cars to sweep the tracks, but the horses still bolted their traces with alarming results:

"The narrow-gauge railroad company is prostituting a thousand-dollar circus horse to the menial task of drawing a streetcar," declared the *San Jose Daily Morning Times* on July 6, 1882. Startled by a firecracker thrown under his heels, the horse in question freed himself from his car and bolted down Fourth Street, the conductor in hot pursuit. Veering sharply, the animal raced toward the porch of the Edward Johnson cottage where Johnson and his son in law, Oliver Chapman, were whiling away the afternoon. The two men barely scrambled out of the way. The horse cleared three porch chairs and, entering the house, knocked down Mrs. Chapman in the doorway to the kitchen. Undaunted, he then chased two screaming little girls across the yard into the stable, where he dumped them unceremoniously. Only then was the horse secured and led back to his car. Fortunately, related the *Times*, there were no serious injuries, Mrs. Chapman and the girls suffering only minor bruises.

12. Bishop-Rich Merger

By February 1882 Rich owned or virtually controlled all the city's horsecar roads except Bishop's San Jose and Santa Clara, against which the Rich-McMurtry narrow-gauge Peoples line to Santa Clara was in fierce competition. Pending was another decision by the California Supreme Court about the parallel trackage on Santa Clara Street (that old five-block question). The *Times* on February 3 described the extent of horsecar service then available to the community:

A narrow-gauge horsecar on The Alameda near Stockton Avenue, San Jose, about 1883. Note that the car, originally the property of Peoples Horse Railroad, is now relettered San Jose and Santa Clara Horse Railroad.   (San Jose Historic Landmarks Commission)

"Five lines of horse railroads are in operation now. The two going to Santa Clara are the principal. The one along The Alameda, of which Samuel A. Bishop is president, is five miles in length. Ten cars are constantly running on it every 15 minutes and about 40 horses are in use. The other Santa Clara road through Stockton Avenue and the Chapman tract is owned by Jacob Rich & Co. This is about five miles long. Seven cars and 30 horses are engaged running over it. The other roads are the North-Side, the First Street and the Willow Glen. Jacob Rich is a stockholder of the last named and the owner of the others. The North-Side Railroad has two cars running every half-hour, and employs eight horses. The Willow Glen road has two cars and six horses, and that on First Street has three cars and fourteen horses. The North-Side runs to the corner of San Fernando and Second Streets. The Willow Glen and the First Street runs (sic) from the S.P.R.R. depot, the former to the corner of William and Lincoln Avenues, the latter to the end of First Street. The length of these three aggregates about eight miles.

"Travel during this part of the year is light. The comparison with other months is best seen on the Santa Clara lines, the others not getting many passengers at any period of the year. The privilege granted to the former owner (Baker) of the First Street line to extend the track to Oak Hill Cemetery is not likely to be used at present."

The Bishop-Rich feud ended abruptly in April 1882. Tiring of the legal maneuvers and failing to find any more laws to throw at Rich, Bishop instead threw in the sponge and took his opponent into partnership. The merger was announced April 14:

"The San Jose and Santa Clara and the Peoples Horse Railroad Companies of this city have consolidated. Jacob Rich will be president of the new company; S. A. Bishop, superintendent, and J. W. Morris, ticket agent. Four or five of the through cars on the narrow-gauge line will be discontinued, and the terminus for them will be at the University of the Pacific. The two roads running in opposition did not pay. Hence, the consolidation. The combination includes all the street railway lines in the city except the North Side."

The exception was not well taken, and the facts were a bit scrambled. On April 22, franchises, equipment, and property of the North Side company went to the Peoples Horse Railroad for a nominal sum. The Peoples road was then sold lock, stock, and barrel to the San Jose and Santa Clara for $66,666, putting both companies under control of the latter. McMurtry, chief stockholder of the consolidated company (400 shares), was named president of the North Side subsidiary and a director of the San Jose and Santa Clara. Bishop was reinstalled as president of the San Jose and Santa Clara with John Moore secretary, Rich treasurer, and John Auzerais rounding out the directorate.

Bishop dropped his legal action against Rich, resulting May 26 in dismissal of all charges against his new treasurer.

On April 27—a fortnight after the merger—the San Jose and Santa Clara acquired land for new car stables. Chosen as the site was the former San Jose Pleasure Gardens, a triangular plot bounded by Los Gatos Creek and the Guadalupe River and fronting on Santa Clara Street. At the same time, plans were announced to add a third rail to Bishop's standard-gauge tracks on The Alameda beyond University Avenue, allowing Rich's narrow-gauge cars to follow the shorter route to Santa Clara. Standard-gauge service was halted May 1 at University Avenue to permit installation of the third rail. Traffic was restored May 23 to within a half mile of Santa Clara center. The dual line officially opened for business June 20.

Rich's original road west of The Alameda, through the Chapman and Davis tract, was subsequently abandoned and the rails removed.

13. Rich Expands Other Lines

Merger of the Peoples Railroad into the San Jose and Santa Clara had not affected Rich's control of the First Street line nor his holdings in the struggling Market Street and Willow Glen road. He quickly acquired the latter from Gambert, who moved on to become proprietor of a Santa Cruz resort, and set about to make joint operations of the two horsecar companies more profitable. In June 1882 he asked permission from the county supervisors to build a branch on Willow Street westward from First Street, striking the present Willow Glen line near the Bird Avenue stables. He then proposed to abandon the Willow Glen road's unprofitable run through the Hop Ranch, providing service on Auzerais Avenue (formerly San Salvador Street) only to Delmas Avenue.

Approval came in December 1882, Rich standing $125 of the cost to widen the Willow Street bridge over the Guadalupe. On March 7, 1883, workmen began removing the Hop Ranch tracks. The Willow Street branch was opened to Lincoln Avenue April 14, and cars of the First Street Railroad first ran up Willow to Lincoln the following day.

On April 16 the county supervisors voted 3-2 to deny Rich rights to extend his new branch southward on Lincoln from Willow to Minnesota Avenue. It was not until after the 1887 depression that this extension was completed.

April 1883 also marked the start of a new Southern Pacific railroad depot at the head of Market Street (Market Street Extension). The old San Pedro Street depot was relegated to freight service. Rich got approval to remove his San Pedro and Julian Street trackage to the old depot, and completed a spur in Bassett Street from First to Market, though not without objections from the San Jose common council.

In 1888 Rich ran a line westward along San Fernando Street toward the "narrow-gauge" depot of the South Pacific Coast Railroad (absorbed by the Southern Pacific). This branch turned south at Delmas Avenue, tying into the end of the old Market Street and Willow Glen at Auzerais Avenue. Service was then discontinued over his Market Street route and the rails removed from Market, Vine Street, and Auzerais Avenue.

The North Side road remained essentially unchanged throughout this decade, the only item of note being a rerouting of its line east of Twelfth Street from Jackson to Empire.

Bishop and Rich continued to improve service on their San Jose and Santa Clara horsecar line during the mid-1880s, modifying switches and generally ironing out wrinkles in the system.

The running time between terminals was bettered by as much as 10 minutes, though Santa Clara was still 45 minutes from downtown San Jose. Dramatic improvements from the East— steam-powered cars, cables, and electric street railways—had now captured the partners' attention. They were absorbed in plans for what they hoped would be the West's first electric streetcar line. As described in Chapter 2 (The Electric Age), this effort was to prove an ignominious failure in which the partners lost a fortune and, eventually, control of the San Jose and Santa Clara.

14. Last of the Bobtail Cars

The indomitable little horsecars continued to show the way during the electrification period. Slow they were but reliable. They shared rails with their electric cousins well into the 1890s, and there were many instances in which horsecar drivers, plodding up behind stalled electrics, had to maneuver their cars clean off the rails and around the electrics to reach their destinations.

Keeping the horsecars running while bridges were rebuilt over the Guadalupe River and Los Gatos Creek proved one of the company's biggest headaches. The removal of these spans, required by construction of the new electric, not only interrupted service between San Jose and Santa Clara but also isolated the company's main car stables, sitting as they were on land between the bridges.

The first span to go, in the summer of 1887, was the one over Los Gatos Creek. Cars on the San Jose side were now cut off from the main stables. Bishop and Rich halted service on opposite sides of the creek, transferring passengers over a narrow footbridge built by the city. That this new structure also served other purposes was observed by the *Times* in early September:

> "Some complaint has been started that the temporary bridge made for the convenience of foot passengers is being used for horses of the horse cars to the detriment of the safety of the foot travelers. The bridge is but about three feet in width, and there is consequently no room for horse and man to pass. This fact has caused a crushed toe for one man, and an uncomfortable squeeze for another. With a little care on the part of drivers and others who cross the bridge no inconvenience need be occasioned."

The bridge over the Guadalupe was demolished in late September, Bishop and Rich installing a temporary horsecar bridge some 40 feet to the north. Cars from The Alameda and Stockton Avenue passed over this span to the main stables, causing no further inconvenience to passengers or the company.

Travel resumed over both rebuilt bridges in December.

Regular horsecar service continued on Santa Clara Street until March 1888, when workmen began removing Bishop's old standard-gauge tracks east of Market Street. Patrons assumed that the railroad would run its narrow-gauge horsecars eastward on rails of the new electric but were doomed to disappointment, Bishop and Rich choosing instead to bundle the passengers into accommodation wagons. Connections were severed that month between the South East and North Side lines but restored March 30, the company adding a switch at Second Street to permit South East cars to enter tracks of the electric road. In July the standard-gauge horsecar rails were removed from The Alameda.

During the next three months, horses often were pressed into service to replace the failing electrics or haul trailers built for the new road. All branches except the Santa Clara-Alameda main line continued to operate under horsepower. In Santa Clara, where the town trustees never allowed the Bishop-Rich electric into town, passengers rode accommodation wagons or the old standard-gauge horsecars, transferring to electrics at the San Jose city limits. Eventual failure of the electric in October 1888 put horsecars back on Santa Clara Street and The Alameda for more than 18 months. Not until April 1890 did bobtail cars finally disappear from the avenue.

Horsecars were replaced by electrics on Rich's First Street line in February 1891. His San Fernando-Delmas branch was converted to electricity in 1892 and his Willow Street branch— the last of his original horsecar routes—in the mid-1890s. A new line Rich built, out Third and Seventh streets, operated briefly with horsecars, then went to electricity.

The old narrow-gauge Stockton Avenue line to the University of the Pacific operated by horsecar well into the 1890s. Plans to electrify this line, which dated to the previous decade, never materialized, and the franchise was finally abandoned. The same fate befell the old Ninth and Reed Street line (Second south to San Carlos, then east to Ninth), which was abandoned in favor of a route south on Tenth from Santa Clara Street.

Last to go was the moribund North Side road, sold by Bishop and Rich in the mid-1890s to John B. Harmon. Harmon struggled with declining revenues until 1901 before hanging up the traces, making this horsecar company the oldest from the standpoint of continuous community service—26 years.

A horsecar on Santa Clara Street, San Jose, plods past a parade marking the tercentenary of St. Anoysius' death. The date is June 21, 1891.

(San Jose Historic Landmarks Commission)

36-Gun Salute Marked Arrival of First Train

A 36-gun salute was fired in San Jose when the train arrived. Crowds cheered, bands blared, and the California Guard fired its cannon as the bulbous-stacked locomotive came into the San Pedro Street station, dragging six coaches and several boxcars jammed with excited passengers. Speeches were made and a huge, free barbeque prepared for the crowd.

"It should be a source of pride and gratitude to every true American citizen," declared editor J. J. Owen of the *San Jose Mercury*, "that while we, as a nation, are passing through the fiery surges of a terrible war, we can with one hand build railroads and telegraphs, establish schools for the promotion of science, and wrest from the willing soil its rich treasures and bounteous harvests, while with the other hand we can throttle the hounds that are tearing at the vitals of constitutional liberty. The Pacific railroad is no longer an idle dream slumbering in the brain of the statesmen. It has a tangible shape and a visible reality. We hail the consummation of this enterprise as one of the proudest achievements of our state."

It was truly a momentous occasion, marking completion of the first railroad linking San Jose with the outside world. The date was January 16, 1864, and the train belonged to the old San Francisco and San Jose Railroad, completed more or less on schedule but only after a 14-year struggle.

A railroad down the Peninsula from San Francisco to San Jose had been discussed as early as 1849, partly to heal local wounds caused by removing the state capitol from San Jose. An instrument was created two years later—the *Pacific and Atlantic Railroad Company*—whose founders had big plans for extending the road down to Southern California, then eastward over the mountains and deserts to the Mississippi. Financial and other difficulties beset the company, and the transcontinental plans were scrapped. The company reorganized, then reincorporated again under the name *San Francisco and San Jose Railroad*, securing State permission for a $900,000 stock subscription election in San Francisco, San Mateo, and Santa Clara Counties.

Faced with San Francisco newspaper opposition, this new company dissolved in June of 1860.

Then Santa Clara County, by a 722-vote margin, approved $200,000 for building the road. A fourth company was formed August 18 with C. T. Ryland the only local director but four prominent San Joseans among its backers: Dr. Davis Divine, George B. Polhemus, auctioneer Henry M. Newhall, and James Donahue, founder of San Francisco's Union Iron Works. One of the new company's first moves was to hire contractors Charles McLaughlin and A. H. Houston to build the road.

The new company had severe financial woes. Of some $285,000 in private subscriptions, only $100,000 was ever paid. The directors and contractors took up the rest to prevent market manipulation. There were problems also in getting rights of way, especially through the 2,000-acre Stockton rancho near Santa Clara. When first efforts to gain passage through the rancho were deadlocked and the project was near collapse, Polhemus and Newhall bought the entire tract for $110,000, provided the right of way, and subdivided the rest.

Construction began in May 1861. The railroad advertised for laborers to work for $30 a month and board, advising them to apply at the Stockton rancho. By October 1862 the roadbed was graded and bridged, with ties distributed from San Jose to a point 14 miles from San Francisco. The target completion date was January 1863, but rails and materials were in short supply, due mainly to the Civil War. On October 18, 1863, trains began regular runs from San Francisco to Mayfield (now Palo Alto), connecting with stages to San Jose.

At first there was only one locomotive. A second train was added in February 1864, making it possible to commute between San Francisco and San Jose. The first regular freight train went into service in June 1864.

In 1867 the Central Pacific Railroad bought the San Francisco and San Jose and rechristened it the Northern Division of the *Southern Pacific Railroad*, the name selected by Ryland and associates for the extension they planned to build southward to Gilroy. In January 1868 San Jose gave the new company a 50-year franchise to operate trains through the city on Fourth Street. The Gilroy extension was opened March 16, 1869.

—*Information from Patricia Loomis and George H. McMurry*

The old Southern Pacific station at Market Street in San Jose saw the comings and goings of countless San Francisco–San Jose commute trains, as well as the through trains down the Coast. This turn-of-the-century view shows train 24. (Randolph Brandt Collection)

S.P. commute train 171 with engine 3107 in a 1920s era photo between Mountain View and Santa Clara. Housing subdivisions would come later.

Earlier view was taken at the old San Jose S.P. station.

(Both: Randolph Brandt Collection)

Building the "Underground Electric." TOP: Construction on Santa Clara Street between First and Market. ABOVE: The line extended out The Alameda; note narrow-gauge horsecar at the extreme right, entering from Stockton Avenue. INSET: Samuel A. Bishop, central figure in San Jose's early traction fortunes.

(All: William A. Barstow from *San Jose Mercury News*)

2. The Electric Age

An early view of the narrow-gauge San Jose & Santa Clara line on The Alameda, in the 1890s.
(Vernon J. Sappers Collection)

BY THE MID-1880s San Jose was well on its way to becoming California's most prosperous boom town. The economic storm clouds of recent years had blown away in the winds of optimism. A flood of fresh Eastern money was sending property values soaring once again. Real estate offices were swamped. Hotels and boarding houses were full. Each day brought trainloads of prospective settlers into the Southern Pacific depot, bent on establishing their local fortunes. The newcomers swung down into the dusty streets, got their bearings, and set off on a feverish property hunt, often before they secured lodging. Quite a number went home disappointed; many stayed on.

Mayor C. W. Breyfogle and city officials, determined to keep San Jose abreast of the economic boom, launched a massive improvement program that included six new bridges, paving for the city streets, a new city hall, schools, and more than six miles of sewers. Efforts were made to attract new industry. Advertisements appeared in Eastern newspapers extolling San Jose's charm, equable climate, rich soil, abundant water and, above all, business opportunities.

The time had come for Bishop, Rich, and associates to consider updating the city's antiquated horsecars with something newer, more modern, more efficient. They stood ready to pour up to $500,000 into improvements when and if the governing bodies concurred.

1. Birth of the Underground Electric

Bishop set out first to gauge the response of city and county officials to the idea of modernizing local transit. Then he made a general proposal: an electric road rather than a cable road, with power supplied through overhead wires. Opposition developed. Emotions ran high. Cable proponents pointed to the successes of San Francisco's flourishing cable roads and held out for cables even for San Jose's flat terrain. Supporters of electrification split into two camps: those favoring overhead wires and those opposing them on grounds of danger and unsightliness, who wanted the wires safely buried and out of the way. This latter view became the majority opinion among city councilmen and county supervisors. Bishop's efforts to gain an overhead electric franchise thus came to naught.

Undaunted, the big man intensified his search during 1886 for a motor and power system that would win the approval of city and county officials. One of his trips took him to St. Louis where an experimental three-rail electric streetcar system was being demonstrated, the product of an ambitious 27-year-old Detroit inventor named Frank E. Fisher. Bishop liked the demonstration and accepted Fisher's invitation to visit Highland Park, Michigan, where a full-scale system was being built.

Fisher told him the Highland Park line would save 60% over horsecar operation and 25% over present cable operation. He estimated a 20-minute travel time for his system from downtown San Jose to Santa Clara, compared with Bishop's 45-minute horsecar run.

The San Josean was intrigued. Conversations were sparked, during which Bishop outlined his needs and problems. As he spoke, an idea sprang to the mind of the young Easterner that piqued his inventive curiosity: why couldn't the live power (third) rail, which in the Highland Park system was mounted above ground, be mounted in San Jose below ground, protected from public tinkering? "Hiding" the third rail would for all time assuage the doubts of San Jose's councilmen and supervisors. The men sat down to plan in earnest.

Cars of the new road would run on 20-pound steel rails mounted at street level in the conventional manner. (Bishop chose a three-foot gauge for the new line to make its operations compatible with those of the Stockton Avenue horsecars.) The third rail could be fabricated from 14-pound bar iron and mounted beneath the street in a concrete culvert, or tunnel, cemented on the bottom. Glass insulators could be used to mount the third rail and a companion 5/8-inch copper wire added to improve the iron's current-carrying capacity. Power would be drawn by the car through a slot in the street, similar to the slot of a cable road, by a "contact carriage" attached to the underside of the car.

Manholes would have to be provided at appropriate distances throughout the system, for access to insulators and the third rail. Provision could be made for flushing out the culvert end-to-end with water, to remove mud and debris.

Power would be supplied by a single 250-horsepower dynamo weighing 4½ tons, which if contructed would be the second largest such engine ever built. A dynamo of this size would be capable of maintaining the entire system. Speed would be controlled at the dynamo and in the individual cars, which should be able to average 25 miles an hour over the length of the line.

The men chose the cars they would use: lightweight affairs resembling those of the San Francisco cable roads. Chicago's Pullman Manufacturing Company had prototypes available. Some of the cars—"dummies"—would be equipped with electric motors, while others would be unpowered "trailers" attached to the "dummies" to make trains up to four cars long.

Fisher estimated costs for the complete system at around $500,000. Though the initial cost for the underground conduit would be high—probably about $30,000 a mile—the comparable costs for a cable road in San Jose could run up to $1 million. In conclusion, Fisher offered the full facilities of the Detroit Electrical Works, of which he was manager, to build the necessary equipment and install the system in San Jose.

Bishop bought the idea. Thus it was that an ambitious young inventor, who without benefit of college training had risen from apprentice electrician to head his own firm, came to design San Jose's first electric street railway.

2. Building the Road

Armed with plans, specifications, and financing, Bishop hastened back to the city council and county supervisors for the necessary approvals. It was his hope, he said, that San Jose, rather than San Diego or some other Western city, might have the first electric streetcar line west of the Rockies. Despite opposition, he won his franchises early in 1887.

Bishop and associates now moved with dispatch, reorganizing the company and expanding its capital to $500,000. Contracts were let to Pullman for 12 cars (five of them powered dummies) and to the Detroit Electrical Works for all equipment except the cars. At Fisher's recommendation, the San Francisco Electric Improvement Company was hired to build the road. August J. Bowle, secretary of that firm, was named construction superintendent. Fisher himself became the general operating superintendent.

This was the equipment used on the Fisher Underground Electric Railway in San Jose in the late 1880s.   (Vernon J. Sappers Collection)

Skeptics of the scheme, mainly those who favored cable lines or overhead electrification, publicly expressed mistrust of the "Fisher road" and took the governing boards to task for allowing it to be built. Santa Clara's town trustees demurred on awarding a franchise, claiming they needed more time to study the system's merits.

Though the franchise terms required an early completion of the road, construction was slow to begin. Most bothersome was an acute shortage of cement for the conduits, a concern also of the contractor building the new city hall. The company finished its survey work during the summer and built a section of the road on stilts in front of its Santa Clara Street horsecar stables to show its manner of construction. Opponents took advantage of the delays to level criticism at Bishop and company, sharpened when Fisher wrote from Detroit that "a large number of orders from other electric roads is necessarily delaying the work on the San Jose enterprise." Rich, speaking to a reporter from the *Times*, took occasion to chastise the critics thusly:

> "We must impress upon your mind, and through you the mind of the public, that this matter of building an electric road is no small undertaking. The streets are being improved in such a manner as to be in fine condition for a quarter of a century at least, and therefore, every step must be carefully looked to. The same is true of our road. We are not going to build it for temporary use, but for years of constant service. Therefore, the work, in order to ensure success, must be done well from the foundation upwards."

Construction actually got under way October 5, 1887, crews starting to excavate for the underground conduit on Santa Clara Street between Second and Third. Three miles of rail were reported on the ground, ready to be spiked down as the conduit was completed. Work soon spread to the bridges over the Guadalupe River and Los Gatos Creek and also to The Alameda, where a public hue and cry attended removal of the historic center line of willows. By year's end, much of the road was completed, somewhat quieting the critics. However, political hay was made of an announcement from San Diego December 29 that an electric streetcar in that city had recently climbed an 8½% grade (440 feet to the mile). "The (San Diego) line is four miles long and a decided success," reported the *Mercury*. Thus was San Jose deprived of the distinction of operating the West's first electric traction line.

A slowdown in the road's construction during the winter of 1887-88 was accompanied by news that a prospective rival, the *San Jose and Santa Clara Cable Road Company*, incorporated the previous June, might soon commence building a competing line from San Jose to Santa Clara out North First Street, Hedding Street, and Union Avenue. Lined up behind this venture were some of San Jose's most prominent citizens: State Railroad Commissioner James W. Rea; his real estate partner Thomas S. Montgomery; Almaden Mines Manager J. B. Randol; Santa Claran Frederick C. Franck, later a state senator; and William P. Dougherty, an incorporator of the old North Side Horse Railroad. This group posted a $10,000 performance bond with the city to guarantee completion of the line, which drew considerable popular support.

Bishop, Rich, and associates now pressed for completion of their road. Their first test took place March 16, 1888, at 12:20 a.m., too early in the morning to attract much public attention. Dummy No. 5 left the car stables bound for the Santa Clara town line, carrying 43 passengers who clung to whatever handhold they could grab. One reporter found himself distracted by the pinging of gravel on the car's underside. At length, some 150 yards short of the Agricultural Park, the car slammed to a halt when its contact carriage (or trolley, as it had come to be called) struck the protruding metal cap of an insulator. This abortive trip was the forerunner of trials to come.

Testing of the line continued well in July, unearthing a variety of operating problems. Regular service began in halting fashion July 28 from the car stables to the Santa Clara town line (that town's trustees still reserving judgment on the underground electric). In September the entire road—from Coyote Creek to the Santa Clara line—went into operation, marking the high point in fortunes of the underground electric. Fisher, now on the scene as operating superintendent, gleefully proclaimed that the road had carried 40,000 passengers during Fair week alone, its nickel fare to downtown San Jose decimating hack service to and from the fairgrounds.

3. Failure of the Underground Electric

The underground road continued to be peppered by public criticism both in and out of the council chambers. In August 1888 the city council ordered Bishop to lower his tracks along Santa Clara Street some nine inches "in conformity with the official grade," revising its own December 1887 instructions now claimed to be "unauthorized." This action and others prompted Stephen W. DeLacy, publisher of the *Times* and a supporter of the underground electric, to vent a scathing attack on the road's critics:

> "No one can recall an instance in the history of public enterprise in this state when the founders and projectors were beset with more opposition from the majority of the press and people," DeLacy wrote. He noted the proliferation of rival companies and counter franchise proposals. "The Board of Trade even went so far as to petition the Board of Supervisors if not directly against our home company in favor of a combination without any degree of standing."

Critics gained support as mechanical failures eroded service over the underground road. Its electrical system shorted out time and again, bringing all cars between Santa Clara and East San Jose to a halt. Some of the incidents were particular vexsome, such as one recalled by Mrs. Lida May Gillette, a staunch member of the Women's Christian Temperance Union. On her very first trip, the car on which she was riding stopped in a shower of blue flame and sparks at the corner of Cinnabar Street and The Alameda. "We had to get off," she said, "right there in front of the Fredericksburg Brewery. I was never so mortified in all my life."

On August 7 the city was saddened by news of the death of young Francis L. Grozelier as a result of the electric railroad construction. In February this lad, the only son of ex-councilman Simon G. Grozelier, had fallen into an open trench on Santa Clara Street, sustaining injuries that led to an amputation August 5. After the operation he had weakened and died, the first casualty of the underground electric. The only other known casualty was Edward Jenkins, a workman killed by an electric car the following November while cleaning mud off the tracks.

Operating problems continued to mount. By mid-October 1888, the road was near a complete standstill. Horsecars returned to The Alameda to spell the troubled electrics.

The failure count was nearly unbelievable. Wires burned and broke in the electric motors. Dislodged wires sometimes charged the cars with electricity, shocking motormen and passengers alike. The underground rails expanded and contracted with changes in temperature, cracking or dropping away from the glass insulators; the next car promptly tore out the rails, broke its trolley, and drew up disabled. The failure of one car often put the entire line out of commission. The third rails proved inadequate to carry the required load; double copper wires had to be installed the length of the system. The big dynamo, pride of the Detroit Electrical Works, failed at its job and had be replaced by two, then three, smaller engines. Mud and stones gathered in the conduit during the winter rains, far beyond the capacity of the flushing system.

Public curiosity and malice also played havoc with the underground electric. Malicious damage was reported to rails and connectors. In one case, stones were piled on the tracks, perhaps in hopes of derailing a car. Last, but not least, pedestrians adopted the unfortunate habit of poking their metal umbrella handles into the conduit slot to see the sparks fly. Sparks they saw, and streetcars stopped all along the line.

The shutdown of the electric road led to some fiery debate in the council chambers. "If some action is not taken immediately," declared one councilman, "everybody will have to walk in another week." Tempers were rekindled by failure of the cable road to materialize. By December 1888 this latter road was seen by the council as a speculation—a swindle, some said—to which several councilmen had been privy. One irate councilman had now discovered he couldn't get his money out of land bought along the proposed cable route. He moved for immediate forfeiture of the promoters' performance bond but failed to carry his case; Rea, Montgomery, Randol, and company got back their $10,000.

Bishop, Rich, and associates staggered through the first six months of 1889, absorbing disastrous operating losses and periodically renewing their shaky franchises. By July 1, 1889, bankruptcy was near at hand. The partners that day assessed a $3 per share levy against their capital stock, to be paid before August 5 under threat of sale by public auction. Rumor had it that the city fathers and county supervisors would soon revoke the charters of the San Jose and Santa Clara Railroad. A showdown was imminent.

On July 17, Bishop addressed an urgent petition to the city and county governing boards:

> "Some time since, upon the collapse of our costly endeavor to lay down and operate an electric railroad on The Alameda and through San Jose and Santa Clara, we procured at your hands an extension of time to complete the double-track road to the boundary line of Santa Clara on the west and put the same in good operating order, and are now operating it, we think, in a satisfactory manner. We have also completed the east end of the road to McLaughlin Avenue, which is in successful operation, and have now in good order a double track from said avenue to Santa Clara ready for any motor that will prove satisfactory to the people. We have been corresponding and seeking to procure a satisfactory motor, one better for public service than horses, and we expect to succeed, but as yet have not been able to do so. We feel, however, from the outlook, that we shall be able, in the near future, to obtain one satisfactory to us and to the public.
>
> "We, therefore, respectfully ask that you allow us to continue the use of horses on our said road until such time as a motor can be procured that will be more satisfactory to us and to the public."

July 22 brought the stunning news that the San Jose common council had rejected Bishop's petition and directed him to remove his tracks from the city streets. Bishop revealed his dismay. "Were we permitted to put in operation the overhead wire system we could make the road a great and triumphant success," he asserted. He told of the company's continuing experiments with "smokeless, noiseless steam engines" and disclosed efforts to peddle the underground electric to promoters of the cable road. "Negotiations with these people have not yet broken off," he added tersely.

The county supervisors, more lenient than their city brethren, voted August 6, 1889, to grant Bishop another 60-day extension. The following day, however, a voluminous complaint was filed against the railroad by the San Francisco Electric Improvement Company, alleging $20,000 in unpaid billings and materials over a two-year span.

Bishop washed his hands of Fisher and the San Francisco company in a bitter denunciation August 15: "We have done with the system, and we have done with Mr. Fisher. The system is a failure, and if we should be such fools as to trust him again we would be failures, also." He branded the underground road "an experiment by men who were ignorant of mechanical laws, however well they might be acquainted with those of electricity.... The Electric Improvement Company, finding that we would not accept the road, threw up the job. We went on by ourselves." He and his associates, vowed Bishop, were now resolved to tear up the entire road and start again with an overhead electric system, the local authorities permitting.

Toward this end, Bishop arranged a trip to Seattle in late August to investigate an overhead system installed by the Thomson-Houston Company of Boston, a forerunner of General Electric. Invited as his guests—all expenses paid—were a San Jose councilman, a Santa Clara trustee, and a county supervisor, whose eyewitness accounts he hoped would swing franchise votes in his favor. In this stratagem Bishop was partly successful. The county supervisors in September gave him a 35-year franchise with full rights to develop overhead power. On the strength of this franchise he signed contracts with Thomson-Houston and began removing his slot rails from The Alameda. Santa Clara's trustees followed with a franchise in November, an action that was later overruled by the town president. San Jose's councilmen stood pat, awaiting further developments.

4. Henry Buys Bishop Road

The developments were not long in coming. November 27 brought news of the outright sale by Bishop and associates of the underground electric, Stockton Avenue and Ninth Street horsecar lines. The price was $229,000 and the buyer a well-heeled ex-banker named James H. Henry, who had come to San Jose a year and a half earlier obstensibly to retire. Henry divulged that he owned every outstanding share of stock in the San Jose and Santa Clara and planned to press forward to completion of the overhead electric road.

The story soon got around that circumstance and Henry's impatience had combined to bring him ownership of the railroad. On coming to San Jose from Walnut, Iowa, where he had been president of the Exchange Bank, he fully intended to enjoy life as a retired capitalist. He bought a home on The Alameda, involved himself in local politics, and joined the exclusive Sainte Claire Club, where his custom soon became an afternoon game of cards with his cronies. Never a man to flaunt his wealth, Henry developed a habit of riding the horsecars home for dinner after his card game.

One afternoon, so the story went, he stood fuming at the corner of First and Santa Clara waiting for a car. This particular afternoon the car was more than characteristically late, and the later it got, the more impatient he became. Finally he spun on his heel and walked over to the real estate office of his friend, C.W. Wooster, near the corner. "C.W.," he said, "I'm tired of waiting for those darn cars. Buy up the line for me as fast as you can. I'm going to see what I can do about it."

As we know, Wooster was successful in his charge.

Henry quickly reorganized the San Jose and Santa Clara with himself as president and Wooster, Samuel F. Leib, Franck (of the stillborn cable road), and Campbell T. Settle as directors, W.N. Sheaff was brought in as general superintendent and F.K. Bowden as electrical superintendent. Dropped from the company's directorate were Bishop, Rich, Hiram Mabury, and Ferdinand Brassy, severing for Bishop a 21-year association with the company he helped found. The big man, now in his mid-six-

The electric generators for Henry's road were housed in a brick building on West Santa Clara Street during the 1890s, before power arrived from the Sierras. This retouched photo shows Machinist Percy Carman, Blacksmith Charles Coryell and Engineer George Coleman with the generators.

(F. K. Bowden Photo from *San Jose Mercury News*)

ties, thereafter concentrated on real estate, selling his mining interests but retaining stock in the Sierra Lumber Company. With Rich and others he tried his hand at promoting a local winery whose failure cost him $30,000. At the time of his death— June 3, 1893—Bishop was developing property on Cinnabar Street as a real estate venture. His passing, mourned by the city, closed a colorful chapter in San Jose history.

All told, the partners in the ill-fated underground electric counted their losses at $300,000, Bishop, McMurtry, Rich, and Moore standing most of the deficit. Rich later told confidants that he alone dropped something like $40,000.

On December 11, 1889, with Henry now in control of the San Jose and Santa Clara, the San Jose city council granted a 35-year franchise for overhead power. Santa Clara's town trustees followed suit, this time for real. The Alameda portion of the line went into operation first, on April 4, 1890. By August the road was running full length from Coyote Creek with overhead electrification.

5. Problems of the Overhead Electric

Not that Henry, like his predecessors, did not have his problems with streetcar pioneering. One immediate quandary was the issue of side poles versus center poles from which to hang his trolley wires. Henry preferred side poles, with which the city council concurred. But the county supervisors, backed by San Jose's Board of Trade, insisted on center-pole suspension down the middle of The Alameda, between the double tracks. This had been a condition of their September 1889 franchise agreement with Bishop, said the supervisors. So Henry elected to dig

up the light rails from the unused underground system, from which he made T-poles. They did not last long. Young folks racing their buggies down The Alameda Sunday afternoons ran into them. Sometimes, despite all a conductor could do, a passenger got off the wrong side of the car and got clobbered by a pole. So the county supervisors finally relented, allowing Henry to hang his trolley wires from crosswires as in the city. The T-poles disappeared from The Alameda.

Merely keeping the electric motors in operation was a chief order of business for Henry's electrical shop. The Thomson-Houston G-30 motors were too large for Henry's narrow-gauge cars and, consequently, were mounted too close to the car's wheels on each side. During stormy weather, water sloshed up into the motor, causing shortcircuits. When protective curtains were installed, the motors overheated. Henry's crews finally devised a way to tunnel air to the motor between the curtains but only after several costly experiences with burned coils and armatures.

Also, there was no way to reverse the motors. At the end of each run—rain or shine—the motorman had to get out and reverse his brushes, a time-consuming job. The German-silver rheostat, in a grille cage just behind the middle seat in the cars, was another trouble spot. One day a Normal school girl, her long curls flying loose, had her hair set afire when it worked itself into the grille and touched hot resistance wires inside the cage.

One of the motor problems—a recurring one—led to a San Jose invention later incorporated into streetcars everywhere as standard equipment. As Henry's crews soon discovered, the bone-jarring stops and starts of the early streetcars crystallized and broke wires inside the motor that connected its four armature coils with the commutator. The connections then

A California-type double-trucker of the Alameda Electric Railroad, circa 1899. (Randolph Brandt Collection)

arced, burning the insulation, and nighttime always brought more coils to be wound. The solution was a flexible armature coil devised in 1890 by Bowden, the company's electrical superintendent.

Working late one night in the old brick powerhouse on Santa Clara Street, Bowden found himself weary of making the same old repairs, night after night, to keep the road's six G-30 motors in operation. He was pondering the problem when his hand struck a coil suspended near the worktable. With it came his sudden idea for a flexible coil that could absorb the shocks.

"I told Mr. Henry about it the next day," Bowden recalled, "and he said he was willing to try anything once and to go ahead on the new installation with his blessings." Henry did more than authorize a local experiment. He wired Thomson-Houston to delay shipment of the four additional motors he had ordered until the flexible coil idea could be tested. The Boston firm checked out the invention and later incorporated flexible-coil armatures in their WP motor, successor to the G-30.

6. Rich Electrifies First Street Lines

Henry's successes with the Santa Clara road had meanwhile spurred efforts by Jacob Rich to become a full-fledged competitor. Humbled but not beaten by his failure with the underground electric, Rich retained his holdings in the First Street and Willow Glen lines. He now proposed to electrify the First Street road and extend it northwest across county lands to the corner of Hedding Street and The Alameda, near the University of the Pacific. Permission was tentatively granted December 1889 by the city and county pending the outcome of Henry's efforts on The Alameda. Rich and his young secretary, Eugene M. Rosenthal, used the intervening months to make a strong financial connection with the German Savings and Loan Society, San Francisco, securing its support and a pledge of $225,000 in mortgage money. In March 1890 he incorporated his First Street and Willow Glen properties as the *First Street*

Railroad, the same name as Bishop's early unincorporated horse railway.

On March 29, the Alameda road standing ready to open, the city fathers gave the new company a franchise to electrify its First Street line. Rich signed contracts with Thomson-Houston, hired Archibald Ford as his superintendent, and electrified and double-tracked the road from Taylor Street to Almaden Avenue (now Alma Avenue). Specifications were for 35-pound T-rail and a 3'6" gauge. The company built a new carbarn and powerhouse at First and Oak Streets where Hazel-type boilers and Crockton generators were used to produce 500-volt dc power for the overhead system. According to Edward Derbridge, a horsecar driver and armature winder for Rich who later worked in the Key System shops, the boilers were fired by wood at first, consuming about 15 cords a day. Eventually they were converted to oil burners.

February 20, 1891, marked the first trial run of the new First Street electric road, attended by an enthusiastic crowd. Three open-platform closed cars with single 16-horsepower GE motors—convertible to open cars for the summer service—commenced regular runs the following day.

Rich continued to electrify his lines. On August 7, 1890, the county supervisors gave him rights to build his Hobson Street branch to The Alameda. Work was soon under way on this line, which opened late the following year. By then 12 cars were in service, of which seven were powered. On September 1, 1891, the city council franchised Rich to electrify his San Fernando-Delmas branch, the terms calling for work to be completed within 18 months. This line, roughly paralleling the old Market Street and Willow Glen horsecar road, opened in 1892. G. K. Edwards replaced Ford that year as superintendent, giving way in turn to Archie D. Foree. Three city franchises were awarded November 14, 1892: Second and San Fernando Streets to Third and Reed, First and Reed Streets to Seventh and Keyes, and Willow Street within the city limits. Another came January 20, 1893, covering Julian Street from First and St. John to Coyote Creek. These franchises also required construction within 18 months. On February 14, 1893, the county supervisors gave

First Street Railroad: Single-truck car 13 is shown on First at San Fernando Street, San Jose. (Randolph Brandt Collection) **BELOW is narrow-gauge car 16 at First and Jackson Streets. First Street cars then ran from Hedding Street and The Alameda to Oak Hill Cemetery via Hobson Street, First Street and Monterey Road.** (Tom Gray Collection)

All is peaceful and quiet, with nary a pedestrian to break the calm along First Street near Hobson, 1892, as narrow-gauge car 11 hums along.

(San Jose Historic Landmarks Commission)

Rich rights to extend his Delmas and Willow Street lines to Lincoln and Minnesota Avenues. This work—the Third-Seventh line, Julian Street, and the Delmas-Willow extension—was completed in 1893-94. The county approved an extension of the First Street line out Monterey Road to Oak Hill Cemetery, and the city sanctioned a line from Second and San Fernando Streets out San Fernando and Cahill Street to the South Pacific Coast (narrow-gauge) railroad depot. By year's end 1894, all trackwork being finished, Rich was operating 20 single-motor cars, plus trailers, over more than 17 miles of narrow-gauge electric lines.

7. Quincey Builds Steam Road

The early 1890s also marked the birth of another local road, a steam-powered line to Alum Rock Park in rugged terrain some eight miles east of San Jose. The idea of building a railroad to the city-owned canyon park, a widely acclaimed beauty spot, had interested San Joseans for the better part of a decade. Various schemes had been set forth including a recent steam-railroad proposal (1888) by Hanford L. Gordon, Alexander E. Mintie, and Charles H. Gordon to promote the latter's

$110,000 property investment near the park. Thus far, none of the proposals had borne fruit.

The author of a new plan, in 1891, was a Canadian-born local wood and coal dealer named Richard H. Quincey who, on a shoestring budget, secured a county franchise in May to build a narrow-gauge road eastward from the corner of Santa Clara Street and McLaughlin Avenue, terminus of the San Jose and Santa Clara. Motive power was not specified. Among conditions for the franchise was a pledge by Quincey to pay $3,000 toward rebuilding Alum Rock Avenue, a county thoroughfare alongside which the new line would run.

Quincey hired R. P. Buswell, a former engineer with the Illinois Central Railroad, to superintend the construction and started laying rails May 11 despite the lack of a franchise to enter the park. Money soon ran out, and construction was halted June 26, the line finished only out to White Road. Thereafter Quincey took to working the line alone with a pickaxe and shovel.

Financial backing finally came from wealthy San Franciscan named John Center, a Scot who had settled in that city before the 1849 gold rush and amassed a fortune in Mission District real estate. The Quincey-Center venture was formally incorporated November 1, 1893, as the *Alum-Rock Railway Company* with capital of $300,000, of which $7,500 was actually subscribed. Quincey himself put up $7,300 of the total. Great plans were projected and rolling stock was put on the line, including San Jose's one and only gasoline-powered streetcar (a failure). There matters ended, the nation's 1893 financial crash just around the corner and gathering momentum.

8. Depression of the Nineties

Henry was in good position to ride out the financial storm. He had left San Jose temporarily in 1890 to build a trolley line in Sacramento, putting the local road in charge of his son Will and his close friend and former Iowa banking associate John P. Burke. Returning, he secured a city franchise in September 1891 to electrify the old horsecar line to Ninth and Reed Streets, rerouting that branch directly down Tenth from Santa Clara Street. (This line was extended to Keyes Street in 1895 after a city franchise the previous December.) Now, facing the stormclouds, he again reorganized the company, intending to electrify the Stockton Avenue line and build branches elsewhere in San Jose. Henry, with 1,513½ shares of reorganized stock, continued as president, his friend Wooster staying on as a director. Added to the directorate were Jacob Rich, Burke (1,000 shares), and Henry's poker-playing crony from the Sainte Claire Club, former San Jose mayor Bernard D. Murphy (1,514½ shares). Business declined sharply when the depression hit, and the expansion plans had to be dropped, but the crisis failed to upset Henry's customary afternoon poker games at the club. It is reported that one of these sessions led to the end of his friendship with Murphy.

The stakes that afternoon at the club were especially high, so the story goes, and all but Henry and Murphy had thrown in their cards. "Tell you what I'll do," Henry is reported to have said. "I'll make it my streetcar line against your Atascadero Ranch." Murphy bet and lost. Rumor had it that he later urged Henry to call off the wager but was refused.

Whatever the truth of the story, Henry did turn up owner of the 22,000-acre Atascadero spread about that time—and his poker face stood him in good stead a short while later in its sale.

The Army had been seeking a tract for a maneuvering ground, so Henry put on his top hat and went to Washington to see what was what. Things moved slowly in Washington that year, and the bill to buy the rancho for $20 an acre got hung up after passing the House. Henry went home.

It was not long before a real estate man brought an Eastern investor to call on Henry. "How much do you want for the ranch?" he was asked. Henry put on his best poker face and reluctant seller pose. "Forty dollars an acre," he said.

"Sold," said the Easterner—and instead of $440,000 from Uncle Sam, Henry supposedly got $880,000, thanks to Congressional dilly-dallying.

9. Rich Fails

If Henry had weathered the depression well, not so Jacob Rich. The 1893 crash caught him in a vulnerable position—land-poor, overextended, and $75,000 the poorer for the winery venture that cost Bishop $30,000. To make matters worse, the president of the German Savings and Loan Society had died, leading to reorganization of its board of directors. Friends and supporters of Rich were replaced by new directors who had no personal commitment to him and refused to honor a $100,000 second-mortgage pledge by the old board.

Rich mortgaged everything he had to stave off the crash, reincorporating his lines September 1894 as the *San Jose Railroad Company.* Now represented on the board of directors were two San Franciscans, Wendell Easton and Moses L. Levy, with Rosenthal secretary and James W. Findlay of San Jose treasurer. Rich continued as president of the company.

A sharp decline set into the company's business revenues during the mid-1890s brought about in part, according to superintendent Foree, by a sudden bicycle mania that swept the city. "There was never another craze like it in San Jose," Foree reflected. "Everyone—young and old; man, woman, and child—was riding bikes. Our cars, which had been averaging $35 a day in fares, suddenly dropped to $3.50."

By 1897 Rich, who had once turned down $325,000 for his streetcar lines, was forced into court with a petition of insolvency. The railroad went into receivership and was eventually secured at foreclosure sale by the German Savings and Loan Society for $225,000, the amount of its first mortgage bonds. That was in May 1899. Rich's mortgaged properties were sold at a fraction of their previous worth, due to the depressed prices of the time. Rich himself was pursued into court by one company that was dissatisfied even by his bankruptcy. He finally extricated himself from the court in December 1900 and went home, free of obligations, to die. His passing January 6, 1901, of general debility, revealed an estate comprised solely of his home and personal possessions, valued at less than $10,000.

10. Center Acquires Alum Rock Road

Another financial casualty of the 1893 crash was Quincey, whose operation of the Alum Rock line had never been successful. Backer John Center foreclosed the road in 1894 and promptly sold it for $1 to one of his favorite nephews, Hugh Center, who was then managing a sugar plantation in Hawaii. Just as promptly the younger man returned to the mainland to put his new property in order.

Center's first acquisition was a little eight-ton steam engine by which he restored service to the road. With his uncle's assured backing, he soon got franchises to enter Alum Rock Park via Kirk Avenue and private rights of way through the olive groves. Steep grades near the park entrance compelled him to build two tunnels and prompted the addition of another locomotive when the line opened in 1896 with a 25¢ fare to the park. The new engine was a 15-ton Baldwin compound reportedly once used to pull trains out to Cliff House in San Francisco. Center later added a 25-ton locomotive and still later converted his engines to oil-burners.

Curt Bailey, an early-day rider, later remembered that the train started from a roundhouse on the north side of Santa Clara Street at the present-day Western Pacific crossing, being told that the reason it did not start downtown was objections by the Santa Clara Street residents to the noise and cinders. "The train ran out Alum Rock Avenue to the present Kirk Avenue," he recalled, "then turned left in front of what once was the Santa Clara Country Club golf course. Crossing McKee Road, it entered an olive orchard. We enjoyed reaching out the windows and picking olives on the way. At Penitencia Creek, where a waiting station was located, it turned right and proceeded through a tunnel, where we were told not to have our arms outside the cars. It proceeded up the canyon, crossing the creek near the present parking facilities to the Alum Rock station located against the hill across from the present road into the park. One of the scenic spots the line passed was the meteor, a big chunk of manganese later sold by the San Jose city council to help the war effort."

E. A. Danforth of Santa Cruz recalled that the train consisted of a small locomotive, passenger car, and flat car. "At the park, men loaded the flat car with rock," he remembered, "to hold the passenger car on the track while it crossed the bridge. Well, one day the car jumped the track on a bridge as we were coming back from the park. It didn't drop to the creekbed, because it was held by the weight of the engine and flat car. We got back by a thrilling ride on the engine. That must have been about 1898 or 1899."

The Alum Rock line had many such Toonerville-trolley characteristics, remembered William D. Hatch, one of its engineers. Business was sparse during the week but boomed on weekends, when multiple-car trains were crowded with picnickers out for a lark. Minor disasters were commonplace and treated with merriment. What matter that the trains sometimes parted company from the light rails and hung up, disabled, for an hour or two? Or that sparks from the engine burned holes in the turn-of-the-century skirts of the young ladies in the cars? These were indignities to be expected. Most of the passengers endured them with equanimity.

Above all, the locals enjoyed a good joke. Their favorite vic-

tim was any newly arrived Easterner who happened to be aboard. When the train stopped amid the Pala Rosa olive grove, knowing riders would urge the newcomer to taste a "ripe olive" and laugh at the wry face he made. It was on such a train that traveling French journalist Amaury Mars in 1901 journeyed to the park: "The trip by rail is particularly enticing, and gives rise to sensations that are altogether unusual; it is an uncommon sight to see a steam engine vomiting forth its dingy smoke in the silence of those covers, as it drags along the three or four cars, laden with pleasure-seekers."

"The road seems to have been constructed for the convenience of this diminutive motor, for it undulates along its way, in the midst of shrubs and foliage that rustle gently in the breeze, as the cars glide swiftly by them; and at times your head seems to twirl, as you go crashing over a bridge that trembles beneath its human load."

Certainly Mars could not imagine how soon his pastoral idyll was to undergo a metamorphosis.

The earliest service to Alum Rock Park was via the steam dummy, shown here at the park in early 1900. A lady is boarding the open trailer, which later was used by the Peninsular Railway behind the electric motor cars.
(Vernon J. Sappers Collection)

Passengers disembark from a steam train at Alum Rock Park about 1900. The line to the park was completed in 1896 and electrified after the turn of the century. (San Jose Historic Landmarks Commission) **BELOW: Motive power for the steam trains is represented by steam dummy locomotive 2. The unit was disguised to look like a streetcar so it wouldn't scare the horses.** (San Jose Historical Museum)

"Narrow-gauge electric" reached Alum Rock Park in 1902, replacing the steam road built in 1896. TOP: Ex-Salinas narrow-gauge car 32 or 33 emerges from a tunnel near Alum Rock Park. ABOVE: Narrow-gauge car 32 and its trailer are at the Park terminal.　　(Both: Charles Smallwood Collection)

11. Centers Buy Out Henry

At the turn of the century, South Bay residents were becoming aware of a spectacular boom in electric railroading all over the state. Down south, Henry E. Huntington was pushing expansion of his new Pacific Electric system. Several smaller roads were prospering. Closer at hand, an association headed by utility promoter John Martin was preparing to pour $2.5 million into standard-gauging and electrifying the old North Pacific Coast steam road out of Sausalito. Over in the East Bay another powerful syndicate headed by Francis M. (Borax) Smith, John Coleman, and William G. Henshaw, backed by Smith's reported $30 million from borax discoveries, was completing an eight-year consolidation of the Oakland street railways and hinting at big interurban developments to come that might involve San Jose.

Also within striking distance was the San Francisco and San Mateo Electric Railway built by Behrend and Isaac Joost in the early 1890's out to Baden (South San Francisco), upgraded and extended in 1896 after sale by its bondholders, and ready for another push, judging from its recent (May 1900) franchise to operate on the San Mateo city streets. The Joost brothers had tried unsuccessfully to reach San Jose. Informed sources now said the road was for sale again and eyed by Eastern capitalists with ambitions to run it to the South Bay and the East Bay.

These were but a few of the rumors circulating Santa Clara County, many of which reached the sanction of public print. Speculation was in the air. There was talk of an electric road over rugged terrain to Sempervirens Park (Big Basin) 20 miles southwest of San Jose. Another fanciful yarn told of the Santa Fe railroad, which had just punched through the Southern Pacific's curtain of steel around San Francisco Bay, building a high-speed electric main line over Pacheco Pass out to the ocean and thence up the coast to San Francisco, with a branch line through San Jose and up the peninsula. That one sent South Bay residents scurrying to their California atlases to study prospective routes. Generally there was enough plausibility to the rumors to keep the local politicians and businessmen jockeying for position among the various schemes, standing as they did to gain from playing their cards (or guessing) right. There was no doubt but what electric interurbans were coming to the county, probably down both sides of the Bay. The only questions were when and by whom financed.

Always the speculations turned to the powerful Southern Pacific, toward which public and private attitudes were ambiva-

Cars 27 and 29 of the narrow-gauge electric are both carrying respectable crowds in this 1903 view. (Randolph Brandt Collection)

lent. For more than three decades the S. P. had dominated California both politically and financially, employing whatever means best served its corporate ends. That story with its many ramifications is well documented. In the process it had acquired many retainers, some in high places, but also a large body of detractors made up mainly of populists and those whom the railroad had hurt. Their attitudes were hostile, and their voices were heard. Thus the politicians of the day, especially county and local officials who lived close to public censure, walked a careful tightrope regarding the railroad: to openly profess one's loyalty was to invite public disfavor, but not to gain its support was to court political suicide.

Businessmen were in a similar quandary, victims as it were of the carrot and stick syndrome. The railroad had power to reward its friends with lucrative contracts, real estate deals, and the like. It also had power to punish its enemies through political and economic sanctions such as opposition to local franchises, bureaucratic delays, court challenges, threats of competition, intimidation of one's financial backers, or, in extreme cases, outright interference with one's right to do business. Cry as they did about the S. P.'s tactics, most businessmen went where the railroad went because it promised them prosperity. Even those stung by the railroad yesterday were likely to be back at the hive today looking for honey, human nature being what it is.

Astute observers also saw that the railroad had interests to protect in the Santa Clara County and a long history of intervening where its interests were threatened. Its corporate strategy, deeply rooted in the personal philosophy and business acumen of Collis P. Huntington, held that nothing short of total domination of California public transportation was tolerable. Huntington had devised this strategy and honed it to perfection through 30 years of political maneuvering. All local transit systems—short lines, riverboats, ferries, steamships, street railways—were viewed as feeder lines for the larger S. P. enterprise and, hence, targets for its concern. In practical terms this translated into a corporate dedication to buying out or inhibiting not only competing main line railroads but also independent local transit systems intent on operating outside the company net.

To maintain its position the S. P. could be expected to use every financial, political, and legal tool at its command, plus whatever other advantage it could muster. Thus far it had not meddled with the South Bay local lines but that day was soon to come, touching off the most tumultuous decade in local transit history.

That, then, was the setting when, in mid-summer 1900, South Bay residents learned that a group of Baltimore industrialists was planning to buy the San Francisco and San Mateo Electric Railway and also had taken options on two San Jose properties: Henry's street railroad and the city light and power company. No offer had been extended to the San Jose Railroad; the asking price was said to be too high. Local sentiment generally ran in favor of acquisition. The present streetcar systems—Center's Alum Rock road, Henry's San Jose and Santa Clara, and the San Jose Railroad—were considered adequate but small diggings compared with the elaborate schemes described by the Bay Area press.

County residents were ready for dramatic progress. Instead they were dealt a setback. February 1901 brought news that representatives of the Baltimore syndicate had been in town,

Narrow-gauge First Street car 16 advertises its destinations. (Charles Smallwood Collection)

surveyed the local situation, and decided to drop the local options, although they still intended to buy the San Mateo road. That $1.2 million deal went through in April, the syndicate expressing interest in certain San Francisco properties and hopes for extending the road to San Jose and Oakland. Their San Francisco plans matured the following year, leading to formation of the United Railways of San Francisco, but they stopped talking about South Bay or East Bay extensions.

There was more to the story, of course. The S. P.'s Collis Huntington had died in 1900 and been succeeded in 1901 by Edward Henry Harriman, no slouch himself at running a railroad. The change at the helm did not change the corporate strategy. In dealing with the San Mateo problem the railroad had simply met with the Baltimore people and reached a compromise, the S. P. agreeing not to build a competing electric line down from San Francisco and the Baltimore syndicate agreeing not to extend the San Mateo road. This was known as eliciting cooperation by threat of paralleling. Complicating the issue locally had been the open hostility between Henry and Bernard Murphy, rekindled during the negotiations. Henry favored selling. Murphy, who had other plans, opposed the sale. Murphy went to court to block Henry from selling, an action Murphy dismissed when the option was dropped. The "other plans" now came to light.

Hugh Center, owner of the Alum Rock road, had been watching the local developments and discussing them with his brother, George L. Center, a Belmont resident and former San Francisco supervisor. George Center, privy to the San Mateo situation and probably hoping to profit from ambitions of the Baltimore group, had quietly bought up 1,000 shares of San Jose and Santa Clara stock. Now, the Baltimore options expiring, the Center brothers offered Murphy $45,000 for his 1,514½ shares, enough to give them more than half the road's 5,000 outstanding shares and, hence, control. This time it was Henry who initiated court action, fighting to block Murphy from selling. At length, however, Henry capitulated. Transfer of control to the Centers was announced April 26, 1901. Formal reorganization took place the following August, George Center (3,737½ shares) becoming president of the combined Alum Rock-San Jose and Santa Clara operations. A. F. Morrison was named vice president and Hugh Center general manager. John T. McGeoghegan, cashier of San Jose's Garden City Bank, became secretary. W. W. Skinner was the chief engineer and P. Carmen the electrician. In November all assets of the Alum Rock road were deeded to the San Jose and Santa Clara for $10,000, completing terms of the merger.

Henry retained but 10½ shares of stock and dropped from active management of the company. He maintained an interest in local politics for a decade or so but eventually quit San Jose in favor of Portland, Oregon, where he died in 1939. John Burke sold his stock, moved to Southern California, and went back into banking.

In November 1901 the Centers placed $50,000 in first mortgage bonds with the Mercantile Trust Company of San Francisco, the first step in their plan to electrify the Alum Rock road and combine its operations with those of the San Jose and Santa Clara. Franchises were awarded and work begun on the park line the next month, including construction of an electric station at the mouth of Alum Rock canyon, powered by gasoline and said to be the largest on the coast at that time. The "nar-

Passengers disembark from San Jose & Santa Clara car 32 at East San Jose, circa 1900. (Vernon J. Sappers Collection)

row-gauge electric," as the line came to be called, was completed in April 1902, through trains operating for the first time from downtown San Jose to the park. The company now operated 16 powered cars (GE motors) and 4 trailers, all built by Fitzgerald in Sacramento, over about 12 miles of narrow-gauge lines, mostly of 35-pound T-rail.

One of the few electric fatalities in the Santa Clara Valley occurred in June 1903 when a runaway trailer plunged down the grade from Alum Rock Park. The car was on a siding at the top, being loaded, when it broke loose. One person was killed outright; two more died later.

The San Jose Railroad meanwhile had reorganized, George L. Barker becoming manager, R. S. Weldenberg secretary, and George Tourney resident superintendent, with F. Thurber the chief electrician. On January 21, 1901, it abandoned its unprofitable Hobson Street branch beyond the corner of Hobson and Walnut Streets, the city insisting that service be maintained out to Walnut. In November 1901 the company placed in service car No. 26, its "fastest ever"—a 24-horsepower two-motor unit with twice the running speed of the standard one-motor cars. At year's end it reported 23 powered cars equipped with rheostat controls and Brill and McGuire trucks. Also on the roster with four unpowered trailers used for special occasions.

12. Birth of the Interurban

By 1902 Borax Smith and associates had completed their Oakland street railway empire by acquiring the Oakland, San Leandro, and Haywards electric road, last of the big East Bay

independents. That deal was engineered in July 1901 and consummated the following September. To consolidate his properties, Smith created in March 1902 a giant holding company—Oakland Transit Consolidated—which gave way June 11 to his $5 million San Francisco, Oakland and San Jose Railway, whose corporate objectives included not only building suburban lines all over the East Bay but also broad-gauging the Haywards line, extending it to San Jose, and running branches out to Santa Clara, Los Gatos, and Saratoga, where Smith owned the former Farrington mansion on Saratoga Avenue. The implications were not lost on South Bay residents, who looked forward to the start of construction.

The action was now under way, but, unexpectedly, it came from a new quarter. In fall 1902 a syndicate of local citizens headed by dairyman-realtor James W. Rea and transit promoter F. S. Granger put together plans for an 18-mile road called the *San Jose, Saratoga, and Los Gatos Interurban Railroad Company.* Rea, author of the abortive 1887 San Jose-Santa Clara cable road scheme, came armed with strong local family connections and promises of solid political and financial backing from the community. Granger offered impressive credentials as an operator of electric traction systems. Plans called for a standard-gauge 600-volt overhead interurban road leaving San Jose via San Carlos Street and Stevens Creek Road and proceeding to Meridian Corners, Saratoga, and Los Gatos by the "most advantageous" route, thus anticipating the branch lines announced earlier by Smith and associates.

One feature was a short spur running up the canyon behind Saratoga to Pacific Congress Springs, a resort community created in the mid-1860s by Darius O. Mills and mining tycoon Alvinza Hayward and operated since 1872 by the Lewis Sage family. This resort, famous for the quality of its mineral springs

The main hotel at Congress Springs, built in 1872, was gutted by fire in June 1903. Plans to rebuild and expand the resort were announced, but never materialized.

(San Jose Historical Museum)

and affluence of its clientele, housed its patrons in guest cottages and a handsome 14-room hotel patterned after Congress Hall in Saratoga Springs, New York. In all these plans, Rea and Granger were told they had the blessings of local politicians, other transit operators, and, most important, the Southern Pacific.

On September 19, 1902, A. T. Herrmann and crew were seen near Meridian Corners (Saratoga Avenue and Stevens Creek Road) surveying for the new road. The company was incorporated October 17 and soon obtained county permission to start building. Financial support was pledged by several local investors including Oliver A. Hale, son of a California merchant and owner himself of a prosperous San Jose department store. One account says Hale was a large investor and thus influenced early decisions affecting the road.

In any event, construction began in January 1903, Rea and Granger choosing county roads as the most advantageous route to avoid the costs of private rights of way. (This move was hailed as shrewd business at the time but later proved a fatal mistake.) Optimism ran high, but when the pledges were called in, very little cash was forthcoming. That was in February 1903. The partners also ran into perplexing delays trying to get a city franchise, made all the more so because Rea was on friendly terms with J. O. Hayes, co-owner of the *San Jose Mercury* and a power in local politics. Eventually the partners were forced to call a temporary halt to construction.

They refused to quit, however. Early in 1903 they set themselves up as the Saratoga Construction Company, with power to execute contracts for the new electric line. In April they reincorporated the road as the *San Jose-Los Gatos Interurban Railway Company*, Rea again serving as president and Granger as vice president. In June Rea succeeded in placing $500,000 worth of bonds with the Germania Trust Company of St. Louis. The Western Electric Supply Company of St. Louis got a contract to supply everything from spikes to cars and ordered 30 large interurbans from the American Car Company, costing $3000 apiece. A week later the order was cancelled in favor of 12 handsome cars originally built for a narrow-gauge road out of Detroit. George W. Elder of San Francisco got the construction contract for roadbed, track work, and the overhead system. Construction resumed June 13 with an elaborate ceremony, the feature of which was the driving of a silver spike.

13. Battle of the Campbell Cutoff

Not widely known at the time and only later appreciated was that the Southern Pacific was behind most of the troubles experienced by Rea and Granger. Pressures had been brought on certain investors to default on their pledges. The S. P. and the San Jose Railroad, which had some interurban designs of its own, were jointly responsible for stymieing the partners' efforts to get a city franchise. Rea and Granger having secured backing, these tactics no longer worked.

On July 7, 1903, the city council gave the interurban rights to enter the city on San Carlos Street and proceed via San Carlos and Market streets to the S. P. depot. Amicable arrangements were made by the new road to share rails with the San Jose and Santa Clara on North Market Street, the interurban promising to pay for the broad-gauge line and the Center brothers to pay for adding a third (narrow-gauge) rail for their equipment.

In June 1903 the main hotel building at Congress Springs burned with no loss of life but damage estimated at $50,000. Rea and Granger announced a $1 million program to rebuild and expand the property, using the remaining buildings as an annex. This plan never came to fruition, although a combined restaurant and clubhouse was built for social functions.

Construction meanwhile was proceeding full bore, aided in no small way by work motor No. 101 from the San Mateo electric road. Gangs were busy at many points. By mid-August, construction trains were rolling through Meridian into Saratoga, where an immense cut, 70 by 600 feet, proved necessary. In San Jose a carhouse and shop building were taking shape. At Saratoga the system's substation was well along; Westinghouse apparatus, including a rotary converter with a 225-cell storage battery, were features.

The nearing certainty of competition hardly suited the San Jose Railroad, which did not relish giving up any local fares, or the S. P., which had larger issues at stake. So, as the construction proceeded, they sought ways to vanquish the interurban. How better, they reasoned, than to establish a shorter and quicker San Jose-Los Gatos route than that chosen by Rea and Granger?

The San Jose Railroad thus sought franchises in October for an electric line linking the two cities by the two-mile-shorter Campbell cutoff. Rea and Granger at once countered by announcing their own line to Los Gatos via Campbell, making use of the "Dunlap franchise" route for they had reportedly paid $5,000. (This franchise, originally costing $250, was one of four obtained by George T. Dunlap in August 1901 from the county supervisors covering some 90 miles of proposed electric railways.) The battle waxed hot for several weeks, and the interurban was saved only when its backers publicly pledged $2 million if necessary to quash the opposition. The San Jose Railroad, unable to muster this kind of money, let the Campbell cutoff route go by default to Rea and Granger in November 1903 but not until after a bizarre meeting of the county supervisors at which the first Campbell franchise (requested by the San Jose Railroad) was awarded by sealed bid, then by open bid, and finally not awarded at all in favor of Rea's "Dunlap franchise."

The S. P. threw in some heavy interference of its own. According to local accounts, trains of cars were left standing on track crossings for long periods to hinder work on the interurban. There were hand-to-hand conflicts between working crews of the two companies. As a parting shot, the S. P. and the San Jose Railroad engineered an injunction that blocked the interurban for some time from operating its cars on Market Street in San Jose.

Despite all, Rea and Granger had rails laid all the way through Saratoga to Los Gatos by the end of 1903 and had the short spur to Congress Springs ready for steel. In February 1904 the 12 big cars arrived from St. Louis and proved to be all the company desired: guaranteed to do 30 mph on level track and sightly enough, with their dark green decor, to please even the most jaded traveler. Given names and numbers, the six motor cars were 2 (Rea), 4 (Granger), 6 (Edith), 8 (Florence), 10 (Los Gatos), and 12 (Germania, named for the bankers). The six trailers were numbered 3, 5, 7, 9, 11, and 13. With the passenger cars came an express car, No. 1, for the partners were determined to get their share of baggage and freight hauling.

The gala first trip over the San Jose-Los Gatos line took place March 19, 1904, marked by festivities all along the line and a banquet at Los Gatos' Lyndon Hotel, opposite the terminal. How the oratory flowed, commented one writer, now that the interurban had arrived!

Regular service began the following week, the big green cars rolling out Market and San Carlos streets past O'Connor Sanitarium and the orchards beyond to Meridian Corners, thence along gently winding Saratoga Avenue past the old Moreland School and Quito to the Saratoga station in the town square. There the line swung eastward, curving through the foothills past Glen Una, Nippon Mura, and Austin down into Los Gatos—right down its main street. The cars ran on an hourly

San Jose–Los Gatos interurban car 101 provides the motive power for a crew stringing wire between San Jose and Saratoga about 1903.

(Charles Smallwood Collection)

schedule and were a great success from the start, usually with every seat taken.

Enthused by the hearty response, Rea and Granger set about building their Campbell cutoff, which left San Jose via Park Avenue, Josefa Street, San Carlos Street, Bird, Coe, and Lincoln avenues, and Willow Street. They also ordered plans for an extension into the Big Basin country west of Saratoga, which would have involved the Congress Springs line.

14. S. P. Acquires Interurban

Rea and Granger had earned their day in the sun, but competitors stood ready to cash in on their success. One was the *Santa Clara Valley Transit Company*, a million-dollar corporation formed in February 1904 to build north from San Jose to San Francisco. In the style of the day, this company neither confirmed nor denied rumors it was backed by the Western Pacific, a main line challenger to S. P. dominance in the Bay Area. Such canards were often helpful in getting franchises and other local support. In this case they proved unfounded, and the company faded away.

Another prospective foe was the *Palo Alto and Suburban Railway Company* formed in November 1903 by John F. Parkinson, G. F. Gray, K. H. List, and W. P. Gray of Palo Alto, G. S. Parkinson of Mountain View, and L. N. Hobbs and W. E. Crossman of San Jose to build a streetcar system in Palo Alto, a growing community above Mayfield, in the shadow of Stanford University. Parkinson, founder of two local banks and a thriving lumberyard, was president of the new company, with List treasurer. Already in hand was a local franchise (August 1903)

for a line northward up the county road (El Camino Real) from the Mayfield town limit to University Avenue, eastward on University through the business district to Waverley Street, and south on Waverley to Embarcadero Road, the Palo Alto town limit. Capital was set at only $100,000, but it was rumored that the company intended to build southward from San Mateo to San Jose, filling the gap left when the Baltimore group failed to extend the San Mateo electric. Under consideration were real estate developments and an expansion of Parkinson's lumber business. Local backers in addition to Parkinson were Albert T. DeForest, president of the U. S. Steel Corporation's Columbia Steel affiliate, and Frank H. Dohrmann of the influential Dohrmann family of San Francisco. This trio, known locally as the Parkinson syndicate, were said to be supported by Eastern investors worth millions.

Still to be reckoned, too, was the Southern Pacific, set back temporarily at San Jose but not deterred in its monopolistic ambitions. Its officials were frankly beleaguered. Pushing for entry was the Western Pacific. The San Mateo electric road was a gadfly and so now was the San Jose-Los Gatos interurban. Over in the East Bay was the biggest headache: Borax Smith and company's new Key system, opened for business from the Key Route Pier in October 1903 and pitting fast, modern electrics against the S. P.'s venerable old steam trains in a battle for suburban patronage. This was territory held by the S. P. for 25 years, yet the electrics were winning big. For the first time, the railroad had serious competition in its own backyard.

It was in this context that S. P. officials met in 1904 to map a comprehensive Bay Area strategy said to be blessed by President E. H. Harriman and backed by his injunction to spare no expense. In brief, the plan called for acquiring the San Jose-Los Gatos interurban, electrifying all East Bay suburban steam lines, and building new electric roads from San Francisco and Oakland to San Jose, down both sides of the Bay. In this way the S. P. could undercut all its electric adversaries at once.

The railroad's main coast line down the peninsula to Los Angeles, opened for service in 1901, would be shortened by building the so-called Los Gatos cutoff, a double-track high-speed route leaving the present main line at San Carlos and proceeding southeasterly 50 miles in a straight line to a junction with the San Jose-Santa Cruz line (former South Pacific Coast road) at Vasona, just outside Los Gatos. The new route would then proceed over the mountains to Santa Cruz, rejoining the present main line via Watsonville. That would leave room for the electric development. There were other features, such as an electric railway of the Pacific Electric's Mt. Lowe type to be built to Lick Observatory on the summit of Mt. Hamilton, 26 miles east of San Jose. Details of the overall plan were not made public but allowed to leak piecemeal.

Acquisition of the San Jose-Los Gatos interurban was made easy by threatening the Germania Trust ompany with a railroad war. Rea and Granger had no personal fortune with which to fight, and their bankers had no taste for such combat. So, on April 9, 1904, the trust company sold out to the S. P. Rea retired to real estate and dairying. Granger moved on to Santa Cruz, where he took over the Santa Cruz Electric Railway in late June and helped merge it with a competing line to form the Union Traction Company, the last streetcar operator in that community. He bought a theater in downtown Santa Cruz and gave every indication of staying, but December 1904 found him in San Luis Obispo promoting an electric road to Avila Beach. In 1907 he was seen in Hanford, California, on a similar adventure.

In July 1904 he and Rea were targets of a lawsuit by H. K. Gilman of St. Louis alleging nonpayment of debts. Details were reported by the *Santa Cruz Sentinel*: "The complaint alleges that in April 1903, Rea and Granger, doing business as the Saratoga Construction Company, entered into a contract with the San Jose and Santa Clara Valley Railroad to construct the road; that afterward Rea and Granger entered into another contract, with the plaintiff, for the supplies to be sent and that the total amount used was $250,248.72 in value, and that of this sum only $201,961.30 was ever paid. When interviewed, Mr. Rea called these supplies second-rate materials and threatened to have Mr. Gilman arrested if he ever sets foot in California." The outcome of this suit is not known but may have gone against the partners, judging from Granger's hasty departure from Santa Cruz.

New management had meanwhile been announced for the interurban. Now in charge was none other than Oliver A. Hale, erstwhile associate of Rea and Granger, with Frank E. Chapin Jr., a 30-year San Francisco streetcar veteran, as his vice president and general manager. F. H. Dearborn was named general engineer. Hale's presidency gave the road a brief hometown flavor, but any doubt as to the real ownership should have disappeared in the summer of 1904 when Paul Shoup, the S. P. district freight and passenger agent, stopped off in San Jose to inspect the road. The Southern Pacific tieup was underscored by news that once the Campbell cutoff was done, the construction crews would be sent off to work on the Stockton Electric, a known S. P. subsidiary. Shoup discussed the possibility of a Mt. Hamilton line to be built by the Eastern corporation operating the Pike's Peak railway.

The Campbell cutoff opened for service November 26, 1904,

The new interurban line was as straight as the wagon road was crooked. This construction scene of the San Jose–Los Gatos Interurban was taken near Saratoga in 1903.
(Randolph Brandt Collection)

New Cars for San Jose-Los Gatos Railway

This company have lately added to its equipment 12 fine cars built by the American Car Company of St. Louis. The cars present an attractive, imposing appearance with the steam-coach roofs, twin windows, vestibules, and pilots, and have pleasing interiors finished in handsomely carved cherry. They seat 52 passengers; seats are of the walk-over type, 33 inches in length, and the aisle 22 inches wide. Over the crown pieces the cars measure 45 feet in length and over the end panels 36 feet. The width over the sills is 8 feet 3 inches from center to center of posts 2 feet 5-1/2 inches in thickness. Corner posts are 3-3/4 inches and side posts 2-1/4 inches. The side sills are 3 inches by 7-3/4 inches, with 8-inch by 5/8-inch plates on the outside.

The end sills are 5-3/4 inches by 7-7/8 inches. From the end panels over the vestibules is 4 feet 6 inches. The step heights from the rails are respectively 16-1/4 inches, 12-1/2 inches, and 12-1/2 inches. The entrances are equipped with sand boxes of the American Car Company's make and Brill's angle-iron bumpers, Dadendi gongs, and folding gates. The trucks are 27-G with a 4-foot wheelbase and 33-inch wheels. Motors have a capacity of 45 horsepower.

— *From* Street Railway Journal, *February 20, 1904*

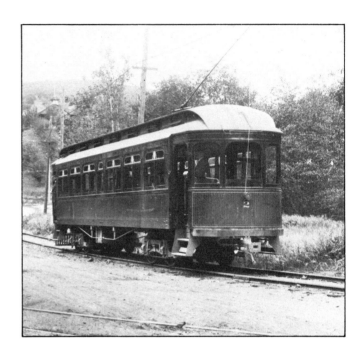

The new cars of the San Jose–Los Gatos were as handsome as any in the land. Motor 2 takes the loop at Congress Springs Park, while car 6 (at one time called the ''Edith'') pauses for a photographer along the line.

(Both: Vernon J. Sappers Collection)

Cars 5 and 7 are at Congress Springs Park with a distinguished-looking crowd about 1905. Could it have been a picnic? (Randolph Brandt Collection)
BELOW: A rare photo of car 4, the "Granger." (Lorin Silleman Collection)

1905: The San Jose and Los Gatos Interurban Railway Company

One of the evidences tending to verify the prediction made long since that all the important railway communities of California were destined to be connected by interurban electric railway systems before the end of the first decade of the twentieth century is found in the system of the San Jose and Los Gatos Interurban Railway Company, at San Jose, Cal.—a system which in less than two years had made itself indispensable to the needs of the 50,000 or more people resident within its sphere of operation.

The "Los Gatos Interurban," as it is locally termed, is distinctively the investment of sturdy businessmen whose thorough familiarity with the country served and its possibilities of development gave them every confidence in the enterprise. As a result, it consists of a line of railway that is sound in its engineering, intelligent in its operation, satisfactory in its service, and profitable in its undertaking. It is distinctively a passenger road, though considerable freight is hauled during the fruit season, with every prospect of a steady growth in this class of traffic; but it typifies more strongly than perhaps any other line of railway in California the fact that it is possible for a well-conducted interurban line to work its way in the favor of a community in which it had always been believed that the good old horse and buggy had come to stay forever, to the exclusion of any such an innovation as a railroad.

One need not extol either the beauties or the enterprise of San Jose, the "Garden City" of California, whose fruits alone have brought world-wide fame, nor the charm of Los Gatos, so cosily ensconced in the foothills of the Santa Cruz Mountains. Between them, as far as the eye can reach, are all but countless thousands of fruit trees. Here and there a grove of eucaplyptus trees rise, as do poplars elsewhere. Ownerships are in small tracts of 100 acres or so, although many large farms are passed, so that it is a community of a practically continual settlement between the terminii.

The trip over the road is at all times a very enjoyable one. On Sundays the patronage is especially large, and during weekdays the travel to and from the city is unfailing. The territory invested in the system as at present operated is fully detailed below, but, as the growth of the system is inevitable, it may be assumed that it will eventually form a connecting link in the chain of electric railways that will encircle the Bay of San Francisco.

The Los Gatos line begins at the broad-gauge Southern Pacific depot at the head of Market Street, San Jose, and continues thence down the latter thoroughfare around City Hall Plaza, opposite which the company's offices are located, and thence along San Carlos Street to the junction known as Bird Avenue. This is a distance of 1.58 miles from the starting point, and thus far the road is double-tracked, but at Bird Avenue the loop in the line begins, that on the westerly side being known as the Saratoga branch, while that on the east is distinguished as the Campbell branch. Taking up the Saratoga branch first, it constitutes the original line, and its length from the Southern Pacific depot in San Jose to Los Gatos is 15.56 miles.

From Bird Avenue the line follows the Stevens Creek road four miles, diverging therefrom at Meridian Corners in an almost southwesterly direction along Santa Clara and Saratoga Avenues to the old town of Saratoga, located a distance, by way of the road, of 11.24 miles from the San Jose depot. At Saratoga a branch line 1½ miles in length follows up the scenic canyon of Saratoga Creek to Congress Springs, a naturally beautifully wooded resort.

From Saratoga to Los Gatos follow approximately 4-1/3 miles of that which is undoubtedly the most attractive part of the line, for as the road winds among the foothills the vista presented in the low-lying Santa Clara Valley, ensconced from the outer world by the Coast and other ranges of mountains, of which famous Mt. Hamilton forms the peak, is a landscape of rural and urban and mountain beauty seldom equalled. Here the forests of Santa Cruz fringe the orchards of Santa Clara, and ever and anon are pastoral spots that fill the city heart with covetousness—notably at Nippon Mura, where a bit of transplanted Japan gives restfulness and refreshment to those wayfarers who come recommended.

The return from Los Gatos to San Jose, if made by the Campbell branch, is over 10.7 miles of single track to Bird Avenue Junction as before, and thence along the 1.6 miles of double track to the starting point at the Southern Pacific depot, making the entire length of the Campbell branch to be 12.3 miles. The total length of the loop, including the double track in San Jose, is, therefore, 27.86 miles, the stations passed on the return being Leno, Mains, Campbell, Hamilton, Fairfield, and Lincoln.

Between Campbell and the station known as Los Gatos and San Jose Road the track is operated conjointly with the Almaden branch of the narrow-gauge system of the Southern Pacific Company through the laying of a third rail, the distance of this joint track occupancy being 1.64 miles. Obviously the trip can be made in either direction and, in point of fact, cars leave the San Jose depot on the even half-hour, beginning at 6 a.m., the last car leaving at 11:30 p.m. Those leaving on the even hour go to Los Gatos by way of Campbell, returning via Saratoga, while those leaving on the half-hour travel in the opposite direction. Some cars make the round trip in an hour and three-quarters, although most of them require an hour and fifty-five minutes, the schedule depending largely upon the amount of traffic. The trip to Los Gatos takes either 50 or 60 minutes by either route, according to the train.

As is the case with all well-regulated interurban electric railway systems, the so-called Los Gatos line is handled by a train dispatcher located in the general office of the company at San Jose. Dispatching is done by telephone, Stromberg-Carlson apparatus being used throughout, but the system under consideration is a radical departure from that ordinarily used in this respect. It is the almost invariable rule everywhere that the train orders are given by the dispatcher to the conductor, who repeats them to the motorman. This verbal repetition of orders ofttimes results in mistakes or confusion, as is evidenced by the occurrence of several accidents therefrom during the first months of operation of the road.

Instructions were then issued making it mandatory for dispatchers to give orders only to motormen, thus placing the entire responsibility for the running of the car (other than that for the accuracy of train orders) upon the motorman. Experience has proved the wisdom of this innovation, for not a single accident has occurred during the year or more since the order referred to has been placed in effect. The procedure is simple. Acting under orders, all cars on either branch that are traveling from Los Gatos to San Jose are regarded as eastbound, and all cars approaching Los Gatos are termed westbound cars.

Such eastbound cars, in passing switches, take sidings, while westbound cars keep on the main track at the sidings. On arriving at a switch the westbound car continues on the main track until reaching the center of the switch, opposite which the telephone station is placed on a pole. Its conductor thereupon advances to the switch ahead which he throws in order that the coming, or eastbound car, will take the siding, after which he returns to his car, whereupon its motorman goes to the telephone box, rings up the dispatcher, gives his train number, and receives his train orders, returning to the car to await the arrival of the eastbound car.

On the other hand, when the eastbound car reaches the siding, the switch of which has been turned as stated, it is compelled to slow down in order that the conductor may drop off, as he is under orders to stand by the switch in order to open it, so that the westbound car may proceed. The conductor of the eastbound car is further obligated to advance to the westerly end of the siding to throw its switch, in order that his car may advance on the main track, and after this is done he opens the switch, leaving a clear track, and returning to his car proceeds on the journey. All switches, frogs, and turnouts are in strict accordance with the specifications of standard steam railroads. They are of steel, the switches being in target design. In fact, the Los Gatos road is operated throughout under standard steam railway rules, and all of its employees are not only required to be conversant with the rules and signals of railroading but must pass the required examinations when called upon. If in doubt as to the meaning of these rules and signals, they must apply to the proper authorities for explanation.

The thoroughness of organization under which the line is operated is shown by a review of some of the special orders issued. In the matter of joint occupancy of track with the Southern Pacific

The firehouse Dalmation looks on as San Jose–Los Gatos car 2 makes its way along a muddy street in Los Gatos, 1906.
(Charles Smallwood Collection)

Company, for instance, the interurban runs 44 cars over it each day, each in a direction alternating from its predecessor, while the Southern Pacific Company runs thereover but two trains daily, these being known as Nos. 803 and 804, respectively. Under the joint track rules all Southern Pacific and interurban trains must come to a full stop at the junction of the joint track, whereupon if the line is clear they may then proceed at a rate of speed not to exceed 10 miles per hour.

The Southern Pacific trains have the right of track over all interurban cars over the joint track between Campbell and Los Gatos and San Jose Road, the Southern Pacific trains registering at the two stations just named. The interurban motormen must examine the registers at these points, and if the northbound Southern Pacific train No. 804 is not registered, the interurban train must wait 10 minutes, after which it must flag over the joint track under the usual rule. The same procedure is followed with reference to sountbound train No. 803, but if the motorman of any interurban trains finds that the Southern Pacific train is not registered at either Campbell or Los Gatos and San Jose Road, the interurban train flags over the joint track in accordance with the usual rules, without waiting the 10 minutes prescribed when Southern Pacific trains are registered.

Interurban trains that are carded to follow the Southern Pacific trains, and which find that the last trains mentioned are not carded, must place two torpedoes not over 200 feet apart by day and a fusee at night, at a point on the engineer's side of the track five telegraph poles beyond junctions, before going onto the joint track. When it becomes necessary to flag over the joint track against a Southern Pacific train coming or due to come from the opposite direction, the interurban train must wait 10 minutes before following its flagman, and must not run at a rate of speed in excess of four miles an hour while being flagged over the joint track.

In addition, after the interurban motormen have examined the registers referred to, they must at once notify the dispatcher as to whether the Southern Pacific trains have registered or not, and they are not at liberty to proceed over the joint track under any conditions until given orders to do so by the dispatcher.

The train dispatcher's telephone system consists of 30 standard Stromberg-Carlson sets, with 2,000-ohm ringers and five-bar generators. Three separate lines enter the dispatcher's office, two of which come direct from Los Gatos, one being via the Saratoga branch and the other, which is known as the short line, being via Campbell. The third line, which is not used in train dispatching but is devoted exclusively to the needs of the power service, begins at the substation near Saratoga and is run direct to the Otterson Street station of the United Gas and Electric Company, whence it is continued to the business office of the United Gas and Electric Company on Market Street.

Power for the operation of the system is taken from the standard transmission line of the California Gas and Electric Corporation, at the Otterson Street station of the United Gas and Electric Company, this station being also a steam auxiliary plant with a capacity of about 2500 kilowatts. In addition to the steam-driven railway generators that it contains, aggregating a capacity of 500 kilowatts, its substation contains three motor-generator sets having a combined output of 1,200 kilowatts for 550-volt power and railway service.

From this plant current is supplied for the operation of the electric railways of San Jose, with the exception of the Santa Clara line, but, in addition to it, the Los Gatos Interurban line maintains a substation located on its main line about midway between its Fruitvale and Saratoga stations. This substation, which is of brick and concrete construction, takes power from the 10,000-volt distributing circuit of the United Gas and Electric Company through six 100-kilowatt, air-cooled, oil-insulated Westinghouse transformers, arranged in two sets of two each. These transformers deliver three-phase current at a potential of 377 volts for the operation of two Westinghouse rotary converters, of a capacity of 150 and 250 kilowatts, respectively, at a potential of 550 volts. The substation is complete in every way and contains ana excellently apportioned battery room which, however, is not occupied at present.

The carbarns of the company occupy the southeast corner of Sunol and San Carlos Streets, which is on the Saratoga line, a distance of two miles from the San Jose depot. The carbarn proper consists of a corrugated iron building, 200 by 80 feet in ground dimensions, in the front center of which is a repair pit 45 by 100 feet in size. Six tracks enter this building. Adjoining the carbarn in separate structures are the machine shop, 32 by 155 in size; the armature house, 18 by 40 feet in size; and the storehouse, measuring 30 by 80 feet.

The track consists of standard T-rails in 60and 70-pound weights, laid through tieplates on split redwood ties, placed two feet between centers. Throughout its entire length the track is ballasted with creek gravel, an excellent quality of which is available from the bed of Los Gatos Creek, which the road crosses.

The main feeders of the system are mainly of stranded aluminum cable. Those from the substation having an aggregate cross section of 948,000 circular mils keep in the direction of Los Gatos, while those extending thence toward San Jose aggregate 431,000 circular mils in cross section. From the United substation in San Jose, the area of the feeders is about 300,000 circular mils in copper. The trolley wire is No. 00 hard-drawn copper wire, and the overhead construction is both thorough and modern in every respect.

The rolling stock consists of nine passenger cars and two freight cars equipped with Westinghouse 38 motors, and five passenger cars equipped with 56s, two of these equipments being double and the rest quadruple. Ten 27G Brill trucks and four CX Peckham trucks are used.

Westinghouse K-14 controllers are used on the quadruple-equipment cars, and the double-equipment cars are provided with K-11 controllers. All equipments are geared to a maximum speed of 35 miles per hour, and in operation the cars show an average energy consumption of 1878 watt-hours per car mile. The grades over which the line operates average 2%, the maximum gradient being 7%, and the sharpest curve has a radius of 50 feet.

The Los Gatos Interurban line is operated throughout under the management of F. E. Chapin, a street and interurban railway man of many years' experience. J. H. Parsons is its chief electrician.

— From The Journal of Electricity, Power and Gas, *July 1905*

---

the parlor car Edith making the first trip. Hourly alternate service was established in December over the two Los Gatos routes, later reduced to half-hourly alternate. A unique feature of this line was its shared trackage south of Campbell with the S. P.'s New Almaden branch as far as the San Jose-Los Gatos road, where the interurban resumed its own right of way southwesterly into Los Gatos. This shared trackage was laid on what is now Camden Avenue. Also opened was the Congress Springs line, running from a wye at Saratoga up the canyon to a spot just below the site of the burned hotel. Cars began regular runs from Congress Springs to San Jose and also to Los Gatos, where the big green cars of the interurban met the S. P.'s narrow-gauge steam trains from Oakland and other East Bay communities.

Hale, a versatile and witty planner, made his first local moves about then to implement the S. P.'s grand scheme, asking the county for rights to extend the interurban west along Stevens Creek Road from Meridian Corners to Cupertino. That was to expedite construction of the Los Gatos cutoff, which he described December 13 as a "Palo Alto line" taking off north from the Stevens Creek extension, skirting El Monte Canyon and on to Palo Alto. Materials had been purchased for this line, Hale said, and some right of way obtained.

Also requested were a city franchise eastward on San Fernando Street from Market Street to Coyote Creek and county franchises from that point to Evergreen, Berryessa, and Alum Rock Park. The proposed route was along Jefferson Street in East San Jose to McLaughlin Avenue, curving northward to Wright Avenue and eastward to King Road, jogging southeasterly along King a few hundred yards, and then eastward over private right of way to Capitol Avenue. The company asked permission to build southeasterly along King and Evergreen Roads to Evergreen, northwesterly along Capitol Avenue across Alum Rock Avenue to the S. P. tracks near Wayne Station, and northeasterly along Alum Rock and Fleming Avenues from Capitol to the southern limit of Alum Rock Park.

"Personally I have great faith in the east side of the valley," Hale declared, "and the building of railway lines in that section means much to San Jose and the county. These roads will give a continuous, rapid and first class service between the eastern foothills and the western boundaries of the county; they will afford equal transit facilities from one side to the other. We expect to make the run from Los Gatos to Alum Rock Park in one hour, and from Palo Alto the park without change of cars. The inevitable result will be to bring the populous centers close together, to develop traffic between the different points, and to disperse population more equally over the whole county by radial roads."

Hale disavowed ownership of the proposed Mt. Hamilton road but noted that his line would tap the survey of that road.

"We expect to reap advantages from that connection," he observed. "In all probability inter-traffic arrangements between the two lines will be possible to the pecuniary benefit of both."

Surveyors were seen in the Diablo Range later that week working the terrain from Smith's Creek to Hall's Valley, laying out the Mt. Hamilton route. By year's end the interurban had spent $700,000 for some 27 miles of electric line linking San Jose with Meridian, Sorosis, Saratoga, Congress Springs, Los Gatos, Campbell, and The Willows, important destinations of the day.

15. Parkinson Pushes Santa Clara Interurban

Parkinson and associates had not been idle in the meantime. They had solidified their support in San Mateo County and upper Santa Clara County, paving the way for their new line. Opportunity then arose to buy up the San Jose and Santa Clara electric road from the Center brothers at a favorable price, guaranteeing entry of the Palo Alto and Suburban into San Jose. Unaware of the full scope of S. P. intentions, Parkinson tested the South Bay political winds, was satisfied, and laid out, with DeForest and others, a $50,000 option on the San Jose and Santa Clara, subject to forfeiture. On all sides Parkinson found himself warmly congratulated by local officials, politicians, and citizens. Among those with the most cordial offers of support were E. A. and J. O. Hayes of the *San Jose Mercury*, the former a congressman and the latter aspiring to be governor of California. Hale assured Parkinson he would not object. The outlook seemed rosy.

In November 1904 Parkinson applied to the San Jose city council for a single-track standard-gauge line on Julian Street to Santa Teresa Street, looping through downtown San Jose on St. James, Second, and Julian streets back to Santa Teresa. He then awarded a construction contract to the Warren Improvement Company of San Francisco and proceeded December 19 with incorporation of the *Santa Clara Interurban Railroad Company*, a $5 million concern whose directorate comprised Parkinson, Dohrmann, San Jose attorney E. M. (Ed) Rea, and San Francisco attorneys J. C. Campbell and W. H. Metson of the firm of Campbell and Metson, said to be representing the Eastern backers. Plans called for a road down the peninsula from San Mateo through San Jose to Gilroy, with various branches including one to Stanford University.

The motive power was to be steam. This stipulation seemed strange for an aspiring electric road but had legal implications, as soon to be seen. The *Palo Alto Times*, announcing formation of the company, said it understood but had not confirmed that J. W. Gates, president of the U. S. Steel Corporation, was interested in the new road. That was a gratuitous boost to enhance the company's fortunes.

All had gone well thus far, but Monday, January 9, 1905, was to be a fateful turning point. That morning a construction gang of 50 men started grading for the Santa Clara Interurban along the county road outside the Stanford University gate. The San Jose franchise went through that evening without a hitch, its terms calling for the city to get 2% of the line's gross receipts after five years. Attorney John E. Richards filed Parkinson's acceptance and posted his $5000 performance bond.

The big action, however, took place at Mayfield, just south of Palo Alto. There, the town trustees, expected to give the company a routine franchise, balked, claiming that state law required them to advertise for bids before making the award. Hale attended that meeting, expressing interest in the franchise in behalf of his San Jose-Los Gatos interurban. "It's rumored that the Mayfield trustees won't give the franchise to the Parkinson people," reported the *Times* on January 11, "and that the Southern Pacific is behind the obstruction." That was the first public mention of possible S. P. involvement in affairs of the Santa Clara Interurban.

Parkinson exploded in anger. "We shall go clear around Mayfield before we will pay one cent for a franchise," he declared. "The Seale tract (a large parcel south of Embarcadero Road and east of Alma Street) would be a good route for the road, anyway." Then, in a calmer mood, he added that he would institute mandamus proceedings in Judge Rhodes' county court asking that the franchise be given him without advertising. If so, he said, the company would build through Mayfield in 40 days. Parkinson arranged a "first spike" ceremony January 12 in Palo Alto, attended by all five Santa Clara County supervisors, then left for New York to buy supplies and attend to other business matters.

The January 9 Mayfield meeting turned out to be merely the prelude to a stormier session the next week at which the town trustees pressed on with their determination to advertise the franchise. Representing the San Jose-Los Gatos interurban this time were Hale, Chapin, Dearborn, San Jose merchant Gustave F. Lion, W. C. Andrews of the Farmers' Union, A. E. Wilder, cashier of San Jose's Garden City Bank, and attorney Victor Scheller. Representing the Parkinson interests were Frank Dohrmann and attorney Ed Rea. The proceedings drew a large local audience.

Rea offered to pay for the franchise, thus saving the Mayfield trustees the costs of advertising. Scheller said no, that the law was explicit and the Board must advertise. The Board agreed.

Rea then observed that the Santa Clara Interurban was incorporated as a steam railroad. "The law allows a franchise award without advertising to a steam road," he told the trustees. "Then we can change it to electric. Fresno gave the Southern Pacific a steam road franchise without advertising."

"But they were a bonafide steam road," Scheller objected.

Hale suggested that the Board might be liable for criminal prosecution if they gave the franchise to Parkinson without advertising. He was willing, he said, to post a $10,000 bond to be forfeited if the road were not started in four months and completed within the year.

"You still don't have Stevens Creek yet," Rea observed.

"You know the law," Hale retorted. "A franchise can't be granted for 70 days after an election. Today is the 69th, and we shall get it tomorrow. There is but one bid in."

"I heard there were two," responded Rea.

"You know better," replied Hale, somewhat nettled. "You mean two envelopes, one with your bid and the other with our currency to back our bid."

What followed next was a long period of legal wrangling finally interrupted by Hale, who said, "Give me the franchise, and I'll build the road while these lawyers are arguing." That

John F. Parkinson, "father of Palo Alto streetcars." This portrait was taken about 1906. (Palo Alto City Library)

brought a general laugh, according to the *Times*.

The Board chose to advertise, the bidding to be open with each party allowed to raise the other to his heart's content and pocketbook's contents. Rea was offered a chance to share in setting terms and conditions of the franchise, which he refused. Finally Rea got up with Dohrmann to leave.

"If you don't want our road," he told the trustees, "I'll go out that door and will not trouble you again." There was no reply. As he and Dohrman reached the door, Rea turned to the assembled townspeople and, pointing in the direction of the Seale tract, delivered a parting shot. "When a fine town is built up to the south of you, I'll drive over some time and visit you people of Mayfield."

"We'll be here," said a member of the Board, and, the franchise matter settled, the trustees turned to commonplace matters of business which, noted the *Times*, were decidedly dull and dry compared with the exciting railway legislation.

The pace of battle had now quickened. The Santa Clara Interurban got an injunction from Judge Rhodes prohibiting Mayfield from selling or advertising its franchise while the court considered implications of the company's steam charter. The S. P. got an injunction preventing Parkinson from crossing its tracks at the so-called Bonair switch in the county road midway between Palo Alto and Mayfield, claiming that its intent was not to obstruct but rather to ensure proper placement of the switch and proper liability for accidents. Ed Rea answered with a demurrer. On January 23 the county supervisors gave Parkinson legal rights of way over county roads from Palo Alto to San Jose except for Mayfield. The *San Jose Mercury* published a telegram the next day from J. W. Gates, disassociating himself and the U. S. Steel Corporation from any California street railway proposition. Construction was meanwhile proceeding; double tracks had been laid from the Stanford University gate to the intended S. P. crossing at University Avenue, and grading was finished on the other side of the crossing down to Mayfield. Crews were said to be moving next into Mountain View for further grading and track work.

More trouble was brewing. In Palo Alto, some University Avenue residents opposed the streetcar line running in front of their homes. Urged by these property owners and stirred by the proceedings at Mayfield, the town trustees met quietly January 20 to hear arguments by certain of its members that Parkinson's local franchise was illegal and contrary to state law as to the conditions under which it was obtained. They referred the matter to the state attorney general for resolution. Stanford University's trustees turned the company down cold on a request to run its line onto the campus, affirming their earlier stand against electric roads entering the University grounds. Then January 30 brought news that Hale and W. C. Andrews had posted a $5,000 bond with the Mayfield trustees guaranteeing completion of their road through the community if the San Jose-Los Gatos interurban won the franchise.

Parkinson halted construction pending resolution of financial and legal questions. On February 20 came word of a further setback: California Attorney General U. S. Webb had filed suit to set aside the Palo Alto franchise. That prompted Parkinson's return to New York and led to hopeful tidings in the *Palo Alto Times* March 2 that the local man had interested Wall Street investors in the new electric road and satisfactorily settled all financial matters. "As soon as he gets here," said the *Times*, "work on the road will be commenced and rushed as rapidly as possible."

Parkinson came back March 6 reluctant to discuss the details of his Eastern trip. He told reporters he was sure that road would go through, then uncharacteristically declined further comment. This was a silence that was to last several months, during which work was suspended on the road and the legal matters, including the Bonair switch, remained unresolved.

From another source—*The Palo Altan* of January 19, 1906—we know what really happened on that trip. Despite growing evidence that the S. P. stood firm in his path and didn't intend to budge, Parkinson, who may not have wanted to believe it, apparently misread the signals. Arrangements had been made through a Judge Geary of New York to sell enough Santa Clara Interurban bonds to a security company to cover the costs of buying and improving the San Jose and Santa Clara electric road. Parkinson had gone to New York to close the deal and bring home the money. He was amazed when Judge Geary drew from his desk a map showing that the Alum Rock line was to be paralleled by an extension of the Hale-S. P. road. "My company cannot fight the Southern Pacific," Judge Geary said. "We cannot buy your bonds. Your road is to be paralleled."

"Impossible," said Parkinson, astounded. "The Southern Pacific has nothing to do with this."

Whereupon Judge Geary produced a large stack of letters and telegrams. They were from Southern Pacific officials, San Jose politicians, and others, all knocking the Parkinson scheme. Among the telegrams was one from San Jose Congressman E. A. Hayes. Parkinson came home, said *The Palo Altan*, a sadder and wiser man.

Judge Geary's information was, of course, essentially correct. Neither Hale nor the S. P. had hidden their immediate plans. On January 30, 1905, Hale had secured his Stevens Creek Road franchise, the new line to run along the south side of the road with stations no more than a quarter-mile apart, all trains to stop on signal. This opened the way to Palo Alto. In March he had obtained a San Jose city franchise covering lines eastward along San Carlos and San Fernando Streets, opening the way not only to Evergreen and Mt. Hamilton but also to Alum Rock Park. The S. P. had divulged plans to electrify its Oakland and Berkeley local steam lines, to meet Key Route competition. There were scattered hints that the railroad had other lofty ambitions, such as a high-speed electric road down the peninsula from San Francisco to San Jose. Pieces of the plan were being revealed, although the grand scheme was not yet totally visible.

On June 30 *The Palo Altan* reported that parties unknown had secured a local right of way through Hopkins Place and the Seale tract. Presumably these parties were the Hale road, if so blocking Parkinson's exit to the south. In August an official of the San Jose-Los Gatos interurban claimed that Stanford University would soon grant that company a right of way through the campus. Company surveyors were seen on the University grounds. Mayfield had not yet awarded a franchise; the present intent, said this official, was to bypass Mayfield to the west. The ring around the Parkinson road was drawing inexorably tighter.

Yet Parkinson, on September 29, broke silence by announcing that electric cars would be running on the Palo Alto streets by July 1, 1906. Final details were now being worked out, he said, to resume the construction to San Jose, probably with a branch to Woodside and other branches in Palo Alto. Reporters found him of cheerful demeanor, as if a heavy weight had been lifted from his shoulders.

16. Hanchett, Martin Enter Scene

Parkinson was indeed happier, for reasons that now came to light. On October 12, 1905, he announced the sale of his company and option on the San Jose and Santa Clara electric road, plus all other rights and interests, to a local syndicate headed by San Jose capitalist Lewis E. Hanchett and San Francisco utility magnate John Martin. "The price was not given out," said *The Palo Altan*, "but will probably reach $500,000." The newspaper attributed the immediate cause of the sale to a failure by Parkinson and DeForest to agree on future plans for the Santa Clara Interurban.

For Parkinson, this meant an end to direct involvement with the company he helped found. He remained a staunch supporter, however, and often is credited with being the "father of the Palo Alto trolleys." His lumber and real estate businesses flourished, then fell into a decline. "I made a fortune in Palo Alto and lost it in Palo Alto," he commented in later years, "but I don't know a better place to do either." His struggle with the Southern Pacific had cost him much but was expensive to the railroad, as well. Invited to the 1940 dedication of the new S. P. depot in San Jose, he was introduced to then-S. P. President A. D. McDonald as the man who had cost the railroad $10 million to stop building streetcar lines. Parkinson acknowledged the introduction as a personal tribute.

Whatever the immediate reason for the sale, it introduced another formidable S. P. foe in the Hanchett-Martin team. Hanchett, beneficiary of a mining fortune and at 33 a seasoned investor with good local connections, was backed by the political and financial clout of Martin, 47, an experienced promoter and developer. The San Franciscan, who had fought to the top from a humble beginning on the streets of Brooklyn, listed his occupation as president of the California Gas and Construction Company, but it was known that he and a partner, Eugene de Sabla, had just put finishing touches on an ambitious scheme to

This view of the San Jose & Santa Clara carbarn on The Alameda shows the sprinkler car on the curve at left, with a Sacramento type at right.

(Randolph Brandt Collection)

fold several large California utilities into one corporate giant, the Pacific Gas and Electric Company. Papers were just going through on this corporation. Martin had widespread local and regional business interests. He was no neophyte at electric railroading, either, having headed the North Pacific Coast until its sale in April 1904 to the Southern Pacific. That transaction had cost him money, so he had a score to settle with the S. P.

Hanchett and Martin announced elaborate plans for developing their new properties, including broad-gauging the San Jose and Santa Clara and extending a new line to Alum Rock Park by way of Berryessa, a large fruit-packing center east of San Jose. They told reporters that the Santa Clara Interurban would be completed, including the Palo Alto local lines, and hinted at transfer arrangements to be set up with the United Railroads at San Mateo. Also on the drawing boards, they said, was a San Jose amusement park of the type then in vogue.

On October 31, 1905, facing expiration of the Parkinson option, they finished buying out the San Jose and Santa Clara for $650,000, of which $400,000 was given in bonds. The deal was consummated November 2, ending more than a decade of Center family involvement with South Bay local transit.

In November Hanchett and Martin jointly formed a real estate venture called the Peninsular Land and Development

Company and bought the vacant 76-acre Agricultural Park fronting on The Alameda opposite the Fredericksburg Brewery. Plans were divulged for developing this prime residential site and opening it for subdivision.

On December 13, the San Jose and Santa Clara was formally reincorporated as the $5 million *San Jose and Santa Clara County Railroad Company*, its board of directors composed of Hanchett and Martin plus Henry Bostwick, Leo H. Sussman, and Karl E. Kneiss, all of San Francisco. The total subscription was $50,000, of which Hanchett put up $48,000. He became the president and chief operating officer, with Kneiss treasurer. Stipulated in the company charter was a standard-gauge interurban road from San Mateo to San Jose via Redwood City, Menlo Park, Palo Alto, Mayfield, Mountain View, and Santa Clara, embracing the routes of the Santa Clara Interurban. Specified also was the new Alum Rock branch.

By now the company had applied for a comprehensive San Jose broad-gauge franchise and other rights, running into resistance in the city council and elsewhere. As before, advance promises of local support melted away in the face of political realities. The S. P., observed a San Francisco newspaper, had directed its engines of war against Hanchett and Martin. Misunderstandings were fomented and magnified. Bitterly criticized

Streetcar mogul John Martin, co-founder of Pacific Gas & Electric Co.
(PG&E)

in as general manager was Richard Emory, an experienced transit operator from the East, with A. B. Southard, a 25-year streetcar veteran from San Francisco, as engineer and construction manager. Despite torrential rains, said to be the worst in 15 years, the changeover to standard gauge got under way April 13, 1906, crews starting from the town of Santa Clara to add a third (broad-gauge) rail to the existing narrow-gauge tracks. Service over the line was slowed but not halted by the reconstruction.

The company also made preliminary moves toward completing the Santa Clara Interurban. On February 5 Hanchett asked the Santa Clara town trustees for 50-year rights to a single-track line out San Francisco Road. The next month he pressed in court to dissolve the S. P. injunction blocking passage of the Santa Clara Interurban at the Bonair switch between Palo Alto and Mayfield. Hanchett also visited Palo Alto in March and April, telling reporters that the main obstacle to starting work there was the lawsuit against the Parkinson franchise. He urged solution of this problem, saying he was sure a compromise could be reached that would prove satisfactory to all.

17. S. P. Creates Peninsular

Taking advantage of Hanchett and Martin's preoccupation at San Jose, the Southern Pacific lost no time in improving its interurban position. A new $5 million corporation, the *Peninsular Railroad Company*, was formed December 21, 1905, with the intent of linking San Jose by interurban to San Francisco. Heading this new company was Oliver Hale, and its directorship was made up wholly of San Joseans: Hale, Frank Chapin, Gus Lion, W. C. Andrews, and A. E. Wilder. Hale subscribed $203,000 of the initial $205,000.

"The Peninsular Railroad," reported a San Francisco newspaper, "proposes to build 200 miles of electric railway. Lines are to be built from San Francisco to San Jose through Stanford University, Palo Alto, Redwood City, and San Mateo. Branches will extend to Los Gatos, Sempervirens Park, Alviso, Oakland, Alum Rock Park, and Lick Observatory on Mt. Hamilton. The first lines constructed will be from San Jose to San Francisco and Oakland, one on each side of the Bay.

"The main coast line of the Southern Pacific will be shortened by a cutoff from Mountain View and the trains for Los Angeles will go via Santa Cruz, while San Jose will be served by the new electric lines of the Peninsular Company. This railway will enter San Francisco through the Mission District using the tracks that are to be abandoned by the steam cars as soon as the Bayshore cutoff in completed. This will obviously render null and void the old agreement with the United Railroads of San Francisco, whereby the latter company would not extend south from San Mateo if the Southern Pacific would not build an electric line from San Jose to San Francisco." Thus was the S. P. master plan at last revealed.

On January 2, 1906, Hale, Chapin, and Senator Louis Oneal, representing the Peninsular, appeared before the San Mateo county supervisors asking rights to a double-track electric road through the county and claiming to have private rights of way from San Carlos to San Francisco and from San Jose to Mayfield, plus public access through Mayfield, Redwood City, and Palo Alto. The claims were premature, since none of these communities had yet given the Hale road a franchise.

On January 4 Chapin and Oneal, a prominent San Jose rancher and attorney, asked for local rights in Redwood City. The next evening Oneal asked the Palo Alto trustees for a single-or double-track line down Middlefield Road to Lytton Avenue, west to Alma Street, down to Forest Avenue, back to Emerson Street, and then south on Emerson to the town limit

by the San Jose Building Trades Council, for example, was the new company's request for a 31-year extension of its city operating franchises. Why should it get such rights without giving up money in return? When Hanchett appeared before this body in December to explain, he found the council's objections rooted in a rumor that the S. P. was backing his company. Not so, he told the council; it's owned by John Martin and me. That satisfied the council, which withdrew its objections.

Many such meetings took place, both public and private. Martin pulled out the stops and applied some political and financial pressures of his own, including a promise to make San Jose pay dearly for power if the franchise requests were ignored. The city council capitulated January 16, 1906, granting the franchise extensions. Final approval came six days later.

Rights to broad-gauge the company's Santa Clara Street and Tenth Street lines came the following week. By month's end Hanchett and Martin had extended city streetcar service on East Santa Clara Street to King Road, formerly served only by the Alum Rock cars, and were well along with acquiring rights of way for the new Berryessa line.

In March the company got permission to run a new broad-gauge line north on Fourteenth Street (now Seventeenth Street) from Santa Clara Street to Berryessa Road, where the new Alum Rock branch would strike out to the east. A construction bond was issued March 29 to pay for this line. Brought at Embarcadero Road. Hale, attending this meeting, told the town trustees that he was indeed the holder of a right of way through the Seale tract.

The Hale-Oneal franchise proposal generated much debate at Palo Alto, including a discussion by the local Board of Trade at which Parkinson contended one should have no faith in S. P. actions. Interests he had formerly owned in Palo Alto were not S. P. interests, he insisted, saying that if the franchise suit were dropped, the Hanchett people would immediately build their line into the community. The Palo Alto trustees evidently endorsed this view, voting January 19 to require a $50,000 performance bond with any new application for a local streetcar franchise.

The San Mateo supervisors decided February 7 to pigeonhole the Hale petition in that county, citing disagreements over the proposed route and sure knowledge that Peninsular agents were still trying to buy up rights of way in both San Mateo and Santa Clara Counties. Hale had better luck in Redwood City and San Mateo, obtaining franchises from both cities and posting a $10,000 performance bond in San Mateo to guarantee completion of his road in that community within 12 months.

Grading was now well along at San Jose for the Stevens Creek, Lick Observatory-Mt. Hamilton, and Park-Josefa lines, the latter paralleling existing rails of the interurban on San Carlos Street and giving it in effect a double-track route from Market Street out to Josefa. Construction began March 4 on the Mt. Hamilton branch, the company laying 60-pound Trilby rail instead of T-rail (the flanged Trilby track being a significant improvement). Market Street was relaid with Trilby. Track laying commenced March 20 on the Park-Josefa line. By then the Stevens Creek line was graded from Meridian to West Cupertino, a distance of 4½ miles. Rails for this portion were due in April. Some work was under way at San Mateo, where streets along the proposed route were being torn up preparatory to grading. No construction had yet begun on the Mayfield cutoff, where company agents were still securing rights of way.

18. 1905 Carbarn Fire

The San Jose Railroad, contending with growing obsolescence and competition from the interurban, had meanwhile suffered another blow. San Joseans awoke the morning of November 9, 1905, to find the company's carbarns at First and Oak Streets totally destroyed by fire. Horses, wagons, and the company's books had been saved, but 28 streetcars had gone up in smoke. Damage was estimated at $136,000 by General Manager George Tourney, who admitted that only $75,000 was covered by insurance.

The cause of the blaze was finally pinned to an electric short circuit. Power to the streetcar system, now supplied by the United Gas and Electric Company, had been shut down the morning of November 9 in accordance with the usual procedures, after all cars were "safely" in the barn. All attempts to restore power, in response to a 4:37 a.m. emergency call from the barn, had failed.

By mid-day November 9, Hanchett had offered the company five of his narrow-gauge cars for immediate use. These were gratefully accepted. By the end of the month the railroad had added a sixth car, obtained from Sacramento and converted from broad to narrow gauge. Thirteen-minute service was now offered on First Street and 30-minute service on Delmas Avenue—which, as the *Mercury* suggested, "is better than walking." By January 6, 1906, the company had procured eight red cars from the United Railroads of San Francisco, to which motors had to be added and the wheels set to narrow gauge. Two more cars were said to be enroute from the East; their ar-

rival would leave the company only two shy of the number it was actually operating before the fire. Service had been improved to a 10-minute headway on First Street and a 20-minute headway on Delmas. The Third-Seventh Street car was operating to no particular schedule.

The German Savings and Loan Society, dispirited by the losses, was said to have the company on the auction block. However, improvements were urgently needed, if for no other reason than to make it marketable. Thus it was, in March 1906, that the San Jose Railroad obtained local franchises and promised immediate action on broad-gauging its 13 miles of operating system. Who could foresee the event soon to happen that would make it impossible for the company to fulfill this promise?

19. 1906 Earthquake

The morning was April 18, 1906, and the time, shortly after 5 a.m. Dawn was lighting the sky over the Diablos to the east, and the cities along the peninsula were slowly wakening. In one moment the day held promise of splendor. In the next, the crushing violence of an 8.25-scale earthquake broke full force along the San Andreas fault, twisting and wrecking and killing. A roar like thunder filled the air. The quake struck once, twice, a third time. In hardly more than a minute, what had been San Jose, Palo Alto, and several other Santa Clara County communities were laid almost to waste. There was no count yet of the dead. Hundreds were injured. Nearly 10,000 were homeless.

This was the famous San Francisco earthquake of 1906, striking with fury to lay a swath of destruction 20 to 40 miles wide, running 200 miles from Salinas in the south to Fort Bragg in the north. No city within that belt escaped damage. Disaster lay everywhere.

In Palo Alto, several business buildings were demolished; total damage was estimated in the hundreds of thousands. Thiele's new $30,000 building and Fuller's new structure on High Street, both of artificial stone, collapsed completely. Fraser and Company's Stanford Building lost walls, as did Simkin's three-story building. The cornice fell from the Mariposa block. Parkinson's block suffered badly, listing to the east. Many residences were damaged, including Albert DeForest's home on University Avenue (incorrect early reports had this dwelling leveled). Particularly hard hit was St. Patrick's Seminary north of Palo Alto, where the tower over the entrance fell at the first shock and the interior was torn up.

Two died and several were injured at Stanford University, where the Memorial Arch lay in ruins. Encina Hall was wrecked, as were the new library and gymnasium then under construction. The dome collapsed at the Memorial Church, where part of the front wall, carrying in mosiac a representation of the Sermon on the Mount, was overthrown. Fortunately the church's interior mosaics and art-glass windows were not badly damaged, and the great organ escaped entirely.

Parkinson, then president of the town trustees and just recovering from painful injuries suffered in an automobile accident the week before, was a powerful force in the community that day, rallying public support and driving up and down University Avenue advising merchants not to raise prices on food and other commodities. Under his direction Palo Alto mobilized its resources, took in refugees, and sent to San Francisco clothing and blankets plus daily shipments of some 7,000 loaves of bread, 900 gallons of milk, and hundreds of gallons of soup.

At Santa Clara, collapse of a steel water tower dumped 180,000 gallons of the precious fluid into the streets. The Pacific Manufacturing Company in that community reported destruction of a mill; damage was estimated at $150,000. Businesses and homes were leveled there as elsewhere. Ralph Van Arsdale, then six years old and living with his grandmother on Stevens Creek Road about a half-mile west of Saratoga Avenue, clearly remembered his bed traveling across the bedroom and slamming into a wall. The door to the room was wedged shut, preventing his grandmother from reaching him.

Mrs. Catherine Gasich of Cupertino, then five and living north of Homestead Road near the present Wolfe Road, recalled being dumped out of bed and running to the dining room in time to see her father, carrying a lighted lantern, thrown into a corner. Her father, a San Jose barrelmaker, held onto the lantern and saved the home from fire. The kitchen was a shambles, Mrs. Gasich remembered, with groceries and dishes strewn over the floor and a leg broken off the wood-burning kitchen range. Both she and Van Arsdale recalled seeing the glow to the north as San Francisco burned.

Florence R. Cunningham, in her book *Saratoga's First Hundred Years*, provides a vivid eyewitness account by a local resident of the damage around that community. "I was spilled out of my bed and then hollered 'earthquake.' I put on my slippers and ran through the house when suddenly my eye glimpsed the kitchen floor. The night before, my mother had canned grapes, filling several dozen half-gallon Mason jars which she had left on the kitchen table. Now they were all over the floor, a mess of grapes, juice, and broken glass.

"Next I hurried out to the front porch, where I heard a roaring sound. Within seconds a flock of chickens was running south trying to escape nature's fury. Then I experienced a dizzy sight. A series of rolling waves made the hillsides planted with fruit trees resemble ocean waves with a constant rising and falling of the terrain. Oak trees lining the gulch down the road were twisted in every direction as though shaken by a savage tornado.

"Later I hitched up the horse and buggy and drove into Saratoga and San Jose. There were big cracks in the roads and some of them were large enough for my foot. Hardly a water tank was left standing in the countryside. Practically each farm had its own water tank, but the violent splashing of the water soon undermined the wooden frame which supported it. Before long the entire structure lay in a wooden heap with miniature floods surrounding it. The steel rails between Saratoga and San Jose were twisted completely out of shape. Some people carried their stoves and bedding into the yard and camped outdoors for a few days. Everywhere there was ruin."

The scene of one of the saddest tragedies was the state mental hospital at Agnews, just a few miles north of San Jose. There, more than a hundred inmates and attendants lay dead, buried beneath the rubble of collapsed walls and towers. Help came

Stanford's Memorial Church sustained heavy damage from the earthquake, but the priceless pipe organ and the art treasures survived.

(San Jose Historical Museum)

from every hand, men walking and running for miles in some cases to be of assistance.

In San Jose, hundreds of walls and buildings collapsed to produce some of the quake's most spectacular wreckage. Damage was estimated in the millions. Beneath the fallen walls of the Vendome Hotel Annex lay a score of persons, all but one of whom were rescued. The St. Francis Hotel was badly damaged, one elderly woman dying there. Other deaths were reported. The annex to Hale Brothers' department store, on First Street, was a total wreck. The new Hall of Justice and several large business buildings stood as shells. The post office building was half demolished. Extensive damage was reported to the Fredericksburg Brewery. Many homes were in rubble. Especially hard hit were the churches, at least five of which collapsed in ruins. The city found itself temporarily without water, power, or gas.

San Jose Mayor G. D. Worswick declared martial law at 6 a.m. April 18, calling out National Guard Company B to patrol the streets, assisted by 500 special deputies. A large part of the downtown section was roped off, and the mayor issued a proclamation warning that crimes and misdemeanors in the city would be punished with a heavy hand.

By mid-morning fires had broken out in several places, including a lodging house at Santa Clara and Locust Streets where seven died, pinioned beneath the timbers. Four fire engines were thrown into an all-day battle against the flames, which were under control by nightfall. St. James Park, opposite the courthouse, was soon full of hastily erected shelter tents.

Hundreds made their way to the park seeking food, shelter, and loved ones from whom they were separated. San Jose was San Francisco in miniature that day, the chief difference being that most of the San Jose water mains didn't rupture. That made it possible to fight fires in the community.

The city's death count the following day stood at 19, a miracle that so few had perished. Property damage was set at $3 million. The streetcar companies counted themselves lucky. Local damage was minor save for distressed roadbeds and the collapse of one wall at the San Jose and Santa Clara's Alameda carbarn at Lenzen Street. Its shops, at Hale and Alum Rock Avenues, were unaffected. Within the city, rails were mostly intact. Cars were undamaged but not running since the wires were down, power had not been restored, and the streets were choked with debris.

During the next week, several carloads of poles and rails intended for broad-gauging the San Jose and Santa Clara were sent by Hanchett and Martin to the United Railroads of San Francisco, to aid in rebuilding its lines. Cars they had on order were also turned over to the United Railroads. The Southern Pacific on its part gave massive help to stricken cities along its right of way down the peninsula, running freight cars into downtown San Jose over the Peninsular's Market Street standard-gauge tracks, once they were cleared, to help in removing the rubble.

Hanchett put a 40-man crew to work clearing debris, stringing wire, and repairing his roadbed. Limited streetcar service was resumed over some lines within the week. Regular 10-minute

The 1906 earthquake destroyed the upper story of the Native Sons Hall at Third and San Antonio streets. The lower floor, occupied by the Santa Clara Valley Wine Co., suffered little damage. Note pictures still hung on the exposed wall, center. (California Collection, San Jose Public Library)

service was restored April 27 on the lines to Keyes Street and East San Jose. Hanchett announced that new cars were now on order in Sacramento and St. Louis: 40-footers for the city lines and 45-footers for the new Alum Rock line. All plans would proceed without interruption, he told reporters, including his San Mateo interurban and Palo Alto local lines.

The Peninsular was soon back in operation, too, its crews working feverishly to repair roadbeds and relay rails along Saratoga Avenue and elsewhere. Local service was restored first, then interurban service via the Campbell cutoff. Even as this work was progressing, Hale spoke glowingly of his own intended line to San Mateo via Mayfield, promising to open the line within two years. Once the repairs were done, his crews went back to finishing the Mt. Hamilton and Park-Josefa lines. Construction of the former was halted at San Fernando and Second Streets because of a refusal by the San Jose Railroad to broad-gauge its San Fernando tracks from Second to Market Street, despite an agreement to the contrary. The latter was extended out Park Avenue to Meridian Road, rejoining the original line at Meridian and San Carlos.

The San Jose Railroad also worked feverishly to restore service, hampered by the heavy rubble along First and Second Streets. Physical damage to the system was slight, but the earthquake forever shattered the company's dream of major improvements. San Francisco demands on the German Savings and Loan Society completed the financial rout. No money was available for modernizing. Plans to broad-gauge the system were scrapped, leading to abrogation of its agreement with the Peninsular.

20. Hanchett Builds Palo Alto Lines

Even as San Jose was digging out from the wreckage, Hanchett's crews went back to work broad-gauging the San Jose and Santa Clara, using 70-pound T-rail beyond Orchard and Fourth Streets instead of the 60-pound Trilby specified in the new franchises. That was partly because Trilby was hard to get after the earthquake. Over the next few months the partners double-tracked the Tenth Street and East San Jose lines and bought 15 new wood-body California cars from the Sacramento Gas and Electric Company, equipped with rope brakes, rebuilt diamond-archbar trucks, and twin GE 25-horsepower motors. Thirteen of these were 40-footers for full service; the other two were 28-footers for feeder lines. The overhead supply system was standardized at 600 volts, same as the Peninsular. New generators and other equipment were installed in the San Jose and Alum Rock powerhouses. A big tract of land was obtained for the new amusement center, Luna Park, running from Old Oakland Road to east of Fourteenth Street along the north side of Berryessa Road, sufficiently removed from downtown to require a ride on the cars.

Well along by now was the Hanchett Residence Park, whose grounds were designed by John McLaren, superintendent of San Francisco's Golden Gate Park. Reportedly the partners had spent $100,000 there on improvements. Features were ornamental trolley poles, cement rock streets, and electric street-lights. "We challenge comparison with any subdivision offered any place on the peninsula, as far as the quality of the improvements and location of the tract are concerned," stated the developers. "This is the only subdivision ever placed on the market in California with a modern septic tank sewerage system and flush tanks." Part of this work involved building a short street-car branch, the Hanchett Park line, under private agreement with the Peninsular Land and Development Company. When this line was finished, Hanchett Park cars began operating from Tillman and Park Avenues through the tract to Tenth and

Keyes Streets, alternating through downtown San Jose with Santa Clara cars to East San Jose.

Martin widened his transit interests during this period, buying Santa Cruz's Union Traction Company in July 1906 and broad-gauging and extending the system. He served as president of Union Traction until 1912. Commanding his attention also was the rebuilding of the Pacific Gas and Electric Company, which had suffered heavily in the earthquake and was forced to borrow $1.4 million over a nine-month period to reconstruct its facilities. There were other money problems at P. G. and E., so Hanchett had to proceed almost alone in developing the Santa Clara Interurban and Palo Alto city lines.

In May 1906, facing a court test of the Parkinson franchise, Hanchett proposed a compromise settlement to the Palo Alto trustees, offering to pay court costs, reimburse the city for up to $500 in attorneys' fees, and post a $20,000 performance bond to guarantee completion of the road by November 15. The trustees agreed, but California Attorney General U. S. Webb insisted that the case go to trial. It did, on June 12, Hanchett and the town trustees solidly supporting each other. The court ruled a week later in favor of the validity of the franchise.

By now Hanchett had ordered cars, rail, switch points, ties, poles, and other materials for the road, many of which were in short supply. So he was forced to cool his heels while a potential competitor, General W. H. H. Hart, won a Palo Alto franchise for double-track lines up Middlefield Road and Alma Street, plus other routes on cross streets. That was July 18. Rumor had Hart backed by James J. Hill, the Great Northern railroad magnate, as part of a plan for the Great Northern to invade California against the opposition of the Southern Pacific. Hart posted a $2,000 performance bond with the Palo Alto trustees in September but failed the following month to get a Redwood City franchise even though there were no other bidders. He threatened to file suit against that community but never did. He never built any Palo Alto lines, either, despite promises to do so.

In August Colonel T. M. W. Draper of San Francisco, hired by Hanchett to oversee his Palo Alto construction, told local reporters that Charles Weiner had contracted to build the road and would be working with company foreman Archie D. Foree, former superintendent of the San Jose Railroad. Four carloads of rail had been shipped, Draper said. Already on hand were 3500 ties, with 2500 more to come. Draper spoke of a concrete-ballasted roadway with tracks set flush to the street, using 91-pound Trilby for the double-track University Avenue line to Waverley Street and 60-pound rail for the single-track lines down Waverley and out University to Marlowe Street, just west of San Francisquito Creek boundary between Palo Alto and Ravenswood.

Crews began grading September 12 at the Embarcadero Road end of the Waverley Street line, shifting over a few days later to University Avenue. Plans were announced for a "diamond track" near the Southern Pacific depot in downtown Palo Alto, into which the double tracks on University would converge and run almost to the S. P. right of way. Track laying commenced October 10 on University Avenue with a brief ceremony at which Weiner drove home the first spike and Foree the second. Some 60 men were now at work on the road.

On October 4 the Palo Alto trustees, without benefit of franchise, gave Hanchett permission to build a single-track line from University Avenue over Emerson Street and Hawthorne Avenue to Alma Street. The purpose of this short branch, known as the Hawthorne Avenue line, was to connect to the carbarn and transformer station Hanchett planned to erect at Hawthorne and High Street, on land secured from Parkinson.

Rights were also given to the California Gas and Electric Corporation to string a feeder line from Embarcadero Road up Middlefield Road and Hawthorne Avenue to the transformer station. These actions were needed, said the trustees, for Hanchett to meet the November 15 deadline, the regular franchise procedure being far too long. Several protests were lodged, including one from General Hart that the feeder line might pose a hazard to his trolley wires along Middlefield Road.

The trustees nevertheless stood firm, publishing an opinion by the city attorney that their actions were legal and ratifying the Hanchett permit three times, the last on November 5. By then the transformer station was taking shape and Hanchett was preparing to install the old generating equipment from his Alum Rock powerhouse. This equipment had to stand out in the open, because the transformer station was not yet roofed.

Over Hart's objections, the trustees also gave Hanchett rights to a 60-foot-wide subway under the S. P. tracks at Hawthorne Avenue, which Hanchett accepted reluctantly and never intended to build. His plan was a grade-level crossing at University Avenue. Emory and attorney Ed Rea spoke out against the subway, triggering resistance by the trustees on other matters. Political prudence compelled Hanchett to put this issue on the back burner.

Five new California-type cars arrived October 24 at the Palo Alto S. P. freight house, painted buff and light green, numbered 1-5, and lettered San Jose and Santa Clara Railroad Company on their side panels. These were handsome cars, reported *The Palo Altan*, with headlights, basket fenders, lever brakes, outward-facing end seats, and operating side windows in the closed center section. Puzzling to the newspaper, though, were the side-panel markings. With permission, Colonel Draper laid a temporary track along S. P. property and Alma Street to move the cars onto University Avenue. Then he explained the markings. This was a manufacturer's mistake, he said. The cars were eventually intended for San Jose but should have been lettered Santa Clara Interurban Railroad Company because they would be used temporarily at Palo Alto. They would be relettered. Ultimately they would be replaced by other cars, probably of similar design.

Track laying was now nearly done, the company bonding its rails by a new method—Brown's bonding—in which the fish-plates were soldered to the rails with mercury alloy instead of the conventional copper alloy. Frogs, switch points, and curved rails for Hawthorne Avenue, Waverley Street, and the diamond

track had not yet arrived, leaving the road a collection of isolated single-track lines. Also missing were the poles for the overhead trolley wires, prompting the trustees to give Hanchett permission in November to use the city poles temporarily. As crews began stringing the wires, Hanchett named Charles C. Benson of Redwood City as his operating manager at Palo Alto, reporting to General Manager Emory in San Jose. Final touches were put on plans for the November 15 opening-day celebration, at which 30 young lady volunteers would collect fares on the cars, all proceeds going to the Palo Alto churches. Other activities were scheduled, such as a parachute leap and balloon ascension.

An abortive attempt November 12 to get the cars running was followed two days later by a successful test. At 2 p.m. on the 14th, Parkinson, officiating as motorman, ran the first car, loaded with local dignitaries, from University and Ramona to the end of the University Avenue line. The car then returned to Waverley Street, where the passengers transferred to another car to travel south to Embarcadero Road. No problems were encountered; the roadbed was reported smooth and the cars comfortable. Regular service began that day at 3 p.m. All was now in readiness for the opening festivities.

The official opening day—November 15, 1906—dawned grey and rainy, but this failed to dampen the enthusiasm of the Palo Altans, many of whom turned out to ride the cars and take part in the celebration. Games, races, and refreshments were offered at the end of the University Avenue line. Merchants gave discounts, and the S. P. offered reduced rates for the day on steam trains from San Francisco and San Jose. School children got a free holiday, the boys spending their nickels riding the cars. The balloon ascension and parachute leap, originally set for 11 a.m., were postponed to 2:30 p.m. because of the rain.

Two streetcars ran in the morning and three in the afternoon. Conductorettes on the first shift were Misses Heddum, McGilvray, Albee, Moore, and Zschokke, who took in $45.81 for the first three hours. Total receipts for the day were $527.61, many people contributing much more than the regular fare (Hanchett himself gave $100). Advertising space in the cars was well used, observed *The Palo Altan*, which philosophized that "the inclement conditions made us appreciate the streetcars just that much more."

Santa Clara Interurban car 2 at The Circle, Palo Alto, about 1906. Charles D. Whittaker is the conductor. (Wilbur C. Whittaker Collection)

This photo was taken about 1947. John F. Parkinson, then 83, holds a 1906 poster announcing the official opening of Palo Alto streetcar service. (Palo Alto Public Library)

Twenty-minute headway was established on the University Avenue and Waverley Street lines, passengers on the Waverley line transferring to University Avenue cars because the frogs and other paraphernalia for the switches still had not arrived. Outbound University Avenue cars ran on the wrong side of the double-track line for the same reason. Materials for the Waverley switch were delivered in mid-December, together with the missing trolley wire poles. By year's end the switch was installed and Waverley cars were running directly from the downtown Palo Alto to Embarcadero Road. The headway had now been reduced to 15 minutes on each line, effecting 7½ minute service through the downtown section. The new poles were in place and the city streets almost repaved. The transformer station was nearly under roof.

Remaining to be completed were only the diamond track, the double curve at Emerson Street entering the Hawthorne Avenue line, and the carbarn, a 70- by 100-foot wooden structure with a sheet-iron coating, adjoining the transformer station. B. F. Gerow, boss carpenter on the transformer station, had the contract for this building. B. F. Stanton had replaced Benson as operating manager at Palo Alto as a result of Richard Emory's unexpected death November 25 in San Jose. Benson had moved down to San Jose, succeeding Emory as general manager of all Hanchett-Martin lines in Santa Clara County.

The road was appreciated and well patronized when operating, as one observer noted. The chief problem was keeping it in operation, a fault of the winter weather and the antiquated generator. The streetcars often stalled because of power failures, once for two days when a storm blew down the lines to the transformer station. "It is a difficult thing to criticize and at the same time to praise," commented *The Palo Altan* late in December. "Our new streetcar system is quite an ornament, at times a great convenience, and likewise frequently a source of no small irritation. It does, however, frequently happen that the moment we are congratulating ourselves that we have a street-car line and that a long walk through the rain and mud is avoided, presto chango, the power is cut off, or a fuse blows out, and we sorrowfully wend our way home, soliloquizing (some may swear a little) on the vicissitudes of life and the uncertainty of electric juice."

Early in February 1907 the company installed a 110-kilowatt generator bought from the Farnsworth Company, San Francisco. That solved the power problem. Work began in mid-April on the double curve at Emerson Street and May 1 on the carbarn. With the line smoothly in operation and nearing completion, Hanchett was in better position to press for a crossing at University Avenue; the diamond track was supplanted in company plans by double tracks up to the S. P. right of way. This time the Palo Alto trustees didn't object. The railroad also yielded. Rails of the Santa Clara Interurban crossed those of the Southern Pacific May 29, the crews then moving to extend the interurban southward along the county road (El Camino Real) toward Mayfield. Hanchett again spoke of a branch line onto the university grounds, although the Stanford trustees were still opposed. Now on order from the St. Louis Car Company were a dozen large interurban cars of the California type—powerful 50-footers with four 100-horsepower motors—underscoring Hanchett's determination to complete his Santa Clara Interurban.

Important events were also transpiring in San Jose, where Hanchett's crews were building the double-track Fourteenth Street branch from Santa Clara Street out to Berryessa Road. That was in April 1907. Cars were soon running over this line. Under construction at Luna Park—Fourteenth and Berryessa Road—were an amusement park, theater, skating rink, and baseball stadium. The company started sponsoring dances that month at the pavilion in Alum Rock Park. Hanchett told reporters that he and Martin had already poured $600,000 into the San Jose developments and estimated their total investment at $1.5 million when the present work was done, including the Alum Rock Park line via Berryessa.

The biggest news, however, had been a tentative move by the Peninsular in January to acquire the moribund San Jose Railroad, currently in trouble with local officials over paving the city streets. Hanchett also coveted the San Jose Railroad. So, to meet the Peninsular's move, he had countered with a paralleling scheme of his own, obtaining city franchises for six miles of lines intended to compete with the narrow-gauge system. Features were a north-south route from Eighth and Jackson Streets through downtown to Second and Virginia Streets, and a branch from Fifth and Santa Clara Streets to Fourteenth and Jackson. On March 29 he had transferred the franchises to a new $1 million corporation, the *San Jose Traction Company*, personally subscribing $298,000 of the $300,000 initial capital and serving as president. Martin became vice president and Sheldon S. Baldwin of San Jose secretary-treasurer. Benson and Ed Rea rounded out the directorate. Hanchett said he would start building the new routes once his other commitments were fulfilled.

21. S. P. Buys Santa Clara Interurban

This represented the high point in aspirations of the Hanchett-Martin electric roads. The S. P. had been preoccupied during recent months, giving the partners a fairly free hand. That was changing. Just around the corner, too, was the depression of 1907, ready to drop its withering hand across the nation.

The Peninsular had now completed its Park-Josefa line and Mount Hamilton branch out to Thirteenth (now Fifteenth) Street, where the track turned south from San Fernando to San Carlos Street. New equipment had been added: two wood-frame Holman city cars, a motorized line car, wrecker, work motor, and sprinkler, the latter built in the company shops. George White got a $1 million contract from the Peninsular to complete the Mayfield cutoff, which was to be double-tracked for the 13½ miles from Mayfield to Congress Junction, outside Saratoga, and single-tracked from there to Vasona, near Los Gatos. This was a important piece of construction to both the S. P. and the interurban. Work was proceeding slowly at this time but expected to quicken in the spring.

Early in 1907 the interurban opened its long-awaited Cupertino branch, running cars out this single-track line to a future Monta Vista junction with the Mayfield cutoff. The Holmans probably were used at first, supplanted that year by new 39-foot city and suburban cars from the St. Louis Car Company. Cupertino service now originated at Meridian Corners. The company also used the new cars to inaugurate Bascome Local service from the San Jose S. P. depot to Meridian Corners.

Oliver Hale continued to discuss his San Francisco extension and make moves in that direction, including an announcement in May that the interurban had secured a right of way behind Stanford University from Mayfield to Redwood City. However, the pace of activity remained slow, reflecting a change in the Southern Pacific's South Bay master plan. The railroad had been ready in 1906 to build the extension. Rails and other materials had been ordered when a catastrophe six months previous and 600 miles away altered its plans. In June 1905 the Colorado River had burst its banks and flooded the Imperial Valley of Southern California, inundating the S. P.'s Los Angeles-Yuma main line. The company was forced to commit millions of dollars to save this line. Special railroads were built to carry rock trains to crucial points along the river, and among the rails commandeered for this purpose were those intended for the Peninsular. The river finally returned to its channel and the Imperial Valley was saved. Most parts of the master plan were salvaged, such as the Bayshore cutoff, Mayfield cutoff, and broad-gauging of the old South Pacific Coast line from Oak-

Palo Alto in 1907. This panoramic view shows the Palo Alto carbarn and transformer station near the tower on Hawthorne Avenue between Alma and High streets, at upper center. In background, left, is the Southern Pacific bridge over San Francisquito Creek near the tall tree—"Palo Alto"—often credited as the source of the city's name.

(George Cody Collection)

land to Santa Cruz, but the price paid for victory over the Colorado River included the San Francisco extension.

Other problems had beset the Peninsular. One was the untimely death July 20, 1907, of Hale, long a powerful voice for its expansion. His replacement was Frank Chapin, reporting to Paul Shoup in Los Angeles. Another was the 1907 depression, now in stride and gaining momentum. S. P. officials, deeming it unwise at that time to push the interurban, ordered new plans which, in brief, called for keeping the old main line through San Jose, temporarily postponing any extension of the Peninsular above Mayfield, double-tracking the Cupertino line from Meridian Corners to Monta Vista to give San Jose a high-speed access, and sharing the Mayfield cutoff—steam trains and electrics—to Monta Vista. From there to Vasona the track would be leased to the S. P. for the exclusive use of steam trains.

Another casualty was the 26-mile Lick Observatory-Mount Hamilton line, which would have been a great attraction. A decision was made to terminate this branch at Thirteenth Street. So the Peninsular instituted loop service over the line—now called the Naglee Park branch—from Second and San Fernando to Thirteenth and back to Market and San Carlos, where passengers could transfer to other lines.

With Hale dead and money in short supply, the S. P. lost interest in buying the San Jose Railroad. The price was right, but the San Jose city council had gone on record requiring any buyer, as a condition of purchase, to broad-gauge the system. Also outstanding was a large paving bill, the city council having ordered the railroad to repair about a mile of First Street at company expense, under threat of voiding its charters. There was the chance of competition from Hanchett's San Jose Traction. The San Jose Railroad was ripe for takeover but not now, decided S. P. officials, in light of the present financial circumstances.

In April 1907 George White, in announcing the resumption of work on the Mayfield cutoff, confirmed that the Peninsular had leased the line to the S. P. for steam service. Crews brought up from the Salton Sea were put to work grading and building bridges. Rail laying began in August. The last bridge, spanning Stevens Creek, was completed in January. The line was previewed April 12, 1908, two S. P. steam trains hustling 16 coachloads of prospective buyers to a barbeque and land sale at Los Altos. Regular service opened April 19 with five trains each way daily, shortening the distance from San Francisco to Santa Cruz by seven miles and meeting the Peninsular at Monta Vista, Congress Junction, and Los Gatos. This boosted business for the interurban.

As the Peninsular had suffered during the 1907 depression, so had Hanchett and Martin, whose resources hardly rivaled those of the S. P. Funding dried up. Martin's first commitment was to the Pacific Gas and Electric Company, which was still in financial straits. He took over briefly as president, poured in $200,000 of his own funds, and righted the foundering utility. That drained him of money, though, for his streetcar projects.

Work was suspended at Luna Park. The partners halted their Berryessa line and Traction developments. The depression and other problems, such as continued refusals by the Mayfield and Stanford University trustees to grant rights of way, also killed their chances for extending the Santa Clara Interurban. Hanchett cancelled his order with the St. Louis Car Company. That left Palo Alto a small system operating three cars over about 2½ miles of track, isolated from the other Hanchett-Martin properties.

The new year brought an economic rebirth and, with it, rumors of fresh rivals. The Western Pacific, it was said, was about to electrify its whole Pacific Coast system, including its lines to San Jose and Oakland. That wasn't true. But Borax Smith and associates, whose Key Route electrics were still win-

ning the battle for patrons over in the East Bay, were indeed preparing to push their long-threatened extension to San Jose. In anticipation, 10 large cars were fabricated in company shops.

The Key Route—San Francisco, Oakland and San Jose Railway—also planned to build a tunnel from Oakland to Yerba Buena Island, shortening its ferry runs and, hence, its total operating time to San Francisco. That would put additional pressure on the S. P. Other East Bay extensions were contemplated. The total cost was expected to exceed $8 million; funds on this scale were not yet available, but the work was expected to begin shortly.

The Southern Pacific responded by reconfirming its own plans to electrify all Bay Area lines, starting in the East Bay. Construction commenced on a large East Bay powerhouse at Fruitvale, lending credence to the claim. By now the railroad had opened its main-line Bayshore cutoff south of San Francisco, touching off new speculations about a San Francisco-San Jose electric road using the old route through the Mission District. Company officials didn't deny the story. With funds again available, a new scheme had been born whereby San Francisco and San Jose would be linked to Oakland by an electric line bridging the Bay from Ravenswood to Dumbarton Point, west of Newark. Chosen for this work was the Peninsular, which presumably would be extended to both Oakland and San Francisco. The S. P. had already filed application for the Dumbarton crossing. Provision was being made at Fruitvale for the increased power load if needed. It was not known yet whether the railroad was serious about the new scheme or merely countering Smith's moves.

The immediate significance, however, was to give special value to the Santa Clara Interurban, lying as it did between Mayfield and the Dumbarton crossing. Whereas Hanchett and Martin now considered the interurban expendable, the S. P. saw its rails over the county road and University Avenue as the natural route to Ravenswood, promising a connection with the Peninsular once the Mayfield trustees granted permission. The equipment and roadbed were in good order. Most of the line was suitable for heavy traffic. The company still held an important franchise from Palo Alto to San Mateo, plus valuable rights from Mayfield to San Jose.

Taking advantage of the opportunity, the S. P. made Hanchett and Martin a tempting offer for the interurban, which they accepted August 13, 1908. The price was not disclosed but conjectured to be $500,000. "Mr. Hanchett stated last night that he sold the road because he does not wish to undergo the worry and trouble of building and financing the line," reported the *San Jose Mercury* the next day. "He expects to leave soon for Europe where, with his children, he may spend a year. Mr. Hanchett wants it understood distinctly that he had not disposed of any part of the San Jose and Santa Clara Railroad, and that he has no idea of doing so." The partners thus breathed easier, freed of their Palo Alto obligations and provided fresh money for San Jose. The S. P. also breathed easier, knowing that the interurban would never be used against it.

22. Peninsular Reaches Palo Alto

Sale of the Santa Clara Interurban spurred new talk of a San Mateo extension. Surveyors were seen working north of Palo Alto, but nothing developed. In April 1909 the Peninsular reconfirmed plans to electrify one track of the Mayfield cutoff down to Monta Vista Junction and double-track the Cupertino line to Meridian Corners. All materials had now been ordered, it said, and the work would start soon. This was followed shortly by announcement of an agreement in principle with the Mayfield trustees for a single-track line down the middle of El

An eastbound University Avenue car nears Hale Street, Palo Alto. (David L. Mitchell Collection)

Camino Real from the north town boundary to Lincoln Street (now California Avenue), curving off westward through the fields to join the Mayfield cutoff. Franchise papers were being drawn. This news plus pressures from the Stanford community encouraged the University trustees to reconsider their opposition to a campus electric line; June 1 found them meeting with S. P. officials to discuss possible routes. The railroad wanted to buy a roadbed, to which the trustees objected. Eventually they agreed to lease the S. P. a campus right of way.

Important events had meanwhile occurred down in San Jose—centering around the San Jose Railroad—that would help shape the final form of the South Bay electric lines. George Tourney was now president as well as general manager of this beleagured road, with W. S. Goodfellow vice president and George L. Barker secretary-treasurer. Under Tourney's direction the company had upgraded its roadbed and successfully negotiated its paving problems with the San Jose city council but consistently refused during 1908 to honor demands to broadgauge at least the First Street line.

At issue was reconstruction of the Hobson Street branch, already unprofitable and sure to be more so with the pending shutdown of the San Jose Woolen Mills. The railroad could hardly afford to rebuild the Hobson Street line. Since this was a city stipulation, however, the 50-year First Street broad-gauge franchise came up for public bid early in 1909. Both Hanchett and the S. P. wanted the franchise. It went, for $11,000, to Jere T. Burke of Berkeley, an attorney for the S. P. The narrow-gauge cars of the San Jose Railroad continued to ply their trade along First Street and the new franchise had doubtful legality, but it clouded the company's titles and added to its other burdens. Implied, also, was that the San Jose Railroad must soon become an S. P. property, setting up another confrontation with Hanchett and Martin.

The situation was in fact a stalemate. If the S. P. exercised its new rights, it faced a legal battle with the San Jose Railroad and also the possibility that Hanchett and Martin might build their San Jose Traction system. On the other hand, the franchise, unexercised, was a curb on the partners' willingness to build the San Jose Traction. Clearly an accommodation was in order, and to this end negotiations started that were to touch off the last big building boom for the South Bay electric roads.

Curiously, not a hint reached the local press. The first word was an announcement June 2 that the S. P., for an undisclosed sum, had bought the 50-year franchise of the San Jose Traction Company. That aroused much interest. It was not until the following October, however, that local residents learned the rest of the deal: that Burke, in return for $16,000 and rights for the Peninsular to use certain tracks of the San Jose and Santa Clara within the city, had turned over to Hanchett and Martin his First Street broad-gauge franchise, giving them a preferred position for buying out the San Jose Railroad.

On June 30, 1909, the S. P. legally consolidated its three South Bay interurban properties—the Peninsular Railroad, the Santa Clara Interurban, and the San Jose and Los Gatos—under one roof, the $12 million *Peninsular Railway Company of California.* Jere Burke signed as president of all three consolidating companies. Capital stock consisted of 120,000 shares: 50,000 each for the Peninsular and the Santa Clara Interurban and 20,000 for the San Jose and Los Gatos. Main offices were established in Los Angeles. The new directors were Burke, Frank Chapin, P. F. Dunne of San Francisco, C. B. Seger of Berkeley, and S. P. official Paul Shoup, who became president.

Chapin, the vice president, remained in charge at San Jose as general manager. E. G. (Ed) Shoup of San Jose was named general passenger agent. W. T. Bailey was the roadmaster and H. J. Rego the master mechanic. J. H. Parsons was the chief electrician. The corporate charter listed about 50 miles of present or intended routes and gave particulars on some lines then in operation:

Saratoga line: starting from a single-track loop at the S. P. depot (Old Market, Bassett, and Market Streets) and extending southward on double tracks along Market to Park Avenue, then westward on a single track up the center of Park to Josefa Street, where the Campbell cutoff turned off to the south. The Saratoga line continued westward up Park to Meridian Road, where it curved south one block up the center of Meridian to San Carlos Street, joining the eastbound single track up the center of San Carlos to Market. To Meridian Corners, where it met the Cupertino branch, it ran out the center of San Carlos and the north side of Stevens Creek Road. At Meridian Corners it turned southwest along the west side of Saratoga Avenue to the Saratoga town center, meeting the Congress Springs branch. Here it turned eastward, running along the north side of the old Saratoga-Los Gatos Road (via the present Austin Way) to San Tomas Aquino Creek and up the center of the road into Los Gatos, where it turned south up the center of Santa Cruz Avenue to its terminus at Broadway.

Campbell cutoff: departing the Saratoga line at Park and Josefa, this single-track line ran south one block down the center of Josefa Street to San Carlos Street, then westward to Bird Avenue. Here it turned in a southwesterly direction, running out the center of Bird, Coe, and Lincoln Avenues to Willow Street, then westward out the center of Willow to Meridian Road. At Meridian it turned south, running along the east side of Meridian to Hamilton, then west along the south side of Hamilton to San Jose-Los Gatos Road (now Bascom

Avenue) and southward along the east side of this road to Campbell Avenue. Here it swung west along the north side of Campbell Avenue to Willets Corners, then up the center of this avenue to Santa Clara-Los Gatos Road, where it turned south again via this road and Railway Avenue to enter the tracks of the S. P.'s Almaden branch. Leaving this branch, the line ran to Los Gatos over private rights of way and San Jose-Los Gatos Road, entering town up the center of San Jose Avenue (now Los Gatos Boulevard) and Main Street.

Congress Springs branch: departing the Saratoga line at the Saratoga town center, this line ran out the center of Saratoga Avenue to Lumber Street and then along the route of the former Saratoga Turnpike to the site of the former Congress Springs hotel.

The *Naglee Park branch* now operated eastward from San Fernando and Market Streets through the Naglee Park tract and back to Market and San Carlos Streets.

One of the new company's first acts, in July, was to order cars for its San Jose-Palo Alto run. The Pacific Electric had just bought 20 of the famous "baby fives" from the St. Louis Car Company, and the Peninsular decided to have five more of these sturdy little cars built for itself. Word now came down to push vigorously on completing all lines. As crews proceeded with double-tracking the Cupertino branch and the Saratoga line between Meridian and Bascom Avenues, poles, ties, rails, and other materials arrived in Palo Alto for the Stanford campus line. The route of this line had now been fixed: from the corporation yard eastward behind the campus bookstore to Galvez Street and Escondido Road, curving northward up Galvez past the football stadium and northeasterly on private right of

The line to Los Gatos through Campbell had numerous twists and turns, including the one in this photo, which finds Peninsular 104 heading a string of cars approaching the Campbell station.
(J.C. Gordon Photo from Henry E. Morse Jr. Collection)

A Peninsular interurban, westbound on the Saratoga–Los Gatos road, slows as it approaches the Saratoga station to the right.

(Lorin Silleman Collection)

Cars 53, 56 and 16 on the wye at Saratoga station, a busy and interesting place, especially in the days before the roads were paved.

(Randolph Brandt Collection)

The Peninsular 100-series cars were big and beautiful. **ABOVE:** The 102 is on the S.P. interchange track near University Avenue, Palo Alto, ready for a "flyer run" to San Jose. (Wilbur C. Whittaker Collection) **BELOW:** Car 112, one of the biggest cars on the roster, is shown on Park Ave. circa 1915. These units wound up on the Pacific Electric. (L. J. Ciapponi)

way to University Junction (El Camino Real about halfway between Embarcadero Road and University Avenue), then northward on El Camino and eastward on University Avenue to the S. P. depot.

Plans called for the Palo Alto streetcars—newly repainted dark green with gold lettering—to share rails with the interurbans from University Junction to the depot. Work on this line got under way August 11 with grading and tree removal in the arboretum. Crews raised the old Parkinson-Hanchett tracks along University Avenue and El Camino Real. Work motor 200 arrived to help with stringing the overhead wires. By September 1 most of the rails were in place and joined with the relaid Parkinson-Hanchett tracks. The ballast had not yet arrived, though, which delayed the line's opening.

On August 16 the Peninsular got its long-awaited Mayfield franchise, opening the way for its San Jose-Palo Alto line. However, to assure the legality of running interurban cars up El Camino Real and University Avenue, the company asked for and received a new Mayfield-Palo Alto franchise covering essentially the same route as the old Parkinson franchise. The cost was $50, and the Peninsular was the only bidder.

October 6, 1909, marked the first trial run over the campus line, which officially opened October 11 with fanfare, speeches, and an enthusiastic turnout of nearly 3,000 passengers. A new bit of color had now been added to the life of a great university, and a new tradition arose—the "Toonerville to Palo Alto"—which a generation of college men fondly remembered. Four cars were placed in regular service: two to the campus from Waverley Street, one to the S. P. depot from Marlowe and University, and one to the campus from the depot, meeting all trains.

W. H. Yount, manager of the Palo Alto division, announced new schedules effecting 15-minute headway through downtown Palo Alto and 22½ minute service on Waverley Street and University Avenue east of Waverley. The first cars left University and Emerson at 6:20 a.m. for the campus, Marlowe Street, and Embarcadero Road, departing those terminals at 6:30 a.m. The last cars headed home at 10:30 p.m.

A second track and spur were laid from Palo Alto to the football stadium in time for the Stanford-California "Big Game" of November 13, 1909, launching another fine tradition. For the next two decades every fall football afternoon saw city and interurban cars rolling up to the bleachers jammed with fans from Palo Alto, San Jose, Los Gatos, and intermediate points. At game's end the cars stood ready to whisk them home. For the fans these were days of great merriment. For the Peninsular, which pressed into duty all its available equipment, they were a headache but also a great moneymaker.

With the campus route open, attention focused on the San Jose-Palo Alto line. San Carlos Street had now been double-tracked out to Bascom and the Cupertino branch in to Meridian Corners, between which lay the old single track of the Saratoga line. (The double-track right of way continued to Bascom but was never finished, the single track being used up to the end.) This work done, the crews moved on to Mayfield, where materials arrived October 13 for completing the Palo Alto extension and electrifying one track of the Mayfield cutoff.

As poles were emplaced and and wires strung from Mayfield to Monta Vista, the old Parkinson-Hanchett tracks were upgraded from University Junction to Mayfield, where the route required excavation to comply with the official street grade. By month's end new rails were in place from Palo Alto to Lincoln Street; crews were installing poles and preparing to make the connection to the Mayfield cutoff. It was now understood that the line's opening depended on completion of a new substation at Los Altos, for which materials had been ordered but not yet arrived. Arrangements had been made there to supply current not only to the electric road but also to the local

community. When finished, this substation would replace the one at Palo Alto unless the Peninsular had immediate plans for building northward.

The five new interurbans arrived in San Jose January 1, 1910, where they were inspected and approved by Peninsular officials. These were handsome cars with Westinghouse air brakes, two-thirds closed and one-third open (for smokers) with rain curtains. In the closed section were red plush seats. In the open section were eight double seats with slatted backs and bottoms. Three had motors (100, 101, 104); the other two (102, 103) were trailers but later motorized. All was in order in the cars, but unknown then to the local brass was the true story of their journey, later told to Ira Swett by S. P. Chief Electrician W. H. Davison.

It seems that the St. Louis Car Company, on completing the cars, had sent all 25 west on their own wheels to Los Angeles, where the Pacific Electric took its 20 and turned over the rest to Davison, who was to be their official escort to San Jose. Just outside Los Angeles a horde of hoboes, seeing all those nice plush seats going to waste, invited themselves aboard as an official welcoming party. Davison introduced himself and let the Weary Willies ride. All the way north they lived the life of Riley.

As the train neared San Jose, however, Davison couldn't help but conjure up visions of his fate if the shiny new cars rolled up to the Peninsular officials full of such unacceptable guests. He nervously explained his plight to the passengers who, moved by a generous impulse, filed out of the cars and disappeared. The cars rolled up to the officials, who blessed them for service—and Davison muttered a silent prayer of thanks.

January 5 brought news that the materials had finally arrived for the Los Altos substation, to be built on First Street where the Safeway store is now. "With the advent of this line will come electric lighting to our little town," declared the Los Altos correspondent of the *Palo Alto Times*. Construction began January 12. By mid-February the station, sans roof and concrete floor, was ready to receive the twin 300-kilowatt generators and accompanying transformers that would power not only the Mayfield cutoff but also the Palo Alto city lines. These were promptly installed. The first inspection trip over the new line came February 21. Five days later a special excursion conveyed 125 Los Altans to Palo Alto and Stanford.

Regular service began March 5 amid a gala celebration touched off successively at each city on the line as a gaily decorated five-car train of the new interurbans progressed north from San Jose bearing railroad representatives and city dignitaries. At University Junction the special train switched onto the Stanford line and officially completed its inaugural run as it pulled up at the Union. There a huge throng welcomed the string of shiny 100's, harbingers of a new convenience in intercity transit.

Hourly service was established between Palo Alto and San Jose with fares ranging from 10¢ between adjacent stations to 55¢ between Stanford and San Jose. Lower rates were in effect weekends and holidays. Monthly commuter tickets ran from $3 (Palo Alto-Alta Mesa) to $6 (Palo Alto-Monta Vista and beyond). Also available were family 30-ride family tickets, good for six months, at rates up to $10. Patronage was good, reported the *Palo Alto Times*, and the service well received, although the San Antonio Country Club went on record protesting the 20¢ one-way fare from Los Altos to Palo Alto.

With the addition of the new "baby fives," the company owned 50 cars, of which 35 were motorized passenger cars. That same month (March) Jere Burke was installed as president and Gerald Fitzgerald as secretary, Chapin continuing as vice president and general manager. The corporate offices were moved from Los Angeles to the Flood Building, San Francisco. With this change in local leadership came word that Paul Shoup was now in charge of all S. P. electric lines on the West Coast, commissioned to improve and extend them as necessary to meet all competition.

One of the Peninsular's tasks, as noted, was to build to the East Bay via the Dumbarton bridge, a long, low structure spanning the Bay from Dumbarton Point to Cooley's Point, east of Ravenswood. That bridge was under construction. So the interurban proceeded at once with plans to extend the University Avenue line from Marlowe Street through the 70-acre Hopkins tract to Ravenswood, where a casino, natatorium (two swimming pools), and recreation park were to be built on the Crowe property. Part of this work required strengthening the new county bridge over San Francisquito Creek, at company expense. Also being developed near the recreation park was a new tract, Sunnymeade, in which the interurban possibly had a financial interest.

Poles and ties for the extension arrived at Cooley's Point in March, from where they were distributed along the right of way. Grading commenced. Rails and more ties arrived May 3, and track-laying began. Within a fortnight the line was finished from Marlowe to the bridge, prompting the Peninsular to announce May 22 as the official opening day for Ravenswood service. Featured were a land sale and through operation of all interurban cars to San Jose, Los Gatos, Saratoga, Los Altos, and intermediate points, with transfers to local lines. The ceremonies drew a large crowd and were quite successful, according to the *Palo Alto Times*, in that 73 lots were sold.

By June 6 the line was completed to a point several hundred feet east of San Francisquito Creek, where construction halted. The Dumbarton bridge opened September 24 with assurances by the Peninsular that work would resume "as soon as there is any demand for it." Ground was broken June 10 for the new

casino and natatorium, which opened the following year. University Avenue cars now provided regular service to the end of the line, alternating with "short-line" cars that terminated at University and Marlowe.

In 1910 the big interurban cars on the San Jose-Los Gatos run were equipped with electric heaters, a welcome convenience. During this year, also, the Peninsular, following the lead of other electric roads of the era, began offering special fares to attract business that otherwise might not come its way. One was a 35¢ Sunday and holiday rate from Palo Alto, Mayfield, and Los Altos to Congress Springs and return. Another was a $1 "Balloon Route" round-trip excursion from San Jose to Los Gatos, Saratoga, and Palo Alto.

Introduced in May was the most famous of all, the $1 "Blossom Trolley Trip" which toured the valley when the orchards were in full bloom and the wild flowers in brilliant array on the hills around Saratoga. Especially breathtaking, it was said, were the vistas from Los Gatos to Saratoga, where travelers looked out over a sea of blossoms to Lick Observatory atop Mt. Hamilton, some 30 miles away. Each year the Peninsular was to carry thousands on this spring pilgrimmage, the biggest event of which was Saratoga's annual Blossom Festival, a celebration of thanksgiving for what the new year had wrought.

Homes and gardens in that community were opened for the festival, the features of which were good food, fine music, and entertainment for the young: jumping contests, sack races, kite flying, and the like, with prizes of bats, balls, and gift certificates donated by valley merchants. So pervasive was the air of celebration that writer and part-time resident Kathleen Norris felt obliged to explain. "Saratoga glorifies the high-tide of fruit blossoms that washes over her like a snowy foam," she wrote. "Every year the little town goes mad with the joy of spring, the

Peninsular cars stand ready to transport passengers home from a special event—perhaps a Blossom Festival—at Saratoga. Nearest car is No. 15; next in line is the 54.
(Lorin Silleman Collection)

Peninsular 100, a "Baby Five," survived this 1910 collision with an S.P. boxcar at University Avenue crossing, Palo Alto.

(Wilbur C. Whittaker Collection)

Palo Alto dinkies were often the subject of ridicule by Stanford students, but they kept going faithfully until the end. Car 32 pauses at the S.P. Depot in Palo Alto.

(Randolph Brandt Collection)

Narrow-gauge car 16 southbound on First and Santa Clara streets, San Jose, about 1910. The First National Bank Building on the corner is nearing completion.

(J.C. Gordon Photo from Henry E. Morse Jr. Collection)

perfume and sunshine and birds, and every year all the neighboring towns pour in to join the festival.''

In March 1911 a group of Stanford students, protesting the constant noise of the streetcar crossing warning bell near the campus bookstore, carried off and destroyed the bell. This prank—the first to reach public notice—was but one of many that would beset the campus line during its 20-year history.

23. Hanchett Buys San Jose Railroad

Before Hanchett bought up Burke's First Street broad-gauge franchise in October 1909, all the evidence—the franchise, acquisition of the San Jose Traction Company, and expansion of the Peninsular—had pointed to an S. P. takeover of the San Jose Railroad. San Jose's councilmen saw all the construction under way and generally favored the takeover, anticipating a unified transit system in which passengers could transfer freely among local lines and from city cars to interurbans.

Also afoot at this time was a comprehensive plan to improve the city streets, many of which were full of potholes and flooded regularly with the winter rains. This was a hot political issue to which the councilmen were keenly sensitive. New street grades were adopted and contracts let to install new storm sewers. Thus it was, in early October, that the council ordered Hanchett to lower his Santa Clara Street tracks from ½ to 4½ inches to conform with a new official grade. Hanchett, a recent bridegroom, estimated the cost at $100,000, branded the order ridiculous, and went off on his honeymoon.

While the councilmen fumed, they learned October 29 that he had not only bought the Burke franchise but also purchased the San Jose Railroad from the German Savings and Loan Society for $300,000, the amount of its first mortgage bonds. George Tourney was leaving San Jose to become secretary of the Society. Terms of the Burke franchise called for installing Trilby rail on First Street from Reed Street to the north city limits, the holder also to pay for paving the first 1,000 feet of First Street north of Hobson. Because it required the work to be done in two years and considerable time had elapsed, the *San Jose Mercury* predicted an early start of construction.

However comfortable the new arrangement for Hanchett and the S. P., it hardly suited the councilmen, who hadn't been advised of the impending sale and saw themselves locked in combat with a recalcitrant owner. They filed suit to block the Burke transfer and lift Hanchett's other franchises. He returned from his honeymoon to find himself in court, refusing to divulge his plans or to comment on the city's legal maneuvers.

On December 22 Hanchett reincorporated his new property as *The San Jose Railroads*, with capital of $5 million and himself at the head. The total subscription was $23,000, of which he personally pledged $22,600. Records indicate that John Martin was not directly involved. On January 10, 1910, Hanchett placed $1.5 million in first mortgage bonds with the Mercantile Trust Company of San Francisco, presumably to buy equipment and broad-gauge the company's 10 miles of lines. His investment was now approximately $500,000. W. R. Lawson became general manager of both the narrow-gauge and the San Jose and Santa Clara, supplanting Charles Benson. As before, Hanchett declined all comment, prompting the *Mercury* to observe: "He feels he has been outrageously treated by the present mayor and common council, who have refused him the plainest courtesies. If he keeps his plans to himself right now, it's no wonder."

On February 14 the court found the city's complaints groundless, ordering the council to honor both the Burke-Hanchett transfer and Hanchett's other franchises. That was hardly the end of the trouble, though.

Despite the *Mercury's* prediction of early action, construction was slow to begin. Negotiations were stalemated on Santa Clara Street. Then there was the matter of the unprofitable Hobson Street branch. The San Jose Woolen Mills had closed, and Hanchett, like his predecessors, refused to rebuild this line despite orders to do so. Under mounting criticism from the city council, he continued to run his narrow-gauge cars over all routes: the First Street lines from the north city limit to Lincoln and Minnesota Avenues (via First Street, Willow Street, and Lincoln Avenue) and to Oak Hill Cemetery (via First and Monterey Road); the Julian-Delmas line from the east city limit to Willow and Delmas via Julian Street, Eleventh Street, St. James Street, Sixth Street, St. John Street, Second Street, San Fernando Street, and Delmas Avenue; the S. P. depot line from the depot to Third and Reed Streets via Bassett, First, and Reed Streets; the Third-Seventh Street line from Second and San Fernando Streets to Seventh and Keyes via Second, San Antonio, Third, Reed, and Seventh streets; and the Hobson Street branch from First to Walnut Street.

Ruth Heath, writing in *The Trailblazer*, recalled bright enjoyment those days in riding the streetcars to Oak Hill Cemetery. " 'Bring a lunch this Saturday, and let's go to the cemetery'— this was the request often made by my best friend during 1910 and 1911. If she hadn't suggested it I probably would have. We had hit on a wonderful form of entertainment. We hurried through our Saturday chores and, with our lunches and ten cents for carfare, we were off for a pleasant day.

"Our streetcar was yellow, striped with brown, and we felt very gay as we started from Julian Street. When we reached Chrisman's Hay and Wood Yard on North Eleventh Street, our car would wait at the switch for the eastbound car, or, if we were early, we went on to Sixth Street where it might be waiting for us. We changed cars at First and San Fernando for our ride south, and with one more transfer at First and Almaden we were on our way to Oak Hill Cemetery.

"We always tried to get outside seats. We felt very adventurous as they faced the street and we had to hang onto the posts to keep from falling off. Sometimes we were fortunate enough to ride on a car which was open on both sides with seats across and an isle in the center.

"Occasionally the trolley slipped off the wire, emitting a shower of sparks. The conductor would run to the back of the car, fit the grooved wheel of the trolley onto the wire, and away we would go.

"We rode through Cottage Grove and down Monterey Road. We had a choice of getting off at the first or second gate— Stone Avenue (now Curtner Avenue) or Tully Road. We were cautioned never to ride to the end of the line. If we did this, we were told, it could be dangerous, for here was located the German Beer Garden (Schuetzen Park). We never found out what might happen to us, but the little mystery added to our sense of adventure.

"We usually chose to enter by the second gate, off Tully Road," she remembered. "In that section were our family plots and I never got tired of reading grandfather A. G. Bennett's Civil War record carved on his stone.... We saw many of these stones in the Civil War plot, where we often attended Decoration Day exercises. The war was always kept fresh in our minds by the bearded veterans who visited our school prior to Decoration Day.

"Since we had lived in San Jose all our lives, we recognized many names on the stones as those of relatives of our friends. While we ate our lunch we discussed the part that those now dead had played in the early days of our valley.

"We still had the fun of a ride home and the change of streetcars. We ended a pleasant day with the promise of a repeat trip as soon as possible."

Another bright spot was the grand opening in April 1910 of

Luna Park, the Hanchett amusement complex at Berryessa Road. On the east end were the rodeo grounds and the baseball stadium, opened earlier, where San Jose battled other teams of the California State League. On the north was the exciting Scenic Railway roller coaster, a feature attraction. Scattered between were amusement stands and carnival booths. Towering over the park at its center was the Devil's Slide, an impressive five-story structure resembling a tank house. Inside was a huge, highly polished ribbed-wood slide, with curved walls, running downward perhaps 100 feet through several turns. Fun-seekers climbed a long stairway to the top of the building, where attendants gave them hemp mats for a quick trip to the bottom. The bravest (and most hardy) sometimes made 20 or 30 roundtrips a day.

All summer the arguments raged between Hanchett and the city council, which finally agreed to relieve Hanchett of the burden of rebuilding the Hobson Street branch. Work got under way in November, a 140-man crew ripping out the old First Street tracks and laying new rails from the north city limit to Willow Street. From Bassett to Reed a third (narrow-gauge) rail was temporarily installed to accommodate the depot line. The crew then moved to other lines. By early December the Willow-Lincoln line was completed, two standard-gauge cars operating from First and Willow to Lincoln and Minnesota. Julian Street was retracted, and a standard-gauge car was operating out the Third-Seventh Street line from Second and San Antonio to Seventh and Keyes. North First Street was being paved. All work was finished the following month except for Hobson Street, which remained an isolated narrow-gauge spur. Hanchett announced that transfer arrangements would go into effect May 1 between his Santa Clara and First Street systems and also between his cars and those of the Peninsular within the 5¢ limit area, when that company agreed. The improvements were said to have cost him $1.5 million, the amount of the first mortgage bonds.

Hanchett needed broad-gauge equipment for his new lines. Although details are sketchy and certain cars have never been traced, it seems likely that he refitted some of the old equipment for standard-gauge service, especially the United Railroads cars originally built for broad gauge. The passage of a city ordinance November 7 regulating such matters as air and hand brakes, cleansing and disinfection of cars, and mandatory filing of quarterly accident reports supports this idea. Hanchett probably lumped most of the old equipment into a new "51" class obtained by adding a hundreds digit to the original number. Among these, Nos. 105, 107, 109, 112, 113, 116, 118, and one other are believed to have been United Railroads standards. Nos. 101 and 102, built by Hammond, were most likely those obtained from the East. No. 115, of unknown ancestry, was another survivor. Of these cars, six—Nos. 101, 102, 107, 113, 115, and 118—were broad-gauged; another survivor, No. 55, probably was refitted and used on the First Street line. Car 52, probably a former United Railroads long, may have been operated both broad-gauge and narrow-gauge. Nos. 106, 108, and 110 were of unknown origin. Hanchett planned to supplement these with cars leased from the United Railroads of San Francisco, of which at least five (Nos. 560, 562, 762, 803, and 813) were delivered to San Jose in 1910 and 1911.

24. S. P. Acquires Hanchett Lines

Hanchett and the city council were still at loggerheads over lowering the track grade on Santa Clara Street. On December 12 the city added another argument. The terms of Hanchett's 1906 broad-gauge franchises required him to use 60-pound Trilby rail in rebuilding his San Jose and Santa Clara lines. He had com-plied on Santa Clara Street between Orchard and Fourth but elsewhere had laid down 70-pound T-rail, which caused no problems at the time but now drew bitter attack as he prepared to pave between the rails on Santa Clara Street (another requirement of his franchises). So, with the city voicing threats and the work needing to be done, Hanchett went to Federal court for a restraining order and put his crews to work pouring concrete. The city also went to court, again seeking to void his franchises. Ignoring the uproar, Hanchett's crews proceeded imperturbably about their business of paving the streets.

On December 20 Hanchett admitted himself ready to compromise on the paving and the regrading of certain tracks if the city would relent in its demand for Trilby rail. There were no takers. Seven days later the city won complete victory in San Francisco's Circuit Court—"the franchise terms are clear and unmistakeable"—then learned perhaps for the first time that it no longer had the unilateral power to order Hanchett or anybody else to pack up his rails and go home. The court, and the court alone, would decide in person whether "the tracks are in a condition to possibly injure a citizen." If such were the case, vowed the judge, the city would be perfectly within its rights to "abate a public nuisance."

Getting the decision was one matter, enforcing it another. As the crews went on pouring concrete after December 27, the council met in stormy session January 3, 1911, determined to strip Hanchett of his right to run streetcars in San Jose. Mayor Charles W. Davison opposed the move, urging moderation, whereupon the angry councilmen voted to hire their own attorney to start disenfranchisement proceedings. On January 5 the councilmen made ready if necessary to arrest Hanchett's workmen one by one for tearing up the city streets. Peace was restored January 26, Hanchett agreeing to install Trilby on the most heavily traveled parts of Santa Clara Street and generally following the lines of a compromise suggested months earlier by the *Mercury*.

Hardly had this matter been decided, however, when flood waters from Penitencia Creek, swollen by the heavy winter rains, washed out Hanchett's narrow-gauge Alum Rock Park line, the soggy hillside caving in one of the tunnels. That was in March. William J. Mendia, motorman of the last car through the tunnel, vividly remembered its collapse. "My orders were to run cars through it until there was no tunnel," he recalled. "There were chills up my back as I drove the car into the park that morning, but they were nothing compared with taking the car out a short time later. It actually bumped the timbering as it went through the closing tunnel." Service to the park was suspended, and no plans were announced for its restoration.

Maybe Hanchett had hoped to turn a neat profit by selling his streetcar lines to Borax Smith and company, guaranteeing them entry into San Jose. Rumors circulated to that effect, though nothing developed. More likely he was just tired of battling the city and disheartened by loss of the Alum Rock line. In any event, in hand was an attractive offer from the S. P., one of several received during recent months. This time he succumbed. On April 7 came word that he had sold the San Jose and Santa Clara and the San Jose Railroads to the steam road for a sum "in excess of $4 million," making it master, at last, of all the South Bay electric lines.

The following day Chapin was named manager of all San Jose lines, with Ed Shoup the operating superintendent. Paul Shoup announced that the narrow-gauge lines would be standard-gauged, new lines extended to Alum Rock Park and Mt. Hamilton, and the Palo Alto line connected with the United Railroads at San Mateo "in sufficient time."

To its stockholders the railroad explained the purchase as follows: "The suburban districts of California are developing and the population is increasing rapidly; therefore it is believed that the lines will soon not only become profitable in and of themselves but will be of very great value as feeders to S. P. steam lines. For this reason the company acquired control of the Peninsular Railway, owning 51.62 miles of single track and 14.97 miles of double track serving the cities of Palo Alto and San Jose and the country adjacent thereto, and of the San Jose Railroads, owning 15.81 miles of single track and 11.73 miles of double track serving the cities of San Jose and Santa Clara and the country adjacent thereto.''

The San Jose city council was jubilant. Hanchett declined to comment on either the transaction or his future plans. Shortly

thereafter he left town for some Southern California real estate developments that finally led to the consolidation of five railroad terminals under one roof, the Los Angeles Union Station. He died in 1956 a wealthy man. John Martin retired from P. G. and E. in 1914, also a wealthy man. In 1928, at the time of his death, he was heading the Mid-Continent Utilities Corporation, a company with sizeable holdings in the Central and Southern states. Their passing from the local scene, which ushered in the "corporate era" of South Bay transit, was observed in relative silence.

Looking eastward along Santa Clara Street from River Street during the March 1911 flood. Water came from the Guadalupe River about a half block west of River Street.

(San Jose Historical Landmarks Commission)

1910: San Jose and Santa Clara County Railroad

San Jose has in the San Jose and Santa Clara County Railroad system one of the best in the state. The roadbed is solid. The service is good and frequent, comfortable and up-to-date cars are used on its lines, and the conductors and motorman are courageous, careful, and diligent in their desire to please the public. Two of the men, Mr. H. F. Kelley, motorman, and Mr. S. W. Wilkinson, conductor, have over 20 years of efficient service to their credit.

Points of interest reached by the railroad include Santa Clara College, in Santa Clara, known as college-town; University of the Pacific; State Normal School; San Jose Driving Park; Luna Park; and Alum Rock Canyon, which is San Jose's extensive and beautiful reservation. This is one of the most delightful places on the Pacific Coast for seekers of health and pleasure, only eight miles from San Jose and reached in 40 minutes. Not only does it attract by reason of its picturesque glimpses of woodlands, hill, and stream, with nodding grasses and waving ferns, but because of its numerous mineral springs, exceeding in number, quality, and variety those of any resort of a similar nature in California.

From San Francisco or Oakland these springs may be reached in a very short time and persons seeking health or pleasure may leave either of these cities on the morning train and return the same evening after spending the greater portion of the day in the canyon wandering along the shadowed paths, drinking from the various springs, refreshing themselves in tub or plunge, and enjoying an outing unrivaled for variety of its pleasures and the ease of its entertainment.

Taking the San Jose and Santa Clara County cars at the Southern Pacific West San Jose depot, going east on Santa Clara Street through the business section of the city, passing the splendid building of the State Normal School, the High School, and the Carnegie Library, all situated on Washington Square one block to the south of the carline, you will be carried past beautiful homes surrounded by spacious grounds. East San Jose will be reached and, beyond that, a beautiful avenue. Between the trees you can catch glimpses of thrifty orchards and pass through one of the finest olive orchards in the state, known as Pala Rosa. This orchard covers 75 acres.

A little beyond, the road enters the canyon, leaving the San Jose Rifle Range on the left and the heights of Mulchera on the right. One charming vista after another delights the eye.

Passing the Alum Rock, a 2000-ton meteor standing like a gigantic sentinel at a gateway so narrow that it was necessary to tunnel through the rock, and winding along the banks of the beautiful Penitencia Creek with cliffs towering hundreds of feet above it, again the canyon widens considerably. It is here along the creek and at the base of the cliffs that bubbles the most remarkable variety of mineral waters in the West: hot and cold sulphur, soda, magnesia as well as a mixture of the above, arsenic, iron and their sulphates, all unequalled for their strength and beneficial effects. One remarkable spring furnishes a mixture of sulphur, magnesia, and arsenic which is found very beneficial for rheumatism, Bright's disease, and other stomach and kidney troubles, malarial afflictions, etc. The flows are so copious that baths may be supplied from nearly all of them.

The pleasure-seeker returning from the Park to the West San Jose Depot may find he has time before his train leaves to make the trip west over the carline, traversing the beautiful winding Alameda. Along this delightfully shaded "El Camino Real," laid out and cared for by the Mission Fathers, meandered the lovers and sweethearts of 100 years ago. Later the road was remodeled, and now it is lined with handsome residences.

A short distance out to the first bend, or the junction of Martin Avenue with The Alameda, is the entrance to the Hanchett Residence Park, the highest development of a modern residential tract. The beautiful winding curves of well-constructed streets give it a tone of individuality seldom attained in a strictly residential locale. This park opened only recently, yet there are many beautiful homes already completed, with others in process of erection.

A little further west you pass through College Park, the home of the University of the Pacific. This university, founded in August 1852, is located between San Jose and Santa Clara within 10 minutes' ride of either city. Beautiful avenues and comfortable homes, a healthful, mild, and invigorating climate, and a high moral and intellectual tone make College Park a most desirable place to live. The university

AN ECONOMICAL OUTING
TWENTY-FOUR MILES FOR TWENTY-FIVE CENTS
ON THE SANTA CLARA AND SAN JOSE ELECTRIC RAILWAY

FROM SANTA CLARA AND SAN JOSE TO

ALUM ROCK PARK AND RESERVATION

lying on the eastern edge of Santa Clara Valley. At the terminus is found a variety of remarkable mineral springs, including hot and cold sulphur, soda, magnesia, arsenic, iron and other combinations unequalled for their beneficial properties. There are private sulphur, turkish, plunge and tub baths, and the largest public mineral swimming bath in America, containing natural sulphur water and covered with an immense glass roof. The scenery is unsurpassed both in the park and on the line of the electric road and its proximity to San Francisco and other central California towns makes it possible to visit this attractive resort and return the same day. Send for booklet.

H. CENTER, Mgr.   First and Santa Clara Sts., SAN JOSE campus, comprising about 17 acres, commands a splendid view of the Santa Cruz and Diablo ranges, on either side of the beautiful Santa Clara Valley.

Journeying further to near the last wind of The Alameda, you pass the Pacific Manufacturing Company plant, the largest wood-working establishment in the state, employing several hundred Union men who work under the shadow of the Old Mission, well worth a visit though all but its interior has been restored. Built in 1776, the church was found in danger of decay and was covered with another structure; within, however, it is as the Indians built it under the direction of the Padres, who also labored with their hands. The frescoes and other decorations do credit to the neophytes who executed them.

Santa Clara College, whose building occupies several acres on the lands of the Old Mission, should not be missed. Here the stranger will be greeted by courteous Priests who will guide him through the buildings, showing books, yellow with age, brought from Spain when the Mission was young, and numerous relics and objects of interest, the likes of which can only be seen about an Old Mission.

The town of Santa Clara invites one to stroll through its streets. Here are homes that once sheltered Spanish grandees and their households: some occupied, some falling into decay, but vine-covered and filled with romantic interest. Behind the fluttering vines and embowered porches one can fancy seeing the bright eyes of the senoritas and hearing the whispered cooings of love that so softly filter from ruby lips, even hearing above the sanctified strains of music, "Ah, Juanita, star of Cordoba! Come, let us dance!"

Should one meet an old resident, he will hear stories of dons and alcaldes that will hold him rapt. Once this little town was as gay as it is now serene. Romance still centers about its ancient families, and now there is seeming revival of the old, happy life. On Saturday evenings when the band plays in the Plaza, lighthearted youths and maidens again wander along flower-bordered streets; still there are whispering and cooing and bright eyes, new hopes, new thrills in other hearts.

But here is our car. We must catch the 8:30 train. I am sure you will say, "How we have enjoyed our trip to San Jose, Santa Clara, and Alum Rock Park."

— *From the* Labor Day Historical Review, *1910*

No traffic jams in those days! San Jose and Santa Clara car 2 rumbles down Santa Clara St. between Market and First, San Jose, in 1907.

(Vernon J. Sappers Collection)

OPPOSITE: A 1925 advertisement in *Sunset* **magazine.** (Magna Collection)

TOP: Maybe they weren't a part of Teddy Roosevelt's Rough Riders, but this Army contingent seems ready for a parade, anyway. A former Los Angeles Pacific car looms in the background, at the same Market and Santa Clara location. Note that the streetcar is partially hidden by the base to the big tower. (Charles Smallwood Collection) **ABOVE: A northbound 50-class Peninsular car stops at Market and Santa Clara streets, San Jose, about 1908 in the shadow of the gigantic electric tower built in 1881 to light all of downtown. The tower survived the 1906 earthquake but collapsed during a windstorm on December 3, 1915. Notice that there's a fire going on down the street.** (Randolph Brandt Collection)

3. The Corporate Era

Peninsular 105 rolls north from Mayfield Junction to University Junction, at the Stanford University campus. (J. C. Gordon Photo from Lorin Silleman and Wilbur C. Whittaker Collections)

DURING the 28 years it controlled the South Bay interurban and streetcar lines, the Southern Pacific was to raise local service to its peak, then find itself presiding over the death of electric traction in the Santa Clara Valley. The high-water mark came about 1915—before any abandonments—when the San Jose Railroads operated some 46 miles of lines and the Peninsular about 80. From 1911 through 1923 the railroad poured millions into new equipment, roadbeds, and paving for the city streets. Much of this went for naught when, in the 1930s, the depression brought staggering losses to the local lines, setting the stage for their demise. It took the resources of a giant corporation like the Southern Pacific to maintain service through the years of losses, and to effect an orderly transition to buses when electric transit proved uneconomical.

All in all, this was the era in which corporate vision replaced the fierce personal pride and competition of previous decades. The corporation responded to the beat of a different drummer, measuring its choices against the cadence of what was best for its corporate growth. Its power and size gave it virtual immunity from local politics. It had resources far beyond those of any individual. It transferred equipment among subsidiaries and ordered cars in wholesale lots. The corporation alone could deal with such far-reaching problems as assessing the impact of private autos on its transit systems and deciding when to stop sending good money after bad. It had the detachment needed to sacrifice local interests, if need be, to larger corporate goals. That's what happened during the 1930s when the Southern Pacific gave up the South Bay traction systems to help salvage its Pacific Electric empire in Southern California.

These problems lay ahead, however, as the S. P. took over the Hanchett lines. There were urgent needs for new equipment and complementary operations between the city and interurban lines. Service had to be restored to Alum Rock Park. Other projects were envisioned. All this was set in the context of a mammoth expansion program for the S. P. electric roads involving not only the Santa Clara Valley but also Los Angeles (the Pacific Electric), Portland (the Portland, Eugene and Eastern), and the East Bay (the Oakland-Alameda-Berkeley electrification project). Millions had been set aside for this development, the plans for which had been approved by E. H. Harriman before his death in 1909 and endorsed by his successor, William Sproule.

1. Peninsular Expands

Over in the East Bay, the S. P., under Paul Shoup's direction, had been preparing for a frontal attack on Borax Smith's prosperous Key Route system (San Francisco, Oakland and San Jose Railway). In 1910 Smith and F. C. Havens had folded this railway and other holdings into their $200 million United Properties Company, second largest corporation in the state. Assets included properties from Contra Costa County to Gilroy. Their plan was to invade the fields of water, power, light, and real estate on a grand scale.

With respect to the Key Route, Smith and associates had thus far managed only to finish the Claremont branch and open interurban service from Claremont and College to the pier. However, they were now said to be within $200,000 of the funds needed to complete the San Jose extension and build some other lines. There was even talk of running the railway eastward to Sacramento if conditions were right.

This time the S. P. was ready. Already holder of a Berkeley electric road franchise, it was about to spend $3 million on electrifying and extending its East Bay local lines. First to be completed would be the Alameda lines. Then would come new routes to Berkeley, San Leandro, and downtown Oakland, thrusting deep into Key Route territory. The battle was set to begin.

The S. P. drew first blood in 1911 by opening its Alameda Encinal line from the pier to High Street station. That was June 1. Next came the Alameda Lincoln Avenue line August 1, the Oakland Webster Street line October 28, and the Oakland Seventh Avenue line to Melrose station November 29. In December the railroad opened two northward-thrusting lines to Berkeley: Shattuck Avenue December 23 and Ellsworth Avenue December 28. Smith countered June 11, 1911, by opening

his Key Route line to Northbrae. This was followed September 28 by the Twelfth Street-downtown Oakland line to First Avenue, November 15 by the Sacramento Street line to Northbrae, and December 20 by extension of the Northbrae line to San Pablo and Albany.

The S. P. onslaught continued into 1912. January 1 saw completion of its California Street line to Thousand Oaks (North Berkeley), followed February 1 by its Solano line to Thousand Oaks. That finished the Berkeley extensions. The Seventh Avenue line was pushed southward to Havenscourt. Then came the $900,000 Sixteenth Street depot line, which opened March 12. This downtown Oakland line—2.27 miles of main track and 2.09 miles of secondary track—was franchised and built by the Peninsular as part of its goal to extend the East Bay routes to San Francisco and San Jose. Streets covered were Fourteenth and Franklin to the depot, to Eighteenth, Brush, Twenty-First, and back to the starting point. Streetcar service over this route commenced August 1, 1913, using cars of the Oakland-Alameda-Berkeley electrification project.

Deep cracks had now developed in the structure of the United Properties Company, partly because Smith and Havens had vastly different management ideas. The main problem, though, was Smith's inability to deliver blocks of transportation stock pledged as collateral on loans. That put an unbearable financial strain on the company, which collapsed in 1913. Smith was forced into bankruptcy; the Key Route went into receivership the next year. Money was not forthcoming for further construction. Needless to say, the big cars built in 1908 for the Oakland-San Jose extension ran out their allotted years considerably nearer Oakland than San Jose.

With one opponent dispatched, the S. P. flexed its muscle toward another, the United Railroads of San Francisco. A new scheme was drafted whereby the Peninsular's oft-proposed San Francisco extension would leave the system at Los Altos, pro-

Peninsular 107 rolls past High Street trailing an eastbound city car on University Avenue, Palo Alto, circa 1910.   (David L. Mitchell Collection)

ceed north via Stanford University through Woodside, and turn eastward at Redwood City toward the S. P. mainline, which it would parallel to San Bruno. From there the cars would run to San Francisco through the Mission District. At issue again, of course, was the San Francisco company's thriving San Mateo suburban line.

Seeing trouble in the fruition of this scheme, the United Railroads promptly bought up the Pajaro Valley Railroad, a narrow-gauge steam road out of Salinas, and announced plans to broad-gauge, electrify, and extend the road northward about 80 miles to San Mateo via Gilroy, San Jose, and Palo Alto. As a feeder, the Monterey and Pacific Grove Railway, a local streetcar system also controlled by the United Railroads, would be extended from Monterey to Salinas. This ambitious project by a powerful competitor gave the S. P. much food for thought.

The outcome was an offer by the Southern Pacific to include the United Railroads trackage from San Mateo to San Bruno in its new route, paying for trackage rights. The San Francisco company had no objection; the Peninsular thereupon ordered eight large, fast interurbans from the Jewett Car Company. These were heavy 64-passenger cars with four Westinghouse motors, dynamotor compressors, and Brill trucks, leased from the parent S. P. through a trust fund and identical to 45 others bought by the Pacific Electric (its 1000 class).

All 53 cars came west from Ohio in mid-1913, via Texas, by two special trains. At the Pacific Electric shops in Los Angeles, the Peninsular cars were given ornate paint jobs, numbered 105-112, and sent north in custody of S. P. Chief Electrician Bill Davison. Motors were installed in San Jose. The cars were exhibited for several days at San Jose and other cities along the Peninsular, then put in revenue service from September 1913 through May 1914.

One who vividly recalled the arrival of these cars—the so-called "Big Palys"—was Russell "Monty" Morgareidge, a journeyman motorman, conductor, armature-winder, and electrician who worked for the Peninsular and several other Western electric roads during the early 1900s. As he later explained to Vernon Sappers, after Davison and the crew installed the motors, they couldn't get the cars to run. Down came the Westinghouse engineers from San Francisco. They couldn't find the problem, either. Davison and Morgareidge began checking the cars detail by detail, finally coming to the dynamotor compressors. There they found that the clutch plates had been installed backwards, so not enough air passed to operate the switch groups. The two men reversed the plates, then took all eight cars, coupled together, on a high-speed run from San Jose to Los Altos, reaching about 80 mph.

With the Oakland construction finished and plans shelved for the San Francisco extension, the Peninsular's construction crews got busy on four important South Bay projects. One was the so-called Santa Clara depot line intended to provide that town and Saratoga a shorter route to S. P. steam service. The county supervisors gave approval September 5, 1911, allowing the Peninsular four years to complete a single-track line out Saratoga Avenue from the Santa Clara town limit to Meridian Corners. Grading began January 4, 1912, the roadway being torn up for several hundred yards. The Santa Clara town trustees awarded a franchise April 8 covering Franklin Street from the depot west to Grant Street and from Franklin southward on Lincoln Street, then westward on Bellomy- Street and Saratoga Avenue to the town limit. This route required the use of existing rails on Franklin from Grant to Lincoln. The city portion opened in 1913, car No. 13 making the franchise run and then hanging around the depot to meet all trains, which was its chief assignment. This 28-passenger car was new to the Peninsular roster: a single-truck unit with hand brakes and Westinghouse 56 motors, obtained from the United Railroads and refitted with double trucks. Expectations that the Santa

Clara depot line would be extended to Meridian Corners ended that same year with word that the Peninsular didn't want to borrow the $20,000 needed to finish it.

The second project was extension of the well-patronized Waverley Street branch, up in Palo Alto. Work was still halted on the University Avenue line, but on August 7, 1912, the Santa Clara county supervisors gave the Peninsular rights to extend the Waverley Street branch across Embarcadero Road into the Seale tract. This was followed August 9 by an agreement with Alfred Seale allowing the Peninsular to build a single-track 0.9-mile line south to Oregon Avenue (South Palo Alto) with turnouts at Embarcadero, Melville Street, and Oregon. Construction began August 12. Cars ran out about halfway (to Lowell Avenue) that fall, then in 1913 all the way to Oregon.

Schedules now called for 20-minute headway between Waverley Street and the campus from 6:30 a.m. to 10:30 p.m. and similar headway on University Avenue between Ravenswood and the campus from 6:40 a.m. to 6 p.m. After 6 o'clock the campus and Ravenswood cars ran hourly schedules on University, the campus car terminating at Marlowe Street and the Ravenswood car at the S. P. depot. The last campus car to Waverley Street left the campus at 10:10 p.m. The last campus car downtown (to the carbarn only) left at 11:20 p.m. The last car from the depot to the campus departed at 11:10 p.m.

The third item—a priority piece of construction—was the creation a new route to Alum Rock Park. Among the assets acquired from Hanchett had been his unused franchises and rights of way along the south side of Berryessa Road and the banks of Penitencia Creek to the park entrance. While the old narrow-gauge line to the park was still operating out to Toyon and could be rebuilt, the Peninsular saw opportunity in the new route to profit from freight movements to and from Berryessa as an adjunct to the passenger trade. One of Chapin's first acts on taking charge had been to solicit approval to enter the park, delayed by a $2,500 price tag hung on the franchise by the San Jose city council. He had gained rights, however, for the streetcar company to haul gravel over its East San Jose lines, partly to help in building the new road. These rights were not seen as significant at the time but were to have important consequences.

In February 1912 Chapin told reporters he expected the Alum Rock line to open in three months. No franchise had yet been awarded to enter the park, although final approvals were under way for the Peninsular to build this trackage. Crews began grading east from Luna Park for rails that would tie into city tracks at Fourteenth Street and into an S. P. freight line at Tenth Street. On April 22 the Alum Rock franchise ordinance, giving San Jose 2% of the line's annual receipts, cleared the city council. The Peninsular accepted four days later.

Chapin's prediction of a three-month completion was grossly optimistic. Work continued all that year and into the next, crews installing 70-pound rail and preparing the line for heavy-duty service. A wooden footbridge was built across Penitencia Creek from Toyon to accommodate passengers transferring from the narrow-gauge electric. The Alum Rock line opened September 2, 1913, the Peninsular offering through service from San Jose and other South Bay cities via the San Jose Railroads' Luna Park line. Construction had proved expensive, with several bridges and fills. Interest on the bonds alone was said to run to $50 a day.

Also completed that month was electrification of the S. P. steam line from Monta Vista to Congress Junction, another priority task. The railroad discontinued local steam passenger trains between Palo Alto and Los Gatos January 4, 1914, when the Peninsular opened direct service between those cities.

The system, valued at about $4.5 million, now consisted of two main lines: Palo Alto-San Jose and Palo Alto-Los Gatos. Next in importance were the twin routes to Los Gatos from San Jose. Then came the city lines—two in San Jose and three in

A Peninsular car on the Bonnie Brae trestle between Saratoga and Los Gatos. The photo dates to about 1912, shortly before track was relocated and the trestle removed.

(Charles Smallwood Collection)

Palo Alto—plus the new Alum Rock line and the Congress Springs spur, served mainly by a shuttle that ran according to demands of the traffic. The Peninsular, with its many connections and almost limitless variety, had become a model railroader's dream.

Daily schedules adopted in 1914 called for about 100 runs. Northbound from Los Gatos direct to Palo Alto were six cars from 6:05 a.m. to 5:20 p.m., plus six more from Meridian Corners and an owl run at about 11 p.m. Southbound runs were similar: seven cars direct to Los Gatos from 8:15 a.m. to 7:15 p.m., plus five to Meridian Corners and an owl run via Meridian at 11:45 p.m. Even though this service often required a change of cars, it was better than the former five-train schedule of the S. P. steamers.

Direct service was more frequent between Palo Alto and San Jose, nine cars operating northward from 6:40 a.m. to 6:15 p.m. plus one from Monta Vista and an 11:20 p.m. owl run. Southbound were 12 cars from 6:55 a.m. to 7:15 p.m. plus one from Monta Vista and an 11:10 p.m. owl run. Also scheduled were two daily round-trips (morning and evening) between Palo Alto and Los Altos.

Westbound from San Jose to Los Gatos via Saratoga were 10 cars from 6:55 a.m. to 11:20 p.m. plus two morning departures from the Sanatarium (San Carlos Street west of Meridian Road). Eastbound were 10 cars from 6:55 a.m. to 12:15 a.m. plus two morning departures from Saratoga. Westbound from San Jose via Campbell were 10 cars from 6:35 a.m. to 11:20 p.m. plus three terminating at Campbell. The 5:20 p.m.

express to Los Gatos skipped all stops from San Jose to Campbell. Eastbound, likewise, were 10 cars from 6 a.m. to 12:15 a.m. plus five starting at Campbell. The 5:20 p.m. inbound express to San Jose skipped all stops after Campbell.

In addition to shuttle service, regular runs were maintained between Los Gatos and Congress Springs. Westbound to the resort each day were four cars from 7:35 a.m. to 3:30 p.m. plus one regularly scheduled trip from Saratoga. Eastbound were four cars from 9 a.m. to 5:25 p.m. plus one trip terminating at Saratoga.

One feature of the new timetable was distressingly obvious: namely, that it dovetailed neatly with the S. P.'s steam train schedule—"coordinating the service," it was called then. Palo Alto, which didn't consider this policy in its best interests or those of the Peninsular, complained to the California State Railroad Commission. Through an exhaustive study of steam road and interurban timetables, the city proved that many Peninsular cars left Palo Alto immediately after an S. P. train, both headed for San Jose. Because the S. P.'s route was but 16.8 miles and the Peninsular's 20.9 miles, with running times of 40 and 58 minutes, respectively, was it any wonder, asked the city, that passengers gravitated to the steam road?

These facts of course merely illuminated the S. P.'s view that the interurban was but a convenience for its steam passengers bound for such intermediate points as Los Altos, Monta Vista, Cupertino, and Meridian Corners. After weighing the evidence, the Commission reached a similar understanding: "The S. P. has practically abandoned all its steam service on the cutoff be-

TOP: The Alum Rock Park line was originally laid to narrow gauge, but was broad-gauged about 1912 with the help of this steam shovel. (J. C. Gordon photo from Wilbur C. Whittaker Collection) **ABOVE: View look westward along the Peninsular line near the entrance to the park. Cars used to stop there so that passengers could gawk at Alum Rock, which is to the right.** (Charles D. Whittaker photo from Wilbur C. Whittaker Collection)

Cars 16 and 53 are stopped on the bridge near the entrance to Alum Rock Park, about 1913. (Norman Holmes Collection)

San Jose Railroads tried the stepless center-entrance car, which was designed so that women in the ''hobbleskirt era'' could easily board. This is shown on First near Santa Clara on the Cottage Grove line, circa 1914. (Randolph Brandt Collection)

Passengers could practically pick fruit from the trees while riding the Peninsular. Here is car 108 eastbound from Cupertino on the high-speed Stevens Creek line, about 1914.
(San Jose Historic Landmarks Commission)

tween Mayfield and Los Gatos and hires the Peninsular to do that service for it, further strengthening the conclusion that...the Peninsular is not operated in such a manner as to secure all the traffic possible.''

2. San Jose Gets New Equipment

In March 1912 the S. P. reincorporated the San Jose Railroads to include Hanchett's other two properties, the San Jose and Santa Clara County Railroad Company and the San Jose Traction Company. As per custom, the parent company kept absolute financial control over the offspring. Months earlier, however, management had examined the rolling stock it inherited, hadn't liked what it had seen, and laid out a program to replace it with equipment similar to that being purchased for other S. P. subsidiaries.

The first step was to return Hanchett's five leased cars to the United Railroads. That accomplished, the company acquired three small California-type cars—Los Angeles-Pacific 36, 38, and 39—with transverse seating and wire mesh to the belt rail in the open ends. This was in July 1911. Probably only the bodies were sent north, the trucks remaining in Los Angeles. These cars, which were to log many years of faithful service, ran over the local lines for some time with their original designations but eventually were converted to one-man operation and reidentified as San Jose Railroads 2, 3, and 31, the numbers they carried to the end.

The next acquisitions were in a sense fortuitous. Before the Southern Pacific bought the San Jose lines it had ordered seven 100-horsepower city cars under the Peninsular's name. Numbered San Jose Railroads 120-126 and introduced during March and April 1912, these 40-passenger cars looked like those obtained by the steam road since 1906 for its other properties but also resembled those of the United Railroads. They had the six-window closed center section of Hanchett's Sacramentos. Built by the American Car Company (J. G. Brill), these cars had General Electric motors, Westinghouse air brakes, Brill trucks, two swinging gates, and two Brill folding gates. The cost—new—was about $5,700 apiece. They were used on the Santa Clara and First Street lines.

That same year the S. P. ordered 18 similar cars from the Jewett Car Company. Resembling the 120 class, these were pure ''long Huntington standards'' with a little more zip (120 horsepower), a four-window steel-sided closed center section, and outer sections enclosed to the belt rail by wire mesh. Of the 18 cars, San Jose got four (Nos. 127-130); the others went to Fresno and the Pacific Electric. These 40-passenger cars, introduced in April 1913, were equipped with GE 201 motors, Westinghouse air brakes, lever-operated wire mesh gates, and wood pilots. The cost again was about $5,700 each. These cars, too, were used on the First Street and Santa Clara Street lines.

Eastbound San Jose Railroads car 129 is at First and Santa Clara streets, circa 1913.

(J.C. Gordon photo from Charles Smallwood and Henry E. Morse Jr. Collections)

The wire gate is closed on car 126 as the two-man crew poses. The year is about 1915 and the car is on the San Jose Railroads Willows line.
(Randolph Brandt Collection)

There was still more equipment to come. Because of the growing national enthusiasm among transit people for low-level center-entrance cars, the S. P. ordered 36 of its own version in 1913, including six for San Jose. Nicknamed "hobbleskirts" for their convenience for the ladies, these cars resembled New York's "Broadway battleships" and Boston's subway-surface cars of the period. A highly advanced design, they loaded and unloaded quickly, and San Jose's six (131-136) were promptly placed on the First Street lines, heaviest in the city. The others went to Stockton, Fresno, and the Pacific Electric.

Thus, by year's end 1913, the Southern Pacific had given San Jose a streetcar system to rival the best in the country. The paint scheme was the familiar S. P. traction red with gold lettering and trim, applied mainly to the new equipment, to trailers, and to the older cars only when converted to one-man operation, which became a major task of the mid-decade. Most of the others were doomed to live out their lives in the increasingly weatherbeaten Hanchett light green. The Sacramentos now were the system's secondary car, some becoming surplus for parts cannibalization or body modifications. The other cars inherited by the S. P. gradually disappeared.

In 1912 Chapin suspended service on the narrow-gauge Hobson Street line from First out to Walnut Street. However, city pressures forced him to back down. The line's single car was restored May 1, 1913, over Chapin's protest that it never took in more than $1.50 a day. Agnes Ryan of Santa Clara, whose home was then on the corner of Walnut and Polhemus Streets, recalled that the streetcar was always stopped for the night at the corner of Hobson and Vendome Avenue. That was because the motorman lived on Vendome, a short distance from Hobson. Ben Estruth, then living on Hobson, remembered him well. "We kids had lots of fun stealing a ride on the rear of the car," he recollected. "Later I became friendly with the motorman. He was an old Confederate soldier and had fought with Robert E. Lee. The tales he used to tell us kids! Then I did odd jobs for him in his garden. In the evening I would listen to his phonograph, an Edison with a horn and cylinder records."

In January 1913 the San Jose Railroads announced some construction of its own: conversion of Hanchett's old Alum Rock Avenue line to standard gauge out to Linda Vista. Work got under way that year, and the line opened for service June 23, 1914. Specifically ignored was the narrow-gauge spur running north from Alum Rock Avenue to Toyon station, whose traffic had dried up once service began on the Berryessa line.

Failure to include the Toyon line in the broad-gauge package prompted some local residents to file a grievance with the State Railroad Commission. After hearings, the Commission told Chapin to standard-gauge the spur and connect it with the Berryessa line at Toyon. This order was subsequently modified to cover only the Linda Vista line (already done), the Toyon line remaining an isolated narrow-gauge shuttle.

Frequent service was maintained over the system's six main lines: Santa Clara-East San Jose, Hanchett Park-Tenth Street, Julian-Delmas, Third-Seventh, First Street-Willow Glen, and First Street-Cottage Grove, terminating at First and Almaden Avenue (now Alma Avenue). The S. P. depot car to Third and Reed Streets, like its Santa Clara cousin, was tied to arrivals and departures of the steam trains. Certain other city schedules complemented those of the Peninsular and were printed in its timetable, such as downtown San Jose service to Oak Hill Cemetery (Scheutzen Park) and to Linda Vista/Toyon. Cars on the Oak Hill line ran from about 6 a.m. to midnight, providing half-hour service. Those to Linda Vista and Toyon also ran half-hourly from 5:45 a.m. to 6:15 p.m., then hourly to 11:15, the last car terminating at Linda Vista and returning home at 11:45 p.m.

The Peninsular offered 15-minute headway on its Naglee Park branch, with service from 6 a.m. to 11 p.m. Cars departed from First and San Carlos Streets on the hour and half-hour and from First and San Fernando Streets on the quarter-hour. This branch also now provided half-hourly Bascome local service from about 7:30 a.m. to 6:30 p.m., the Naglee Park cars continuing on to Bascom Avenue via San Fernando, Delmas Avenue, and Park Avenue and returning via San Carlos, Delmas, and San Fernando. From 6:30 to 7:30 a.m. and after 6:30 p.m.

(hourly to 11:30 p.m.), Bascome locals ran to and from the S. P. depot via Market Street.

An interesting wrinkle was joint operation by the Peninsular and San Jose Railroads of the Alum Rock line. Generally speaking, the S. P. tried in San Jose to follow its traditional Los Angeles practice of separating city lines from interurban lines, carefully refraining from amalgamating the properties. Since the local operations interlocked, however, this distinction was often lost. Sunday and holiday trade on the Alum Rock line was heavy, but weekday traffic was quite light.

So the Peninsular took charge Sundays and holidays, running its cars from downtown San Jose to Seventeenth (formerly Fourteenth) Street and Berryessa Road over the city company's Luna Park line. For this right it paid the San Jose Railroads 4¢ per car mile for use of its tracks, power, etc. On weekdays the roles were reversed; the city company ran the service and paid the Peninsular 4¢ a car mile from Seventeenth and Berryessa. That was per agreement of March 17, 1914. Tickets to the park or intermediate points on the interurban were apportioned 75% to the Peninsular and 25% to the San Jose Railroads. Sunday service was frequent from about 6 a.m. to midnight. Weekdays the first car to the park departed downtown San Jose at 6:30 a.m., the second at 7:12 a.m., and subsequent cars hourly from 8:30 a.m. to 6:30 p.m. From then until 10:30 p.m. they ran hourly service terminating at Noble Avenue, nine minutes west of the park. The last car to the park left downtown San Jose at 11:12 p.m. Returning schedules were similar: hourly from 7:05 a.m. to 7:05 p.m., then hourly from Noble Avenue only and a final car leaving the park at 11:47 p.m.

A similar accommodation was reached regarding freight movements. The Peninsular owned no freight cars but did a modest business hauling oil, fruit, gravel, and other cargo, meeting the Southern Pacific at Palo Alto, Mayfield, Campbell, and San Jose (the so-called Tenth Street transfer). It had spur tracks at several locations, and Stanford University depended on it to bring oil to the campus powerhouse.

Motive power was provided chiefly by a 1,000-horsepower, 60-ton steel Baldwin-Westinghouse locomotive (No. 4) acquired in 1912 and a 1450-class box motor (No. 2) built for the interurban by the Pacific Electric the following year. As expected, the Berryessa packing center generated considerable traffic. The San Jose Railroads supplied power for Peninsular movements serving this trade. In theory neither company should have benefitted from the 1914 agreement; in practice the Peninsular usually came out ahead.

The city lines' paint shop and office space served both companies, as did the interurban's shops and stores on San Carlos Street: three buildings in a row containing a car overhaul and machine shop, an electrical shop, and the storeroom. Maintenance performed at San Jose included heavy repairs. Adjoining the shops was the Peninsular's six-track carbarn used in 1981 as a garage by the Santa Clara County Transit District. Numerous storage tracks were built on the property, as was a connecting track to the S. P. Both companies bought power from P. G. and

Since the topography was pretty rugged, not too many photographers could duplicate this rare view of two of the 50-class "standards" in Alum Rock Canyon, on their way to Alum Rock Park on a busy Sunday. The lead car is pulling a trailer. (Vernon J. Sappers Collection)

E., delivered to substations at Berryessa, Saratoga, and Los Altos.

Except in San Jose the interurban shared stations with the parent S. P. at all cities served by both steam trains and electrics; there the Peninsular had its own downtown station, first at 143 S. Market Street and later at 65 S. Market. The interurban and city systems often traded equipment, and it was even possible to see city cars, thronging with passengers, whizzing down country lanes toward special events like Saratoga's annual Blossom Festival.

3. 1915 Blossom Festival

The 1915 Blossom Festival seems to stand out in people's recollections for a couple of reasons. That was the year, on the eve of World War I, in which the festival coincided with the Panama Pacific International Exposition, which opened February 20 in San Francisco. President Woodrow Wilson had hoped to attend the Exposition but dared not leave Washington in view of the rapidly changing world situation. In his stead he named Vice President Thomas R. Marshall, who agreed not only to welcome foreign dignitaries in San Francisco but also to visit Montalvo, Senator James D. Phelan's home in Saratoga. In connection with the latter, the vice president sent word that he and his party would attend the festival and address the celebrants. Enthusiasm ran high in the local community, as one would surmise.

Also, the exposition was a splendid forum for the Peninsular to display its virtues and peddle its wares. To San Francisco it sent one of its big Jewett cars, No. 112, gussied up for the occasion with an ornate paint job and brass fittings on the corners. Another exhibit that drew great interest was an operating model of a 50-class car set against a painted backdrop of the Santa Clara Valley.

According to Harry Rich, long-time conductor for the Peninsular, that was hardly the end of its efforts to entice visitors down to the peninsula for a ride on the cars. In March 1963, then retired and living in Pacific Grove, he described those efforts to *San Jose Mercury News* columnist Dick Barrett: "Mr. Chapin, general manager of the Peninsular, sent one of my best friends, Jerry Locke, to the Fair. He was very good at meeting people to advertise and sell tickets to all those he could interest. Jerry was very successful at selling the trip to Easterners and many times we would have as many as 200 passengers. It happened to be my good fortune to be the conductor many times, and my motorman was generally V. M. Hollenbeck. Holly was always one of the neatest dressed of us. We tried to make a good impression on those out-of-towners." On both counts, then, Saratoga expected a record turnout for its 1915 festival.

Florence R. Cunningham tells of preparations for the event, which had been held previous years on the village green, in the Bell-Wood tract. This year, decided the festival committee, the village green would be too small, so they chose a new site across the road just east of the Saratoga Inn, between the road and Campbell (now Saratoga) Creek. A large platform was built for speakers and guests, and the hillside was prepared for seating the audience. Between the platform and hillside the ground was leveled for the children's pageant and folk dances. The probable speakers were Vice President Marshall and the eloquent Franklin D. Roosevelt, then assistant secretary of the Navy, with Senator Phelan in charge of introductions. It was believed that Interior Secretary Franklin K. Lane and Assistant Secretary of State William Phillips might be encouraged to say a few words.

The Peninsular was also busy preparing for the event. Not only were its nine flat cars seated and railed for passenger serv-

Horses, buggies and the newfangled auto kept the dirt packed down on Lincoln Avenue prior to World War I. Car 125, inbound from The Willows, is coming toward the camera. (San Jose Historical Museum)

ice (a common practice for the festivals), but plans were made for the interurban cars to haul several S. P. passenger coaches as trailers.

The chief complication was the weather. Most of the week, conditions were right, but on Friday rain fell almost everywhere in Northern California except Saratoga. Overhead the skies darkened. Saturday morning brought an urgent last-minute appeal by the *San Jose Mercury* to attend the festival.

As people began arriving, some by automobile but more by electric cars, a few fat, lazy raindrops splashed down. Then more fell. The Fifth Regiment Band played on as the committee awaited developments. They soon discovered that Vice President and Mrs. Marshall, on learning that the festival program would have to be modified, had cancelled their Saratoga visit. However, Roosevelt and several others were now at Montalvo, ready to speak if the rains abated.

Instead of abating, they became a torrential downpour swirling under winds of near hurricane force, collapsing the carousel tent and pelting the crowd. Nearly three inches of rain fell that day. Many discouraged visitors headed home. Others sought

Baldwin–Westinghouse locomotive 4 heads a paving train on East Santa Clara Street, San Jose, about 1915. (Charles Smallwood Collection) **BELOW: Box motor 2 has a short freight train at San Carlos and Page streets, San Jose. From left to right are Motorman Harry Drew, Conductor Bill Rasmussen (in blue serge) and Brakeman George Smith. The motor became the property of San Jose Railroads in 1934.** *(San Jose Mercury News)*

shelter from the bone-chilling rain in stores and churches. The Saratogans, besides being drenched and chilled, were thoroughly dejected. This festival, which was to have surpassed all former celebrations and perhaps all future ones, had instead resulted in failure. Also for naught, of course, were the many preparations of the Peninsular.

Harry Rich, reflecting on his own Blossom Trolley Trip experiences, observed that rains were not uncommon that time of year, though not in the amounts delivered in 1915. "Those trips were really something," he told Dick Barrett. "We would start out at San Jose and go by way of Campbell to Los Gatos, then to Saratoga, Congress Springs, and back to Saratoga, then to Congress Junction and over to Monta Vista, Los Altos, Mayfield, Palo Alto, and Stanford, where we gave them a conducted tour, then home by way of Cupertino. It was really one of most beautiful trips that anyone could wish for.

"We used to run two- and three-car trains from San Jose to Saratoga-Los Gatos, or Campbell-Los Gatos-Saratoga back by Meridian Corners. In those days the prune trees would be in full bloom, and of course they were not cut out and houses built in like they are now. And how those people would ride the cars! There was only one thing wrong. It seemed that it always rained through the three days, but the entire community would get out and go anyway."

Another who was intrigued by that particular trolley trip was railfan-publisher Ira Swett. "Getting off the train at San Jose," he wrote in later years, "you buy your ticket from the S. P. ticket agent, walk out the opposite door of the station and board big red car No. 110, standing impressively in the street. At exactly 1:30, two bells, and the trip begins. Passing through San Jose's business section, through the Willows and Campbell, Los Gatos is reached in exactly one hour. From Los Gatos the trip leads up into the higher foothills, giving you on one side a fine panoramic view of the Santa Cruz Mountains and on the other vistas of the valley and San Francisco Bay. You can easily spot Lick Observatory, standing on Mt. Hamilton across the way.

"At Saratoga, the 110 leaves the main line and plunges into a wooded canyon to Congress Springs, a noted mineral springs resort, popular because of long aisles of leafy walks and many shaded picnic places. Leaving Congress Springs at 3:30, you resume your foothill route through Los Altos, past section after section of garden-like homes to the college town of Palo Alto. At University Junction you are switched to the Stanford line and ten minutes later, at 4:40, roll to a stop in the midst of the large sandstone buildings. After visiting Stanford's famous chapel, you leave at 5:30 arriving at the end of the trip at 6:30. The fare for the Blossom Trolley Trip was only a dollar, and saw 65 miles of views difficult to equal elsewhere.

"Those who desired could take the San Francisco Blossom Trolley Trip," Swett related, "so-called because it began and ended at Palo Alto, making close connections there with Southern Pacific trains. This trip began at 10 a.m. and included first an hour at Stanford, a fast ride to San Jose for lunch, there joining the regular Blossom Trolley Trip at 1:30. The regular itinerary was then followed until the arrival at Palo Alto at 4:30, whereupon the San Franciscan bade goodbye to the Peninsular and boarded the S. P. for home."

The Blossom Trolley Trip continued as a special car movement until 1924, he recalled, when it was made a part of the regularly scheduled cars. Thereafter, passengers bought a coupon book of tickets covering the parts of the system formerly visited by the special car. In effect this considerably increased the number of daily trips, one leaving hourly. But when the coupon book came in, the trolley trip car went out, and with it went most of the glamour of the idea.

In 1915 the Peninsular withdrew from Oakland by selling its depot line to the S. P. for approximately $900,000, the con-struction cost. That same year, explaining that it was over-stocked with cars, it sold two of its famous "baby fives"—Nos. 102 and 103—to Fresno Traction, which leased them in turn to the Fresno Interurban Railway for the seven-mile Fresno Beach line. The price was $13,000, close to the original figure. These cars later went to the Pacific Electric upon collapse of the Fresno Interurban.

4. The War Years (1916-1918)

In 1916 the Peninsular, ordered by the county to pay part of the costs for maintaining the San Francisquito bridge at Palo Alto, halted service on its Ravenswood line at University Avenue and Pope Street, just west of the bridge. The cars continued to offer 20-minute headway on University to downtown Palo Alto and the Stanford campus but stopped running about 9:30 p.m. Ravenswood residents, forced to walk about eight blocks further to catch the cars, appealed to the Railroad Commission but failed to carry their case. Service was abandoned east of Pope. Clearly the interurban no longer entertained ambitions of reaching Oakland via Dumbarton.

These actions, in truth, marked abandonment by the S. P. of plans for extending it not only to the East Bay but also to San Francisco. The electric road had now reached full growth, contrary to the belief of almost everyone in the South Bay who cherished hopes of someday riding the big red cars to the city. Work was suspended on the San Francisco extension, but Peninsular officials preferred to call it a postponement due to the wartime steel shortage. "Wait 'til after the war," they said, "and we'll see about getting to San Francisco."

It was not to be. Some years later, in writing to railfan Lorin Silleman, then S. P. President Paul Shoup gave his reasons why: "At the time we built it (the Peninsular) and when we acquired the San Jose roads, we had plans to build into San Francisco and also possibly into Oakland from San Jose. We acquired rights of way, and I even went so far as to acquire options on terminal rights of way in San Francisco. The decision of the Supreme Court directing the Union Pacific to sell its Southern Pacific stock in 1912 upset all our financial plans and made necessary deferring any action.

"Then the Government's attacking the Southern Pacific for the purpose of tearing our system in two (the attempted split of the Southern Pacific and Central Pacific in 1914) kept us in a state of uncertainty and in the courts until 1923, deferring action in the territory where the lines of the two companies, the S. P. and the C. P., were so closely interwoven.

"That problem was finally disposed of satisfactorily, and chaos in California's major transportation system was avoided. But in the meantime, the automobile and motor bus traffic had developed to a point demonstrating that the electric interurban lines almost without exception could no longer be made profitable, and that the capital invested in them had a perilous chance of being entirely lost."

Other forces probably were at work, too. For one thing, all the S. P.'s traction opponents of former years—Hanchett, Smith, the United Railroads—were now either gone or dispatched, so there was no compelling reason to proceed. Also, the interurban was seen as by the steam road as subordinate, not meriting full attention. The financial picture was as described by Shoup, the Peninsular showing net operating gains each year through 1918 but large overall losses when debts to the parent S. P. were taken into account: for example, a $13,000 operating profit in 1915 but $220,000 overall loss including interest paid to the steam road. The 1917 tally was similar: a $20,000 operating profit but $290,000 overall loss. Operating deficits of $48,000 in 1919 and $23,000 in 1920 did not change the picture, just added to the burdens. These facts had been known and understood, however, for many years. It seems in retrospect that the chief difference may have been a change in attitude by the S. P. following the death of E. H. Harriman; he might have built the San Francisco extension because he chose to maximize profit, whereas his successors didn't because they chose to minimize risk.

In July 1916, its work force reduced by war work, the Peninsular cut its daily trips from 100 to about 80. Then Camp Fremont opened, near Palo Alto, offering a steady stream of military passengers. In September 1917 the company inaugurated a motor coach service from the camp to Palo Alto, which ran about six months. Two vehicles were used: an 40-hp "Fageol" with 18 seats (an early example of the Fageol Brothers' coachbuilding skills), and a 38-seater built on a two-ton Moreland truck chassis. Doughboys paid a 10¢ fare but were allowed a free transfer from the Palo Alto city cars. Although this route operated over paved highways, maintenance costs were high and the revenues insufficient to cover expenses.

In an effort to cut costs, Chapin experimented briefly with an eight-mile Peninsular bus line to Campbell and Los Gatos from the terminus of the Bascome Local (San Carlos Street and Bascom Avenue). This service proved a financial disaster and was soon abandoned. He also tried a gasoline-powered rail-bus on the Alum Rock line, an old idea in S. P. circles. Chapin extolled the virtues of his steel-wheeled hybrid, but the public (and his own maintenance crews) were harder to please. They shunned the bus, which disappeared, to be seen no more. It was scrapped during the 1920s.

Car utilization rose sharply during this period, holding at 1.91-2.33 passengers per car mile through June 1918. It was during this time, too, that the Peninsular refitted its original Rea-Granger cars (1-12), renumbering them 50-61. Also, following the city lines' lead, it moved quickly toward one-man PAYE operation. Cars 15, 16 (renumbered from 14), and 19 were converted in October 1916. Orders came down a year later for Palo Alto cars 22-26, which were also fitted with air gates and steps. Car 17 was converted to one-man operation in December 1917 and cars 18 and 20 in August 1918.

One car was accidently lost: a wrecker sitting disreputably in the San Carlos Street yard while company officials debated its fate. "It was filthy, in horrible shape," recalled Monty Morgareidge, who happened to be working in the yard when an order came down to retire the car. "We were told to get rid of it. So we splashed it with about 20 gallons of gasoline and touched it off. That was a sight. While it burning merrily, there came a phone message; old man Chapin wanted to counteract the order. 'Sorry, Mr. Chapin,' I told him, 'you're too late; it's burning right now.' He wasn't too happy about it, but what could he do?" Morgareidge was later fired by the Peninsular for a rule infraction not related to the incident. "I did a lot of things contrary to the rules," he later explained to Vernon Sappers. "I guess I had it coming."

Conversion work was also well along by the San Jose Railroads. Most surviving members of the 101 class had now been one-manned, with hand-operated collapsible gates and folding steps, giving the company a roster of 10 one-man cars. Sacramento cars 14 and 15 were shortened to their closed sections plus short end platforms with air-operated wire mesh folding gates, folding steps, and doors on the right end of each end for one-man operation. Sacramento car 21, renumbered from 4, was not shortened but altered for one-man operation with sid-

Rubber-tired transport came early to the Peninsular. This unique tractor-trailer bus was built in 1916 by affiliated Pacific Electric and sent north to work in the San Jose area. A duplicate was built for SP-owned Fresno Traction.

(Magna Collection)

SAN JOSE RAILROADS REVENUES 1912-20

Source: California State Railroad Commission

| Year | Revenues | | Expenses | Net after Taxes |
	Passenger	Total		
1912	$197,000	$213,000	$147,000	$ 58,000
1913	347,000	367,000	251,000	101,000
1914	342,000	359,000	241,000	100,000
1915	332,000	347,000	242,000	85,000
1916	314,000	330,000	232,000	76,000
1917	295,000	309,000	250,000	38,000
1918	297,000	302,000	232,000	51,000
1919	344,000	352,000	253,000	79,000
1920	394,000	402,000	298,000	82,000

ing extended to rear corners, transverse seating, and air-operated folding gates and folding double steps up front.

Operations remained profitable at San Jose during the war years (see accompanying table), although passenger revenues and net profits declined sharply in 1917-18 from their respective 1913 peaks of $347,000 and $101,000. The wartime conditions encouraged Chapin to make some overdue changes in San Jose service. In 1916 the Hanchett Park and Oak Hill lines became shuttles operating single cars, respectively, from Martin and The Alameda to Tillman and Park Avenues and from Almaden and Monterey Road to Scheutzen Park. Some Tenth Street cars now originated in Santa Clara and some in downtown San Jose.

On June 19, 1916, the company filed application with the Railroad Commission to abandon its Hobson Street branch, formerly served by two-man equipment but now as an economy move by a one-man car running on a 20-minute headway. The stated reasons for abandonment were declining patronage and deficits of over $3,000 yearly. Chapin proposed replacing the car with a 12-seat converted Ford truck operating on a 30-minute headway, which he did when approval was given February 26, 1918. According to Agnes Ryan, Warren McGrury was the bus driver for several years. He later joined the California Highway Patrol.

In June 1918 the company filed two more applications for abandonment: the narrow-gauge Toyon branch June 3 and the broad-gauge Oak Hill (Scheutzen Park) line June 21. The *Mercury* unsuccessfully opposed both applications. As regards the Toyon branch, which ran from Linda Vista via Alum Rock and Kirk Avenues to McKee Road, thence over private right of way to Toyon station near Penitencia Creek, the company insisted that it was in very poor physical condition and, moreover, served only a farming community that had not developed into a residential district. The projected cost to convert the line to standard gauge was $26,000, representing an annual loss of $3,700. This argument carried.

The proposed abandonment of the Oak Hill car stirred public dismay, but, as Chapin observed, it had run at a "dead loss" of $6 a day since the closing of Scheutzen Park and the San Jose Driving Park. He pledged "experimental" bus service as a Sunday and holiday substitute. Approval to abandon the streetcar came on July 30. Coach service began Sunday August 25, using the 40-hp Fagoel from Palo Alto. The fare was 10¢, with free transfer to the city cars. Chapin later suggested, to a select audi-

ence, that these abandonments represented a rather novel application of motor coach technology to provide euthanasia for "desert" streetcar lines, which might have wide applicability to the industry.

Another casualty of the war years was Luna Park, which failed because of declining trade and the difficulty of getting workers to man the attractions. According to Clyde Arbuckle, the site stood idle for several years before the National Axle Corporation moved in. In 1981 it was occupied by the Giacomazzi warehouses.

The city lines—San Jose and Palo Alto—got a boost August 12, 1918, when local fares were increased from 5¢ to 6¢. The 30-ride family, 62-ride daily, adult 46-ride monthly, and 50-ride commutation fares gave way to 60-ride individual and 46-ride school children's individual commutation fares.

5. Coyote Bridge Disaster

Fall 1917 brought a railroad tragedy to San Jose called its "greatest catastrophe since the earthquake of 1906." On October 30, at 5:17 a.m., the Coyote Creek bridge on East Santa Clara Street gave way under the weight of three heavily loaded S. P. freight cars. Cars and bridge went crashing down into the creekbed, conductor Harry Rich clinging to the steps of the middle car and escaping with barely a scratch. Not so fortunate was 12-year-old Larry Foster, who at that moment was cycling over the bridge on his morning milk-delivery route. The lad died of his injuries.

An aroused city demanded explanation. Why was a freight train allowed to operate on the city streets? By whose permission? The explanation was as follows.

This early morning westbound freight was a routine movement by the railroad, its cars bound for the Tenth Street transfer to S. P. tracks. Contrary to its franchise terms, which stated no freight was ever to be hauled over the city streets, the railroad had been operating such trains for many years with the full awareness of city officials, who were reluctant to put obstacles in its path. Some precedent had been established in 1911 when the railroad obtained rights to haul gravel, but these rights were thought to have expired.

The State Railroad Commission, investigating the accident,

The 1917 bridge collapse spilled cars, contents, concrete rails, and wooden walkway into Coyote Creek. Conductor Harry Rich stayed aboard one of the cars and came through unscathed, but a 12-year-old boy died of injuries. (Albert Whiteaker Collection)

later reported that condemnation of the bridge had been discussed as early as 1911 when the gravel-hauling question arose, then put aside and forgotten. "It is purely a matter of luck," said the Commission in its summary report, "that these loads (that caused the failure) were not further increased by a street-car on the eastbound track or by an automobile or two, which would have caused increased loss of life or serious injury."

Within a week the company had established a temporary bus route across the creek from the end of its Julian Street line, routing every second car on East Santa Clara Street to the Julian terminus. While city and company crews removed the wreckage, a wooden footbridge was hastily erected at the site and streetcar service restored to both ends of the bridge.

As work began on the new Santa Clara Street bridge, city and company responsibilities for the tragedy were hammered out in a series of meetings convened by the State Railroad Commission. Agreement was reached November 18, 1918, limiting the hours and conditions of freight movements and citing other improvements to be carried out by the city and the railroad. Signatories were Chapin, engineer Henry Lynch of the San Jose Railroads, and city engineer F. M. Nikert.

Within the city, freight hauling would henceforth be restricted to Berryessa Road and a route westward on Santa Clara Street from King Road to First Street, north to Bassett Street, over Bassett and down Market Street to Park Avenue and San Carlos Street, then westward on San Carlos to the carbarn and on Park and Meridian Road to Meridian and San Carlos. Transfers to the S. P. would be permitted only at Tenth Street and the carbarn. The former privilege of hauling freight on Seventeeth Street was now curtailed.

In January 1919 the city opened its new span over the Coyote, dubbed the "Teddy Roosevelt" bridge in honor of the ex-president who had died shortly before. Streetcars began operating over the new bridge in mid-February, at which time the Julian Street emergency bus service was ended.

6. S. P. Acquires Birneys

On June 19, 1919, came news of another tragedy when Ed Shoup, operating superintendent of the Peninsular and the San Jose Railroads, lost a leg in an interurban collision. The accident happened just outside Saratoga when car 51 overlooked a meet order and plunged headlong into car 109.

A San Francisco newspaper described the wreck in vivid detail: "Car No. 109, a big interurban almost twice the size of No. 51, swept down a grade and around a curve and caught the smaller car before either of the motormen could stop their cars. The smaller car was thrown on end and nearly every seat torn to pieces. That many were not killed outright is considered remarkable." Shoup's leg was later found in the wreckage of car 51, according to Lorin Silleman, and buried out behind the San Carlos Street carbarn. The superintendent was laid up for some time but eventually returned, continuing to serve the company despite his handicap until his death in the 1930s.

That accident called forth memories of previous wrecks, two of which had occurred the same year (1910) at the University Avenue crossing in Palo Alto. The first involved car 100, one of the "baby fives," broadsided by a boxcar soon after the Stanford-Palo Alto line opened. She was too well built to be badly hurt, however, and quickly cleared the San Jose shops. Not so lucky was car 5, clobbered by a locomotive two months later just moments after being abandoned by its passengers and crew. That car had to be scrapped.

Another unusual accident involved car 105, one of the big Jewetts. One day, while traveling down the twisting grade from Congress Springs, she got to moving too fast and threw her motorman from the cab on a particularly sharp curve. Onward she raced, finally leaping the track and overturning on a country highway. Though badly damaged, she was restored to service.

Car 109 was repaired soon after the Saratoga collision, but No. 51 sat in the San Jose yards many months while company officials debated whether she was worth rebuilding. That gave railfans a chance to prowl through the wreckage and do some "moonlight requisitioning," as later told to Ira Swett by Lorin Silleman: "While traveling over the line in 1919 a week after the disastrous 109-51 cornfield meet, I saw wrecked car 51 in the yards near the Peninsular shops.

"My twin brother, Ben, and another friend were with me, and of course we were eager for souvenirs. We came on the bright long air whistle of 109, lying in the rubble. Our minds acted as a committee of one—'Take it!' We did and, on our return to San Francisco, boarded one of the former very large cars of the United Railroads San Mateo line. We knew the conductor and offered him the whistle if he would guarantee to put it on one of those cars. Next day we were delighted to hear 'Big Sub' No. 9 with the Peninsular whistle. That was a thrill, to hear that tone on that line!" Silleman got back his whistle when No. 9 was scrapped and has it to this day. The eventual decision on car 51 was affirmative; she was rebuilt and restored to service.

In May 1919 the Peninsular, trying to attract more passengers, adopted faster schedules, reduced its round-trip rates, and increased the number of daily runs from 80 to about 120. Main line schedules now called for 32 one-way trips daily between San Jose and Palo Alto, 55 between San Jose and Los Gatos (27 via Saratoga, 28 via Campbell), and 20 between Los Gatos and Palo Alto, all but two of which required a change of cars. Ridership increased somewhat, but car utilization declined to 1.58-1.93 passengers per car mile.

That led to a 20% hike on through fares October 16, 1920, widely advertised in the local press: "No increase of the one-way 6¢ fare or the school commutation $1.85 fare between San Jose and Bascom Avenue, San Jose and Cherry Avenue, Naglee Park line, Stanford University line, Waverley Street line. San Jose Railroads, no fare increase at all." Passengers were asked to cooperate. "Fares in many instances end in odd cents," they were told. "Will you please assist conductor with exact change?" The net gain to the Peninsular was a 26% boost. In some cases schedules were also slowed slightly to improve the utilization factor.

It wasn't enough, though, as company profit-loss statements mutely testified. So in December the Peninsular and San Jose Railroads went to the State Railroad Commission requesting a gradual rise in local fares to 10¢, with tokens five for 35¢. They asked for adjustments in the 46-ride school commutation rate, the $1.85 fare increasing to $2.22 but the $2.70 and $3.60 fares declining to $2.63 and $3.48, respectively. The city company asked to boost its fares to Capitol Avenue from 10¢ to 12¢ and to Linda ista from 15¢ to 18¢. It asked approval to cancel its 125-ride cash coupon fare, substituting a 30-ride family commutation ticket at 20 times the one-way fare if in excess of 12¢. These hikes would affect only local lines; no increases were sought for through service.

The proposals were accompanied by promises of important operating changes in San Jose. During 1920 the city company had evaluated five one-man Birney safety cars (27-31) sent to the Peninsular in January as part of the S. P.'s first Birney order. The cars, painted yellow at first and called "canaries," were initially tested in Palo Alto, then in San Jose on the Naglee Park branch and in weekday service on the Alum Rock Park line. Results were obtained from actual experience, taking into account anticipated passenger loads and track conditions, which

Paul Shoup held a distinguished and long-lasting career on the Southern Pacific, rising to the top. He had been South Bay district freight agent and figured in many low- and high-level decisions affecting San Jose traction operations. At one time Shoup headed the giant Pacific Electric system.   (Southern Pacific)

were rated only fair. The projected annual saving from the Birneys in San Jose was $15,000, of which about $2,500 was expected to come from reduced power consumption (the 1920 power cost was $42,119, declining to a projected $39,500 in 1921 if the Birneys ran). As a result, 22 more were obtained for the San Jose Railroads as part of the S. P.'s second order. These cars (137-158), leased from the parent company at 7½% per year of the purchase price, were intended to be standard 28-footers but were equipped at the factory with a "duckbill" over-size anticlimber for better collision protection, increasing their length to 29 feet 9½ inches. Also, for base service on the Santa Clara Street lines, the 120- and 127-class cars were one-manned about this time by removing rear steps and immovably fastening the former swinging gates in the rear openings.

7. 1921 Route Revisions

The promised changes took effect May 1, 1921. The San Jose Railroads made sweeping revisions that day, consolidating some of its routes and improving the headway on major lines

The Birney safety car came to San Jose in a big way. Unit 150 bounces along The Alameda opposite Hester School in 1922. BELOW: A couple of pass-riding U.S. mailmen board a sister car at First and San Fernando streets.   (Both: J. C. Gordon photo from Henry E. Morse Jr. Collection)

Notice the extra-heavy-duty anti-climber on San Jose Railroads Birney 145, shown on North First Street in San Jose, circa 1925. This was characteristic of Birney cars on several Southern Pacific traction properties. (J. C. Gordon photo from Henry E. Morse Jr. Collection)

from 10 minutes to 7½ minutes. Details of the routes after May 1 were as follows:

Line 1—Linda Vista/King Road. Originating on Santa Clara Street at Market, operating easterly on Santa Clara Street to King Road on 10-minute headway 6 a.m. to 8 a.m., and easterly on Alum Rock Avenue from King Road to Linda Vista on 30-minute headway 6 a.m. to 6 p.m.

Line 2—Tenth Street. Originating in Santa Clara at Franklin and Jefferson Streets, operating easterly and southerly along The Alameda, Santa Clara Street, and Tenth Street to Keyes Street, then easterly along Keyes to Cedarbrook Park (the city limit). This line operated on 15-minute headway 6 a.m. to 3:30 p.m., then 12-minute headway 3:30 p.m. to 8 p.m.

Line 3—Seventeenth Street. Also originating at Franklin and Jefferson, operating southerly and easterly along The Alameda and Santa Clara Street to Seventeenth Street, then northerly on Seventeenth to Berryessa Road. This line also operated on 15-minute headway from Santa Clara, alternating its operation with Line 2, thus effecting 7½ minute headway between Santa Clara and San Jose through most of the day. Once each hour a car of the Seventeenth Street line ran through to Alum Rock Park over tracks of the Peninsular Railway except weekends and holidays, when Alum Rock service was provided by the Peninsular at more frequent intervals.

Line 4—Hanchett Park. Shuttle service through Hanchett Park residential section on 15-minute headway, originating at the corner of Race Street and The Alameda and proceeding via Martin and Tillman Avenues to the corner of Race and Park Avenue.

Line 5—Santa Clara Depot. Originating at S. P. depot, Santa Clara, operating westerly and southerly to Saratoga Road and the Santa Clara town limit. Irregular service 6:30 a.m. to 7 p.m., meeting all important S. P. trains.

Line 6—First Street-Cottage Grove. Originating on First Street at the north city limit, operating southerly along First Street to the south city limit (Almaden Avenue) on 12-minute headway 6 a.m. to 8 p.m. This was the heaviest short-haul line in the system.

Line 7—First Street-Willow Street. Also originating on First Street at the north city limit, operating southerly and westerly along First and Willow Streets to Lincoln Avenue, then southerly along Lincoln to Minnesota Avenue. This line also operated on 12-minute headway 6 a.m. to 8 p.m., alternating its operation with Line 6, thus effecting six-minute headway on First from the north city limit to Willow Street.

Line 8—Delmas Avenue-Julian Street. Originating on Delmas Avenue at Willow, operating northerly and easterly through downtown San Jose and along Julian Street to east city limit. This line operated on a 10-minute headway 7 a.m. to 8 p.m.

Line 9—Seventh Street. Originating at First and St. John Streets, operating southerly and easterly to Seventh and Reed Streets, then southerly on Seventh to Keyes. This line operated on 30-minute headway.

Line 10—Hobson Street. This bus route operated on Hobson from First to Walnut Street, on 30-minute headway.

Line 11—Oak Hill. This bus route operated Sundays and holidays only from the Cottage Grove terminus of Line 6, running southerly along Monterey Road to the entrance of Oak Hill Cemetery (Stone Avenue). The line usually maintained 30-minute headway.

In addition to these were Peninsular city service on the Naglee Park and Bascome local lines and weekday San Jose

Railroads service to Alum Rock Park. According to Curt Bailey, the westbound Alum Rock cars came in on Santa Clara Street, turned right on Second Street, left on St. John, left on First Street, and left again on Santa Clara Street to complete their loop. He recalled their being quartered at The Alameda carbarn. The one-way fare to the park was 20¢. Norman Holmes remembered the motormen transporting a quilted ice cream box up front—containing ice cream and dry ice—its top folded over.

New equipment was introduced that day on all routes. Before May 1 the Santa Clara Street lines (1 through 4) were served mainly by the 120 and 127 classes and by the two-man Sacramentos, now considered to have inadequate power and braking capacity for high-speed street work. The First Street lines were served by the 120-127 classes and 131-class dragons, and all others by the 10 older one-man cars and leased Peninsular Birneys. After May 1 the Sacramentos were replaced except during rush hour by the Birneys, considered safer and more capable of handling the traffic. Now assigned to the Santa Clara Street lines were the 120 class, three cars from the 127 class, four Birneys, three cars from the Peninsular 17 class, and car No. 10, a two-man Sacramento. Most other routes were served by Birneys, including the four leased Peninsular Birneys on the Delmas-Julian line. Car No. 14, a one-man Sacramento, was used on the Seventh Street line and 107, an older one-man car, on the San Jose depot line.

All other cars were classified as spares except one Birney and two older one-man cars leased to the Peninsular for San Jose city service. The dragons, which could not be converted for one-man operation, were sent by the S. P. to the Pacific Electric, where they served with other P. E. and Stockton dragons on the Long Beach and Edendale lines until retired in 1934. Car 135, one of the dragons, was badly damaged in a colli-

sion with an S. P. locomotive at Fourth and Santa Clara Streets and was scrapped.

Investigations by the State Railroad Commission into the December 1920 rate increase proposals had prompted a comprehensive engineering study of operations of the Peninsular and San Jose Railroads published in July 1921. At that time the city system had 36.834 miles of track (25.3 miles in paved streets) varying from 60-pound T-rail to 127-pound Trilby. The Commission recommended abandoning the Hobson Street bus line and urged the companies to consign Alum Rock passenger service full-time to the San Jose Railroads, with freight service maintained by the Peninsular.

It also proposed boosting the track charge for Alum Rock service to 8¢ per car mile, double the current rate. Funded debt for the Peninsular, said the Commission, now consisted of ·$500,000 par value bonds issued in 1903 by the San Jose-Los Gatos Interurban Railway Company, maturing May 21, 1923, and bearing 5% interest. These bonds, held $379,000 by the S. P. and the balance by the public, had been assumed by the Peninsular under terms of its 1909 consolidation. The Commission suggested abandoning the Santa Clara depot line and the southern leg of the Naglee Park branch (on San Carlos Street), substituting 15-minute headway on San Fernando Street from First Street to Fifteenth and San Carlos Streets.

Palo Alto was treated separately. The University Avenue line was served by two cars offering 20-minute headway from the Ravenswood Bridge to Stanford University. The Waverley Avenue branch was served by three cars on a 20-minute headway from Oregon Avenue to the university. Tracks and paving, declared the Commission, were not maintained at a high standard. It observed that the local lines were earning 8%, not justifying a rate increase, and suggested as an economy move that the com-

Remodeled older cars worked alongside the Birneys as the 1920s wore on. Here is SJRR car 6 westbound on Santa Clara Street near Market in San Jose. Note that the back door is gone, pilots have been added, the car sits higher on its trucks and the end is "modernized" to at least vaguely resemble the Birney.
(J. C. Gordon photo from Henry E. Morse Jr. Collection)

pany reduce its number of cars on the Waverley Street branch from three to two, since there was a 12-minute layover at the end of each round trip.

This reduction could be achieved by cutting back service from Oregon Avenue to Lowell Avenue and/or by moving a motor-generator set from the Los Altos substation to Palo Alto, thereby increasing the voltage by 20% and the car speed from 10 to 12 mph. P. G. and E. already used part of the carbarn as an 11-kilovolt substation, the Commission noted, facilitating installation of the motor-generator set.

These recommendations were not mandatory and served mainly as guidelines for changes or abandonments the companies might want to pursue. Despite the Peninsular's projected $362,000 loss for 1921, the Commission, after weighing the evidence, decided November 29 to deny the fare increases.

That year the Peninsular sold its three remaining "baby fives"—cars 100, 101, and 104—to the Pacific Electric, which renumbered them 468-470. That left it with the 12 original Rea-Granger cars (50-61) and the eight big Jewetts (105-112), plus trailers, to handle its interurban passenger traffic. Weekdays it had nine cars running in main line service with 11 in reserve. Sundays and holidays, 19 operated with only one in reserve.

The eight Jewetts were leased from the S. P., as were three trailers from the city company. The Peninsular owned two trailers outright. In city service were eight cars, all arranged for one-man operation: five in Palo Alto, two on the Bascome local line, and one on the Naglee Park branch. The roster of city equipment listed two double-truck cars owned outright, two standard cars leased from and four to the San Jose Railroads, and one Birney leased from and five to the San Jose Railroads. Its express car (No. 1) was not much used. In service were three 240-horsepower locomotives (Nos. 9, 200, and 201), the Peninsular having succumbed to a fine offer to lease its Baldwin-Westinghouse locomotive to the Pacific Electric, which renumbered it 1618.

Other equipment included line car 14, sprinkler 12, service car 5, and the nine flatcars (300-308). Box motor No. 2 now became the system's heavy power, regularly hauling 10 or 12 boxcars. When its chores at Berryessa prevented it from working elsewhere, the Jewett cars were pressed into duty as switchers, especially No. 111.

Daily schedules adopted by the Peninsular October 1, 1921, called for hourly runs northbound between San Jose and Palo Alto from 6:40 a.m. to 7:25 p.m. with 9:25 and 11:25 p.m. cars and a 5:55 a.m. car Sundays and holidays. Southbound the service was hourly from 7:45 a.m. to 8:30 p.m., then at 10:20 p.m. and 12:20 a.m. plus a 6:55 a.m. run Sundays and holidays. Most cars connected with the S. P. steam trains at Palo Alto.

Direct northbound service was now offered hourly between Los Gatos and Palo Alto from about 7 a.m. to 5 p.m., then at 9:10 p.m. via Meridian Corners. The southbound schedule was similar: hourly from about 8 a.m. to 8:30 p.m., then at 10:20 p.m., with 7:05 and 8:30 p.m. runs via Meridian Corners. This was a vast improvement in through service, most Palo Alto-Los Gatos runs formerly requiring a change of cars.

Cars no longer operated between Los Gatos and Congress Springs. However, scheduled each day between the resort and Saratoga were three cars eastbound (11:15 a.m., 5:15 p.m., and 7:05 p.m.) and two cars westbound (11 a.m. and 5:14 p.m.). New to the timetable was San Jose service to Congress Junction and Sunny Brae. Eastbound from Congress Junction were cars hourly from 6 a.m. to 2:30 p.m., then at 5:30 and 7:16 p.m. Westbound was a 6 a.m. car followed by hourly runs from 8 a.m. to noon, then cars at 2, 3, 5, 7, and 7:30 p.m. From Sunny Brae eastbound was a 6 a.m. car followed by hourly service from 8 a.m. to 1 p.m. and cars at 4 and 6 p.m. The westbound schedule to Sunny Brae was similar.

One of the more obscure San Jose local lines was the stub to Hanchett Park. Here, in 1923, Peninsular car 14 careens around the curve at Park Avenue and Race Street.   (Vernon J. Sappers Collection)

8. Peninsular Builds King Road Line

In 1922 the San Jose Railroads took steps to solve the difficulties of its 127-class cars, which had superior mechanical qualities but closed center sections that were too small for the cool South Bay climate. The open end sections were enclosed to the belt rail with steel siding; sash and glass were not added. The rear door openings were not enclosed, however. In 1923 Sacramento cars 6, 9, 10, and 12 were rebuilt for one-man operation on the Santa Clara Street lines by installing transverse seating, extending the siding to the rear corners, and installing new motors, brakes, and air-operated folding gates and steps. The company styled the ends of these cars like the Birneys, using curved steel sheeting and large end windows with a flush-mounted roller destination sign on the right.

Sacramento car 3 went to the Peninsular where it was converted for one-man operation, retrucked, renumbered 32, and put to work on the Palo Alto campus line. This car came back to San Jose in 1930 after abandonment of the campus line.

An important fact had emerged from the Railroad Commission engineering study of 1921: namely, that 75% of the people now left the San Jose business district by automobile and only 25% by streetcar. Coupled with this was a new dedication by the city, under the direction of city manager and former city engineer Clarence B. Goodwin, to paving its streets, less than 37 miles of which were hard-surfaced at the start of the decade. Pressure was brought on the San Jose Railroads and the Peninsular to pave between their rails as required by their franchises; the projected cost was $600,000 just for the main routes. The companies agreed to do this but, understandably reluctant to pour further sums into marginal routes, also promoted some abandonments.

The first to go was the Keyes Street line from Tenth Street east to Cedarbrook Park (Coyote Creek). Advised that the city wanted to pave both Tenth and Keyes Streets, the San Jose Railroads requested this abandonment January 4, 1922, noting that the 0.4-mile line served only 23 residences. The company also asked permission to convert the Tenth Street line from double to single track south of Reed Street before the paving began. These requests were approved April 12 and the work done at a cost of about $12,000.

The Railroad Commission that day approved abandonment by the Peninsular of the Santa Clara depot line out Franklin, Lincoln, and Bellomy Streets to Saratoga Avenue, one of the routes earmarked by its 1921 engineering study. Serving this line was car 13, one of the Peninsular's oldest. Receipts were said to total only $1.20 a day. No immediate action was taken on the abandonment, but service abruptly ended January 27, 1923—with informal approval by town officials—when old No. 13 gave up the ghost.

Apparently it wasn't missed, because no complaints were lodged. Two years later the town launched a paving program of its own. Costs to resurrect the line now amounted to $32,000, which the company was unwilling to pay. So the abandonment became final. In April 1926 the rusted rails were declared officially dead.

On April 12, also, the Peninsular asked permission to abandon its San Carlos Street line from First to Fifteenth Street, another of the Commission's recommendations. Approval was given and the rails removed, cars maintaining a 15-minute headway on San Fernando Street in lieu of the former loop service over San Fernando and San Carlos Streets.

On October 7, 1922, facing an additional $100,000 in paving bills, the San Jose Railroads asked the city for rights to haul freight at night over the Seventeenth Street line, a former privilege. The immediate purpose was to serve the California Prune and Apricot Growers' Association plant at Alum Rock and Capitol Avenues. The city turned down the application. So the Peninsular asked rights from the city and county to build a new single-track passenger and freight line up King Road north from Alum Rock Avenue to Berryessa Road, where it would join the existing Berryessa line.

San Jose gave its approval March 26, 1923. The county followed suit April 2. Crews then installed rails along the east side of King Road from Alum Rock Avenue to McKee Road, crossing over to the west side from McKee to Berryessa Road. On July 18 the Railroad Commission gave the Peninsular a certificate of authority to operate the new route.

On the opening of this line—the last major construction undertaken by either the Peninsular or the San Jose Railroads—weekday service to Alum Rock Park was rerouted from Seventeenth Street to King Road. A single Birney now traveled a U-shaped route from Linda Vista west to King, north to Berryessa Road, and east to the park, returning by the same route. City cars to East San Jose, which now terminated at King Road, bore placards "Berryessa" or "Linda Vista" to denote which direction the Birney would be going when the cars met at the transfer point. The Berryessa signs were white with black letters. The Linda Vista signs were blue with white letters.

Hanchett Park service was suspended in the summer of 1924 when local residents asked the Peninsular to remove its tracks on Martin Avenue while they repaved the street. A bus was substituted, the swap becoming official in April 1926. Costs to restore the car were then said to be about $23,000, a sum not justified by the traffic. The removal costs amounted to $17,000. Fred Griffin, a company official, later told the Railroad Commission that revenue from the line dropped 50% when the bus started operating, even though it performed the same service as the car and charged the same fare.

Buses cost more than streetcars to operate, he said—21¢ versus 17¢ a mile—and were not as well patronized. One reason for the decline, he suggested, advanced by a Hanchett Park woman and supported by her neighbors, was that people in that section depended on hearing the car pass on its outbound trip and preparing to catch it when it returned. When the bus went by they didn't hear it and consequently missed the return.

Railroad Commission figures for 1924 credited the Peninsular with 80.48 miles of lines and the San Jose Railroads with 46.23 miles. By now there were some further equipment changes by the city company. All 101-class cars, those inherited from Hanchett, had been scrapped, including cars 101 and 102, which were never one-manned. In that year, also, the San Jose Railroads bought five newer Birneys from the San Diego Electric, numbering them 159-163. An improved car, these Birneys had a small window located forward of the front door for better visibility. They went to work on the First Street lines.

9. Buses for Palo Alto

On April 7, 1924, the Peninsular applied to the Commission for approval to substitute buses for streetcars on its University Avenue and Waverley Street lines. To cope with the burgeoning automotive traffic, the city had just launched a massive repavement program that would force the company to spend large sums for paving between and beside its rails. This was money it could ill afford, the company claimed, in view of the operating losses it was experiencing.

City officials prevailed on the Peninsular to withdraw its application while joint efforts were made to attract more business. Public attention was called to the situation, and attempts were made to popularize the service. Five cars now ran regularly instead of three, the local fleet consisting of the five original cars (22-26) plus the two converted Sacramentos (14 and 32). Twelve-minute headway was offered on Waverley Street before 6:30 p.m. and 15-minute headway thereafter. There was no change in service or headway on University Avenue, the cars continuing as before to terminate at Pope Street.

And all to no avail. There was no influx of passengers. On May 13, 1925, the city council passed an ordinance requiring the Peninsular to re-lay its roadbed with 127-pound girder rail and pay its share of paving costs, estimated to be around $230,000. This was some 30% more than the company's total investment in the local system.

"Present indications are that the struggle to retain the streetcar system has been lost," reported the *Palo Alto Times*. "The Peninsular Railway Company officials have definitely decided to renew their abandonment proceedings, which require nothing but the consent of the Railroad Commission to effect a conclusion. To those who have watched the situation closely, the decision of the railway company is no surprise. The inevitable has happened. The city in its long-continued effort to hold the streetcars has been met more than halfway by the railroad company. Whoever has observed the large number of streetcars passing by, empty and near empty, is prepared to accept the railroad company's figures which show a financial loss on the local investment. In the face of this condition there can be no logical expectation that the Railroad Commission will rule otherwise than to grant the company's application for abandonment."

This assessment was correct. Company records proved that monthly gross receipts from the two lines came to $1,700 against operating expenses of $1,750, leaving less than nothing for interest payments. Moreover, most of the traffic originated

A steam engine and other heavy equipment struggle to remove the Peninsular rails from lower University Avenue, Palo Alto, in 1925.
(George Cody Collection)

in the business and depot areas bound for the university over the campus line. Costs for removing company property from the city streets and repaving some sections were estimated at about $10,000. The Peninsular asked for a 12-month test of coach service, with right to discontinue the service if revenues were insufficient to pay operating expenses, depreciation, taxes, and a 6% return on its investment. The Commission agreed July 9. The company then secured four buses from Pacific Electric, which arrived in Palo Alto July 16.

University Avenue was the first line to go. The last car ran Sunday July 19. A bus went into service the following morning from the S. P. depot to Ashby Avenue, some 2000 feet short of the Ravenswood bridge. In time this route was extended to Ravenswood. As workmen began removing the rails from University Avenue, final plans were laid to abandon Waverley Street.

"Old red trolleys pass into history here next Monday," advised the *Times* Thursday September 24. "Beginning next Monday, the streetcar service in Palo Alto will give way to that of motor buses. This is the announcement of Dwight Ross, superintendent of the Peninsular's local system. Two buses will be placed on the Waverley Street line, and the present one will continue to serve the University Avenue section. An additional bus will be held in reserve. The route on Waverley Street will be from the S. P. depot on Alma Street to Hamilton Avenue, to Cowper Street, to Tennyson Avenue, to Waverley Street, and to the terminal at California Avenue.

"During the day 12-minute service will be given, and after 6:12 p.m. the buses will run every 20 minutes until 11:30 p.m. Removal of the streetcar tracks on Waverley Street and University Avenue is proceeding with all possible dispatch in order that paving of the avenue from The Circle to Middlefield Road may be completed by December 1."

The buses began rolling September 28 on Waverley Street, at which time the bus fare was upped to 10¢. The campus trolley line kept its 6¢ fare. Patrons had to walk over the S. P. tracks, about 100 yards, to transfer from the buses to the campus cars.

Transfers were given, but streetcar passengers had to pay an additional 4¢ on boarding the bus. The *Times* treated the situation with equanimity. "For months, nay, years," it observed, "Palo Alto has had the phantom of car-less streets hovering over it, and the possibility of being left without proper means of conveyance has not been conducive to peace of mind. Perhaps anticipating the unpleasant eventuality of having to walk, we naturally were fearful lest we should be deprived of that symbol of modern life—rapid transportation. When it became unmistakeably clear that the streetcars must go, some of us were abashed at the thought of motor buses (electric cars do look more citified), but upon mature reflection we became resigned, wisely concluding that buses are better than bicycles, and carriages are out of the question.

"But these bugaboos may be laid away now. We have a number of first class buses. The streetcar rails are to be removed; indeed, on lower University Avenue the work is well under way. It was really a momentous occasion when the city council adopted resolutions and ordinances clearing away the last legal obstructions to the removal of the car tracks and the actual improvement of the avenue from The Circle to Middlefield Road.... The council and the Chamber of Commerce, collectively or as individuals, have been unsparing of effort in working for a satisfactory solution of the transportation difficulty....

"The company has said it does not anticipate with any pleasure the prospect of operating a transportation system which is financially unprofitable. We can at the same time respect the feelings of the company, which appears to hold little hope for buses as a business enterprise here, and do our best toward making such an undertaking justify itself."

Still unresolved was the question of where to house the campus cars once the rails were removed from lower University Avenue. The company had asked to keep the Emerson Street carbarn line but yielded to a city request to abandon this track, too. Several schemes were proposed, including storage at Mayfield. The solution was to park the cars in the Stanford corporation yard. On October 8 the switch was removed at Emerson and University Avenue, cutting access to the carbarn. Company equipment was taken out and the building sold. In August 1947 it was torn down to make way for a new structure housing taxis and the garage of a local automobile dealership, Hagen and Bell. Also vacated and sold was the old substation, which served many years as an auto-repair shop. Today the building has new life as an office complex, thanks to Palo Alto architect George Cody.

"When I looked into the space for the first time in 1973," Cody told the *Palo Alto Times*, "its last tenant, an auto-repair business, had vacated two years before. As I studied the cracked concrete walls painted with aluminum paint, iced with grime, dead in the dim light of decades of dirt over windows and skylights, I noticed the peculiar roof structure, the delicate strength of a great iron truss that spread across the middle of the space, and I wondered how one could resurrect the spirit of the place." In brief, he did, converting the building into the "Old Trolley Barn" complex now shared with other tenants.

10. The Middle Years (1925-1929)

As the years rolled on and the Peninsular sank deeper in debt, the S. P. continued to meet the deficits. William F. Herrin was now president of the interurban, reporting to the S. P. corporate offices in Los Angeles. In 1925, to gain better control of the interurban, the steam road transferred its main office to San Francisco under the direction of F. W. Webster, who had succeeded Paul Shoup as head of all S. P. electric traction except the Pacific Electric.

A new deal was effected whereby the Peninsular's financial structure was revised and it could start anew the amassing of a deficit. All payroll, audit, and purchase functions for the Peninsular and San Jose Railroads were now carried out by the Pacific Electric, which performed like duties for other S. P. electric roads—the Stockton Electric Railway, the Fresno Traction Company, and the Visalia Electric Railway. As regards San Jose expenses, the wealthier San Jose Railroads paid all local office costs for itself and the Peninsular. The interurban made all major streetcar repairs.

The salaries of officers serving both companies, including those of the superintendent and chief engineer, were divided equally. The two assistant superintendents, mainly serving the Peninsular, were each paid $400 a month; of this, $150 was charged to the San Jose Railroads. The attorney's retaining fee of $175 a month was split evenly.

Of greatest concern to the Railroad Commission were the continued inequities in charges for Alum Rock service, which was still operated daily by the San Jose Railroads and on Sundays by the interurban. The companies had adopted the 8¢-per-car-mile track charge proposed by the Commission but had not turned the service over to the city company, as recommended. Since 1923 the San Jose Railroads had paid almost $7,000 a year for track fees, plus car costs and some 90% of the power costs. The annual expenses amounted to $19,000 versus revenues of about $4,000, producing an net loss of $15,000 per year for the city company.

Frank Chapin suffered a stroke in late 1925 and was removed to the S. P. hospital in San Francisco, where he died January 5, 1926, at age 69. His loss was deeply felt by the community where he had served for more than 20 years. Webster succeeded him as vice president and general manager of the Peninsular and the San Jose Railroads, remaining in this capacity until 1931.

On July 19, 1925, a bizarre accident at Alum Rock Park, resulting from a broken trolley wire, claimed three lives. Sometime that afternoon a boulder or branch, dislodged from high up the canyon wall, crashed down, snapping the wire and touching off a small grass and brush fire. Several people were trapped by the heat and smoke. All were rescued, but three men, including a city fireman, died from smoke inhalation. Two others rushing the fireman to a local hospital were injured when their car ran off the tortuous road near the park entrance.

In August the city renewed its demand that San Jose Railroads lower its tracks on Seventeenth Street to the approved grade; no further time extensions would be allowed. The company responded by asking the council for the right to rebuild its double-track line on Seventeenth into a single track, which was granted October 12 as a franchise amendment. On March 2, 1926, the Railroad Commission gave its blessing. The work cost about $12,000. In December the company also got

General Manager Frank Chapin posed for this greeting card picture shortly before his death in 1926. Clyde Arbuckle noted an extraordinary resemblance between Chapin and Superintendent Ed Shoup, with whom Chapin worked closely.

(Lorin Silleman Collection)

permission from the Railroad Commission to abandon and remove its Julian Street track from Seventeenth Street to Coyote Creek (Twenty-first Street). The city prevailed on the company, however, to maintain this line at least temporarily.

The following year (1927) brought a citywide track improvement program that included suspension of service over the old Seventh Street route (Third, San Antonio, Second, and St. John streets) in favor of a new route to the S. P. depot via Reed and First streets. Ten-minute headway was now maintained during business hours on the three Santa Clara Street lines: Santa Clara-East San Jose, Tenth Street, and Seventeenth Street. After 6 p.m. the headway was 15 minutes on the latter two lines.

The Tenth Street cars, which formerly had originated in Santa Clara, now started in downtown San Jose at Market and Santa Clara Streets, as did the Seventeenth Street cars. On alternate trips these cars ran out to Tenth and Keyes Streets and to Seventeenth and Berryessa Road, reducing the layover time at the terminals. From 3 to 6 p.m. the western terminus of the Seventeenth Street line was Hedding Street, thus effecting a five-minute headway on Santa Clara Street from Seventeenth to Hedding. The Linda Vista-Alum Rock car ran an hourly schedule in both directions from the King Road transfer point. In service on these lines were cars 6, 9, 10, 12, 120-126, 127-130, and Peninsular Birney 19.

On First Street were three routes operating successively in chain-gang fashion from the northerly city limit to Willow Glen (Lincoln and Minnesota Avenues) and Cottage Grove (Almaden Avenue) and from the S. P. depot to Seventh and Keyes Streets. Twelve-minute headway was maintained on each line, thus effecting four-minute service from the depot through downtown San Jose to Reed Street, where the Seventh and Keyes cars turned off toward the east. Eight-minute service was provided between the S. P. depot and northerly city limit and also between Reed and Willow Streets, where the Willow Glen cars turned off toward the west. All the cars serving these routes were Birneys: 137-149, 151-158, and 159-163.

Ten-minute headway was maintained during the day on the Delmas-Julian line (Willow and Delmas to Julian and Twenty-first), with 15-minute service after 8 p.m. The cars on this line were Peninsular Birneys 28, 30, and 31. The Hanchett Park bus line offered 30-minute headway, as did the Oak Hill bus line, which operated only Sundays and holidays from 9 a.m. to 6 p.m.

A Railroad Commission engineering report that year generally complimented the local streetcar operations though noting almost duplicate service by the San Jose Railroads' Tenth and Seventh Street lines and by its Delmas Avenue and Santa Clara Street routes and the Peninsular's Cherry Avenue and San Fernando Street (Naglee Park) routes. However, all of these except Santa Clara Street were now one-track lines, observed the state engineer, so no further efficiencies were possible except the elimination of one or more of the duplicated lines.

In December 1928 the San Jose Railroads began operating an experimental feeder bus route out Lincoln from Minnesota Avenue to Curtner Avenue. This line was discontinued early in 1930. In April 1929 the company was authorized to discontinue its Hanchett Park bus service, rerouting it via Park Avenue and Hedding Street.

The Peninsular, in connection with 1927 plans to one-man its entire system, needed a new type of car for its Campbell cutoff line, so it bought the San Jose Railroads' 127 class and four sister cars from Fresno. It repainted and then rebuilt them by completely enclosing the siding and installing glass windows with sash, eliminating the rear door openings, and replacing the wire gates with a folding glass door in front. This series, dubbed "Comfort Cars" by the Peninsular, didn't get the extra two motors per car needed for interurban service, although the Pacific Electric had scrapped enough of its sister cars to provide

A campaign photo for Motorman L.J. Edwards, who was running for office in the trainmen's union. Peninsular car 111 is spotted on the San Jose–Palo Alto main line between Meridian and Monta Vista.
(California Railway Museum Collection)

them. The remodeled class, renumbered 70-77, lasted in Los Gatos service until 1930.

By now the San Jose Railroads had scrapped all its remaining two-man Sacramentos plus one-man Sacramentos 15 and 21. The 120-class cars had been recalled for installation of sash and glass in the open end sections, again without closing the rear door openings. In 1928 more capacity was needed for the First Street lines, so the S. P. transferred four double-truck cars from Fresno. These had the same look as the 120 and 127 classes but were medium-platform PAYE cars. Siding was extended to the rear corners without sash or glass in the open sections; folding front gates were installed. The cars were renumbered 164-167 and put to work amongst the Birneys.

The color was also changed about then to the familiar S. P. traction yellow with tile red roofs, maroon window and door trim, and company initials monogrammed on the side. Car numbers were maroon. Within the monogram, the "S" was maroon with a brown outline and the "JRR" was brown with a darker brown outline. The striping was maroon with a brown outline, replacing an earlier aluminum stripe with red outline. The Peninsular repainted its Birneys and 17-class cars to conform, although most of its cars retained the traditional red. Destination signs added another bright touch. Tenth Street cars displayed red signs with white letters, marked 10th & Keyes St. on one end and Hedding Street on the other. The Santa Clara Street destination sign was green with black letters, marked Santa Clara on one end and King Road on the other. The San Fernando Street car carried a yellow sign with black letters marked Second & St. James. Most Peninsular destination signs were black and white.

Do the two canines really want to board the Birney for Cottage Grove? The motorcycle cop is keeping a wary eye on them, lest they do anything illegal here at First and San Fernando streets in downtown San Jose. The view was taken around 1925. The Birney car is southbound at First and San Fernando streets.
(J. C. Gordon photo from Henry E. Morse Jr. Collection)

Streetcars were an intimate part of the everyday school and work life of the community during these years, recalls Dorothy Keeler of San Jose. "In 1917, when I was six years old, my family moved from Berkeley to Los Altos. Palo Alto was our shopping center. I remember the big red electric cars and how they went through what seemed to me orchards and didn't stay on the regular streets as the cars I was used to." In 1922 the family moved again, this time to Michigan Avenue in Willow Glen, and she began riding the cars to school.

"The line ended at Lincoln and Minnesota," she remembers, "and went to the S. P. depot on Bassett between First and Market. The rails weren't always smooth, and many areas were only single track with special double tracks for passing. If the passing car wasn't right on time, especially in the morning, everyone became edgy as they might not get to school or work on time. The cars stopped at all corners to let passengers on and off. The regular conductors knew most everyone who rode their cars. If you usually took a car at a certain time they watched for you—even waited for you to run the last block."

The cars were both were a reward and an adventure, she says. "Many of the grammar-school ends of activities for the seventh and eighth graders were to take the car to Alum Rock Park for a picnic. It was a big event, and often some kids had never been there. The other year-end treat was to take the big red cars—as we used to call them—to Congress Springs for a picnic. It was a long ride to us and a real experience." Later there were trolley-car romances: "Your dates took you out on the streetcar and had to get you home early enough so they could get home on the streetcar, too." In between was some frivolity. "I believe all streetcars with overhead trolleys were a big temptation to the bigger boys to pull the trolley off the wire so the conductor would have to get off the car and put it on again. A few of the conductors who could reach out the back window of the car and put the trolley back were bothered very little; that was no fun."

In 1926 Ms. Keeler got her first job, at a cannery in Campbell near the railroad track, north of the Campbell Avenue. "At 15 years old, to start out and walk to Lincoln and Willow to catch the big electric car at 6 a.m. was quite an experience. It was the way most cannery workers got to and from work. You worked 10 to 12 hours, so all hoped we wouldn't have to wait too long at night for the next car. If you were very late, the cannery hired someone in your place, as all the fruit was processed by hand and paid for by piece work; no hourly rate governed fruit workers. There really was double pressure: you might lose your job if you were late, and the earlier you got there the more you earned."

To her, spring was the best time of year for riding the big red cars. "They took you past orchards of apricot and prune trees in bloom; the air was pungent with their fragrance. The grass in the unplowed fields was dotted with wildflowers, especially the California poppy." The cars also brought workers to the prune orchards, she remembers, and to the larger groves that had cutting and drying sheds for apricots.

Another with lively recollections is George C. Praisewater of San Jose, who says that the trip on a Delmas Avenue Birney through the Gardner district was always one of the most interesting. "Settlement of the street in 'soft spots' had included not only the roadway but also the streetcar tracks," he recalls. "The cars were the small single-truck jobs: four wheels per car. The design was such that the wheels were near the center of the car, and there was considerable projection of the front and rear ends beyond the truck. On level track the ride was quite stable, but on Delmas Avenue and similar streets the little cars plunged up and down like a boat in a choppy sea. A common phrase of the day was, 'Here comes the streetcar bobbing along.' "

Particularly vivid in his memory is one especially brisk spring morning in 1928. "It was about 7:20 a.m.," he says, "as I stood on the corner of Twenty-sixth and Santa Clara Streets waiting for the big red car to take me downtown to work. Soon it came rumbling along and stopped opposite me with a swish of airbrakes. It was one of those big interurban types with a truck at each end. I climbed the steps into the car and put my coin in the box. The conductor greeted me with a cheery, 'Good morning.' It was very cold and, although he wore a heavy overcoat, he beat his gloved hands against his body to stimulate circulation.

"The conductor's area, while protected from the elements by glass panels in front, was open to the outside atmosphere since there were no doors on the passenger entrance. Rather than going back to the seating area, I stayed with the conductor, talked with him, and watched as he controlled the big car with hand-operated airbrakes and a huge drumlike affair with a handle on top. I was his first passenger. As we rolled downtown, picking up occasional passengers, he told me he had left the car-barn at 6 a.m. and that it was very cold at the Alum Rock end of the line. He explained that his 'run' was from the park to Santa Clara. Our conversation was cut short by our arrival at my destination, Third and Santa Clara Streets, from where I walked one block to my job with the King-Russell Electric Company, on the northeast corner of Third and San Fernando Streets."

Elwyn E. Overshiner of Santa Rosa, who then lived near Lincoln Avenue and Malone Road, especially remembers the high jinks that brought consternation to the motormen but delight to the perpetrators. "Transportation to the Willows from downtown San Jose consisted of dinky little streetcars that rattled down a half-dozen different streets to terminate at Lincoln and Minnesota," he recalled in a recent letter to Wes Peyton, chief editorial writer for the *San Jose Mercury*. "On this corner, opposite the school, stood Alex Gordon's grocery store. It was a favorite late-evening gathering place for adventurous locals, who made the trolley cars provide entertainment as well as transportation. The most ambitious action was the night they soaped the tracks between Minnesota and Brace Avenues. The last little car rattled out from San Jose at 11:30 p.m., applied his brakes at Brace—and nothing. The car slid along smoothly, left the tracks, crossed Minnesota Avenue, and plowed into a huge eucalyptus tree. Nobody got hurt, but it caused quite a commotion.

"On another night," Overshiner continued, "someone stuffed the ceremonial cannon at the base of the McKinley statue in St. James Park with gunpowder, rags, and a sledgehammer head. The resulting explosion shook downtown San Jose. The sledgehammer head narrowly missed a streetcar on North First Street and shattered a window in the County Courthouse across the street."

During the late 1920s the San Jose Railroads found itself maintaining a profit of about 10% on its annual operating revenues. Like those of other city systems, however, the revenues were in a steady decline. One solution was to boost local fares, which the city company and Peninsular jointly proposed to the State Railroad Commission early in 1927. Hearings began June 9 in San Jose. It wasn't until April 1928, though, that permission was given to hike the rate from 6¢ to 10¢, four tokens for a quarter. By then the Commission had approved a similar statewide increase to become effective June 1. The local companies delayed their action to coincide with the statewide boost.

Total receipts of the San Jose Railroads for 1927 had been $367,000, a figure that would have been higher except for the construction that year. The operating income, after taxes, was $35,000. For 1928 the corresponding figures were $359,000 and $40,000. For 1929 they were $349,000 and $32,000. A special Railroad Commission bulletin issued November 2, 1929, noted that the flat-rate increases in street railway fares throughout the state had failed in almost every case to produce the expected increases in revenue or volume of travel. During the first year

San Jose had experienced a 4% decrease in travel but a 6% increase in revenue. "The downward trend of local travel has continued since then," commented the *San Jose Mercury-Herald*, "with the result that revenues are now less than prior to the fare increase."

Similar experiences were reported elsewhere. The Commission called attention to the fact that 17 California street railway systems, with an investment of approximately $130 million, were now facing "a problem of major public importance in meeting the competition of the private automobile." This might result in the abandonment of streetcar service in some smaller cities, it predicted, but probably not in the major cities. "With fares adjusted on a proper basis and service modernized to meet public demands," the Commission declared, "it would appear that this essential type of public service can be conducted so as to produce a reasonable return to the owner. It is apparent that a system of fares will not, of itself, solve the electric railway problem. Service is also of paramount importance. Within the limits possible, service must be improved or maintained. Any lessening of schedules or slowing of running times may be as disastrous as an improper adjustment of fares. Likewise, the type of equipment operated materially affects the volume of traffic."

One of the cities facing a crisis of confrontation with the private auto was San Jose, which according to State Highway Commission reports now had California's highest weekday automobile traffic count. Another was Palo Alto. Good times had brought to the South Bay an average of one auto for every 2.92 persons, crowding into the city streets and pushing out the trolleys.

11. Last Run of the Toonerville

In Palo Alto, the introduction of buses on University Avenue and Waverley Street, coupled with the 10¢ fare, had resulted in a significant decline in revenues. Operating costs were greater with buses, but the chief reason was a 16% drop in patronage during the first year of coach operation: from 80,000 passengers a month down to about 67,000. The deficits mounted, contributing to the financial woes of the Peninsular. Efforts were still being made to promote local travel on the big red cars, as for example a 1929 advertisement in the *Palo Alto Times* announcing a new "Travelectric" Congress Springs season to open March 24, featuring John McDonald and his orchestra. The round-trip fare from Palo Alto to Congress Springs was 50¢; admission to the resort was free to car passengers.

Service over the road continued to be good and well appreciated, as recalled by *San Jose Mercury News* columnist Dick Barrett: "Aside from the fact that a car occasionally picked off a farmer in a Model T at a rural crossing, the Peninsular had a pretty good record. I remember riding one of the cars to Palo Alto to usher in Stanford Stadium the day Herbert Hoover accepted the nomination for president. It was a lovely trip and a pleasant experience, with the chugging of the compressor underneath, the roar of the wheels, the deep-throated cry of the air whistle, the rocking of the car, and the sight of fruit trees fleeing past."

The deficits at Palo Alto were, of course, cause enough for concern. But now a more serious crisis had emerged. Since 1925 the State Highway Commission had been pushing to widen El Camino Real (Highway 2) from the San Mateo-Santa Clara county boundary to Matadero Creek, on the outskirts of Mayfield. In 1929 this became an ultimatum to the company to move its single-track line from beside the road—either to take to the fields or to clear out altogether. The debt-ridden Peninsular couldn't begin to afford a new right of way, so there was no choice but to abandon. Not only did this mean the end of the Palo Alto through service but also the campus route, which met the main line at University Junction and traversed it to the S. P. depot.

Agreement was reached September 30 between Peninsular officials and A. E. Roth, the Stanford controller, to substitute bus service to the campus via Palm Drive. The start date was to be October 21. Made public at this time was a letter from B. F. Burckhalter, general manager of the S. P., granting Palo Alto an easement over its right of way in the Plaza and promising to make other improvements if the city bore the expense of developing the right of way. The *Times* editorially supported the company in this matter and sounded a wistful note of concern for the future: "While officials of the bus company are not optimistic over present prospects of making an extensive bus service in Palo Alto and environs pay, we are sufficiently sanguine to believe that considerable could be done in this direction by a concentrated effort."

Final plans were now drawn—by the students as well as the Peninsular, it developed—for the last commemorative midnight run of the Toonerville October 20. In anticipation were recounted many highlights of the line's history: the steam trains running over its tracks at Big Game time, the annual serio-comic efforts of later years to immortalize the Toonerville in a blaze of glory as a preview of the pregame bonfire, and the runaway oil car that slipped its moorings one afternoon at the powerhouse and chased the streetcar halfway to Palo Alto.

Told again were stories of the student pranks: of stealing the warning bell from the car crossing, greasing the rails, and pulling the trolley poles off the wires. One such incident had resulted in the pole getting caught in the span wires, causing it to be ripped from its base.

Among those with poignant memories was Charles D. Whittaker, motorman of the Toonerville for nearly 20 years. In his car had ridden many distinguished passengers, including a U. S. president and the secretary of the interior. He'd had plenty of trying experiences with students "crashing the gates" and "beating" their way to town and back. There were times, he recalled, when the trolley came limping out of its encounters with turbulent youth with broken windows and other marks of battle. But those were mostly in the "good old days"; of late, the students had been more sedate, perhaps out of respect for age.

Undoubtedly that had been true, but, as the end drew near, rumors got around that certain students had in mind cremation rather than veneration of the ancient car. Word also reached company officials. "At about 10 o'clock last night," reported the *Times* October 21, "a procession of collegiate mourners boarded the car, operated by John Peterson, the night motorman. Some wore bands or scarves of crepe; others were in gloomy academic gowns. All were in the proper dramatic spirit. So bowed with grief were they, in fact, that many refused to be distracted with such trivialities as paying fares although they declared their intention of riding throughout the sad, sad night.

"But fate, in the form of a company official who was on the car unknown to the 'mourners,' intervened. Perceiving the situation and having heard rumors of the elaborate 'rites' destined for the last trip of the car, he murmured in the motorman's ear, 'This'll be the last trip.' " Thus the Toonerville got home safely to the corporation yard, thwarting the scheme of those who intended its demise.

That wasn't the end of the last rites, however. "Sometime between dusk and dawn," related the *Times*, "the old campus terminal was bedecked with serpentine, and at 2 o'clock this morning a ceremony of cremation was performed by the side of the rails east of the University library. There were no mourners present when the campus fire department arrived to find a pile of barrels, railroad crossing signs, and grass burning. The signs were but slightly charred, and three of them remained to tower above the ruins like grim scaffolds." To which the *Stanford Daily* added its own touching farewell: "No funeral wake with its mourning procession followed the last car to its final resting place. No one was present to weep at the passing of the creaking old 'Dinky.' Unmourned, the old car wavered down the track, out of the life of Stanford. The 'Dinky' is dead, fellows. Brave old buggy!"

Bus service replaced the Toonerville October 21. Work began that day to remove the streetcar tracks from University Avenue between the railroad and El Camino Real, making way for the Plaza improvement project. With the closing of the Palo Alto line, Mayfield became the transfer point for S. P. patrons. Service north of Mayfield was provided by buses, which proved far inferior to the big red cars.

12. Peninsular Calls It Quits

In 1930, with the Palo Alto line shut down and the great depression of that decade rolling in over the South Bay like a tidal wave, the Peninsular retired its big Jewetts (105-112) because the traffic no longer warranted the use of such heavy equipment. They were stored in San Jose and their runs taken over by the 50-61 class, rebuilt that year into one-man cars. Other runs were handled by city cars from San Jose. Needless to say, business was not improved by the use of inferior equipment.

Confronting the parent Southern Pacific in San Jose that year was a problem of a different sort related to operations of its electric roads. A decade of negotiations between the city and the railroad on relocating the S. P. main line in San Jose had led to victory for the company. The price, however, included eight underpasses to be built at company expense, one at Willow Street. The impending construction and city demands to pave that street led October 30 to a joint request by the San Jose Railroads and the Peninsular to abandon service on Willow west of McLellan Avenue. The First Street cars that had formerly served Willow Glen would now terminate at McLellan. Willow Glen service would be provided from downtown San Jose by cars operating over the Peninsular's Campbell cutoff line: San Carlos Street and Coe, Bird, and Lincoln Avenues. Also retained would be the Peninsular's Cherry Avenue local, operating over the Campbell cutoff.

The companies in their application said the improvement project would require the San Jose Railroads to spend $30,000 to pave between the rails and that the line's revenues—less than $1,500 during 10 months of 1930—did not justify the expense. Also, as Superintendent Ed Shoup noted, the project would force the company to relay the line with new ties and heavier rail, an added burden.

Hearings took place in December. Both San Jose and Willow Glen opposed the application, the latter insisting that the street be paved at company expense even if the line was abandoned. The Willow Street merchants east of Lincoln threatened if necessary to start a competing bus line. The abandonment was

The look of the transportation future in 1929. Owned by the Peninsular, it awaits passengers at the S.P. station in Palo Alto with an interurban car in the background, shortly before rail service was abandoned.   (Lorin Silleman Collection)

An unidentified crew awaits departure on the final day of South Bay service for Peninsular 109. According to railfan Lorin Silleman, who has the original whistle from car 109, this was the only "Big Paly" with a horn. It was given to the Peninsular in the hopes that other cars would be similarly equipped.

(Lorin Silleman Collection)

approved by the Railroad Commission in March 1931, but a local compromise was not reached until the following August, at which time the streetcar companies agreed to pay $2,500 toward paving Willow Street and to regrade the Peninsular's tracks on Willow west of Lincoln. Rails were taken up between McLellan and Lincoln, a connection was built between the Peninsular and San Jose Railroads at Willow and Lincoln, and the new Willow Glen service went into effect.

By then the depression, poor rolling stock, and competition with the automobile had put an unbearable strain on the Peninsular. Many of the routes traveled almost exclusively by the big red cars in former years were now clogged with trucks and private autos. Pressures had been exerted on the State Highway Commission to improve highways all over the state; that body responded locally by asking the interurban to quit the Campbell cutoff line on San Jose- Los Gatos Road (Highway 5) between Hamilton and Campbell Avenues, as part of a plan to widen that road.

Because this line no longer paid operating expenses and acquiring a new right of way was out of the question, the Peninsular decided to let it go, applying in October 1931 for permission to abandon it from the corner of Lincoln and Willow, in San Jose, to Rinconada Station, at the Los Gatos city limits. Approval came the following March, and service ended April 1, 1932. Also wiped out by this cutback was the Cherry Avenue local. Interurban schedules on the Saratoga-Los Gatos line were rearranged to compare favorably with those that had been eliminated. Work of removing the Campbell cutoff began at once; within two months the last traces of this once-important trackage were gone.

Another 1932 casualty was the Alum Rock line. Annual deficits on this line, said the companies, came to $13,000. Less than 7,000 passengers had been carried during a recent five-month test period. These reports preceded a public meeting in January 1932 at which plans were announced for suspending passenger service to the park and freight service east of Noble Avenue. Little opposition was voiced. The abandonment was approved March 28; the last regular car ran to the park June 11.

There was a bit more to this story. With special permission by the city, a few cars ran to Alum Rock in fall 1933 to carry Civil Works Administration (CWA) crews rebuilding the park. In May 1934, however, workmen began removing the rails, and that was that.

By 1933 the Peninsular was ready to call it quits. Plans were announced to substitute buses for cars on all interurban routes and to merge its city operations with those of the San Jose Railroads. In February the Interstate Commerce Commission approved the abandonment of the Meridian Corners-Congress Junction and Monta Vista-Congress Junction-Saratoga-Los Gatos lines. The State Railroad Commission quickly followed suit. The first to go was the Saratoga line March 12. Work then moved to the other routes, the rails being torn up immediately as the motor coaches went into service. By June the company's bus mileage exceeded its rail mileage. The rolling stock now

On the final day of Campbell cutoff rail service, the motorman of Peninsular 59 is about to receive a bouquet of flowers from a sentimental passenger.
(Lorin Silleman and Randolph Brandt Collections)

consisted of 18 passenger cars, box motor 2, wrecker 201, and line car 14.

The big Jewetts were sent to the Pacific Electric. One by one they were coupled onto S. P. freights and headed south but, according to Ira Swett, had to be cut off at various points between Salinas and Paso Robles because someone had forgotten to pull the pinions. Eventually they got to Torrance and were put in dead storage until 1937, when they were resurrected as Pacific Electric 1050-1057.

The Peninsular had meanwhile asked for and received permission to abandon its Palo Alto bus routes. A buyer was found, so bus service was maintained in that community. By year's end all that remained of the once proud Peninsular were its San Jose-Mayfield line, San Jose city routes, and freight line out Berryessa Road to Noble Avenue.

On May 15, 1934, the State Railroad Commission approved abandonment of the Berryessa line. In September it gave permission for the Peninsular to halt all operations except those of its San Jose city lines. Service ended on the Mayfield line at midnight October 1. The company continued its San Jose city runs for another couple of months but formally conveyed its 11.68 miles of city lines to the San Jose Railroads November 30 along with some city cars, the box motor, the wrecker, and the line car. Because the city company had no wish to go into the freight business, the profitable Berryessa freight service went by default to another S. P. subsidiary, the Visalia Electric, to be operated for 3½ years as the "San Jose District of Visalia Electric."

On June 12, 1935, the Peninsular Railway was legally disincorporated and its properties and assets, valued at $955,000 and including the 16.68-mile Los Gatos cutoff, were conveyed to the parent S. P. by authority of the Interstate Commerce Commission.

One who remembered those final days was Harry Rich, who worked for the Peninsular almost to the end. "If it was still in existence," he later told Dick Barrett, "they would have to double-track every place, and how the people would ride those cars now. Of course, they would get an auto at least once a day. I went back in 1933, and in six months I had 13 accidents. If I didn't hit them, they would hit me while standing still. The last accident I had, the car ran across the wrong side and took the steps off my streetcar. I never reported it, and about a month after I quit Fred Watson asked me if I had had an accident on my last trip. I told him I had, and that was the end of my railroading."

13. Resettlement Franchise

The tidal wave of the depression was also pounding the foundations of the San Jose Railroads. Passenger revenues had declined 12.6% in 1931, some 3% more than the statewide average, leaving the company with an operating deficit. The following year brought eclines of 24.3% in traffic and 24.6% in revenues, the severest losses for any streetcar company in the state. Curtailments were clearly in order.

Looking north along the Mayfield cutoff near Los Altos. The eastern track was used by commute trains of the Southern Pacific's Los Gatos branch line to San Francisco. The other track, owned by the Peninsular, was removed in February of 1935.

(J. C. Gordon photo from Wilbur C. Whittaker and Henry E. Morse Jr. Collections)

The company applied February 6, 1933, for permission to abandon service on the Oak Hill and Hanchett Park bus routes. Receipts from the latter had amounted to only $3,784 during the past year, it told the Railroad Commission, against expenses of $7,800. Service ended on both routes April 26 without protest by the community.

As an "economy measure," the company also applied February 24 for rights to suspend service on Seventeenth Street between Santa Clara and Julian streets and on Julian between Seventeenth and Twenty-first. "If permission is granted," said Superintendent Ed Shoup, "the company will reroute cars over the Delmas-Julian line out North Seventeenth Street to Berryessa. The Market to Seventeenth Street line will be discontinued, and plans call for the Tenth Street line to be extended to Santa Clara during peak traffic hours." On March 8 the company got a go-ahead from the Railroad Commission. Before the new plan could be implemented, however, the Peninsular halted service on its Saratoga line west of Bascom Avenue. These two events combined March 21 to produce a consolidation of five operating lines into two, the San Jose Railroads absorbing the Peninsular's Naglee Park and Bascom Avenue city lines.

Effective that date, the Bascome local, formerly a Peninsular car, was re-routed from San Carlos Street north along Delmas Avenue to San Fernando Street, then east along the old Julian Street line to Seventeenth and north to Berryessa Road. The Delmas Avenue car from Willow Glen, instead of terminating at Second Street, now continued east out San Fernando to Fifteenth and south to San Carlos. Both new lines were set to operate on a 12-minute headway, effecting a six-minute schedule through the downtown area.

Ed Shoup died that year, being succeeded as operating superintendent by Arthur L. Wood. The president of the San Jose Railroads was now W. A. Worthington, with C. R. Harding vice president and P. L. Billingsley general manager.

Early in 1934 the company took careful stock of its position. Revenues were increasing but not enough to project a profit from present operations. Pressures were being applied by local merchants, city officials, and the State Highway Commission to clear the streets for automotive traffic. Another problem of growing importance was damage suits, many of which asked small awards but required the company to defend against the action.

Commenced in June were negotiations between City Manager Goodwin and Worthington, Harding, Billingsley, and Wood of the San Jose Railroads on a blanket resettlement franchise that would allow buses to be substituted for streetcars on all local routes. The scheme called for combining some 29 existing franchises into one comprehensive document. Commented the *Mercury-Herald*: "It is understood that this will include removal of the tracks on Market Street from Park Avenue to San Carlos Street, leaving a clear front for the Civic Auditorium, and also removal of the tracks on First Street from Reed Street to the south city limits. This is in accordance with a California Highway Commission ruling, as that street is a portion of Highway 2." That this plan met with at least token approval by the company was intimated the following month when city officials were treated to a ride in a new 42-passenger motor coach which, as the newspaper wryly observed, "happened to be in San Jose at this time on a manufacturer's demonstration tour."

In November a city proposal to replace all First Street cars with motor coaches was being considered by S. P. and San Jose Railroads officials. "The council pointed out that the new franchise called for operation of both motor buses and streetcars on First Street," reported the *Mercury-Herald*, "and felt that this duplication of service would add to the existing traffic congestion on the street." The council was now said to favor the new franchise, questioning some details but concerning itself mostly with who would pay for repaving the streets once the rails were removed. The company had acknowledged itself "financially unable to repave on a wholesale scale in abandoning its tracks."

A satisfactory solution to this problem was soon found. The company agreed to donate its rails and fittings to the city, which in turn would sell them as scrap to meet the paving costs. Furthermore, the city would receive enough funds—about $75,000—from the State Emergency Relief Administration (SERA) to start the project. "This is not only working out to the advantage of the city and the railroad," reported the *Mercury-Herald*, "but will furnish more employment than if the railroad did the repaving itself. Because it is a SERA project, the requirement is that the maximum of hand-labor be employed. Not even compressors are to be used in breaking out the pavement."

The pattern had been set for eventual abandonment of all local streetcar lines. Crews removed the abandoned rails and fittings by hand labor (later with the help of compressors and jackhammers), pouring concrete in the troughs and covering the roadbed with asphalt. As many as 900 men at a time were employed chipping out the rails and repairing the streets. Sale of the rails brought in more than enough to cover the costs of their removal. Sales of salvaged copper and scrap aluminum alone paid for all the paving materials. The resettlement franchise became law in December 1934 and was approved by the Railroad Commission the following February. Its terms allowed the city and railroad to substitute buses for streetcars on other lines without further consulting the Commission.

In November 1934 the city announced its first sale of scrap rail—120 tons at $9.50 a ton—to be salvaged from the Alum Rock line. Removals began December 18. The buyer was R. L. Martin, an Oregon merchant, who announced that the rails would become part of a shipload of scrap iron he was sending to Japan. That called forth some eloquent prose from the *Mercury-Herald*: "Old steel rails that for 48 years carried picnickers to the leafy glades of Alum Rock Park may next year be carrying Japanese through cherry-blossomed vistas in Nippon, or Russians, Chinese and Japanese across the plains of Manchuria."

A second contract was awarded, in February 1935, to San Jose's West End Junk Company, this time for $8.06 a ton. "About 40% of the rails have already been removed from the streets by SERA workers," reported the *Mercury-Herald*, "and it is expected that the remainder will be out by the end of this month. The total to be removed will exceed 1,000 tons."

City equipment obtained from the Peninsular in November 1934 were the 70-class cars and the Birneys (27-31). The former were repainted yellow from the Peninsular's green and cream and placed in service on the Santa Clara-King Road line. The latter went into storage and probably were never used. As noted by Henry Morse, there are some puzzling differences in appearance of the fully enclosed cars 126 and 70-77 during these final years, as compared with earlier periods. Charles Smallwood recalled that the company, in the early 1930s, fully enclosed its four Fresno cars (164-167) like the 70 class. When it got the 70 class from the Peninsular, cars 70, 71, and 73—ex-San Jose Railroads 127-class equipment—were inoperable. The main office told San Jose to scrap car 72 (the remaining 127), as well as all 120-class cars except 125 and 126, to be kept as spares. However, car 72 was in better condition than 126, so the latter was scrapped, one of the 164-class cars renumbered 126, and the other cars of this class renumbered 70, 71, and 73. Thus, the non-Birney fleet then consisted of ex-Fresno cars 126, 70, 71, and 73, ex-Fresno cars 74-77, ex-San Jose Railroads 127-class car 72, and car 125, retained as a spare.

In 1935 revenues were up 9% over the previous year; in June the company cut local fares from 10¢ to 7¢. Wages generally remained low, streetcar and bus operators earning 53 to 56¢ an hour and track crews and shop workers 42 to 59¢. Employees worked six- to nine-hour days and six-day weeks. Labor disputes were rare. Obsolescence and capital investment were matters of growing company concern, however. A 1935 property valuation, for purposes of local taxation, came to about $190,000, a figure challenged by the railroad. Among evidence it presented was that its rolling stock, assigned a replacement value of $272,000, actually had a salvage value of less than $10,000. The financial facts of life about the railroad's operations were encouraging its officers to endorse the city's goal of "everything on rubber."

14. Beginning of the End

"Shiny red buses" replaced streetcars on the Tenth Street and Delmas-San Fernando lines at midnight February 23, 1935. Mechanic William H. Humrichouse won local distinction as the first passenger to board one of the new coaches. On April 15 three "large yellow buses" with a six-inch white stripes along each side replaced streetcars on the First Street route, one running out to Seventh and Keyes from the S. P. depot. Only three car lines were still in operation: Bascom Avenue-Seventeenth Street, Santa Clara-Linda Vista, and Willow Glen from the S. P. depot via Market Street. A large hole was being dug in front of the San Carlos carbarns to accommodate two gasoline storage tanks with a combined capacity of 25,000 gallons.

On May 20 the company asked San Jose and Willow Glen for approval to substitute buses for streetcars from San Carlos Street and Bird Avenue to Lincoln and Minnesota Avenues (the southern end of the Willow Glen line) and from Park and Delmas Avenues via Market Street to the S. P. depot, including the loop on Bassett, Little Market, and Julian Streets (the northern end of the line). Permission to halt streetcar service was granted June 10 by both cities. Willow Glen approved the bus route June 24. Motor coaches went into service June 28 on the northern end of the line, beyond City Hall; the last cars ran on the southern end July 25.

Streetcar service continued in San Jose during the mid-1930s. **ABOVE: A Birney car is southbound on First Street.** (J. C. Gordon photo from Henry E. Morse Jr. Collection) **BELOW: Wet weather could occasionally play havoc with the schedules, such as when a flooded underpass halted eastbound traffic on Santa Clara Street, San Jose, at the new Southern Pacific underpass.** *(San Jose Mercury News)*

San Jose Railroads Birney 161 is westbound on the Linda Vista line at Alum Rock and Kirk Avenues, near the end of the line.

(J. C. Gordon photo from Henry E. Morse Jr. Collection)

In June City Manager Goodwin reported that $17,500 had now been recovered from the rail project. That was enough, he said, to pay all costs of materials for the repaving program, which had employed 300 to 900 men during the past five months. Received from SERA that month was an additional grant of $39,000, including funds for 207 workers to remove the rails on Market Street from San Antonio to Bassett and on Park Avenue from Market to Delmas.

On July 10 the company extended its Linda Vista service to provide a 6 a.m. car and five new evening runs, the last departing downtown San Jose at 11:47 p.m. The first car formerly had been at 7 a.m. and the last at 6:14 p.m.

The next abandonment came in 1936. City and company officials agreed in March to substitute buses for streetcars on the Julian-Seventeenth Street line. On April 1 workmen began gadding out the pavement around the rails. The last cars ran over this line April 26, leaving only two routes in operation: Santa Clara-Linda Vista and Bascom Avenue-Second and St. John Streets. Most of the Birneys were now considered surplus. Cars 137 and 141 went that year to the Sacramento Northern; most

others went to the Stockton Electric. Other Birneys on the property were stored in a semi-dismantled condition. The main operating Birney class after 1936 was the 159 class. Two more "S. P.-look" medium-platform PAYE cars eventually joined the San Jose Railroads from Stockton, retaining their former numbers (22 and 23). The Pacific Electric inspected box motor 2, used for the Berryessa switching district, to see if it was fit for Southern California service. It failed the test, however, and was scrapped in 1938.

The constant pepper of damage suits against the company, formerly an annoyance, became a heavy burden during this period. In September 1934 a local worker filed suit for $86,000 claiming injuries to his spine—believed to be permanent—as the result of being thrown against the side of the streetcar in which he was riding when it collided with a meat truck on San Carlos Street. Filed the following year was a $12,000 complaint by a San Jose woman claiming injuries sustained when the car she was driving and in which her two sons were riding as passengers was struck by a trolley at Stevens Creek Road and Arletta Avenue. Another large action, filed December 1936 in

Superior Court, resulted from a spectacular truck-streetcar crash that month in the Park Avenue subway; three of the six injured victims sued the San Jose Railroads and the truck owner for $61,000. Co-defendants with the railroad in this action were R. L. Jameson, the streetcar motorman, and Alfred Cornwell, the truck driver.

On February 25, 1936, a wage increase of 2½¢ an hour was won by San Jose Railroads employees as a result of friendly negotiations between union and company officials. The wage for streetcar and bus operators was boosted from 56 to 59¢, depending on length of service. Track crews and shop employees now received 44 to 61¢. The question of hours was not involved in the new contract, the workers continuing as before to put in from six to nine hours daily on a six-day week.

15. Farewell to the Trolleys

The Bascom-downtown and Santa Clara-Linda Vista lines moved closer to abandonment during an April 1937 meeting of city, railroad, and taxi officials at which C. R. Harding, now vice president of the S. P.'s traction systems, announced its willingness to "spend $200,000 making San Jose 100 percent buses the second you pass an ordinance that suits us." The most important link to be replaced, observed the *Mercury-Herald*, was Sam Bishop's original route: the double-tracked Santa Clara-Linda Vista line extending from Santa Clara to King Road, then by single track to the foot of the Country Club hill.

The city soon obliged with a suitable ordinance. On March 7, 1938, the Railroad Commission approved the final abandonment of South Bay electric traction.

San Jose and Santa Clara bade farewell to their streetcars the evening of April 10, 1938, in colorful festivities commemorating 70 years of service. Civic leaders, city officials, railroad employees, and people of all ages who loved trolleys came to join in the ceremonies—a funeral cortege with mingled gaiety and sadness—the cars offering free rides from 9 p.m. to the final trip of the last car at midnight. An atmosphere of yesteryear prevailed, as when horsecars first appeared on The Alameda. Costumes of the nineteenth century were worn; prizes were given for the best garb.

Pranksters played tricks as in days of yore, pulling the trolleys off the wires and stalling the cars. Some enthusiastically started removing pieces of the cars for souvenirs. Among the celebrants were those who remembered the dinky little horsecars and Bishop's calamitous underground electric, who had known Jacob Rich and ridden the rickety rails of Hugh Center's Alum Rock line. There were many who had played hi-jinks with the Birneys and thrilled to the deep-throated call of the Peninsular's big red cars.

Many genuine mourners were among those who found seats in the "funeral procession" that departed Santa Clara at 9 p.m. to pass in review through the Alameda underpass in West San Jose. Included were all cars then in service on the Santa Clara-Linda Vista line.

After midnight came silence. On hand to greet patrons the following morning were 14 new buses costing $11,500 in all.

Youngsters jammed the cars and clung to whatever handholds they could find on the last day of San Jose streetcars, April 10, 1938. The company offered free rides on all cars from 9 p.m. to midnight.
(San Jose Mercury News)

Twelve days later the San Jose Railroads abandoned its last 8.24 miles of track, used for freight.

There was another "last day of operation," if it could be called that. On the evening June 14 several cars cut down to floor level passed through the city decorated as floats for a parade. Thereafter, all that remained was the mopping up. Track removal was performed by 400 Works Progress Administration (WPA) workers under a program sponsored by the Federal government and run by the cities. In November the courts settled their last streetcar case, an $84.41 damage suit that found the company blameless. On December 29 City Manager Goodwin announced that all tracks had now been removed from the city streets.

There was a final cheery note. The price for steel scrap having risen sharply, the city wound up more than $27,000 to the good when the last rail had been taken and the last asphalt poured to cover the passing of streetcars from the South Bay scene.

16. The Transition Years

Traces of the Peninsular's right of way from Palo Alto to San Mateo were seen as late as 1940, recalled Ira Swett. Old maps given by mistake to census takers that year showed the right of way as one boundary to be followed. The census people, puzzled at first, dutifully followed directions on the maps and found several weatherbeaten surveyors' stakes in the country north of Stanford University. In abundance elsewhere for another decade or so were old carbarns, powerhouses, stations, way structures, rails, and concrete ribbons in some streets to show where the tracks had run. As late as 1971 one could trace the route of the Peninsular on Josefa Street and Meridian Road from Park Avenue to San Carlos Street, San Jose, sure that he was negotiating the same turns as the big red cars.

Most physical remains soon disappeared, victims of the South Bay's huge population growth. Survivors include the old Hanchett transformer station in Palo Alto and the former Peninsular station in Los Altos, once a restaurant and now a financial institution. In San Jose are the San Carlos Street carbarn used in 1981 for buses and, nearby, traces of two concrete strips up the middle of the overpass built by the S. P. in the 1930s to bridge its main line. In Alum Rock Park are several remains including a concrete bridge and the old powerhouse, once a nightclub and now a private residence.

Still in use by the S. P. are the Tenth Street transfer along Berryessa Road and one track of the Mayfield cutoff from Monta Vista Junction to Vasona Junction, where it curves into the former San Jose-Santa Cruz line. Its junction with State Highway 85 (Sunnyvale-Saratoga Road) is yet called Azule Crossing, harkening back to days of the Peninsular. North of Monta Vista the Mayfield cutoff was gobbled up by the Foothill Expressway. South of Vasona the San Jose-Santa Cruz line is long gone, in part under the muddy bottom of Lexington Reservoir.

Prized today is a pair of shining rails protruding from the pavement of Austin Way at Quito Road, near State Highway 9 between Los Gatos and Saratoga. Railfan Willys Peck recovered the old Nippon Mura station from the opposite end of Austin Way; it is alive and well in the backyard of his Saratoga home.

Soon gone, too, were most cars of the South Bay electric roads: scrapped, cannibalized, or abandoned. The bodies of some survived a decade or two as diners, outbuildings, and the like. Railfan Norman Holmes remembers seeing the remains of San Jose Railroads 10 off Cheynoweth Avenue, 73 and 124 off Almaden Road (still there in 1981), 120 off Pickford Avenue, 159 and 161 off Downer Place (later moved to Madrone), and 160 off Moorpark Avenue between Meridian and Bascom (later moved to the foothills). He also recalls seeing Peninsular 56 off

McCreery Avenue, 57 and 59 off Coyote Road, and 60 off Hamilton Avenue. More fortunate were Peninsular 52 and 61, both of which are now in the California Railway Museum at Rio Vista Junction, State Highway 12 east of Fairfield.

Car 52, once transformed into a sewing room on a ranch west of Santa Clara, was located by Charles Hopkins of San Jose, rebuilt by the railway museum to its former glory, and dedicated for service in May 1976. Car 61, owned by Lew Bohnett of San Jose and later by railfan Charles Smallwood of San Francisco, is being restored as a trailer.

As the physical evidences faded away, so also with the passing years did the private traction companies that once battled for business on both sides of the Bay. In April 1921 the United Railroads of San Francisco folded into the newly organized *Market Street Railway Company*, which served that city for more than two decades before yielding, in turn, to the publicly owned *San Francisco Municipal Railway*. In May 1944 San Francisco voters approved purchase of the Market Street company for $7.5 million. The company's directors agreed in July and the stockholders in August. The sale became official in September 1944.

East Bay transit ultimately went public, too, although by a more tortuous route. The S. P. electric lines, still struggling with the Key System, were formalized in November 1934 as the *Interurban Electric Railway*, a wholly owned subsidiary. Jointly with the Key and the Sacramento Northern, the IER gained access to San Francisco in January 1939 over the new San Francisco Bay Bridge. The continuing East Bay competition proved deadly, however; in December 1939, the IER reported a $1 million annual loss compared with $200,000 for the Key. Early in 1941 it terminated service except for two Berkeley lines and filed for abandonment; the Key consolidated lines and acquired the major IER routes the following July. This ended direct S. P. involvement in East Bay local transit. After 1939 it got out of the electric traction business altogether by disposing of its Stockton and Fresno properties and eventually dismantling the Pacific Electric.

The Key System operated in receivership for some nine years starting in 1914, then underwent a reorganization in June 1923 as the *Key System Traction Company* with John S. Drum as president. In June 1929 the company defaulted on its bonds and fell back into receivership. The new operator was *Railway Equipment and Realty Company, Limited*, through a subsidiary—*East Bay Street Railways, Limited*—headed by Alfred J. Lundberg. There were other corporate entities including a reborn Key System. These companies operated successfully through the war years but began phasing out local streetcars, upon a change in ownership, early in 1946. The last local cars ran in November 1948. Declining revenues, traffic congestion, and the obsolescence of equipment and roadways, including the bridge railway, led in April 1958 to the end of Oakland-San Francisco electric rail service. The *Alameda-Contra Costa Transit District* (AC Transit), formed to maintain local and transbay bus service, bought out the Key in May 1960 for $7.5 million. The last of its initial bonds were retired in 1980. Eventually born in the East Bay, also, was the *Bay Area Rapid Transit District* (BART), which built 71 miles of high-speed heavy electric rail, opened service in 1972, and reached San Francisco in 1975 through a transbay tube, realizing Borax Smith's loftiest turn-of-the-century ambition.

In the South Bay, after abandoning the Peninsular and San Jose Railroads, the S. P. upgraded its San Francisco-San Jose commute rail line and maintained rail service until an orderly transfer could be effected to public hands. Several new private bus companies emerged, among which two were to serve area residents for more than 35 years. The final result of these transition years was to introduce the "public era" of South Bay transit.

After abandonment, removing the rails from San Jose streets became a WPA project. Here, the workmen use power equipment to remove rails at Santa Clara Street at the S.P. underpass. Earlier rail removals were accomplished solely by manual labor. *(San Jose Mercury News)*

From Birneys to buses. A crane unloads ex-San Jose Birney cars in the S.P. yards at the West Oakland shops for transfer to the Stockton Electric Railway, which was still a rail operation in 1938. (James Boynton photo from Wilbur C. Whittaker Collection) **BELOW: One of the San Jose Railroads' original transit-type coaches was Twin Coach 240, seen next to one of the parent Southern Pacific's new "Daylight" trains.** (Magna Collection)

For the traction archaeologist, traces of the former electric rail operation remained in the San Jose area for several years. Peninsular tracks in Meridian Road near Willow Street now lie beneath several layers of asphalt. (Norman Holmes) **BELOW: Bernard (Ben) Silleman inspects the old Springer Road station in 1949.** (Lorin Silleman Collection)

Onetime San Jose Railroads car 31 found a second career as the "Espee Diner" across the street from the carbarn on West San Carlos Street.

Peninsular 60 earned peaceful retirement in a cabbage patch, though railfan Norman Holmes managed to salvage panels, pushbuttons and buzzers.
(Both: Norman Holmes)

San Jose City Lines bus 6502 takes a layover at the end of the Linda Vista–Santa Clara line at Franklin Street, Santa Clara, on July 26, 1970. Behind is a "new look" bus.

(Vernon J. Sappers)

4. The Public Era

**When the Southern Pacific exited the local transportation picture, San Jose City Lines took over.
Here is an early Twin Coach westbound on Santa Clara at Fifth Street, circa 1941.**

(Norman Holmes)

IN 1938, when San Jose lost its streetcars, they were a surviving but endangered national species. In many of the smaller cities they were gone, but in most metropolitan areas, trolleys still rumbled through the streets hauling millions of passengers. New to the scene and hailed as the savior of electric traction was the President's Conference Committee (PCC) car, a dependable, rugged vehicle that appeared in numbers before and after World War II.

After 1950, not even the PCC could stem the tide away from electric traction. Maintenance had been sharply curtailed during the war; large capital outlays were needed to refurbish the lines. With fuel, tires, automobiles, and new motor coaches available, trolleys went the way of the nickel soft drink in most American cities.

What was generally true of America was especially true of the South Bay, which became an urban area during the expressway-freeway boom of the 1950s and 1960s. The private bus firms then operating—successors to the Peninsular and the San Jose Railroads—were either city systems (San Jose, Palo Alto) or suburban systems designed to move riders from outlying areas to downtown San Jose, the mercantile heart of Santa Clara

County. For economic and political reasons the new industries attracting thousands of new workers to the county clustered in the north and north-central regions away from the S. P. commute rail line and the established bus routes, which suffered accordingly. For similar reasons housing, mainly single-family dwellings, accumulated on the valley floor to the south and east. Most South Bay residents now drove their private vehicles over Federally funded highways that were the backbone of the transportation system. Public transit weakened and, as some feared, neared death.

This personal transit system worked well—for example, no labor problems or public costs for transit vehicles—but only to a point. New expressways and freeways brought only temporary relief from the congestion. Always needed were more roads to keep pace with the expanding population. Then in the 1960s and 1970s it became obvious that the gasoline engine had limits, after all, in terms of air pollution, energy consumption, and fiscal responsibility. Concern over air pollution and energy consumption tipped the scales back toward public transit.

From that sentiment was born a public transit agency—the Santa Clara County Transit District—which, from a modest

Southern Pacific Station. Palo Alto, Calif. SP 232

Palo Alto Transit bus 114 awaits arrival of train at the new S.P. station, Palo Alto, which officially opened on March 8, 1941.
(Lorin Silleman Collection)

beginning, has become one of the nation's larger transportation systems: all bus at present but with ambitious projects including light rail (a resurrection of the electric trolley) in the wings. County Transit suffered growing pains but now carries more than 75,000 people daily in a service area spanning some 250 square miles.

1. Palo Alto Transit

Before the Peninsular was permitted to abandon its South Bay rail lines, the State Railroad Commission was determined to ensure that substitute bus service would be provided by reputable motor carriers. Two such already served Palo Alto. One was *Pacific Greyhound Lines*, which emerged about 1930 from the consolidation of several operators and ran between San Francisco and San Jose on certificates held by Pickwick Stages System, one of its operators. Pacific Greyhound maintained regular schedules between Palo Alto and Mountain View; among its backers was the Southern Pacific.

The other was *Peerless Stages, Incorporated*, formed in 1921 by an association of six owner-operators who held rights to Oakland-Santa Cruz and Oakland-San Jose service. Its main routes were from Oakland via San Jose to Santa Cruz, but it also operated some South Bay local lines—East San Jose, Cambrian Park, and Santa Clara—and ran a San Jose-Los Gatos suburban service via both Campbell and Saratoga. Since 1927 Peerless had been running buses from the East Bay to Palo Alto and Menlo Park over the Dumbarton bridge.

Although the S. P. was maintaining its steam rail commute service down the peninsula and had restored passenger rail service to the Mayfield cutoff, the Railroad Commission demanded that the Peninsular operate motor coaches between Palo Alto and San Jose via Los Altos, Loyola Corners, Monta Vista, Cupertino, and Meridian Corners, the old electric route. By certificate granted March 7, 1933, the base fare was established at 6¢, climbing at nickel intervals to 55¢ maximum. The coaches ran some nine trips daily (6:30 a.m. to 5:30 p.m.) from the Palo Alto S. P. station to downtown San Jose. Seven of the runs were keyed to the arrivals of the S. P. trains from San Francisco.

Within Palo Alto, the problem was different. For years the Peninsular, legally allowed to suspend local bus service if its revenues did not exceed its costs by a reasonable margin, had run the system at a loss. Now, preparing for final abandonment, it was not willing to continue. For a while it seemed local service would be lost, then a replacement was found. The Palo Alto lines went in March to Floyd B. Pearson's newly formed *Palo Alto Transit Company*, which in December 1934 also took over the Peninsular's Palo Alto-San Jose motor coach service. Under terms of Pearson's agreement with the S. P., his company was paid approximately $1,000 a month based on an assumed passenger count and a rate of 35¢ per S. P. passenger handled by the joint commute tariff.

In 1941 Pearson, while retaining his Palo Alto-San Jose service, sold his Palo Alto city routes to taxi operators Frank Knapp and John P. Demeter, who called their new company *Palo Alto City Lines* and shared garage and work space with Pearson at the old Peninsular carbarn. At this time there were four local routes—South Palo Alto, Stanford, Bayshore, and Veterans Hospital-Stanford Village—carrying 325,000 passengers a year in eight coaches of which, Demeter claimed, no two were alike. Knapp and Demeter added Menlo Park service.

Also serving the community during these years were Peerless, offering five buses weekdays—two on Sundays—from Palo Alto to Oakland via Dumbarton, and R. F. Martin's *Martin Transportation Company*, a Redwood City-based firm with a coach route to San Carlos. In 1949 Demeter and Evelyn Knapp, who succeeded to her husband's interest on his death, bought out Martin and reorganized their firm as *Peninsula Transit, Incorporated*, serving San Carlos, Redwood City, Menlo Park, Atherton, and Palo Alto south to Diss Road. One new route—Embarcadero—was inaugurated in 1950 and two others—East Meadow Road, and Town and Country Village—soon thereafter. The Embarcadero and East Meadow Road lines were then combined.

By 1953 Peninsula Transit, operating from a garage at 1841 Bay Road, was running 27 green Ford buses whose daily aggregate route mileage was 1,158 in Redwood City and 1,386 in Palo Alto. The seven Palo Alto lines carried about 1.6 million passengers that year, a 500% increase over 1941. Demeter nevertheless saw trouble ahead. "Everyone has a car nowadays, and a lot of people have two," he told the *Palo Alto Times*.

Ex-Peninsular motorman and longtime Peninsular Transit employee Lee Harper is at the wheel of 1924 Fageol Safety Coach 216 for the 1963 inauguration ceremony that introduced nine 31-passenger General Motors buses bought by the city of Palo Alto. Coach 216, with sisters 213-215, replaced Peninsular trolleys in Palo Alto. New bus is coach 266. (Jack Perry) **BELOW:** An early Peerless Stages engine-in-front bus is still in service in 1947. (Robert A. Burrowes)

Palo Alto Transit 106, a 25-passenger Gillig–Diamond T coach, in the spring of 1950. (Bob Townley photo from Jack Perry Collection)

"Nobody wants to ride in a bus when he can go by car."

Ridership declined during the 1950s, resulting in the progressive elimination of night and Sunday service and the lengthening of midday headways from 20 to 30 minutes, then to hourly. Attempting to maintain reasonable service, the City of Palo Alto finally came to the rescue, taking over the foundering system December 1, 1963, after a year of subsidies. Peninsula Transit then ran the service under contract. Introduced December 2, to replace the aging Ford buses, were eight city-owned 31-passenger General Motors coaches that paraded down University Avenue behind ex-Peninsular Fageol safety coach No. 216. At the wheel of this 1924-vintage vehicle was Lee Harper, former superintendent of Peninsula Transit and a one-time Peninsular motorman and driver.

Fares were cut from 30¢ to 25¢ under the new arrangement; the basic weekday headways were improved to half-hourly. The Menlo Park line was dropped but the other routes continued. Except for the addition of a Saturday-only 5¢ shuttle from downtown Palo Alto to the Stanford Shopping Center and a short-lived nickel shuttle to Town and County Village, the system remained essentially intact from 1963 to its takeover by County Transit.

2. San Jose City Lines

Down in San Jose, the S.P. sold its properties (San Jose Railroads and the vestiges of the old Peninsular) to Pacific City Lines in March of 1939. In addition to the San Jose system, the railroad succeeded in selling off its unprofitable city operations in Stockton and Fresno at the same time. PCL was originally formed by the principal owners of *National City Lines* when sufficient funds could not be raised by western interests to buy the properties from S.P.

NCL originally supplied one-sixth of the capital, but within a year, PCL was forced to refinance and NCL lost control to the *Manning Transportation Co.* In each of the three cities, an operating subsidiary was set up by PCL to run the local system. The *San Jose City Lines* manager was Arthur L. Wood, former superintendent of the San Jose Railroads, and the company operated 48 buses over seven routes: (1) Santa Clara Street line from downtown Santa Clara to King Road and Linda Vista; (2) First Street line from Second and Rosa Streets to Cottage Grove; (3) Willow Glen line from First and Market Streets to Minnesota and Lincoln Avenues; (4) Delmas-Naglee line from Fifteenth and San Antonio Streets to Curtner and Radio Avenues; (5) Bascom-Seventeeth Street line from Fifteenth and Vestal Streets to Bascom Avenue and Stevens Creek Road, looping either north to Forest Avenue or south to Scott Avenue; (6) Tenth and Keyes line from the S. P. depot via Tenth and Keyes to Seventh and Margaret Streets; and (7) Park Avenue line between Market and Newhall Streets. Ridership was remaining fairly constant although the company pared its fares to a nickel in April 1940 in an effort to stem the tide toward private autos.

Also serving the community during that period, in addition to Peerless, were two smaller local bus firms: *Almaden Stages* to New Almaden and *San Jose Auto Stages* to Alum Rock Park. Bert Smith, owner of Almaden Stages, acquired the Alum Rock service in 1937 and whittled back his New Almaden line to South San Jose. In 1940, for $300, Smith sold his franchises and a 21-passenger bus to Lewis D. Bohnett, Jr., owner of the City Parcel Service and a local service station, who operated the coach weekends and holidays from downtown San Jose directly to Alum Rock Park and also hauled the mail to New Almaden to maintain that franchise.

Two years later, preparing to join the Merchant Marine, Bohnett sold the bus for $100 to a local wrecking yard and his Alum Rock franchise for $285 to San Jose City Lines. The coach was later used to haul walnuts, Bohnett said. Sale of the franchise was arranged through his neighbor Fred Griffin of City Lines, who like Wood was a former S. P. employee. "I was glad at the time to get the $285," Bohnett recalled. "Griffin later told me I might have gotten $15,000."

The advent of World War II—December 7, 1941—brought many other changes. One was the S. P's abandonment the following month of steam passenger service between San Jose and Los Gatos (four trains daily) to conserve equipment and manpower for the defense effort. Peerless buses replaced the trains, offering frequent schedules and 35- to 40-minute service via Campbell or Saratoga over four routes. Four of the coaches (six Sundays and holidays) went on to Santa Cruz via Holy City and Felton. The first outbound bus was 5:50 a.m. and the last 11:15 p.m.; inbound it was 5:50 a.m. and 10:20 p.m.

There was no reduction in passenger rail service over the Mayfield cutoff, and the plan was endorsed by the Los Gatos Chamber of Commerce. One local official, however, called it just "the second step in the S. P.'s plan to remove all passenger rail service from Los Gatos." A hearing on the matter, set for February 1942 in San Jose, was cancelled by the State Railroad Commission at the request of U. S. Army officials.

In January the Interstate Commerce Commission authorized bus companies to hike passenger fares 10% effective 10 days from formal notification. Railroads had earlier been authorized a similar boost. Military personnel in both cases were exempted from the increase. Tire rationing was instituted, and there was talk of gasoline rationing. Organized by the San Jose Chamber of Commerce was a War Transportation Committee to enforce

equalled those of the 7¢ era, prior to the 1940 rollback. City Lines was retrofitting several of its smaller buses to handle from six to eight more passengers apiece, he told the *San Jose Mercury Herald.* He rated as slim the chances of getting new equipment ordered the past year and, therefore, for extending the local routes. There were plans, though, to speed up schedules if the traffic warranted. The advent of tire rationing, Wood noted, had "hastened slightly" the rate of increase in bus travel, which he expected to accelerate as motorists saw their tires wearing thinner. "We're doing our best to prepare for the increase," he declared. "We just hope it doesn't come too fast."

One of the projects of the War Transportation Committee was to keep local homes occupied by residents working at out-of-town defense plants. Discussions with Robert Maxwell, local manager for Peerless Stages, led in August 1942 to inauguration of the San Jose "shipyard bus line": direct 75-minute service to the Moore Dry Dock Company in Oakland. One bus

Twin Coach model 23-R was for awhile one of the basic streetcar replacements in San Jose. Unit 2250 belongs to San Jose City Lines.

(Robert A. Burrowes)

Peerless Stages covered the territory between Oakland and Santa Cruz, but San Jose was the center of many Peerless operations.

(Robert A. Burrowes)

directives of the Federal Office of Defense Transportation (ODT), whose powers included allocations, enforcement of 40-mph wartime speed limits, and regulation of local transit.

In February 1942 Wood reported bus travel in San Jose on the increase but not dramatically. Revenues had not yet

departed San Jose at 5:45 a.m., returning at 5:45 p.m. The monthly round trip fare was $17. Another was begun in September to serve workers on an earlier shift.

Les Harlen and Ken Challen received a certificate from the State Railroad Commission in August 1942 to operate a wartime bus company—called *Victory Lines*—from San Jose, Santa Clara, and Cupertino to the Permanente Metals Corporation plant above Monta Vista. Two new 42-passenger buses were secured for this service, which commenced August 27 with five round trips daily on two routes.

Gas rationing became law in January 1943, boosting bus ridership. Along with it came a "skip-stop" schedule approved that month by the San Jose city council. The schedule eliminated many bus stops to comply with a new ODT order limiting stops to eight per mile in residential sections—in essence, to about one each 700 feet. The purposes were to save rubber and speed travel, allowing the company to carry more passengers. The plan went into effect Monday February 15, company drivers handing out advance copies of a listing of the stops. Wood reported that the new schedule would cut out 206 of the 810 stops the buses had been making. "Elimination of the bus stops does not save mileage," he stated, "but speeds up the service."

Roy A. Hauer replaced Wood that spring as general manager of City Lines and almost immediately faced a wage dispute, the workers asking a 30¢ hourly pay boost (from 80¢ to $1.10) and the company offering just 10¢ on expiration of its contract June

30 with Local 265, Amalgamated Association of Street and Electric Railway and Motor Coach Employees. This controversy went to Federal arbitration, another wartime provision for transportation companies.

In August 1943 Peerless modified schedules of its San Jose, Oakland, and Palo Alto lines to accommodate workers traveling to and from the Waco Chemical Company plant near the Dumbarton bridge. That month, also, at the urging of the War Transportation Committee, San Jose City Lines temporarily extended its service to 1 a.m. to accommodate cannery workers on the midnight shift. All routes were involved except the Park Avenue and Tenth and Keyes lines, which did not serve the canneries.

City Lines also made some route adjustments that included elimination of its former Tenth and Keyes line from the S. P. depot. The new plan established daily schedules on the Santa Clara-King Road line from 5:55 a.m. to midnight with seven-minute headway to 6 p.m. and 12- and 15-minute headways thereafter. Line 2 now operated between Burton and Alma Streets from 5:48 a.m. to midnight on a 10-minute headway to 7:10 p.m. and 20 minutes thereafter. Line 3 ran from Hicks and Mercer to Tenth and Keyes: 12- and 15-minute headways from 5:45 a.m. to 6 p.m., then 20 and 30 minutes to midnight. Line 4 operated from Fifteenth and William Streets to Lincoln and Curtner Avenues (same general schedule as Line 3). Line 5 ran from Bascom Avenue to Seventeenth and Rosa: first bus 5:40 a.m., 12- and 20-minute headways to 8 p.m., and 30-minute headway to midnight. Line 7 ran from Newhall Street to Thir-

A Mayfair Bus Lines Twin Coach is at the San Jose Greyhound Station.
(Robert A. Burrowes)

teenth and Rosa: first bus 6:10 a.m., 20-minute headway to 6:30 p.m., 30-minute headway to about 11:30 p.m. This line had now absorbed the Luna Park bus once operated by a different company. Linda Vista operated as a feeder line between King Road and Miguelito Avenue: first bus 5:50 a.m., 30-minute headway to 7 p.m., hourly to midnight. Shoppers were asked to avoid the rush hour crowds. "Please shop after 10 a.m.," the company advised. "Start home before 4 p.m."

With the city buses jammed to capacity during peak travel periods, Hauer received the welcome news in January 1944 that three brand new 40-passenger General Motors coaches ordered the previous, increasing the local fleet to 51 vehicles. Replacement parts for the older buses were now coming through, he reported. The company's chief difficulty at present was securing and training new mechanics.

February brought word of a new local transit enterprise—San Jose's most innovative solution to its wartime transportation needs—run by Lew Bohnett, former operator of the San Jose-Alum Rock Park bus service. Called "Bohnett's Hacks," it was a collection of electric automobiles, horsedrawn carriages, and even a large haywagon purchased from private owners as far away as Modesto. Bohnett said he was standing by with 20 coaches and 10 drivers ready to carry up to 32 riders from 2 p.m. to midnight daily, at about the same rates as motor taxis. This service lasted until August 1945.

The traffic volume remained heavy on motor and rail lines throughout the war years as companies struggled to make do with equipment that was becoming obsolescent. By 1946 the availability of new buses and used coaches from other operators eased the burdens of Peerless Stages and San Jose City Lines. Paul Steiling, once a driver for Bohnett and later the jury commissioner for Santa Clara County, resurrected Almaden Stages, running buses out to South San Jose and the Almaden Valley. He eventually sold out to Claude A. Kingsbury.

True to prediction the S. P., which during the war had maintained a heavy schedule of trains between San Francisco and Los Gatos via the Mayfield cutoff, halted its rail service. That left Peerless the chief operator to Los Gatos and Palo Alto Transit—still receiving its $1,000-a-month subsidy from the Southern Pacific—the only operator between Palo Alto, Los Altos, Loyola Corners, Cupertino, and San Jose. Pearson sold the latter franchise in 1950 to Nicholas Capraro.

A mood of cautious optimism prevailed immediately after the war about the future of public transit—automobiles being in short supply and the public accustomed to riding trains and buses—but Pacific City Lines was reluctant to expand its base at

Norman W. Holmes owned and operated Mayfair Suburban Lines and Almaden Stages. Photo dates to about 1953.

(Norman Holmes Collection)

Mayfair operated several wartime Yellow Coach TD4505 units, still active in 1960. This photo was taken in Los Altos. (Harre W. Demoro)

San Jose, one of its only paying properties. Restoration of the 7¢ fare in 1947, accompanied by a midsummer strike of bus drivers and shop workers that irritated some 40,000 patrons, was followed two years later by a 20-year city franchise obligating the company to pay a $100 monthly franchise fee.

In April 1950 City Lines commenced bus service to Alum Rock on 30-minute headways eastbound from First and Santa Clara streets 9 a.m. to 5:30 p.m. and westbound from the park 9:45 a.m. to 6:30 p.m. By 1951, in addition to this service, it was operating seven lines reminiscent of its prewar routes: (1) downtown Santa Clara to King Road and Linda Vista; (2) First and Gish Road (north city limits) to Cottage Grove; (3) Tenth and Keyes Streets to Willow Glen; (4) Lincoln and Curtner Avenues via Delmas Avenue and Malone Road to Twenty-second and William Streets; (5) Seventeenth and Berryessa Road to Bascom Avenue and San Carlos Street; (6) Second and Santa Clara Streets to San Jose Municipal Airport; and (7) Thirteenth and Rosa Streets via Park Avenue to Newhall and Monroe Streets.

In August 1953 a new company, Norman W. Holmes's *Mayfair Bus Lines,* began operating coach service from First and Santa Clara Streets to Toyon Avenue and Holly Drive, operating six days a week and offering nine roundtrips daily from about 7 a.m. to 5:50 p.m. Despite strenuous protests by City Lines, the owner, a Western Pacific fireman, obtained an unrestricted certificate from the State Public Utilities Commission—successor to the Railroad Commission in matters governing local transit—allowing him to pick up riders all along his 8.5-mile route out Santa Clara Street to Tenth Street, south to Keyes Street, east via Story Road to White Road, north to McKee Road, east to Toyon Avenue, and north on Toyon to County Club Gardens (Holly Drive). The fare was 10¢ plus another dime beyond King Road. For $400 each plus tires, Holmes

bought two red, cream, and silver Ford 27-passenger coaches in Little Rock, Arkansas, and drove them west to San Jose at 45 mph. One bus worked the route, the other standing by in reserve.

Holmes then added an old Key System 41-passenger Twin Coach and, in 1956, extended his Holly Drive line down McKee and Julian Street to Thirteenth, then south to Santa Clara Street, effecting loop service to downtown San Jose. Two buses now served the line, operating outbound on the hour via Story and White and on the half hour via Julian and McKee. Business being slow, Holmes bought a Greyhound 41-passenger diesel coach and started doing some charter work. He also launched a five-times-daily limousine service between the San Jose and San Francisco airports—using a 1947 Packard and a 1948 DeSoto—that fell by the wayside partly because it was hard to solicit customers at San Francisco.

In July 1957 his company, now called *Mayfair Suburban Lines,* extended its service to Agnews and Alviso, acquiring the certificate and mail and newspaper contracts from former owner Hazel Bushnell. There were five trips daily—7:45 a.m. to 4:45 p.m. from San Jose, 9 a.m. to 5:20 p.m. from Alviso—and seven on Sunday, when business was brisk to Agnews State Hospital. Three months later, on learning that Palo Alto Transit did not intend to restore service from Palo Alto to Loyola Corners—a route it had suspended in late August without Public Utilities Commission approval—he also picked up its San Jose-Loyola franchise from its manager, Vince McQuiggen.

For some months Palo Alto Transit had been locked in combat with the S. P. over their subsidy (joint tariff) arrangement, which had been wiped out by the rail company the previous February without PUC consent. The S. P. had been ordered to reinstate the tariff, which it did in late May, but only after what was viewed as an irreparable loss of motor coach traffic. The

Almaden 15, workhorse of the Almaden fleet, was a Ford 29-passenger coach from Asbury Rapid Transit, Los Angeles. (Norman Holmes)

railroad had subsequently decided to reimburse Palo Alto Transit at its full one-way tariff fares—averaging about 35¢ per passenger—only for the S. P. tickets actually honored. The bus company, in response, had refused to honor any S. P. tickets until ordered by the Commission to do so, then had suspended its Palo Alto-Loyola operation, claiming financial inability.

Holmes started operating the San Jose-Loyola route even before the certificate was officially conveyed, extending it to Mountain View to serve St. Francis and Holy Cross high schools and hoping that his East San Jose patrons would avail themselves of direct service to the large new shopping center at Valley Fair. They still got off mainly in downtown San Jose, however. Holmes later said that his only advantage in owning this franchise was an ICC permit that would have allowed him to run an out-of-state charter service.

Sunnyvale got coach service briefly in 1956 when Raymond Phillips and associates organized a small company to run Volkswagen buses from Washington and Francis, their downtown stop, eastward to Duane and Santa Ynez and westward to Wright and The Dalles. Their firm, which was called *Sunnyvale Bus System,* offered five trips daily in each direction—no Sunday or holiday service—from about 10 a.m. to 5 p.m.

Another company to expand during this period was Almaden Stages, which commenced running in 1954 to Hillsdale Manor (Hillsdale Avenue east of Almaden Road) and to Hacienda Gardens (Foxworthy Avenue and Kirk Road). Reportedly one of its coaches was an ex-San Jose City Lines bus still decked out in original colors, bought from the Navarra wrecking yard on Monterey Road. City Lines supposedly paid to have it repainted after many fruitless complaints to the Almaden management but got the last laugh, after all, when it won the right in May 1958 to operate into Hacienda Gardens (extending its No. 3 line), at which time it also began serving Valley Fair, O'Connor Hospital, and County Hospital (extending its No. 5 line).

A City Lines extension into Hacienda Gardens ended any hopes for profitable operation of Almaden Stages, which had

been purchased from Claude Kingsbury in March 1956 by Holmes and two Pan American World Airways pilots, David Summerville and Wayne Snyder, whom he later bought out. Holmes suspended his Almaden operations in February 1959. Two years later he dissolved Mayfair after two investigations of his buses—in May 1960 and February 1961—led to an April 1961 PUC decision to revoke his operating rights within two weeks. "Enough was enough," Holmes later explained. "My losses were too great. I couldn't fight it, so why carry on? I told the *Mercury* I'd quit the following weekend." Peerless Stages picked up the franchise for a token $100.

Peerless announced the purchase and reported plans to add more runs to the former Mayfair lines: San Jose-Loyola Corners, Agnews, and East Foothills. Mayfair stopped running April 17, supplanted by Peerless. No equipment was involved and the deal seemed straightforward, but it touched off a bitter argument with City Lines in which Peerless President Harry Gaeta, one of that company's founders, successfully defended its right to maintain an exclusive franchise over the Mayfair routes.

The general ridership decline of the late 1950s, as prosperity brought more and more autos to the South Bay, had also affected City Lines. By 1961 Diaz was compelled to negotiate some subsidy payments including a six-month agreement with Santa Clara, at $3,000 per month, to maintain service in that city. The patronage was down to about 25,000 daily. In July 1961 the system experienced a month-long strike during which 90 drivers and 14 maintenance workers—earning $2.23 and $2.47 per hour, respectively—won a 20¢-per-hour wage boost. The local fare was now 15¢.

In 1962 the Public Utilities Commission ordered City Lines to replace 37 obsolete buses within five years. National provided five new buses, which went into service November 1, but sold its San Jose and Stockton interests the following month to *Pacific City Lines* of Oakland—a National affiliate created in 1938 by General Motors and Standard Oil of California—as part

San Jose City Lines bus 6602 was one of the first transit-type General Motors buses on the property. It was a model TD-3609, gasoline-powered, and arrived in 1944. (Robert A. Burrowes) **BELOW:** At the other end of the General Motors spectrum is historical City Lines bus 6512, the last "paired-window" model, a TDH-4512, built by GM before introduction of its "new look" design. It is shown headed eastward on The Alameda in 1971.

(Jack Perry)

One-way traffic moves southbound on First Street across Santa Clara Street—the intersection of San Jose's first two horsecar lines—in May 1967. One-way traffic today moves northbound.

(The Association of Metropolitan San Jose)

of a plan to unload its West Coast properties. The new owners were George H. Hook and Glen Gordon, Bay Area residents both of whom who had been with National. Hook, the president of Pacific City Lines, became vice president at San Jose. William Blair was named general manager of San Jose operations.

In January 1964, on evidence of the company's financial inability, the Public Utilities Commission stayed its 1962 order, also setting aside its requirement that the company put eight more buses into service that month.

Rising costs and declining revenues led to a January 1965 request by City Lines to hike its local fares to 20¢. Permission was given, but the boost was laid aside when the San Jose city council agreed to meet the nickel deficit. Later that year the company asked to reduce service on three main routes and discontinue service on one line after 7 p.m., prompting the *San Jose Mercury* to inquire editorially if local bus service was slowly dying.

Peerless was also encountering major deficits; costs averaged 52¢ a mile, Cole reported, compared with passenger revenues of 28¢. City Lines was maintaining service on seven routes through downtown San Jose weekdays from 5 a.m. to 1 a.m., less often on weekends. Its cost-revenue experience paralleled that of Peerless. Earnings the previous year had amounted to only $8,000, Hook told the *Mercury* in 1967, and things were getting worse. He noted that his franchise was due to expire soon and said he would be happy if the city took over his lines now.

By 1969 the local bus companies were failing. Peninsula Transit and San Jose City Lines lived on subsidies. Peerless grossed only 40¢ a mile from its local routes—San Jose-Loyola Corners, Agnews, and East Foothills—compared with a profitable 80¢ a mile from its main line operations. Enthusiasm had now developed in some quarters for a new broad-based county agency to buy out the local companies and run the buses.

Among the staunchest supporters were Public Works Director James T. Pott, architect of the county's expressway system, and San Jose City Manager A. P. (Dutch) Hamann, who earlier had urged the city to set up some plan—a transit district or joint powers agreement with the county and other cities—to maintain local service. Envisioned was a consolidation of the county's transit, transportation planning, highway, and airport operations in one agency responsible to the general public. Supporting arguments included less air pollution, reduced traffic congestion, and the likely availability of Federal and state money to bolster local transit.

Despite strong political and editorial backing, a 1969 county ballot measure to create the new agency was defeated by cost-conscious voters. Another similar measure went down to defeat the next year. Hook, appearing before the San Jose city council, offered to give his company to any responsible operator. The council responded by paying him to maintain bus service while it explored other alternatives.

3. Birth of County Transit

By October 1971 the financial picture had brightened. Congressional support had now lined up behind the idea of using Federal money to stimulate urban transit development, with emphasis on innovation. Studies were needed to qualify for these funds, but the benefit was Federal willingness to pay 80% of the costs for buying equipment, constructing maintenance facilities, or even building a new South Bay electric rail system. The state legislature meanwhile had passed its own funding measure—the Transportation Development Act (TDA), also known as the Mills-Alquist-Deddeh Act—which applied the state sales tax to gasoline and through a complicated formula channeled the new revenues into public transit.

Transit supporters moved with dispatch to cash in on these opportunities. Created that month was the *San Jose-Palo Alto Transit Authority*, with James Boring as interim director, entrusted with preparing for a countywide election the following year. It lobbied vigorously and effectively for an agency whose philosophy would be to entice people out of private autos onto public transit, which in congested areas would become the chief mode of conveyance. It pledged frequent, modern service to all corners of the county.

This time the campaign bore fruit. On June 6, 1972, by better than a 2-to-1 margin, South Bay voters approved the new *Santa Clara County Transit District*, which was endorsed two weeks later by the county supervisors. The supervisors became the district's governors, supported by a 25-member advisory panel—the County Transportation Commission—whose views theoretically represented those of the county's 15 cities. This was unusual in that the transit agency had no taxing powers and, while supervisors elsewhere in California served on transit governing boards, nowhere else were they the sole bosses.

Incorporated into the new agency were a transportation planning and development division, a road operations division responsible for 68 miles of expressways and 779 miles of other roads, and an aviation division charged with administering the county's three airports: Palo Alto, Reid-Hillview (San Jose), and South County (San Martin). A target date of January 1, 1973, was set for taking over Peninsula Transit, San Jose City Lines, and the local routes of Peerless Stages.

One of the supervisors' first moves was to adopt a general transit plan that remains in effect today. Public transit, it stated, must provide "at least an equal choice" compared with automobiles and, in congested areas, a preferred choice. The plan called first for creating a bus fleet and then for building some sort of county rail network: "an orderly transition to advanced fixed-guideway transit when investigations have been completed which enable the district to secure necessary capital grants." Arrangements were begun to adjust the South Bay transit goals to those of the Association of Bay Area Governments (ABAG) and the Metropolitan Transportation Commission (MTC), whose endorsement is still needed for Federal transit grants in the Bay Area.

To head the new district the supervisors selected public works expert Jim Pott, 46, a prime mover in its creation. Some criticism was leveled because of Pott's inexperience with transit, but such objections weren't wholly unfamiliar to the new director, born in Shanghai to missionary parents and graduated in civil engineering from Stanford. Pott had worked briefly for the City of San Francisco before taking a job with an engineering consulting firm, then come to Santa Clara County in 1960 as assistant public works director for highways despite his lack of highway experience. He had become acting director in 1963 and permanent director in 1964, claiming as one of his major accomplishments the construction of some 40 miles of county expressways before voters called a halt to the system. Always a good problem-solver, he admittedly thrived on controversy. "The only time you have a prayer of developing an efficient shop is when the pressure's on," he said.

Arrangements were now completed for County Transit, as it became called, to absorb the San Jose-Palo Alto Transit Authority and buy out the local bus lines. Included in that purchase were 78 aging General Motors diesel-powered buses, some with more than a million miles, by which the district planned to maintain service. Sixty were from San Jose City Lines, ten from Peninsula Transit, and the rest from Peerless. Added to the county payroll were the drivers, dispatchers, and maintenance personnel from the three companies who wanted to work for the district. AC Transit contracted to run the fledgling countywide system for six months while the district's operating staff was being chosen.

County Transit took over on schedule in San Jose at 6:20 a.m. January 1, 1973. Coaches that had been the property of San Jose City lines, thoroughly cleaned by crews working through the New Year's weekend, rolled away from the San Carlos Street barn that morning proudly bearing the blue and orange County Transit insignia. One of the first riders was Ralph Mehrkens, chairman of the county supervisors. Back in service the next morning were the coaches formerly owned by Peninsula Transit and Peerless Stages. A new 10¢ fare was adopted for riders age 5-17.

AC Transit also leased to the district 18 of its venerable 45-passenger 1947 GM coaches, the same units that had replaced the last of the Key System's East Bay local streetcar lines. These buses were used to launch six "interim routes" July 1, 1973, which were intended to fill in the gaps between the three predecessor systems and provide minimum service to county areas that had no prior local bus service. The system network was thus extended from the Fremont BART station in the north to Gilroy in the south and now included the cities of Sunnyvale, Cupertino, Mountain View, Los Altos, Saratoga, Milpitas, and Morgan Hill. Another line, connecting Alviso with the Kaiser Hospital in Santa Clara, was added the following April. Service on these interim routes was offered only weekdays from 6 a.m. to 6 p.m.; the headways were generally hourly except for the San Jose-Gilroy (46) line, whose solitary coach ran only every three hours.

As soon became obvious, the new district had inherited many problems, not the least of which was maintaining the antiquated coaches. Parts were in short supply or sometimes nonexistent. For example, old No. 268, a 30-passenger bus acquired from Peninsula Transit, threw a connecting rod through its engine block. Attempts to find parts were met with replies that the bus was too old; the parts weren't made any more or weren't in stock.

Mechanics working for Equipment Manager Bob Erickson drew on their native ingenuity and installed a 350-cubic-inch Chevrolet V-8 engine. Old No. 268 thus became the only bus in the fleet in which the driver could tromp down on the accelerator and lay rubber. The V-8 engine was governed down to more sedate limits before the bus went back on line.

All County Transit operations were consolidated at the San Carlos Street barn in central San Jose, which made for considerable deadheading of coaches formerly operated by Peninsula Transit on the Palo Alto local runs. Adding to the complexity was that the San Carlos Street barn stored only diesel fuel, so the gasoline-fueled coaches had to refuel daily at the county's Berger Drive maintenance yard on their way home from work.

Consolidation of the operations showed the inadequacy of the district's storage and maintenance facilities, a problem that was to grow in significance over the years. There was disquiet, too, among the workers. When County Transit took over, the drivers were making $3.98 an hour. They got a big boost—to $5.90 an hour—but felt put upon by their former employers and considered their wages inadequate.

Also, certain problems, mostly political in nature, had evolved from the campaign to create County Transit. Many

Peerless Stages provided suburban service from downtown San Jose to East Foothills, Los Gatos, Saratoga, Los Altos, Cupertino, Sunnyvale and Mountain View. Shown here is coach 246, a GM model TDH-4512 and one of the newest coaches in this service, headed south on Stelling Road in the waning days before County Transit takeover.

(Jack Perry)

The Short Line Varieties

A bewildering mix of equipment was operated over the years by the various Santa Clara Valley bus operators. Even the consolidation of service under County Transit has not brought uniformity. **ABOVE: Mayfair 29 was a World War I Twin Coach and is shown at the company bus yard at McLaughlin Avenue and Story Road, East San Jose.** (Norman Holmes) **BELOW: Not to be overlooked is the small San Jose, Santa Clara, Agnew and Alviso Stage whose tiny bus is shown here.** (Harre W. Demoro)

The Palo Alto fleet was rounded out at 10 units in 1966 with the purchase of coach 269, shown at the S.P. Depot. (Jack Perry) **BELOW: Palo Alto Transit 102 is an early model Flxible Clipper dating to 1941; it was formerly Moyers Stages 81.** (Bob Townley photo from Jack Perry Collection)

Mayfair had one of the more interesting bus fleets. TOP: Unit 81 was a former Greyhound 41-seat Cruiser, and is shown at Pinecrest, California, on a post-snow ski charter trip. CENTER: Mayfair 43 was a Ford Transit, a type of bus well-known on small and medium-sized transit operations, perhaps the closest thing to a "bus-Birney." ABOVE: Unnumbered Mayfair coach was No. 66, a 44-passenger White acquired in 1959 from the San Francisco Municipal Railway. (All: Norman Holmes)

advocates including Pott had sketched glowing scenarios of the service-to-be, assuring the voters of the district's ability to serve an ambitious route schedule. If the system worked as planned, they had said, it would offer "transit opportunity" for 97% of the county's population. They promised Federal grants, economies in fares, and reduced air pollution. These were tall orders, and now it was time to deliver. Truth was that County Transit was a newcomer serving one of the nation's richest urban areas and starting low in priority for Federal funding. Moreover, the TDA required state money to be matched dollar for dollar by local money, with no more than half going into operating expenses. As a new agency County Transit had until July 1977 to comply with the state regulations, but they had to be considered in the district's plans.

Arguing persuasively that an innovative approach was the best entree to Federal funds, Pott urged the supervisors to accept personalized transit—a Dial-a-Ride scheme—as their primary transit program, using small, relatively inexpensive coaches powered by propane to reduce air pollution. The intent of Dial-a-Ride, he said, was to offer on-call, computer-dispatched, door-to-door service within districts or zones around the county, stimulating use within the zones and to the arterial routes, which would be served temporarily by the aging diesels. The arterials would then be adjusted to comprise an arterial-personalized transit (APT) net. In this way, he said, the district could honor its promise of "transit opportunity."

Pott observed that the Dial-a-Ride plan was Federally approved and under evaluation elsewhere, though not on the scale seen for the South Bay. He described the 30-foot propane buses that would be built to district specifications as environmentally safe, efficient, and Federally sanctioned.

The supervisors adopted Dial-a-Ride and so did the County Transportation Commission, though with reservations about the bus size, use of propane fuel, and practicality of Dial-a-Ride. Then came word that the Federal Urban Mass Transportation Administration (UMTA) had approved a $4.5 million

Government Center, north side, San Jose, looking east to the Diablo Range. This 1967 aerial view shows the junction of Hedding Street with Guadalupe Parkway.
(The Association of Metropolitan San Jose)

capital grant to purchase equipment. The district's estimate was $33,600 per unit. Bids were advertised in late August 1973 for 134 coaches, 90 to be delivered within six months of the award and the balance by July 1, 1974. Specifications went out to nine manufacturers, but only one submitted a bid: Highway Products of Ohio (Twin Coach) at $43,000 per unit, totaling $5.76 million.

During October Pott managed to whittle the $43,000 bid down to $35,600. At this point, because of political overtones and fears of kickback charges, the supervisors asked an impartial three-member team to conclude negotiations after the UMTA gave its blessing, which came November 19. Federal spokesmen noted that other agencies using Twin Coaches were having problems but did not withhold their approval. The team went to work, pruning the bid to $35,000. On December 4 the supervisors awarded a $4.7 million contract to Highway Products calling for delivery of the 134 coaches by September 1974, at a cost only $200,000 above the original estimate.

Early in 1974 the supervisors moved ahead with their promised countywide transit assessment. Firms bidding to conduct a first-phase study observed the South Bay's explosive population growth and characterized it as suburban with dispersed low-density housing and scattered industrial parks, shopping plazas, schools, and entertainment centers, requiring a large transit net. Growth was sure to continue, they said, though probably at a slower rate.

The first-phase contract, for $280,000, went DeLeuw, Cather and Company to study how a modest county rail net, coordinated with bus and auto transit, might actually work. The results were to be reported in 1975.

Dial-a-Ride was scheduled to begin in September 1974 when the district took delivery of its 134 new propane-fueled Twin Coaches, expanding the fleet to more than 200 buses. In July, however, labor negotiations with the drivers stalled over union demands for $13.50 an hour—$28,000 a year—by mid-1976. The present rate was $5.90. After negotiation a compromise was reached, but the dispute delayed by about two months the advent of Dial-a-Ride.

The arrival of the Twin Coaches in September coincided with an influx of riders because of a severe gasoline shortage. Daily demand on Dial-a-Ride had been expected to reach 10,000 in two years but now seemed potentially larger. Suddenly at issue was the system's ability to handle incoming calls, schedule problems, and wear and tear on vehicles subjected to longer hours and heavier loads. Officials chose to delay adjustment of the arterial lines—the next step toward APT—until the impact of the new service could be assessed.

In November the district reported its preparations on schedule without a day to spare. Colorful maps and descriptions, with Dial-a-Ride phone numbers, were distributed with local newspapers. There were to be 18 Dial-a-Ride zones (1-10, 12-19) assigned. Hispanic names based on land grants or other historical identities, such as Pueblo de San Jose (1), Rancho San Juan Bautista (2), Potrero de Santa Clara (12), and Rancho de las Llagas (19). The zone name was to be displayed on the coach.

Riders were urged to call the control center or individual zone scheduling stations for a 25¢ home pickup and delivery service to arterial routes, shops, schools, and medical facilities. In mid-November a reporter made a trial trip and declared all in readiness for opening day. On November 18, however, eight local taxi firms filed suit in Santa Clara County Superior Court arguing that state law required County Transit to buy out any transit operation adversely affected by a new public service. The law applied to taxi companies, they claimed, as well as the bus companies already secured by the county from private owners. Judge Marshall S. Hall took the case under advisement. Its potential consequences were unknown.

4. Dial-a-Ride

Dial-a-Ride service commenced November 24 with reservationists, including Spanish-speaking operators, standing by to accept calls at the control center and the zone scheduling stations. The calls started and soon became a deluge straining human endurance and swamping the reservation lines. More than 80,000 tried to reach the control center and scheduling stations that day. Another 80,000 tried the next day and 80,000 more the day after. Many of the calls were for information; others were directed to wrong stations. After two weeks the count was still holding around 80,000 daily.

Operators told reporters that the bulbs on the switchboard were literally burning out faster than they could be replaced. Dispatching problems were monumental, too. Not infrequently the buses ran empty or nearly so. The drivers had to follow orders from computers that occasionally hiccoughed and forgot to pick up or deliver passengers, with results that were sometimes hilarious but usually downright annoying.

Despite all, Dial-a-Ride was serving about 4,500 passengers a day when its formal welcoming ceremonies took place December 14. Hundreds attended. Five thousand antiqued, solid bronze coins were struck to commemorate the advent of APT, its 200-bus fleet the nation's largest. The coins sold for $1 apiece at local city halls, chambers of commerce, and the county service and administration centers in San Jose.

Revised arterial routes went into operation December 21 to consummate the marriage. "To ease the honeymoon," declared the *San Jose Mercury*, "those old fixed routes not covered by the new network will remain in service, at least until Dial-a-Ride starts running smoothly. The problem areas are primarily parts of Palo Alto, Santa Clara, the northern Almaden area, and northeast San Jose. Temporary continuance of parts of the old routes will actually be a shuttle service. Buses will run riders to points where they can board other vehicles on the new routes. About 100 buses will run weekdays on the new arterials. Another 90 buses are operating in the Dial-a-Ride system. Some 60 buses had been running the old arterial routes, which carried about 20,000 passengers a day."

As regards the taxi firms, Superior Court Judge Marshall Hall stated in a preliminary opinion that he supported their claims. On January 9, 1975, he ordered the supervisors to decide in two weeks whether to halt Dial-a-Ride or buy the taxi companies. They responded a week later by announcing purchase plans. No details were given, but a figure of $1.5 million was cited by the press.

By now this issue had taken a back seat to other, more pressing problems. Riders were growing impatient with busy telephones and long waits to arrange service. They were angry when the drivers of near-empty buses refused to pick them up without reservations at shopping centers or arterial transfer points. The drivers explained that they were run by the computers—which was true—but this merely reflected poorly on the whole Dial-a-Ride plan.

On January 8 the supervisors announced a crash program to add more reservation clerks and phone lines, diverting some $1 million tentatively earmarked to fill 50 vacancies in other county departments. Six days later they authorized 70 new Dial-a-Ride aides.

Then came the alarming news that the Dial-a-Ride coaches were logging 833 hours carrying 5,000 passengers daily whereas the arterial buses, logging only 1,000 hours, were hauling about 26,000. Collectively the Dial-a-Ride buses were accumulating some 9,200 miles a day versus 12,500 for the arterials. Even more alarming was incontrovertible evidence that 25¢ Dial-a-Ride service cost $2.69 to $3.09 per mile compared with 59¢ for arterial service.

County Transit brought a new white paint scheme. Ex-City Lines 6643 is at Second and Santa Clara streets, San Jose, in 1973 shortly after being repainted. County Transit's ill-fated Dial-a-Ride venture used 90 of 134 new propane-fueled Twin Coaches. Seen below is empty coach 476 on Hollenbeck south of El Camino Real, Sunnyvale, awaiting a call that may never have come because of communications foulups.

(Both: Jack Perry)

In February the *Mercury* urged the supervisors to abandon Dial-a-Ride, citing excessive costs and the county obligation to buy out the taxis if it continued. The Santa Clara city council also voted for termination despite an impassioned plea from County Transportation Commission Planning Committee Chairman Jack Ybarra, who saw the service as a boon to the aged, the infirm, and the impoverished. On March 11 the supervisors hired Bechtel, Incorporated, a consulting firm, to make a crash study of the entire system. This action was seen as significant.

On April 4 Bechtel recommended scrapping Dial-a-Ride for the "short-term immediate future" except in the South County, though some buses might continue to transport the elderly. The recommendation was accepted over bitter protests by Ybarra and the Planning Committee. Reluctantly the supervisors voted May 5, by a 4-1 margin, to halt Dial-a-Ride within the week in all but Morgan Hill, San Martin, and Gilroy.

Friday May 9 was the final day. Shortly after 10 p.m. the last North County Dial-a-Ride bus rolled into the barn on West San Carlos Street and into a partly finished terminal north of the Bayshore Freeway in Mountain View. Inaugurated the following morning was an ambitious schedule of new arterial routes that spread the system thin and drew on equipment formerly held in reserve. Among the new routes, restructured the following July, were some generally following the old San Jose City Lines routes. Two routes were restored to Palo Alto.

The coaches assigned to several special commuter subscription bus pools, which had been used by Dial-a-Ride during the midday, were now available for other off-peak duties. Between August and October they were deployed over several midday shopping routes, primarily serving South San Jose, Sunnyvale, Mountain View, and the West Valley.

On May 12 Judge Hall decided not to rule on the remnants of Dial-a-Ride. "The court will not substitute itself," he said, "for the legislative judgment of the board of supervisors, sitting as the transit district directors." The taxi companies withdrew their suit.

Improvements had been made as Dial-a-Ride evolved, the *Mercury* reflected, but the major problem—oversubscription— had been beyond any power to rectify. From the start the scheme had been a political compromise to limit fleet size. Demand had been grossly miscalculated; instead of 10,000 riders in two years, it had reached 7,000 in just six months.

Initially bought to spell the Twin Coaches in Dial-a-Ride service, 20 Plymouth Voyager vans were pressed into use on lightly patronized regular routes after Dial-a-Ride's demise. Seen here on December 29, 1975, is VP-24 departing the Sunnyvale Community Center terminus of midday-only routes 98 and 99.   (Jack Perry)

Ridership had declined on the arterial routes. Maintenance was expensive and time-consuming. The 90 buses allotted for Dial-a-Ride could not handle the load. The experiment was "a victim of its own success," the newspaper concluded, "a victim of too much demand with too few resources, a victim of the politics that spawned it."

5. Voters Approve Transit Tax

The demise of Dial-a-Ride was not only embarrassing to transit officials but posed many new problems including maintenance of Twin Coaches required to work arterials for which they were not designed. The district had now received $3.7 million in Federal funds to buy bus benches and finish their 10.7-acre North County coach yard at L'Avenida and Macon Avenues, Mountain View. Completing that yard would add maintenance bays, shorten runs, and relieve congestion at San Jose. Thirty-five more maintenance people were employed. Twenty used GMC coaches were leased for a year from the Sacramento Regional Transit Authority to augment the district fleet.

Other work was meanwhile under way. In May 1975 the supervisors approved the first 18 months of a second major study—a $990,000 Phase II corridor evaluation by ABAG and the Metropolitan Transportation Commission into the social, environmental, economic, and land-use impacts of a Santa Clara Valley rapid transit system. The consultants were also asked to conduct preliminary engineering leading to construction of a "starter segment" or test track. Postponed until November, however, was a scheduled May 27 countywide election authorizing a new ½¢ sales tax to support County Transit.

The need was there but the political climate wrong, claimed the supervisors, coming so close on the heels of Dial-a-Ride. In July they again postponed the election, drawing complaints from the Metropolitan Transportation Commission that the county was attempting a "free ride" in transit. "We've been after them for at least two years," protested MTC Chairman John C. Beckett. Transit Chairman Sig Sanchez, citing "a total lack of enthusiasm" for the November election, responded that it would be foolish to try "knowing full well we're going to lose."

Eventually the supervisors selected March 2, 1976, for the special ballot, eliciting this caution from the *Mercury*: "They have a tremendous educational task ahead of them. It should be clear by now that local tax elections fare badly where the voters are apathetic or downright hostile. At the same time, people will vote tax money to meet what they believe are genuine needs. Adequate public transit is a genuine need in Santa Clara County; the people will buy it—if they are convinced they will get what they are being asked to pay for. It is just here that the...supervisors must make a concerted and effective effort."

That summer DeLeuw-Cather, reporting results of their first-phase study, recommended building 140 miles of automated, elevated, medium-capacity rapid transit lines supported by a vast bus feeder system, at a cost of about $2.4 billion. The study found that no practical form of public transit could draw 30% of all trips but that more than a third of the rush-hour commute trips probably could be accommodated by cars resembling those of BART but smaller. Freeway expansion to meet the same travel demand would cost $2.5 billion but offer none of the environmental or energy-saving benefits of rail. They estimated that automated rail could save commuters from $20 to $70 million a year in the long run.

However exciting the prospect, the costs staggered even the staunchest transit supporters, especially after Pott reported that most funds under the $11.8 billion Urban Mass Transportation Act of 1974 had already been allocated and that the county did not appear to be in line even for the remaining crumbs. Thus, it would take new legislation to get more aid.

Amidst bitter criticism of the study, studies in general, and the lack of Federal funds, the supervisors accepted the DeLeuw-Cather report but voted to shelve medium-capacity transit. This drew cries of mismanagement from a community preconditioned to accept arterial/personalized transit and space-age technology (one widely circulated County Transit advertisement had shown the nose of a BART car with the words, "Guess who is coming?"). Santa Clara County was famous for its technology. It had not seemed unreasonable that workers who built Polaris missiles and spy satellites and digital watches could ride into the future on mass transit that not only equalled but also improved on the automobile.

Pott, whose Washington sources had since told him that Federal authorities now favored light rail (trolley) systems over medium or heavy systems such as BART, tried to quiet the troubled waters. "It's going to be years before a start can be made," he insisted, "but if we don't decide some things as to what we want in this county, we can't even ask." The county was still dedicated to rail, he declared. The apparent unavailability of heavy Federal funding of transit for at least the next five years hadn't materially changed its options for the future. "The only options are to stagnate or to proceed. We can only choose how, not if, to proceed."

In October 1975 the supervisors adopted plans to deploy a 516-bus fleet in a massive countywide grid: 46 lines with 1,300 route miles crisscrossing the county's urbanized area at peak hours. They estimated that only half the $20 million annual revenue to be raised by the county sales tax, if passed, would be needed to operate the expanded fleet, leaving the remainder available for rail. On this basis they asked DeLeuw-Cather to conduct a $100,000 light rail corridor evaluation study due December 1976, drawing another angry blast from MTC Chairman John Beckett. The commission would urge Federal officials not to fund any South Bay rail system until its countywide rail needs assessment was completed, he told the *San Jose News*, branding county estimates as wrong. A report by state legislative analyst A. Alan Post had confirmed MTC's own studies, he said, that it would take $18 million to run the 516-bus fleet, and the remaining $2 million should be held in reserve. Thus, Beckett concluded, if any rail system were to be built in the county, alternate funds would have to be found.

By January 1976 the transit tax campaign was in full swing. Voters were told that, without local revenues, the district would be unable to match state TDA funds, losing millions of dollars a year. Farebox revenues wouldn't come close to supporting fleet operations; the district would be $19 million short in six years operating just 216 buses. Calling the referendum a "do-or-die measure," Pott said that if it failed he would have no choice but to submit a 1976-77 budget aimed at an orderly shutdown of bus operations.

Most doubts seemed to have been assuaged when the voters went to the polls March 2 to determine the fate of County Transit. "Transit Tax Wins Voters' Go-Ahead," announced the *Mercury* in banner headlines the following morning. A simple majority had been needed for passage. From the count it was determined that a 30% voter turnout had produced a 55.3% approval—67,550 aye, 54,403 nay—ensuring that the agency would stay in business and expand.

Later that month Walter Kudlick, vice president of DeLeuw-Cather, cited early results of his firm's light rail corridor evaluation study. The corridor with the greatest potential was the S. P. Vasona Branch line from Vasona Junction near Los Gatos to downtown San Jose. Next came the Guadalupe corridor from Edenvale (Southeast San Jose) to downtown San Jose, a route from Cupertino to Vasona Junction, and one eastward from Vasona Junction to the IBM facility near Edenvale. Some

50,000 jobs—10% of the county total—were within a mile of these corridors, Kudlick announced. Another 80,000 jobs—16% of the total—were accessible via S. P. peninsula service from San Jose to Palo Alto. He estimated that 25 to 50% of the potential peak-hour riders in all the study corridors would finish their trips using the S. P. "Thus, patronage potential is greatly dependent on the ease of transfer to the Southern Pacific peninsula route and the quality and cost of service offered on that line."

6. The October Breakdown

The final results were available in August 1976. The five corridors had been chosen, said DeLeuw-Cather, because they were either existing rail lines or rights of way for proposed freeways. The best starter segment, they said, would be the corridor linking downtown San Jose with Edenvale, with a branch westward from Edenvale to the Oakridge Mall shopping plaza, Pearl Avenue at Blossom Hill Road. The estimated cost was $170 million in inflated dollars of 1981, the earliest anticipated start date.

There were a couple of hitches. Although light rail was found marginally feasible in each corridor, ridership would finally depend on land-use planning to cluster apartments and industry along these corridors; the county had no official land-use policy. Also, UMTA later refused to accept this study as a basis for applying for Federal funds. Local officials claimed that the Feds had switched signals. Said Supervisor Dom Cortese: "We were relying on UMTA directives that light rail money would be available."

In March 1977, following local assurances from Transportation Secretary William T. Coleman Jr. that more Federal money would be available for transit, came a report by Project Manager Robert Harrison on the Phase II Santa Clara Valley corridor evaluation study by ABAG and the Metropolitan Transportation Commission. Among its alternatives, appropriate for 1.6 million residents in 1990, was a 55-mile light rail network which, when supported by 1,500 buses, offered the highest return on projected investment. The report warned against expanding the highway system beyond the 36% already planned.

The operating focus had meanwhile switched to equipment and maintenance. In May 1976 Federal authorities approved a $4.2-million capital grant for 80% of the costs to replace the 78 ancient diesels, buy fareboxes and radios for the vehicles, and remodel the San Carlos Street and South County bus barns. On October 5 the supervisors awarded a $5.38 million bus contract to Gillig Corporation, Hayward, for 81 new units: propane-powered 35-footers valued at $72,000 each, scheduled to start arriving the following summer.

Pott described Gillig as a long-time "first-line" manufacturer of school buses whose products he termed "quality work." In July the district hired a consulting firm to design a new transit center and repair facility on property that was once part of the east grounds of Agnews State Hospital in North San Jose, bought by the county after it was declared surplus by the state. That month it also filed application for $8 million more in Federal funds to expand the bus fleet by 100 vehicles. Federal approval came in April, at which time the supervisors contracted to buy buses, radios, fareboxes, and support vehicles and purchase land on West San Carlos Street for employee parking. Gillig again got the award, boosting its commitment to 181 units. It now seemed that plans to expand the bus fleet, . made possible by the sales tax measure, would solve the district's problems.

This was not to be, however. For many long months the

The Southern Pacific's San Francisco–San Jose rail commute line was to figure prominently in transit plans for the Santa Clara Valley that were made in the 1970s. Two trains of modern double-decker coaches are shown at the Fourth and Townsend depot in San Francisco, ready for the trip to San Jose.
(Southern Pacific photo by Bill Robertson)

overtaxed system had been operating on borrowed time, teetering precariously between scheduling requirements and maintenance needs. The strains were showing. Too many coaches were running too many hours, straining the maintenance staff. Often the crews were shorthanded; always they had to work in cramped facilities. Reliability suffered. The near-term solution was a temporary service cutback, which for political reasons the district refused to consider. Forced to choose between preventive and corrective maintenance, the crews had to get the buses back on the road, almost guaranteeing further breakdowns.

By July 1977 the breakdown figures—failures to show up for service or to maintain regular schedules—had become ominous. Facing a mounting crisis, the supervisors, still hoping that delivery of the new Gillig coaches would solve their problems, chose to add leased vans and coaches to the fleet rather than reduce services, putting more pressure on the maintenance people. Pott took action, hiring as his fleet operations officer Peter Shambora, a low-key Navy aviation maintenance specialist who had solid experience and lots of plans but was alarmed about what he saw in San Jose. As Pott later recalled, "When I hired Pete Shambora he came to me and said he could respond to the politics or fix the situation but not both. 'I'll take the heat,' I told him. 'You fix the system.' "

Shambora set reliability as his top priority. His approach was unglamorous and deliberate. He instituted a computerized tracking system for problem parts and vehicles, launched an

effort to expand the 129-man work force, and sent his managers and crews back to school. Shambora got full support from the district. The question was whether he could work a turnabout before the roof caved in.

In August the first Gilligs arrived: handsome coaches but with too many mechanical and electrical faults to put them immediately to work. These were first-of-a-kind coaches of unproved design and reliability. Several were rejected. Then in October came a surprise inspection by the California Highway Patrol that turned into a disaster for County Transit. Forty-seven buses were cited for 276 violations. Thirty-six were red-tagged, which meant they had to stay in the garage until fixed. The CHP threatened to sue if the county didn't improve its maintenance.

Service was suspended on some routes and curtailed on others. Angry riders found themselves without transportation or delayed, often for hours, in reaching their destinations. They demanded to know what had gone wrong.

On paper, declared the *Mercury*, County Transit had 216 buses plus a small array of maxivans. Really, 80 of the coaches were 35-foot-long diesel-powered GMC coaches, of which a sizeable number no longer ran. The rest were 30-foot propane-burning Twin Coaches acquired in 1974 to operate Dial-a-Ride. Three of the 134 Twins had been wrecked, including one that had been hijacked in 1976 and gone through a railing at the Highway 17-101 interchange. "Rarely are more than 170 buses in service on any given day because of breakdowns," it declared.

Supervisor Rod Diridon confirmed this report, adding that the district's barn on West San Carlos Street "was built 30 years ago to handle 60 buses, and we're still using it to dispatch and maintain 140 buses, and that's a physical impossibility." He noted that the district had planned to have its new coaches in service by now, but Federal authorities had delayed approving the capital grants.

"We're about six months behind," he told the *Mercury*. "The fleet is falling apart under us, and we're just trying to hold on until the new buses arrive and new maintenance facilities are completed." County Transit was then leasing 30 vehicles, planned to lease 25 more, and hoped to lease others, he said. "We've searched all over for buses to lease and just can't find them."

Fifteen of 25 yellow 16-passenger Dodge maxivans leased from Pinetree Transportation, of Long Beach, went into service October 24, offering free rides because their fareboxes hadn't been installed. These vans, obtained for six months at $400 per month each, were used mainly around Palo Alto. In San Jose the bleak bus situation persisted. October 25 brought word that 54 of 169 runs had been cancelled for lack of buses. Peak deployment the following day found 181 buses serving 39 routes, according to Mike Aro, head of scheduling for County Transit. None of the district's routes was without service now, he said, though the wait time was sometimes 60 to 90 minutes.

District officials reported November 1 that construction was now proceeding well on their new bus maintenance terminal in Agnews. The following day they announced substantial progress on their "crash" plan to ensure the safety of County Transit buses, which they said now looked good. Twenty-two new maintenance workers and inspectors had been hired. It was hoped that the 25 leased maxivans would take up the slack in bus service while about 30% of the larger coaches were being overhauled. Soon to arrive, too, would be the propane-powered Gilligs: 81 replacement units by spring and the balance soon after. The old GMC coaches would be scrapped after delivery of the replacement units and refurbishing of the Twin Coaches, which had literally been run into the ground.

The October shutdown also fired up another smouldering controversy: the choice of propane over diesel engines. Critics led by the *ad hoc* Council for Public Transit renewed their protests that propane engines required much more maintenance, limited the field of bidders, and posed serious safety problems. They demanded that County Transit not buy any more propane buses and retrofit those on hand.

District officials agreed that propane had limited the bidders but defended it as safe and environmentally sound. The maintenance of propane vehicles should be about the same as gasoline or diesel vehicles, they stated. Also, to change fuel systems now would cost a lot of money.

In a draft report November 1, the County Transportation Safety Commission found no evidence to support charges by the *ad hoc* group that the propane fuel used in district vehicles was unsafe. On the contrary, it said, propane might be even safer than diesel or gasoline because its pressurized fuel tanks were sturdier than standard tanks. The commission suggested, however, that the supervisors might want to further investigate

Leased equipment that arrived in the fall of 1977 included 25 Dodge Sportsman Maxiwagons from Pinetree Transportation Company, Long Beach, and 20 GM model TDH-4801 coaches from the Southern California Rapid Transit District's 2300 series. (Jack Perry)

the effects on the overall fleet readiness of maintaining the propane equipment.

Analysis of the ridership figures confirmed the damage done by the summer breakdowns and the October shutdown. Two items stood out: in July, ridership had fallen below that for the same period in 1976 and stayed below, and while 1977 had followed the same pattern of peaks and valleys as in previous years, the seasonal declines since midsummer had been steeper than usual. The system had carried only about 978,000 riders in October 1977 compared with more than a million in October 1976. Current projections now foresaw only 5.48 million for July-December 1977 compared with 5.66 million for the same period in 1976.

In the end, it was the multiplicity of failures that cost Pott his job. Late in October came word that Supervisor Geraldine Steinberg had now joined colleagues Diridon and Dan McCorquodale in opposing Pott. Diridon and McCorquodale, it was reported, had sought unsuccessfully to oust Pott two years earlier after the Dial-a-Ride fiasco. No formal vote had been taken, but action would soon be forthcoming.

On November 22 County Executive William M. Siegel announced that he had transferred Pott to unspecified duties in the county executive's office effective December 1. Siegel also reported he was prepared to ask the transit board for $18,000 to run a nationwide search for Pott's replacement. Until then, Charles Battersby, assistant transportation agency director, would be acting head.

For Pott, it marked the end of an 18-year association with Santa Clara Valley transit. His firing remained a hot issue in the local press for several weeks. Some blamed him for mismanagement during the district's crucial early years. Others saw him as a political tool for the supervisors. He was lauded for his achievements and criticized for his mistakes, among them, it was said, one of the district's most serious blunders: buying the Gillig coaches. Promoted as safe and efficient, they continued to have such problems as poor suspension, improperly fitting windshields, cracked mounting brackets, and premature tail light failures.

Pott, who wryly observed that the volume of service complaints had dried up significantly since his ouster, stayed on as an assistant county executive until the following July, when he announced plans to start work in mid-August as city engineer for Long Beach, California. Reportedly he had been recruited by Long Beach City Manager John Dever, formerly at Sunnyvale. Pott said he would welcome the challenge of his new post.

7. A Time of Recovery

Even now there were evidences of a turnaround in the fortunes of County Transit. To maintain service, nine buses were leased from San Diego and 20 from the Southern California Rapid Transit District, which went into service dressed in their original colors. Shambora's efforts to enlarge and train the maintenance force had also borne fruit; one year saw an expansion from 129 to 206 workers who logged 10,000 hours of training. The computer tracking system was working; Shambora could scan a printout to determine if Coach 641 needed a brake job. McCorquodale, who had headed the transit board during its troubled year, was optimistic. "Overall," he said, "the transit situation is not as bad as it looks. We've begun to mature, tying it in with the cities. We've come to the point where any major project must provide for public transit."

There was no immediate turnaround in ridership, which was down 40,000 in December compared with the previous year. "If you extend the present trendline there won't be any riders at all by August," observed Diridon whimsically. It was noted, also,

that there were lots of diehards who continued frequenting the buses, mostly by choice. District officials were told early in March that riders were slowly returning. That was confirmed April 9 with news of an upswing to 1.089 million passengers the previous month.

In January Diridon, co-owner of Decision Research Corporation and, at 38, the youngest and newest county supervisor, had been sworn in as board chairman replacing Steinberg, who moved on to head up the transit board. That brought to the supervisors leadership from a staunch rail enthusiast who endorsed the planning process and gave it firm voice. In the next few months Diridon would also serve in several other key transit posts: presidency of ABAG, national chairmanship of the National Association of the Counties Public Transportation Committee, chairmanship of the County Supervisors Association Transportation and Public Works Committee, chairmanship of the County Transit board, and eventually membership on the Federal Aid to Urban Systems Advisory Committee to the State Transportation Commission.

Interviewed by the *San Jose Sun* in February, Diridon amplified his views. "At least 25 of the nation's metropolitan areas have or are planning some sort of light rail system using modern vehicles," he declared, urging that Santa Clara's name be added to the list. "Why shouldn't we? A light rail vehicle carries four times the number of people as a packed bus, three times as quickly. That gives us 12 times the commute productivity for only about two-thirds the cost."

While the initial investment in light rail required higher capital costs than an expanded bus fleet, Diridon observed, the difference in operating costs made it more attractive in the long run. "We may pay $500,000 each for new vehicles, but they have a design life of 40 years. So you amortize that expense over the whole period. They just don't wear out like buses. They're electrically powered; you don't have to change the oil, and steel wheels against the steel rails give very good wear characteristics."

Mercury writer Rob Elder was less optimistic about the chances for light rail. As regards the county financing plan, he observed, some $23.1 million in local money was certain—$13 million from the sales tax, $9.6 million from the county gas tax diversion, and $500,000 from TDA funds—to support a $78.6 million Federal grant that now seemed questionable. The new ABAG-MTC study was costing the county $275,000 more.

"Even if it recommends light rail," Elder continued, "no Federal money is now available. It's a problem of county priority versus those of other areas, and Santa Clara is a low-density county. Even if Federal money becomes available, UMTA is not likely to fund a rail system that isn't supported by comprehensive land-use planning. We have no coordinated countywide plan, though we may be moving toward one. Finally, old-fashioned trolley cars may have been cheap, but the new light rail vehicle (LRV) built by Boeing for San Francisco and Boston costs about $500,000 to $600,000 per car. Also, there are bugs in the technology of the new space-age streetcars. A cynical view would be that Federal officials led the Santa Clara County government down a primrose path, and that the county officials lured the public along with them, into a dead end they're not sure how to get out of."

Another important issue had meanwhile emerged: the wisdom of having the county supervisors continue as the transit bosses. In March 1978 a county grand jury transit committee urged that a competent, single-purpose board be named to run County Transit, relieving the supervisors of that duty. The *Mercury* initially found merit in the proposal, which was endorsed by the Santa Clara City Council and by John Beckett, reigning chairman of the Metropolitan Transportation Commission. The County Transportation Commission vascillated a bit, then agreed that the supervisors should no longer wear two hats.

Eventually the issue prompted an inquiry by three state senators to consider whether legislation should be introduced to change the structure of County Transit. Hearings were held locally. San Jose Councilman Jim Self observed that the supervisors had long ignored the Transportation Commission's recommendations on Dial-a-Ride, bus size, and choice of fuel. Transit workers rapped district operations and expressed their desire to see a new district formed with representation from the riders and from the transit union.

Others, however, supported the existing plan. Cupertino mayor Jim Jackson said the most valid criticism might be that the supervisors had "tried to do too much, too fast, with too little professional help." Diridon urged the senators not to change the structure, saying it would "disrupt" transit operations at a time when they just were beginning to function well. The *Mercury* echoed this sentiment, citing recent evidence of improvement and urging the legislators to "give transit a chance." On balance, the senators chose not to press for an immediate restructuring.

District officials had now conducted a public hearing to consider a $21.2 million Federal grant application to buy 155 buses, 210 fareboxes, 245 mobile radios, destination signs, and support equipment including cars, vans, trucks, special maintenance equipment, and spare bus parts. That was in December

1977. In January came an agreement with UMTA to equip the district's 81 Gillig buses with passenger lifts and wheelchair restraining devices. The estimated cost was $952,000, covered 80% by Federal funds.

That same month Battersby told the supervisors that County Transit buses were still breaking down about every 896 miles compared with 14,000 to 17,000 miles for other Bay Area agencies. One-week totals for December had shown that the district's 53 GMC coaches, ticketed for phase-out, encountered schedule delays every 696 miles. That figure climbed to 922 miles when only mechanical breakdowns were counted. The Twin Coaches had failed every 811 miles and the four FMC buses for the handicapped every 444 miles. The district's 46 vans had failed every 1,228 miles. The Gilligs, of which only 16 of 181 were on hand, with deliveries running about four months late, had encountered major problems every 2,643 miles. These coaches, now undergoing shakedown, had experienced schedule delays every 622 miles if all the minor problems were included using the normal criteria. One of the Gilligs—No. 601, the prototype—had broken down so often, it was said, that Battersby ordered it banished forever from his sight. The shop crew renumbered it 600. To this day there's no 601 in the County Transit fleet.

On January 23 the supervisors took firm action, returning all

County Transit's two orders totaling 133 Gillig/Neoplan 35-passenger buses were the largest placed by any operator for this short-lived production model, which combined a U.S. power train with German coachwork. It was also the District's last fling with propane fuel before a policy change that led to cancellation of 50 more Gilligs. Shown here on September 24, 1978, is Gillig coach 656 at Eastridge Shopping Center, also designated Hillview on early County Transit headsigns.

(Jack Perry)

the Gilligs thus far delivered and telling the company they would accept no more defective units. They also authorized Battersby to lease 25 more buses if such could be found. Battersby assured them that he'd be "back in a flash" if he found more than 25. The supervisors had recently authorized him to lease 20 other buses and several small vans, he said, adding that he hoped to eliminate as many of the vans as possible because they weren't suitable for transit purposes.

Gillig was sternly told that no more propane-powered Gillig buses would be accepted until recurring mechanical defects were corrected. The problems had ranged from air conditioning failures to required enlargement and rewiring of the electrical system.

On February 5 Dennis Howard, Gillig's newly installed president, told the supervisors he was highly confident that his firm would meet its commitments. "The 81st coach will arrive by the end of May," he said, noting that he knew of county dissatisfaction over the quality of units delivered thus far under the 81-bus contract. He admitted they had experienced major faults including suspension, throttle, and leakage problems. The company had added shifts and diverted manpower from other projects to meet the county delivery schedules, he said, observing that Gillig had lost $3,000 to $5,000 on every $72,000 bus returned by the county.

The district's decision not to depend solely on propane had satisfied the *Mercury* but not the County Transportation Commission or the Council for Public Transit. In the past four months there had been three fires involving propane-powered Twin Coaches: one December 1, another January 23 on State Highway 85 near Fremont Avenue that gutted the vehicle, and still another February 3 in Los Altos Hills. Now, citing a recent propane tank explosion in Tennessee that had killed several people and injured some 50 others, the Council for Public Transit demanded in March that U. S. authorities suspend all Federal funding until the district stopped using propane. A spokesman announced that loaded Twin Coaches carried 92 gallons and loaded Gilligs 132 gallons, calling the vehicles "rolling propane bombs."

Battersby ordered an investigation. Even while it was proceeding, another Twin Coach was destroyed by fire on Interstate 280 in North San Jose. That was March 20. The engine compartment of yet another burned six days later on Wolfe Road in Sunnyvale, prompting an urgent plea from the Transportation Commission for the district to phase out the Twin Coaches.

On March 29, reporting the results of his probe, Battersby listed four likely causes of the blazes: inadequate engine cooling, combustible material in the engine compartments, leaking oil that ignited on contact with the hot exhaust pipes or manifold, and distributors that could not be properly set for propane, causing the engine exhaust manifolds to overheat at sustained high speeds. The district had limited the Twin Coaches to maximum speeds of 40 mph and banned them from freeways and expressways. Although the problem was not the fuel but rather the basic power train design, he said, the district had decided to seek emergency replacement of the buses.

Another Twin Coach caught fire April 4 in Saratoga. It was only the quick action of driver Lois Cortese that saved this vehicle, the first to escape without serious damage.

On April 20, in a letter to U. S. Transportation Secretary Brock Adams, the Council for Public Transit cautioned that "any fires, loss of property, injuries, and loss of life due to or caused by continued use of the explosive fuel propane by the Santa Clara County Transit District will be on your head for your failure to address our long-festering danger." Six weeks later a local attorney filed a petition with the California Supreme Court demanding an immediate ban on propane buses by reason of public safety.

That was too much for the *San Jose News*, which advised that a total ban would be impractical and hopelessly cripple local transit. "The county supervisors have wisely voted to end additional purchases of propane buses. However, the chief reason for this decision was the unreliability of the propane buses, not public safety."

8. Graebner Heads County Transit

In late March, also, came news that Pott's successor had been selected: James H. Graebner, 37, general manager of the Rhode Island Public Transit Authority, chosen over six other finalists during a two-month talent search by a San Francisco firm. He would take over his new duties in about three months. Praised as competent and creative, he had come to Rhode Island in 1975 when an aging, deteriorating transit system was obtaining some new equipment and the state was getting a new governor and a new transportation administration, according to Peter Stowell, Boston regional administrator for UMTA.

Under Graebner's direction the Rhode Island system had established new routes, vigorously advertised, and increased its ridership by 7%. Stowell, who was familiar with County Transit's political and technical problems and also knew some of the other finalists, said the new chief was "head and shoulders above the others in terms of what you want out there."

The new chief was a tweedy, pipe-smoking, prematurely gray man with an encyclopedic knowledge of transit. The son of a business school dean, he had grown up in various Eastern cities, attended high school outside Philadelphia, and graduated from Valparaiso University in Indiana. His first transportation job had been with Pullman, in Chicago, where he helped design and sell rapid transit cars. He had then moved through industrial jobs in Pittsburgh and Cleveland to become operations manager for the fledgling public transit system in Denver. Four years later he had been named manager of the Rhode Island system.

On June 12 Graebner was officially welcomed by the supervisors, who also took that occasion to commend Battersby for his months of interim leadership. "He gets high marks from the transit brass for bringing the county through a difficult period," commented Lou Montini, deputy director for transportation development. "He did a hell of a job."

Graebner set out first to tackle the two major equipment problems: the Gilligs and the Twin Coaches. Maintenance of the former was still excessive, to the detriment of the rest of the fleet. If maintenance crews were diverted to provide extra care for the Gilligs, they had to be taken away from the Twin Coaches, which the Gilligs were supposed to replace because the Twins were a maintenance headache.

All 81 Gilligs from the first order were on hand by July. The district had hoped to run them 15,000 to 20,000 miles between major breakdowns; however, they had averaged only 6,742 miles. Diridon had meanwhile demanded replacement of the troublesome Twins, which he called "abominable." Graebner agreed, urging a mix of small and large diesels with which the County Transportation Commission heartily agreed.

That same month a plum dropped into his lap. On July 12 AC Transit had been ready to receive 66 new General Motors RTS-2 coaches without wheelchair lifts when handicapped riders staged a widely publicized wheelchair blockade in San Francisco's Transbay Terminal, halting both AC and Muni vehicles and snarling the evening commute. The East Bay agency had responded by postponing delivery of the new buses, which were sitting in a Pontiac, Michigan, parking lot.

Two days later Graebner reported good prospects for buying or leasing them. Local handicapped groups endorsed the purchase. The supervisors promptly authorized negotiations. In August they bought the 47-passenger diesel-powered vehicles for $107,000 each, declaring that deliveries would begin shortly.

On August 14 the supervisors announced approval of a $13 million Federal grant to buy 134 more coaches to replace the Twins. Of these, 74 units would be 45-footers costing $120,000 each and the others 35-footers costing $90,000. All would be equipped with air conditioning and wheelchair lifts. In October both requests—the 134 new buses plus those purchased in August—were folded into a $21.9-million Federal grant to be matched by some $5.48 million from the district. "This grant is for 134 expansion coaches and 66 replacements," explained Montini, who said the district would submit other applications for more vehicles. Ultimately another 300 buses would be added to expand the fleet to 516 vehicles, he said.

There were two other important Federal grants during this period. One led to a $6.2 million contract with GM in January 1979 for 50 new rear-lift buses, approved with some reluctance because county guidelines called for front lifts but Federal standards, which didn't distinguish, required the award to go to the lowest bidder. Flxible's bid for front-lift coaches had been only $17,000 higher.

The other, approved in February, was $8 million for a new 250-coach terminal on Tully Road between Seventh and Tenth Streets, opposite the County Fairgrounds. That terminal, in San Jose's south-central industrial area, would replace the antiquated West San Carlos Street facility. There were mild local protests but none to compare with the previous year's ruckus over a proposed West Valley terminal, defeated by neighborhood complaints. The cost of the new facility was expected to be approximately $11 million, the local share coming from county tax revenues. Some $1.6 million would go for property acquisition. Construction work was also nearing completion on the district's new terminal and major repair facility near Agnews State Hospital in North San Jose.

A few more Gilligs had now arrived as part of the next 50-bus increment, constituting the first genuine additions to the fleet in four years. District officials had also leased 74 coaches from other cities including 56 used New Jersey buses, at Graebner's request, at $620 per month each. These 15-year-old coaches needed work, he said, but his efforts to get delivery on new equipment for immediate needs had been thwarted by heavy nationwide demands.

With these and the 66 buses rejected by AC Transit, the district could eliminate all but 40 or 50 Twins, some of which would still be used in South County Dial-a-Ride service and on arterials running through mostly residential neighborhoods.

January 1979 marked the beginning of three new express bus lines: route 2 from downtown San Jose to the Stanford Industrial Park, route 4 from Berryessa to Stanford, and Express 68 (later route 12) from Gilroy through downtown San Jose to Trimble Road. These three lines joined "Express One," inaugurated in January 1977 from southwest San Jose to Stanford. The cost for premium service was 50¢ each way compared with 25¢ for regular service; it was well received. That same month the supervisors approved $103,000 for a park-and-ride facility at Tilton Avenue and Santa Teresa Boulevard, near Morgan Hill, which opened in February with space for 23 vehicles. Parking was free. The new facility was served by the 68 Local and 68 Express lines to San Jose.

Ridership had also staged a triumphant comeback. The July count was 1.03 million, swelling to more than 1.2 million in August and September. October saw a record 1.3 million, which declined somewhat in November and December but still produced 13.3 million for 1978, up 17% from the previous year. By April 1979 the average weekday count had reached 67,000, up 22% in just one month. In July the monthly ridership topped 1.53 million, nearly half again as large as in 1978. The big ques-

tion now was whether the district fleet of 366 coaches could stand up to the growing demand.

Enthusiasm for light rail had likewise swelled, partly because of County Transit's recent successes but mainly because of a new Federal transit package fashioned by compromise, concession, and some arm-twisting in final hours of the 95th Congress: the Surface Transportation Act of 1978. If the pieces fell together, it was reported, the county would receive nearly double the Federal transit support it used to—and also have a shot at special funds earmarked for projects such as light rail. It was now confirmed that UMTA was steering away from heavy systems like BART and the Washington Metro, a course set in part by a presidential directive to eliminate "grossly overdesigned" transit systems. The act contained dollars for S. P. peninsula commuter service, and potentially, for a downtown San Jose transportation center with light rail. "It's a signal we can move ahead," Graebner declared.

Findings of the ABAG-MTC Santa Clara Valley corridor evaluation study had now been evaluated, and local officials focused attention on the route thought to have the greatest potential: a 10-mile starter segment along the unfinished Guadalupe Freeway (State Highway 87) from downtown San Jose to Oakridge Mall at Blossom Hill Road, extending southward into the Almaden Valley and eastward along the unfinished West Valley Freeway (State Highway 85) to Edenvale. One advantage, Graebner observed, was that the right of way, including the freeway corridors, was already 90% publicly owned. "It's not like we have to go out and gouge a path through an established area," he said. Moreover, the county was far down the state priority list for completing the Guadalupe and West Valley freeways. If properly connected with S. P. rail service in downtown San Jose, the ABAG-MTC study suggested, the starter segment might carry 20,000 riders daily and up to 60,000 daily if the county seriously pursued land-use policies to mix residential and industrial development. By 1990, 25 to 30 light rail vehicles could be carrying 30,000 riders daily, possibly 60,000. At the outset construction would run $8 to 10 million a mile in 1978 dollars, but by the midpoint of construction—five or six years hence—inflation would have boosted this by as much as 50%. The total projected cost was $130-150 million.

The next step was to open the corridor evaluation study for public review and, through the County Transportation Commission, scrutiny by the South Bay communities. "Light rail: it's worth a new look," declared the *Mercury*, but Santa Clara City Councilman Gary Hansen, insisting that mixing housing with industry would not work, called the study "the greatest boondoggle I've ever seen during my time on the council."

Diridon, in talking to the Santa Clara city council, had meanwhile backed extension of the Edenvale-San Jose trolley line to Marriott Industrial Park, which he called "a natural." State Assemblywoman Leona Egeland had introduced a bill opening the way for extending S. P. commuter service to South San Jose, perhaps to Gilroy. Lawrence Dahms, director of the ABAG-MTC study, claimed he would have been "a little surprised" if its recommendations came about exactly as written. "The report is professionally defensible," said Dahms, executive director of the MTC, "but we are bound to learn something else along the way."

In February 1979 came word that two more cities had endorsed the study, bringing to eight the number of approvals. Five hadn't acted, one (Gilroy) had voted against it, and one hadn't taken a stand. On March 19 the supervisors authorized a $500,000 third study into whether light rail to downtown San Jose would be worth the cost. Federal rules required this study before UMTA would consider engineering and construction funds. "The Feds need more convincing to grant funds for light rail," declared a "well-informed" UMTA source. "The county

County Transit's first advanced-design buses came as a windfall when AC Transit of Oakland chose not to take delivery of 66 GM 40-foot RTS-2 models. Shown here on El Camino Real at Wolfe Road on November 24, 1978, is coach 1007.   (Jack Perry)'

is on right track toward building a light rail line, but it isn't far enough along for the Federal government to say if it will pay for it.''

Diridon rated the light rail chances good because recommendations of the ABAG-MTC transportation study had survived the test of political fire, opening the door for Federal funds. If the project passed its next crucial test, he said, the starter segment could be under construction by the mid-1980s and open before 1990.

While the general climate was favorable, there were problems, among them thievery, violence, and a growing volume of service complaints. Seven transit employees—five men and two women, all San Jose residents—were arrested early in August 1978 for investigation of the theft of more than $130,000 in coins from bus fareboxes. Five more were subsequently booked. Charges ranged from stealing money and property (tires and automotive parts) to dealing in drugs. Searches of some of the suspects' homes turned up cash and narcotics. Eight of the employees pleaded guilty. Charges against the other four were eventually dropped.

The thefts spurred heightened security and new procedures for handling cash from the fareboxes, said Frank Lara, the district marketing director. In January the supervisors authorized a new security program aimed at preventing future thefts: hiring a security coordinator, fencing work areas at district yards, restricting access, installing television monitors, and acquiring new farebox equipment. UMTA funds would be sought for this program, they declared.

As elsewhere in the South Bay, violence and vandalism relative to County Transit had also taken a sharp upswing, aimed at riders and drivers alike. In July 1978 a man wounded in a knife attack on a district coach died in a local hospital. October brought news that young toughs, in gangs of up to 50 youths, were plaguing the city center, focusing their attention on Santa Clara Street between First and Second Streets where crosstown buses met on scheduled runs, delivering passengers from outlying districts and picking up outbound riders. There was word of attacks, muggings, and harrassments downtown and elsewhere.

An aroused and fearful public demanded better protection. The security system was far too lax. In July Lara reported that the number of incidents had been declining since May, when the district had hired four firms to patrol the bus yards and authorized a $200,000 annual contract with a security service to protect the buses and riders. The system was now designed so that drivers could radio to nearby security cars when help was needed. Lara said the district hoped to have radios in all coaches by summer's end.

The number of service complaints had likewise risen dramatically, mainly for skipped runs or outright failures of buses to make their appointed rounds. The cause, often lost among the complaints, was proliferating ridership plus maintenance problems, which wreaked havoc on the schedules. About 10% of the coaches were usually out of commission, including those awaiting engines and transmissions. Securing parts for the various equipment types was a burdensome chore. A work dispute with the transit union had prevented district officials from farming out the repairs on the 56 leased New Jersey buses, of which only five were running.

Graebner had explained that it took 60 weeks to obtain new buses and that used equipment, therefore, was the only available short-term option to expand the system. More buses required more repair facilities, he had said, and with present Federal and state planning restrictions, it was taking two years to get a new garage. The supervisors had approved his moves. On June 4, however, while he was away on a combined work trip and vacation in Colorado, they told County Executive William Siegel to draft plans to get the 51 idle New Jersey coaches rolling. Robert Scott, district operations manager, said that work was progressing but had been curtailed of late because of the increased ridership, which created more need to repair other vehicles. Dan McCorquodale complained that he hadn't seen or felt the sense of urgency the agency ought to have.

On June 6 Siegel, told that fleet downtime was now running 13.2%, called Graebner back from Colorado to answer the protests. Two days later the transit chief met with union officials to discuss ways to improve the system, reporting that they were still at odds about contracting for repairs on the New Jersey buses.

On June 13 Graebner suggested that County Transit buy the coaches, noting that even with repairs the district's cost amortized over their lifetime would be less from owning than from leasing: $441 versus $620 a month. He admitted that the repairs would be more expensive than originally believed but said the coaches would be more reliable in the long run than the Twins, the Gilligs, or even the RTS-2's. The supervisors then requested him personally to inspect the buses and arrange for their purchase. Eventually they were bought for $19,500 apiece. With repairs, the estimated total cost was more than $2 million.

What had been a mild wind of criticism against Graebner had now reached gale proportions. "Graebner calm in the eye of transit storm," declared the *Mercury* June 16. The supervisors had been peppering him with questions about fleet acquisitions, performance, and maintenance. He had taken the criticisms calmly, even admitting that many were legitimate. "I try to keep calm under pressure," he related. "It doesn't help much to shoot out in all directions. Rather than making charges and countercharges, what I need to do is get the job done." He was applauded for stimulating ridership and for leading County Transit out of its late 1977-early 1978 abyss of poor service. Yet he had not come to grips with several nagging problems, it was said. The district still had its troublesome Twins. Security at the central yard was lax. Morale was low, and there were still residual weaknesses in middle and lower management despite complaints by the transit union.

The following day McCorquodale said he would seek to replace the transit chief unless things got better. "Graebner says the buses haven't been repaired because a new service facility wasn't done on time," related the *Mercury*. "He says they've turned the corner. They've got the mechanics and the facilities. What they need is time. We hope he's right, that the time he's talking about isn't that much."

Meeting June 25, the supervisors denied a motion to dismiss Graebner and his top staff proposed by McCorquodale, who said the buses were still running late and the schedules were still inadequate. The percentage of lost service had now dropped from 13.2 to 3.8%, it was learned. Two days later the County Transportation Commission gave a unanimous vote of confidence to the embattled transit chief. Jim Self, a member of that body, said he was "appalled" at the board's unprofessional approach. "If you're going to fire Mr. Graebner, fire him," he declared, "but if you're not going to fire him, get off his back."

By July 10 the percentage of lost time had fallen to 2%. Ridership totals through June had shown an amazing 37.6% increase over previous-year figures, prompting Diridon to comment that patronage on County Transit buses was rising "50% faster than any other system in the country." It was now clear that the tran-

sit chief had weathered the storm, though 14.5% of the coaches reportedly were out of service in early September awaiting parts. A task force had been appointed to investigate this problem.

Two "horrendous days" in mid-September saw both the temperature and the number of bus breakdowns to soar to over 100. Some 75 to 80% of breakdowns had been caused by hot engines, Graebner related, many of them on propane-driven buses "which cannot tolerate heat." Almost in response, the engine of a propane-powered Gillig coach burst into flames a few days later. There were no injuries, but the coach was severely damaged.

There were a few more protests. Graebner finally urged the supervisors to "stop flogging a dead horse" over the maintenance issue. By year's end the fleet reliability, once 86% when ridership was going through the ceiling, now stood at 99.4% — "one of the finest in the nation," Diridon enthused.

9. Pointing Toward the Future

In August 1979, UMTA released about $8 million in Federal funds it had pledged eight months earlier to help complete the local fleet expansion. This money was part of its previous $21.9-million grant to pay for 200 new coaches. Specifications called for 40-foot, diesel-powered buses of an advanced design with wheelchair lifts. Graebner announced that either the Grumman-Flxible 870 or the General Motors RTS-2, of which the district was now operating 66, would be suitable, although he preferred the latter so as to build a base of similar equipment. The RTS-2 problems were being worked out, he said; those delivered to County Transit had been among the first, and they had improved. One problem was air conditioning. If it went out, the coach had to be pulled from service because the windows were sealed.

The contract for the 134 additional coaches went to bid in September. On January 28, having gained Federal approval, the supervisors accepted a bid of $19.7 million, at $135,000 per unit, from Grumman-Flxible. Two days later UMTA authorized 85 more coaches — making 219 in all — totaling about $33 million, of which the Federal share would be $25.6 million. Graebner was asked to arrange a contract for all 219 buses to be delivered in about a year. "With the entire order," he declared, "we'll have the coaches needed to meet our 516-bus goal." The fleet then numbered some 400 units, of which 300 were available for daily service. Completion by January 1981 of the new central district yard near the County Fairgrounds would be crucial to the fleet expansion. An architect was designing the new facility; the district was awaiting an additional $8 million Federal grant to help offset the $10 million construction cost.

The National Highway Traffic Safety Administration had earlier refused to make another probe of the propane bus fires, since investigations had already been made by UMTA, the National Transportation Safety Board, the Santa Clara County Fire Marshal's Office, and County Transit. None of these, it claimed, had turned up any evidence that bus fires anywhere in the U. S. were caused by or significantly fueled by propane. Where fires had occurred they apparently had been triggered by nonfuel components in or around the engine compartment.

On December 10, however, the supervisors voted to bring down the curtain on propane for county buses. At Graebner's urging they approved the conversion of four propane-powered Gilligs to diesel at a cost of $14,000 to $19,000 apiece. Diesels made the buses more reliable, Graebner said, and meant more savings in the long run. The propane engines averaged only 3.6 miles a gallon, performed badly in hot weather, and needed overhauls twice as often as the diesels. Eventually he hoped to convert all 133 Gilligs, which made up 40% of the county's active fleet. The oldest among them had now logged 75,000 to 80,000 miles. The total cost for the conversion was estimated at more than $2 million.

Adding the 66 RTS-2's had permitted district officials to smooth out the schedules and offer new services including two more express routes: line 5, from Eastridge to the Mountain View S. P. depot via Santa Clara and Sunnyvale, and line 6, from Campbell to Lockheed-Sunnyvale via Westgate. Line 66 from San Jose to the BART terminal in Fremont was soon to be changed into an express and renumbered line 3. The flood of complaints had now dwindled to a trickle.

At year's end the district was offering service from about 6 a.m. to midnight on some 50 routes running from Menlo Park in the northwest and Fremont in the northeast to Gavilan College, near Gilroy, in the southeast. Its buses met those of the San Mateo County Transit District (SamTrans) at Menlo Park and Palo Alto and those of AC Transit at Milpitas and Fremont. They met S. P. commute trains at several points. Dial-a-Ride service was still available in Morgan Hill, San Martin, and Gilroy. New maintenance and storage facilities had been completed in Mountain View, North San Jose, and San Martin.

In a surprise move, the supervisors had asked William Siegel to study the possibility of divesting them of their transit duties and establishing a new supervisory body. This action had come on a motion by Cortese, who had opposed the move in the past. He was supported by McCorquodale and Steinberg. Diridon, who had formerly opposed a separate board, didn't dissent. Supervisor Susanne Wilson was absent. State Senator Alfred E. Alquist then introduced a bill that would create a new transit board composed of representatives from 11 county districts of equal population, each district providing one representative. No member could hold any other elective office. Plans were revealed in March 1980 to hold public hearings in the South Bay.

Continued violence on the buses had led the district to mount a major offensive. Named to head district security was Augustus "Gus" Bruneman, a retired police commander from the San Francisco Police Department and former security chief of the Golden Gate Bridge, Highway and Transportation District. County Transit reported that it had now ordered radios for all buses. Plans had been laid to install television monitors in coaches serving the most troublesome routes.

Several other issues had now arisen, among them continuation by the S. P. of its San Francisco-San Jose commute service. As described, the rail company had improved and eventually expanded this service, which remained the backbone of public transit along the peninsula. Coveteously eyed by the supervisors for some years, also, had been its freight routes southerly along Monterey Road to Morgan Hill and Gilroy, southwesterly through the Blossom Valley area to the Almaden Valley (the Lick branch), and westerly by a V-shaped path to Campbell, Vasona Junction, Los Gatos, Saratoga, and Cupertino. In 1975 they had voted to open negotiations with the company to establish passenger service along these routes. That effort had gone for naught. Two years later the S. P. had asked the California Public Utilities Commission and Interstate Commerce Commission for authorization to discontinue its San Francisco-San Jose service. With only 7,500 riders a day, it reported, it was losing $12 million a year.

Metropolitan Transportation Commission officials had been determined in 1978 to save the commute service, not so much for the 7,500 present riders as for the thousands of others who would use it in the future. Clearly, if it were to be retained, money would have to be found to replace at least part of the loss the railroad claimed it was suffering. Santa Clara County therefore joined San Francisco and San Mateo Counties in a bulk-purchase ticket subsidy plan, designed by the MTC, which would cost the county some $1.2 million over the next two

years, the money to accrue from its sales-tax light-rail reserve fund.

MTC officials saw this subsidy plan as only a stopgap measure, which it ultimately proved to be. Ridership soared to some 22,000 passengers daily. The S. P. won ICC approval to suspend service effective January 1, 1980, but by then the railroad and the state transportation agency (Caltrans) had approved a 10-year pact whereby the company agreed to maintain and upgrade the service and the state promised to cover its operating losses through a combination of Federal, state, and local funds. Lost was the subsidy arrangement under which Santa Clara and San Mateo counties had been buying reduced-fare tickets.

Diridon had meanwhile taken up the banner for passenger service on S. P. freight lines. Lightly considered among the county's transit alternatives for the Guadalupe Corridor was one that would extend rail service to Bernal Road, about two miles south of Edenvale. He pushed it. Assemblywoman Leona Egelund reintroduced legislation in January 1980 authorizing Caltrans to negotiate for extending the commute service past Bernal Road to Morgan Hill.

In February, responding to requests by the United Transportation Union, the San Jose Chamber of Commerce, and citizens' groups, the board controlling the study of transportation alternatives in the Guadalupe Corridor voted 6-1 to include S. P. rail extensions to Edenvale and the Almaden Valley among the alternatives. The lone dissenting voice was that of San Jose Councilwoman Iola Williams, who said that inclusion of the Lick branch, which had consistently been opposed by area homeowner groups and the San Jose City Council, "really made us angry."

Diridon, whose swing from negative to affirmative had broken a 3-3 deadlock, said he didn't necessarily support using the Lick branch but had switched his vote so the study could continue. The San Jose members later lost another battle to eliminate the Lick branch, coming up short on a 4-3 vote at which Williams, Self, and San Jose Mayor Janet Gray Hayes cast the ballots for exclusion.

In March the supervisors voted to endorse the board's decision, Diridon commenting that if the rail lines were not included, such supporters as the United Transportation Union, the San Jose Chamber of Commerce, and the Santa Clara County Manufacturers Group could sue when it was finished, requiring it to be done over again. The vote was unanimous for the main line but only 3-2 for the Lick branch, Cortese and Wilson voting against its inclusion.

In February, on a motion by Diridon, the supervisors had asked Graebner to prepare a study on the feasibility and legality of extending rail service along three feeder routes from the S. P. depot in San Jose: the main line to Morgan Hill and Gilroy, the Vasona line to Los Gatos and Saratoga, and the Niles line northeasterly to Fremont. The transit chief was asked to develop a plan within 45 days covering such details as timetables, stopping points, and feeder bus routes that could be set up to carry people to the rail line.

The results, reported by a consultant in April, showed the extensions to be "well within the realm of possibility" but likely to be strenuously resisted by the railroad. The expenses for track rework, stations, and other outlays would range from $450,000 for the Gilroy line to $980,000 for the Fremont line. Single-deck passenger cars would cost more than $200,000 each and used diesel locomotives from $200,000 to $400,000 apiece. The Surface Transportation Act of 1978, which helped pay for the peninsula service, might be tapped for this purpose, but with the railroad saying it didn't want public subsidies and preferred to get completely out of the passenger business, it was unclear how this scheme might fare. A collateral question was whether the county's light rail money might be used to finance the extensions.

In 1980 County Transit contracted with Peerless to provide Summit Road (Route 76) service in mountainous terrain behind Los Gatos with suburban-type manual-transmission coaches like 132, shown here on Highway 17 at the Summit Road offramp. (Jack Perry)

Resolved in the negative, for the time being, had been the question of a BART extension into Santa Clara County. In January 1979 the Alameda County representative to the Metropolitan Transportation Commission had proposed that BART expand from Fremont to San Jose. In December had come word that the BART board would ask Santa Clara County to chip in for a new station at Scott Creek Road, north of Milpitas, extending their proposed line to Fremont's Irvington and Warm Springs districts. The Milpitas city council had given its blessing. The cost for the seven-mile extension was estimated at $225 million, perhaps more if it had to go under Fremont's Lake Elizabeth and if BART had to pay to relocate existing railroad lines. The three new stations would yeild more than 3,000 riders daily, it was claimed, producing more than $3 million a year in revenues.

In February 1980, BART officials said they hoped to launch discussions in Santa Clara County to see if local residents were interested in Scott Creek. BART president Nello Bianco put the "buy-in" price tag for extending over the county line at $200 million. Except for Milpitas, county officials were either silent or cold to the idea, observing that only 5% of South Bay commuters left the county and their needs were met mainly by the S. P. A contribution that large would also exhaust all funds for other South Bay work, they said. In April 1980 the BART board adopted a $1.7 billion, 20-year expansion plan that omitted the Scott Creek station.

Resolved in the affirmative had been the question of a transit fare hike, although the boost was less than originally feared. This issue dated back to a 1978 action by the Metropolitan Transportation Commission requesting all Bay Area transit agencies to obtain at least 30% of their operating funds from the farebox. County Transit, like the others, had fought this threat.

However, in 1980 the MTC had modified its request into a demand; not to comply might mean losing the state revenues it was empowered to distribute. The other agencies agreed and so County Transit, which considered doubling the basic fare (from 25¢ to 50¢) before adopting a 10¢ boost to become effective

June 15, its first fare hike since 1973. That was on April 28. The supervisors also agreed to boost the cost of monthly full-fare passes from $10 to $12 and 22-ride passes from $5 to $7. Express bus service went from 50¢ to 75¢. Youth fares (ages 5-17) remained at 10¢; there was no increase for the elderly and handicapped during off-peak hours. Transit officials insisted that the fare increase was needed to keep pace with inflation. The supervisors split 3-2 in their vote: Diridon, Steinberg, and Wilson aye, Cortese and McCorquodale nay.

Plans for a $10 million downtown San Jose transit mall were now moving along, and a White House visit by San Jose Mayor Hayes was seen as the key to a $440,000 first-phase Federal grant to set the mall's scope and cost. After meeting with Transportation Secretary Neil Goldschmidt in November 1979, she had tea with First Lady Rosalynn Carter.

Diridon was cynical. "Both this administration and the last have used the process of Federal transit grants to obtain political support," he declared. "Blatantly. What we're trying to do is not just have the goods; we're also trying to exert some political leverage by saying that Santa Clara Valley is an affluent valley that tends to vote well." A highly placed Congressional source had confirmed Diridon's opinion, claimed the *Mercury*, saying that approval of the mall had been delayed while Carter officials waited for an endorsement from Mrs. Hayes. The prospects now looked good, added the source, in the wake of her meeting with Rosalynn Carter.

In any event, the basic concept—a four-block open-air pedestrian island on First Street from St. James to San Carlos Street—won approval by the UMTA staff later that month. Announced on December 19 was a $760,000 Federal design and engineering grant. If all went well, it was said, the plans would be done and the project ready for bid by fall 1980.

Meanwhile, as regards the Guadalupe Corridor evaluation, the *Mercury* had expressed some concerns. "We've spent a lot of money on studies," it observed. "What do we have to show for it? If the Federal people keep changing the rules of the funding game, then what assurance do we have that they won't keep on doing the same thing in the future, putting the carrot of actual construction always one more step out of reach? If we're going to invest in more studies, let's be absolutely specific about what we're getting for our money, when we can expect to have it, and why we expect the Federal government to come in and help us pay for it."

The newly created seven-member Guadalupe Corridor Study Board of Control, representing several agencies including the supervisors, had reluctantly accepted that this study was needed—the fourth since 1973—before UMTA would provide funds for final engineering and construction. Some $700,000 in Federal money had already been received to conduct it. The supervisors then got $113,000 more, boosting the total contribution to $813,000.

Most of this money—$400,000—would go to the consulting team to manage the study. Another $80,000 was earmarked for a "citizen participation program." The purposes of the study, they reported, were to achieve a "substantial agreement" among the 350,000 residents in the 75-square-mile study area, to comply with state and Federal environmental quality laws, and to meet the UMTA requirements.

Unveiled in August had been nine options including that of doing nothing, as required by Federal guidelines. The one attracting the most attention was a $100 million two-track, light-rail line from Edenvale to Marriott Industrial Park, part of a $400 million scheme that would include more buses, roads, and transit for the 1990's and beyond. Envisioned for the corridor was a highway-rail combination that would have to mean an expressway, reported William Hein, deputy executive director of the Metropolitan Transportation Commission.

Hein, addressing the control board in October, cautioned that an expressway would probably be the largest highway facility that could be built in the corridor because of financial problems. One difficulty was that present Federal policy prohibited funding both rail and highway construction in the same corridor. Another was that state funds to build the Guadalupe and West Valley freeways would not be forthcoming despite previous promises to the contrary. This was borne out several days later when Transportation Director Adriana Gianturco announced that Caltrans would approve no more environmental impact statements or property acquisitions for these freeways.

The announcement brought forth ringing protests and also a plan proposed by San Jose Councilman Larry Pegram that the city sell $35 million in bonds to build a four-lane expressway in the corridor, with an option of adding express bus or carpool lanes, light rail, or some other form of mass transit. Pegram said the project would cost $41.2 million—$12.1 million for rights of way and $29.1 for construction—of which $28 million would come from the bond sale and the remainder from the city's construction excise tax fund and funds set aside to buy rights of way. The proposal called for a dogleg-shaped expressway from Miyuki Avenue near Santa Teresa Hospital west along the West Valley corridor state Highway 85) to the Guadalupe corridor (State Highway 87) near Oakridge Mall. From there it would run north to Curtner Avenue.

The Pegram proposal drew rousing support from the *Mercury*, which, after observing that the state had built only the northernly part of Highway 87 and none of Highway 85 from Cupertino eastward, urged the city council to issue the bonds. Pledge the cash to build the highway, it recommended. Proceed with the environmental impact reports and engineering studies. Continue pressuring the state officials to honor their longstanding commitments to build Highways 85 and 87.

A state treasury official warned, however, that the bond sale would create a burden that would "stretch the imagination" of most experts. The city had pegged the debt cost at $30 million. In the face of rising interest rates, it would find no takers at less than 9%, he advised, which would significantly boost the cost. The city had not made its decision at the time of this writing.

In December the *Mercury News* assembled a blue ribbon panel of authorities to review the present state and future hopes for South Bay transportation. In 1975, it was reported, approximately 650,000 county residents—80%—had chosen to drive alone compared with 81,000 (10%) by carpool, 25,000 (3%) by transit, 57,000 (7%) by other means. By 1979 the total travel had climbed by about 20%; corresponding figures for that year were 810,000 (76%) alone, 135,000 (12%) by carpool, 75,000 (5%) by transit, and 82,000 (7%) by other means, representing a percentage decline in private travel but a huge increase—731,000 versus 945,000—in the number of vehicles on the road.

The 1990 targets were 833,000 (62%) traveling alone, 270,000 (20%) by carpool, 135,000 (10%) by transit, and 108,000 (8%) by other means, again representing about a 20% increase in total travel but skewed in favor of shared ridership. The biggest gain would come from slowing the proliferation of private vehicles. If these goals were met, about 1,100,000 cars would be on the road by 1990, only a modest increase.

Using those data, the panel assessed the choices. Several were opposed to more highway construction. One panelist called it delusion to try making rail transit the dominant form of county transportation, but others supported light rail, among them Diridon, Minister, and Larry Klein, a Palo Alto attorney. "We can get it built here, I know, if we refuse to take no for an answer," Diridon insisted. "Rail is the only means of catalyzing densification that will allow us to stop sprawling all over the place. We're going to have continued growth. We need to shape our future. Our only choice is some kind of guideway system that will tend naturally to centralize people."

Minister saw light rail in the Guadalupe corridor as the equivalent of constructing an eight-lane freeway in terms of providing passenger capacity at a lower cost than buses. "Buses need an extra driver for every 50 to 100 people," he commented, "and those drivers don't come cheap." Klein said he supported light rail but thought that county residents preferred a living style that was not dense.

In January 1980 Frank Sweeney of the *Mercury News* offered a thoughtful review pointing toward the future. "In 10 years Santa Clara County could have a public transit system consisting of a thousand buses and the first segments of a light rail network that some day could crisscross the urbanized part of the valley," he declared. "A key element would be an upgraded S. P. peninsula commute line. The cost will be hundreds of millions of dollars, but we have no choice, transportation planners say. The county's highway system alone cannot carry the load that will be imposed in the years to come. The alternative is intolerable traffic congestion that could strangle the economy of the valley.

"The Santa Clara County Transit District now operates about 360 buses and is well along in a program to expand the fleet to 516 by 1981. The county's long-range transportation plan calls for expansion to a 750-bus fleet by the mid-1980s, and it could reach 1,000 vehicles by 1990.

"A light rail or trolley car transit system might be constructed in the Guadalupe corridor (designated as State Highway 87) that links the sprawling Edenvale-Blossom Valley and Almaden Valley residential areas with downtown San Jose, Civic Center, Municipal Airport, and Santa Clara's Marriott Industrial Park. The rail line would be linked with upgraded Southern Pacific railroad service in downtown San Jose, where planners envision a major transit terminal will be constructed."

An upgraded S. P. could carry 100,000 riders a day compared with the present 15,000, Sweeney said, observing that the S. P. line from San Jose to San Francisco runs within two miles of 65% of all local jobs. Highway projects in the plan included preserving the West Valley corridor, building the Guadalupe expressway, and widening Interstate 280, U. S. 101, and State

Highway 17. "The plan came out of the $1.2 million Santa Clara Valley Corridor Evaluation study. It was approved by most of the county's cities in 1979 after three years of study. The transit system improvements recommended in the study were predicated on a forecast of 715,000 county jobs by 1990, an increase of 115,000 over 1978. But reality is outstripping the forecasts, and there are already 670,000 jobs. The county planning department now forecasts 725,000 by next year and 840,000 by 1990.

"A series of evaluations since the early 1970s, including the valley corridor study, identified light rail as the transit system appropriate for San Jose's Guadalupe corridor," Sweeney noted. "Last year, the county transit district began the final study of what form of transportation actually should go there. The study, to be completed in 1981, may recommend a combination of light rail and expressway, running on the West Valley corridor from Edenvale to Oakridge Mall and north on the Guadalupe corridor to downtown and beyond. The investment could be $100 to $200 million in today's dollars, says David Minister, project director. Federal funds have already paid 80% of the cost of the district's existing bus fleet and will pay a proportionate share of further fleet expansion.

"The Guadalupe corridor study will consider seven alternatives including a freeway, an expressway, a busway, a light rail line, or a combination of rail and expressway. 'The best we could hope for is the first element of light rail in operation in 1985 or 1986,' Diridon has said. The Guadalupe corridor became the prime candidate for light rail because nothing had yet been built in it. 'We have to put something in that corridor or San Jose will literally strangle,' he says.

"Although S. P. is a key element in the county plan," Sweeney concluded, "BART is not. As Graebner has said, 'The dollars are short enough, and to simply take up S. P. and replace it with another form of rail transit doesn't seem wise use of those dollars.'"

As regards the Guadalupe trolley line, nothing is certain yet although the corridor study is expected to recommend it, particularly in light of progress on the downtown transit mall and successful negotiation of the Caltrans-S. P. pact to upgrade the peninsula commute rail service, considered vital if the Guadalupe line is to realize its potential of 20,000 to 60,000 riders a day.

There is still hope that state freeway funds may be freed and UMTA authorities will reverse their present stand against building roads and rail lines in the same corridor. With money scarce and interest rates high, local officials have been reluctant to place construction bonds until these matters are resolved.

Barring a major shift in Federal funding or change in local resolve, it appears likely at this writing that the Guadalupe line will become a reality. The need is there; so, it seems, are the funds. The time may thus be near when another generation can thrill to the rumble of streetcar wheels on steel rails and the whoosh of a passing trolley. Maybe they won't call them trolleys. Then again, how does one sing, "Clang, clang, clang went the LRV"?

Influenced by the factory color scheme of RTS-2 buses, County Transit's paint shop introduced a new "black window" design in 1980, with straight blue-over-orange belt striping replacing the traditional "dip stripe." Coach 6524, one of the newest series of ex-San Jose City Lines buses, displays this livery.

(Jack Perry)

SOUTHERN PACIFIC COMMUTE SERVICE

After abandoning the Peninsular and the San Jose Railroads, the S. P. had no wish to operate any South Bay local transit systems, although it maintained and gradually improved its San Francisco-San Jose commute service. Introduced in 1924 were 60 steam-heated suburban steel coaches—"subs"—to replace wooden equipment. Ten more were added the following year and another five in 1927. At a cost of about $5 million, ten modern "galley-type" double-deck coaches were added in 1955 and 21 more in 1957, bringing the fleet to 31 double-deckers, 75 "subs," and 90 older cars. Nineteen older cars were still running in 1981.

Here as elsewhere on the system, diesels replaced steam engines in January 1957. The motive power then consisted of sixteen 2400-hp single-unit Fairbanks-Morse "Trainmasters" (numbered 4800-4815)

and eight 1750-hp Electro-Motive diesels (3000s), plus other assorted units. Added in recent years have been ten 3600-hp SPD45s (3200-3209), which are the workhorses of the San Jose commuter fleet despite a continuing S. P. need for heavy freight equipment. Passenger demand has risen sharply, and there has been some doubling up of the lighter diesels to maintain schedules. A 1978 trial of 3000-hp General Electric P30CHs ended when these tricolor units leased from Amtrak to relieve the diesel shortage proved to be even slower starting than the 3100s.

Daily commute traffic on the line rose from about 8,000 in the late 1930s (13,000 during World War II) to a 1955 high of 16,000, then fell to 11,500 in 1964 and about 7,500 in the mid-1970s. The railroad sought to abandon the San Jose run, citing some $12 million in annual losses, then negotiated subsidy agreements with state and local officials that seem to have guaranteed it for another decade. In 1978 the line carried more than 3.2 million riders in nine months (January-September). In 1979, with gasoline costly and in short supply, the nine-month total was 4.15 million (22,500 daily), an increase of 28.3%.

For eight decades or more the faithful commuter trains have served the Peninsula between San Francisco and San Jose. The trains are heavily patronized, and run as frequently as three minutes apart in the rush hour. Toward the end of the 1970s, the Southern Pacific attempted to abandon the service due to heavy financial losses, but instead worked out an agreement with a California state agency to continue and upgrade the service, which will tie directly into improved transit service in the Santa Clara Valley. A scene that cannot be repeated, however, is train 147 at California Avenue, Palo Alto, about 1941, with a steam locomotive and the old "Harriman" commute coaches.
(Waldemar Sievers photo from Harre W. Demoro Collection)

Overlap of the new and the old. With two double-decked cars fresh from Pullman–Standard, 4-8-2 Mountain type locomotive 4311 halts at Santa Clara in 1955. The double-deckers, with others added in 1957 and 1969, were still operating in 1981 but the 1924 Schenectady-built steam loco was off the roster in less than a year after the photo was taken.

Interior of one of the double-deck "gallery" commute cars shows how the railroad packs them in on two levels. Caltrans, which now operates the service over S.P. rails, was planning to buy more such cars in the early 1980s.

(Both: Harre W. Demoro)

Even contemporary commute trains mix a bit of the old and new. The heavy-duty SDP45 diesel locomotive and the new gallery cars are spliced by one of the venerable old "Harriman" coaches which have completed nearly seven decades of service. (Southern Pacific)

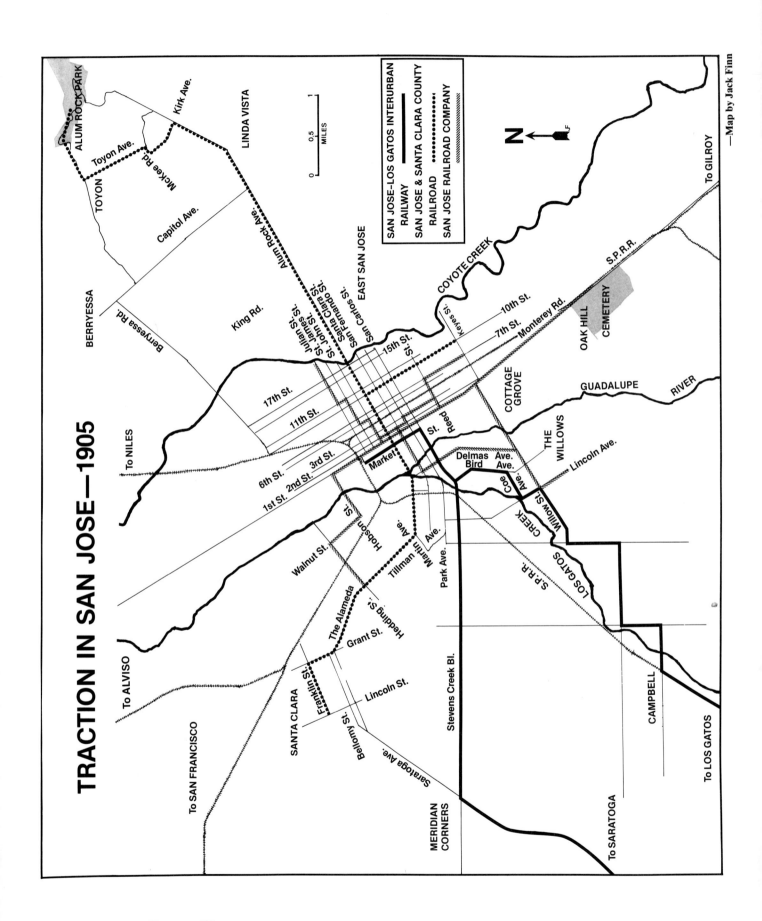

TRACTION IN SAN JOSE—1905

—Map by Jack Finn

N

SAN JOSE–LOS GATOS INTERURBAN RAILWAY	
SAN JOSE & SANTA CLARA COUNTY RAILROAD	
SAN JOSE RAILROAD COMPANY	

1 0.5 0 MILES

ALUM ROCK PARK

TOYON

Toyon Ave.

Kirk Ave.

McKee Rd.

LINDA VISTA

Capitol Ave.

Alum Rock Ave.

BERRYESSA

Berryessa Rd.

King Rd.

EAST SAN JOSE

To NILES

Julian St.
St. James St.
St. John St.
Santa Clara St.
San Fernando St.
San Carlos St.

17th St.

15th St.

11th St.

Keyes St.

10th St.

7th St.

Monterey Rd.

COYOTE CREEK

To GILROY

S.P.R.R.

OAK HILL CEMETERY

CEMETERY

COTTAGE GROVE

GUADALUPE RIVER

6th St.
1st St. 2nd St. 3rd St.

Market St.

Reed

Delmas Ave.
Bird Ave.

THE WILLOWS

Lincoln Ave.

To ALVISO

To SAN FRANCISCO

Hobson St.

Walnut St.

The Alameda

Hedding St.

Grant St.

SANTA CLARA

Franklin St.

Bellomy St.

Lincoln St.

Saratoga Ave.

Martin Ave.

Ave.

Tillman

Park Ave.

Stevens Creek Bl.

MERIDIAN CORNERS

Coe Ave.

Willow St.

CREEK

LOS GATOS

S.P.R.R.

To SARATOGA

CAMPBELL

To LOS GATOS

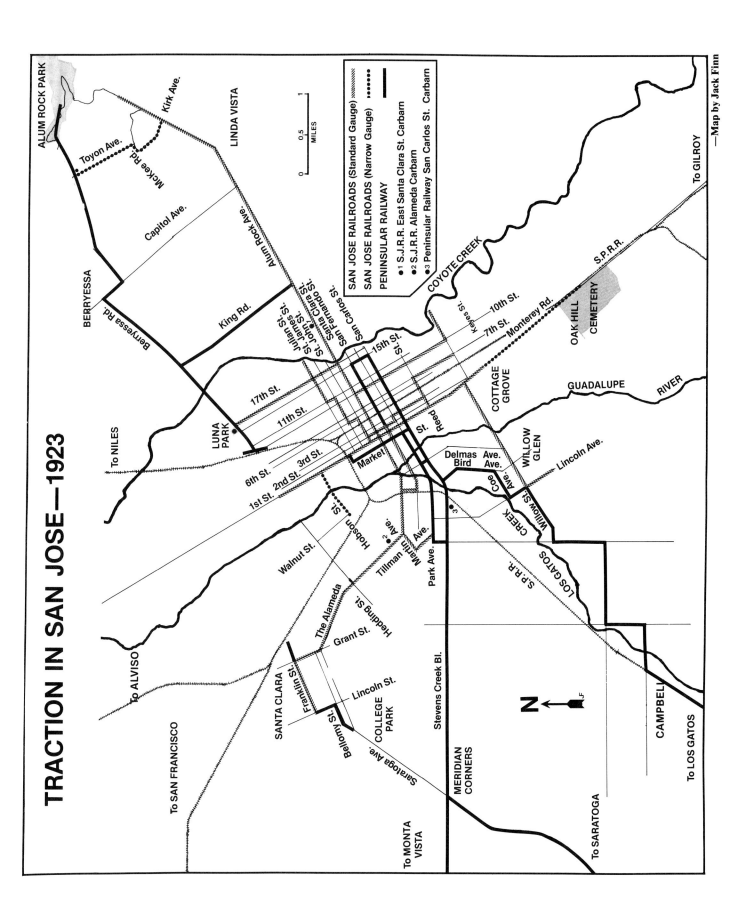

TRACTION IN SAN JOSE—1923

—Map by Jack Finn

SAN JOSE RAILROADS (Standard Gauge)
SAN JOSE RAILROADS (Narrow Gauge)
PENINSULAR RAILWAY

• 1 S.J.R.R. East Santa Clara St. Carbarn
• 2 S.J.R.R. Alameda Carbarn
• 3 Peninsular Railway San Carlos St. Carbarn

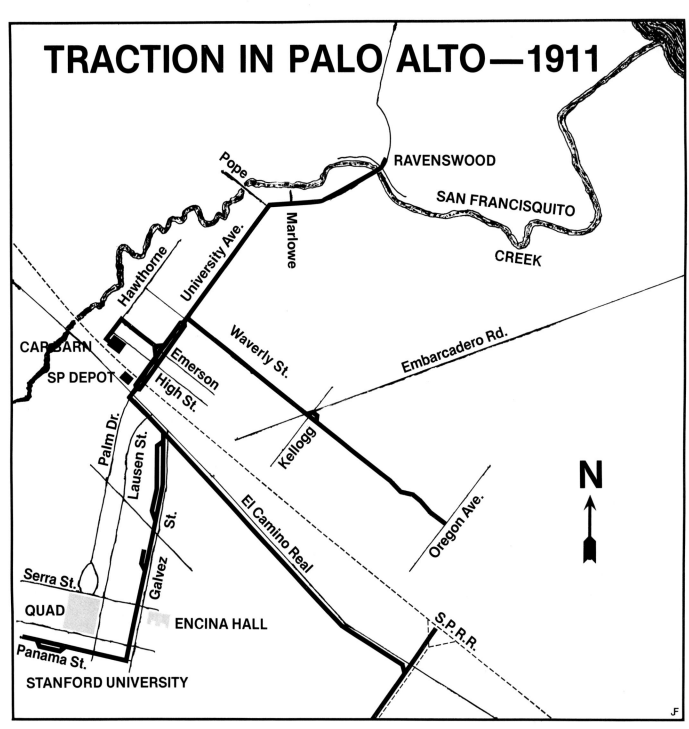

TRACTION IN PALO ALTO—1911

RAVENSWOOD

SAN FRANCISQUITO

CREEK

Pope

Marlowe

Hawthorne

University Ave.

Waverly St.

Embarcadero Rd.

CAR BARN

SP DEPOT

Emerson

High St.

Kellogg

Palm Dr.

Lausen St.

Galvez St.

El Camino Real

Oregon Ave.

N

Serra St.

QUAD

ENCINA HALL

S.P.R.R.

Panama St.

STANFORD UNIVERSITY

—Map by Jack Finn

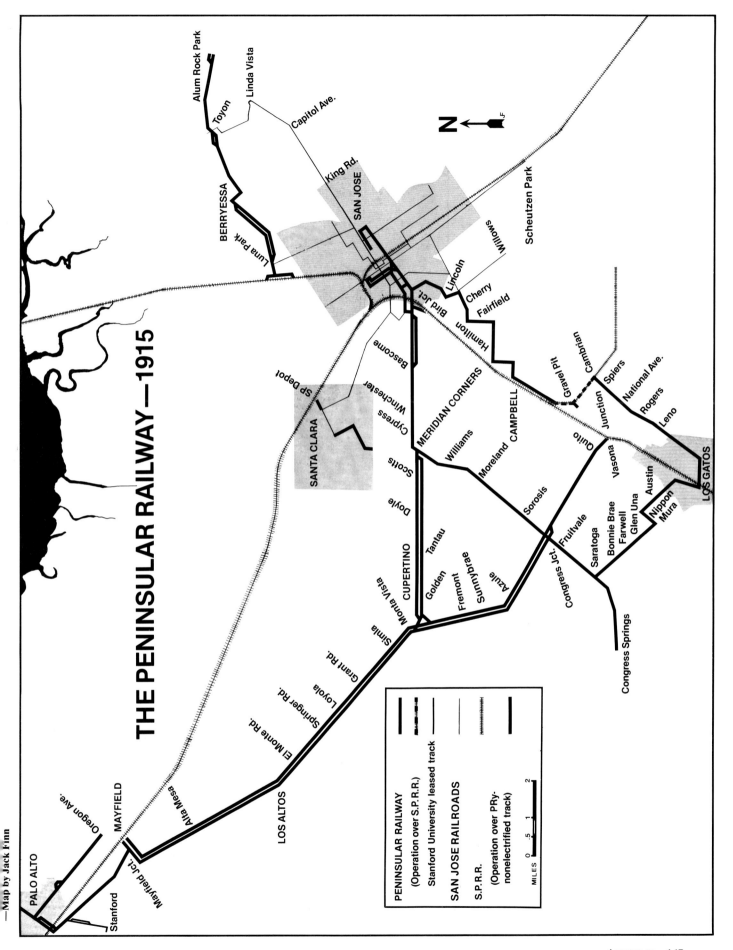

THE PENINSULAR RAILWAY—1915

— Map by Jack Finn

PENINSULAR RAILWAY
(Operation over S.P.R.R.)
Stanford University leased track

SAN JOSE RAILROADS

S.P.R.R.
(Operation over PRy-nonelectrified track)

MILES 0 .5 1 2

Biographical Notes

THE FOLLOWING information is derived from newspaper accounts, city directories, voting registers, death notices, probate and real estate documents, personal interviews, and published biographies. Its completeness and accuracy cannot be assured. It is meant as a guide and supplement to materials available in local libraries and historical collections.

Auzerais, John. b. Normandy, France, 1822. Naturalized April 21, 1879, U.S. Circuit Court, San Francisco. d. December 12, 1887. With brother Edward, went to Valparaiso, Chile, 1849, where he worked for a mercantile firm. Edward emigrated to San Jose in 1850, opening Mariposa Store. John followed in 1851 and, with Edward, established Auzerais Brothers building firm. Auzerais Brothers built many private residences and developed several good commercial properties in early San Jose, including Mariposa Block, Central Block, Pacific Hotel, City Market, and Auzerais House erected in 1864 at cost of $150,000. John sold his interest in Auzerais House to Edward in 1874, devoting final years to vine culture and wine-making on his 100-acre estate east of San Jose, near Alum Rock. He left estate valued at $250,000.

Baker, George F. b. 1850. d. San Francisco March 10, 1882. Graduated U. of Pacific 1870. Superintent of Schools Santa Clara County 1872-74. Attorney San Francisco 1874-77, then returned to San Jose. President pro-tem California State Senate 1880.

Belden, David. b. Connecticut c. 1833. d. May 14, 1888. Defeated Henry M. Moore by one vote 1858 in race for county judge. Judge Santa Clara County Superior Court 1871-1888.

Bethel, Franklin Cloud. b. Indiana c. 1833. Usually referred to as Major Bethel. Registered to vote Santa Clara County March 1871; listed occupation as capitalist. Listed occupation 1877 as merchant.

Bird, Calvert T. b. Oklahoma September 1, 1840. d. December 23, 1910. Came to The Willows 1851 with family. Subdivided and sold property in The Willows 1870's. Admitted to state bar 1882. Served nine years as U. S. Circuit Court Commissioner.

Bird, Isaac. b. England c. 1814. Naturalized April 6, 1857, San Jose. Hop grower The Willows 1852; petitioned Court of Sessions (forerunner of Board of Supervisors) to build road from his place along west side of Guadalupe River "to intersect with the Santa Clara-San Jose Road between the two bridges (Guadalupe River and Los Gatos Creek bridges)." Listed occupation 1866 as grower. Owned coffee plantation Panama October 1879.

Bishop, Samuel Addison. b. Virginia 1825. d. San Jose June 3, 1893, reportedly choking to death on a pine nut shell. Invested in San Jose Savings Bank 1870, serving as vice president several years. In 1870 also acquired San Jose Institute and Business College. President San Jose Homestead Association. Incorporator and long-time director Sierra Lumber Company (founded 1878), which operated in Sierra Nevada and Butte, Plumas, Tehama, and Shasta Counties. President San Jose Agricultural Works, founded 1883. Heavy investor and director Paul O. Burns Wine Company, established 1885 and, before its bankruptcy, said to be largest viticultural organization in Santa Clara County. Bishop was a local pundit and political wit who observed in 1882 that "there is hardly a difference these days in serving the state in Sacramento or in San Quentin." An 1888 account commends his personal charm and record of civic achievement: "Few of the pioneers of California have led a more active and useful life, or contributed more largely toward the advancement of this state to its present proud position than Mr. Bishop. He is endowed with rare natural abilities, and a genial, kindly disposition. The burden of 63 years sits lightly upon him, and his regular habits and systematic activity have solidified and knit into a column of enduring life his whole organization."

At the time of his death, Bishop, said to be in robust health, was developing a subdivision fronting on Cinnabar Street, San Jose. To his widow and children—two married daughters and a 12-year-old son—he left considerable property but less than $3000 cash. Holdings included 609½ shares in the Sierra Lumber Company. His 10,000 shares in the Burns winery were appraised as worthless.

Bland, John Caswell. b. North Carolina c. 1829. Listed occupation 1866 as auctioneer.

Bodley, Thomas. b. Kentucky March 19, 1821. Lawyer and adventurer. State assemblyman 1857; also an early member of city government. Santa Clara County District Attorney 1875. Admitted to bar Louisville, Kentucky, then went to New Orleans, where he joined commissary department, U. S. Army. Fought and wounded in Mexican-American War. To San Jose 1849. Appointed undersheriff Santa Clara County, then entered local law practice. First secretary Saratoga and Pescadero Turnpike and Wagon Road Company 1866.

Bohnett, Lewis Daniel, Jr. b. San Jose June 8, 1917, son of prominent local attorney and one-time state legislator. With brother, John B. Bohnett, also local attorney, operated Bohnett Brothers gasoline station at 227 S. Market Street, San Jose, reportedly city's first "super" station offering mechanics, rest rooms, and garage spaces many of which were leased to the city. Opened relic and antiques business on Almaden Road 1944 that moved in 1949 to Monterey Road opposite Hillsdale Avenue, where Bohnett leased Red Barn restaurant-saloon, opened museum, and built several historical structures later acquired by city. Red Barn was not reopened after major fire in 1976; last remaining structure on property, sold by Bohnett in May 1980, is China Station restaurant.

Boring, Samuel Watson. b. Tennessee 1824. d. Santa Clara County 1903. State assemblyman 1856. State senator 1878. Mayor San Jose 1888-89. Listed occupation 1867 as expressman.

Bowie, August J. Mining engineer often called Colonel Bowie. With J. B. Randol, Fred Sharon of Palace Hotel family, San Mateo capitalist William H. Howard, and others, founded $5 million Electric Improvement Company of San Francisco March 1887 to challenge established California Electric Light Company in that city. With W. P. Dougherty, James W. Rea, and others, founded $100,000 Electric Improvement Company of San Jose October 1889 to complete locally against San Jose Brush Electric Light Company, with Electric Improvement Company of San Francisco holding three-fourths of San Jose stock. Sold San Francisco firm 1892 to California Electric Light Company. Went to Alaska late 1890's to help with mining operations of James R. Keane, New York financier.

Branham, Isaac. b. Scott County, Kentucky, 1803. To Missouri 1824, then to San Jose December 2, 1846. With Captain Julian Hanks of San Jose, built first sawmill 1848 in what was to be Santa Clara County, at Arroyo de Los Gatos above present Town of Los Gatos. Member Los Gatos town council 1878.

Brassy, Ferdinand. b. France 1841. d. San Jose March 7, 1913. To California 1856 and San Jose sometime later. Founded Brassy and Company, wholesale liquor merchants. Director First National Bank of San Jose.

Breyfogle, Charles W. b. Columbus, Ohio. Graduated Ohio Wesleyan University medical school 1865. To San Jose 1870. Organized San Jose Building and Loan Association 1885. First president Garden City National Bank 1887.

Broughton, Samuel Quincy. b. Kentucky c. 1824. Listed occupation 1866 as farmer.

Bryant, Benjamin. b. South Carolina c. 1823. Listed occupation 1866 as physician.

Burke, John P. Twelve-year Iowa banking associate and personal friend of James H. Henry. Resigned as vice president San Jose and Santa Clara Railroad August 1901 to return to banking. Third vice president First National Bank of Los Angeles February 4, 1910.

Burnett, Dwight Jay. b. Tennessee 1831. Rancher. Tax Collector Santa Clara County 1867.

Center, Hugh. One of 12 children of John Center. According to son, late Hugh Stuart Center, worked briefly for Spreckels family in Hawaii managing plantation on Maui. Returned to operate Alum Rock railroad. Hugh's brother David, who took over plantation and died 1901 in Hawaii, fathered George David Center, famous in the Islands for promoting athletics. Hugh's brother Sam was well known San Francisco realtor.

Center, John. b. Scotland. Came to California before gold rush, acquiring large property holdings in San Francisco Mission District. Foreclosed Alum Rock road and sold it to Hugh, his nephew, for $1. At death left $30,000 each to some 35 nieces and nephews he was instrumental in bringing to this country, with balance of estate to four favored nieces and nephews including Hugh.

Chapin, Frank E., Jr. b. Tuolumne County, California, January 28, 1857. d. San Francisco January 5, 1926. Employed Market Street Railway 1874. Mining engineer 1875-79. Joined California Street Railway Company 1879 as conductor, then gripman. Assistant Superintendent California Street Railway Company 1882-1904. To San Jose 1904 as General Manager San Jose-Los Gatos Interurban Railway Company.

Cobb, James Clark. b. New York State 1819. Physician. Contributor to original San Jose statehouse 1849. Secretary Agricultural Society 1857.

Cottle, Oliver. b. Missouri c. 1815. Listed occupation 1866 as stock raiser.

Crandall, Jared. With Warren Hall, bought out Whisman's San Francisco-San Jose stage line 1850 and extended it the following year to Monterey. Partners later expanded, operating stage lines throughout Northern California. Crandall is credited with opening present U. S. 50 route over Sierra in 1857. According to Patricia Loomis, he was driving when he and Governor Peter Burnett beat a rival stage pounding down El Camino Real to bring word to the legislature in San Jose that California had been admitted to the union.

DeForest, Albert Tracy. b. Cleveland June 4, 1863. d. Lakeport, California, September 13, 1948. Son of Capt. Louis Germaine de Forest, Union Army officer during Civil War. Cousin of Dr. Lee T. de Forest, radio inventor, Chicago. Started business career with American Steel and Wire Company, Cleveland. Headed U. S. Steel Products Companies for many years. In 1904 came to San Francisco because of poor health; arranged purchase of the Columbia Steel Company for U. S. Steel. Built home in Palo Alto 1905, University Avenue near Hale Street. President Columbia Steel until his retirement 1932. Moved to Menlo Park 1937 after wife's death.

deLacy, Stephen Walter. b. Louisiana c. 1854. Editor *San Jose Daily Morning Times.*

Divine, Davis. b. New York State c. 1806. Judge Santa Clara County. With Peter Donahue, Henry M. Newhall, and George B. Polhemus, was instrumental in clearing way for San Francisco and San Jose Railroad that reached San Jose January 1864.

Dougherty, William Patrick. b. Ireland 1832. Naturalized by naturalization of father, Edina, Knox County, Missouri, 1849. d. San Jose March 18, 1894. To Santa Clara Valley 1858. Called "lumber king of Santa Clara Valley." Founded Dougherty Lumber Company. Founder and president Santa Clara Valley Mill and Lumber Company. Manager San Jose Brick Company. With Charles Hensley and others, created San Jose's second gas utility, Garden City Gas Company, June 1877. This company built plant on St. Augustine Street to produce gas by Lowe water-gas process, triggering rate war that led to merger of Garden City firm with older San Jose Gas Company about 1879. With August J. Bowie, James W. Rea, and others, created Electric Improvement Company of San Jose October 1889. This company merged into United Gas and Electric Company April 1902. Director Security Savings Bank 1892. Director Loma Prieta Lumber Company 1892.

Emory, Richard. b. Baltimore 1870. d. San Jose November 26, 1906. General manager electric railroads in Baltimore, Nashville, and Columbus, Ohio, before coming to San Jose April 1906 as manager Hanchett electric lines in Santa Clara County.

Fitts, William. b. Maine. d. San Jose c. 1913. To San Jose about 1850. Started San Jose-Santa Clara horse omnibus line about 1861, operating stage on The Alameda until 1869. Drove horsecar for San Jose and Santa Clara Railroad and became superintendent, handling operations until 1890 when electrics replaced horsecars. Elected town marshal Santa Clara April 1876. Ended working career with San Jose Water Works.

George H. McMurry describes Fitts as a good-looking youth who had hardly broken into stages when Sam Bishop's horsecars put him out of business. So Fitts, a resilient young pioneer, became a horsecar driver, thereby winning his wife. McMurry tells the romantic story as follows.

"It was a unique and new occupation to a horsecar driver in San Jose in the 1870s. Fitts was the envy of many a boy and, with his good looks, the cynosure of many a dark eye of the fair young senoritas who boarded his car each morning, headed for classes at the Notre Dame Academy in San Jose.

"Among the fairest was Senorita Dolores Pinedo, daughter of Lorenzo Pinedo of Santa Clara. Now, she was a granddaughter of Jose de los Reyes Berryessa, owner of the rancho on which the rich Almaden mines were discovered. Berryessa, on a peaceful mission to Sonora, had been wantonly shot without challenge by Kit Carson during the Bear Flag revolt, and the family had vowed never again to speak to a gringo if they could avoid it.

"But this was love at first sight and, fortunately, it was no Romeo-Juliet tragedy. Dolores became William's bride, and for years they lived happily on Alviso Street in Santa Clara beside the historic Pinedo home, until she preceded him in death.

McMurry also reports that Fitts, who knew every bump and mudhole in The Alameda, was incredulous when told the avenue was being paved. That was about 1912, and Fitts was fatally ill. "I won't believe it until I see it with my own eyes," he told his family, and he wouldn't rest until they took him out to see the smooth asphaltic panorama where he had witnessed the passing pageant of the years.

Franck, Frederick Christian. b. Waschbaschserhof, Bavaria, Germany, December 23, 1828. Naturalized February 20, 1857, U. S. Circuit Court, San Francisco. d. Santa Clara December 20, 1902. Merchant and capitalist. State assemblyman two terms 1871-75. State senator two terms 1895-99. At age 15, apprenticed to harness and saddle maker, Kaiserslautern. Emigrated to New York 1846, thence to Buffalo, Cleveland, Cincinnati, Louisville, and New Orleans. Arrived San Francisco February 1852, having crossed Panama Isthmus on foot. Worked mines in Mother Lode country for two years, then established harness and saddlery shop in San Francisco 1853, the second such business in that city. To Santa Clara 1855; established harness and saddlery works. Member Santa Clara board of trustees eight years. Chief volunteer fire department six years. Incorporator, director, and chairman of finance committee, Bank of Santa Clara County.

Gambert, Felix. b. France c. 1833. Naturalized Santa Clara County August 15, 1857. Proprietor Gambert and Lemoine City Store, San Jose. To Santa Cruz 1883 as proprietor Pope House, a prestigious coastal resort. Dismissed from Pope House 1884 upon change of ownership.

Goodwin, Clarence B. b. Santa Clara County August 6, 1889. Degree in civil engineering Stanford University December 1912. City engineer San Jose 1920-22. City manager San Jose 1922-38.

Gordon, Hanford Lenox. b. New York State c. 1837. Listed occupation 1866 as orchardist.

Granger, F. S. Railroad promoter described by *Santa Cruz Surf* June 1904 as a "robust man of powerful physique, active, energetic, and forceful." Took over controlling interest that month of Santa Cruz Electric Railway and, in September 1904, merged it with Santa Cruz, Capitola, and Watsonville Electric Railway to form Union Traction Company. Was general manager of Santa Cruz Electric, then Union Traction. Briefly owned Unique

Theater, Pacific Avenue, Santa Cruz. Sold his Santa Cruz railroad interests and theater November 1904. Reported to be in San Luis Obispo December 1904 promoting electric railroad to Avila Beach and in Hanford, California, 1907, on similar adventure.

Hale, Oliver Ambrose. b. Phoenix, New York, March 18, 1852. d. San Francisco July 19, 1907. Director Garden City National Bank 1892. Member San Jose city council 1892. Trustee Agnews State Hospital through administrations of six California governors. Eldest of five sons of Marshall Hale, successful New York and Michigan merchant who came west 1873. With father, on $4000 investment, opened first Hale's department store 1876 in cramped quarters at 140 S. First Street, San Jose, around corner from Lick Stables. Marshall Hale died 1890. San Jose store, renamed O. A. Hale and Company, moved 1890's into two-story building San Fernando Street between First and Second Streets. In 1901 Hale brothers opened San Francisco store Market Street opposite Mason Street. San Jose store moved 1931 to multistory building First and San Carlos Streets, where it remained until doors closed February 3, 1967. Hale's Stores had meanwhile merged (1950) with Broadway Stores, a Southern California firm. San Jose building was sold to Valley Title Company.

Hanchett, Lewis Edward. b. San Jose April 23, 1872. d. February 29, 1956; buried Mountain View Cemetery, Oakland. Son of Lewis James Hanchett, who came west from Michigan 1852 to work mine at Moore's Flat, near middle fork Yuba River; then developed prosperous mines at Silver Peak and Hornsilver (Gold Point), Esmeralda County, Nevada; settled San Jose early 1870's, living on San Carlos Street and listing occupation as mining engineer and capitalist. Nephew of Joseph E. Hanchett, who established San Jose livery stable early 1870's. Miner, real estate promoter, and "father of Los Angeles' Union Station," Lewis E. Hanchett inherited father's interest in Esmeralda mines. Investor and a director, Vendome Hotel, San Jose. In 1907 developed 76-acre Hanchett Park residential subdivision, San Jose, on site former Agricultural Park. Resided 43 S. Priest Street (now Fourteenth Street).

According to grandson, Burke Hanchett, went to Los Angeles after leaving San Jose and bought property on which the city's old Chinatown stood. Later sold part of property as site for Los Angeles Union Station, a project he had earlier proposed to get five railroads off the city streets. Balance of property eventually went to build a Los Angeles freeway. Maintained an interest in Vendome Hotel, which he, J. O. Hayes, and Paul Fratessa acquired February 1919 by trustees' sale for $80,000.

Harmon, John Bowman. b. Ohio c. 1856. Bookkeeper 1892.

Harrison, Cornelius Gooding. b. Illinois 1829. Mill owner San Jose 1867. With Charles Silent and others, founder San Lorenzo Flume and Lumber Company (1874), The Santa Cruz and Felton Rail Road Company (November 1874), and Pacific Avenue Street Railroad Company, Santa Cruz (April 1876), serving as director of all three companies. Also with Silent and others, an early investor Santa Cruz County Bank of Savings and Loan. Filed suit against Silent in San Jose December 1880 claiming misrepresentation by Silent of Harrison's Santa Cruz County investments.

Hayes, Everis Anson. San Jose attorney and businessman-farmer—called "Red" Hayes because of his beard color—who served seven terms in U. S. House of Representatives (1904-1918) and helped write Federal Reserve Act. Son of Anson E. and Mary Folsom Hayes, who according to Wes Peyton developed rich Midwestern iron ore deposits and, in 1887, established residence on 240-acre tract in Edenvale, off Monterey Road, which was rebuilt after an 1899 fire into present-day Hayes Mansion. With brother Jay Orley "Black" Hayes, formed Good Government League to fight corruption in San Jose City Hall. In 1900 the brothers acquired *San Jose Herald* and, a year later, controlling interest in *San Jose Mercury.* The *Mercury-Herald,* and later also the *San Jose Evening News,* continued in Hayes family ownership until 1952, when they were sold. Two years later the family sold their Edenvale mansion.

Hayes, Jay Orley. San Jose lawyer and businessman-farmer: nicknamed "Black" Hayes. Helped organize California Prune and Apricot Growers Association (now Sunsweet Growers) and, in 1918, ran unsuccessfully for governor of California.

Henry, James H. b. Michigan 1846. d. Portland, Oregon, June 22, 1939. Director Security Savings Bank 1892.

Hensley, Charles B. b. 1849, son of Samuel J. Hensley. d. Portland, Oregon, July 1891. Personal income from family sources reported to be several thousand a month. With W. P. Dougherty and others, founded Garden City Gas Company, San Jose, June 1877. In September 1878 sold San Jose Music Hall to Captain C. H. Maddox for $52,500; Hensley was said to have paid $65,000 for the property about 1872. Filed petition of bankruptcy November 12, 1879, listing no assets and liabilities of $153,000. On July 19, 1891, *San Jose Mercury* reported that Hensley and his sister succeeded in bankrupting $1 million estate left them by their father.

Holmes, Norman W. b. San Jose August 15, 1927. Started with Western Pacific in 1945 as engine watchman; became student fireman, then fireman, now engineer. Ran final Saratoga Blossom Festival in 1963. Resided near Santa Clara and Twenty-fourth Streets, later on Casey Road (now Curtner Avenue) in San Jose. Now living in Portola, California, where he avocationally operates Feather River and Western Railroad, full-scale backyard railroad with small locomotive, a caboose, a couple of cars, and a quarter mile of standard gauge track, commissioned during Bicentennial Celebration

January, William Alexander. b. Kentucky. Editor *Santa Clara Argus*, known as a "gentleman of the old school." California State Treasurer 1882.

Leib, Samuel Franklin. b. Fairfield County, Ohio, 1848. LLB University of Michigan 1869. To San Jose 1869; entered law practice with firm of Moore and Laine. Vice president First National Bank of San Jose. Attorney for estate of Samuel A. Bishop 1893. Appointed Judge Santa Clara County Superior Court 1903; resigned same year to resume private practice.

Lion, Gustave F. b. San Jose December 13, 1859. President L. Lion and Sons Company, San Jose, 1890.

Lowe, James R. b. Massachusetts c. 1840. d. San Jose September 23, 1904. To Santa Clara County 1853. State assemblyman two terms 1889-91. State senator 1885-86. Trustee Whittier State School 1889-93.

Mabury, Hiram. b. Pennsylvania 1816. Banker. Listed occupation 1867 as capitalist.

Martin, John. b. Indianapolis 1858. d. May 23, 1928. Entrepreneur, financier, industrialist. With Eugene de Sabla and others, founded Pacific Gas and Electric Company. President North Pacific Coast Railway 1902. President California Gas and Electric Company 1905. Director and briefly president Pacific Gas and Electric Company 1906-1914. President Coast Counties Power Company and Union Traction Company, Santa Cruz, 1906-12. Founder and first vice president Laveaga Realty Company, Santa Cruz, 1907. Retired from PG&E 1914. At time of death was president of Mid-Continent Utilities Corporation, a Midwestern company with extensive holdings in Central and Southern states.

Martin grew up in Brooklyn and, from age 13, had to fend for himself. Real estate experience in Alabama and employment by the Armours in Chicago preceded his arrival in California in 1891. In San Francisco he became a bookkeeper for Husband and Brooks, waterfront coal dealers, who subsequently went bankrupt. He worked as a salesman for the U. S. Cast Iron Pipe Company, then established his own business—John Martin Company—to sell pipe and pig iron. From iron sales he moved into electrical equipment sales, utility acquisition, traction development, real estate development, and finally utility management on a scale realized by few men.

In 1902 Martin and partners, for a "healthy price," bought the North Pacific Coast narrow-gauge railroad, broad-gauged and double-tracked the system, and added a third rail for electrification, the first such system in California. This acquisition was facilitated by a $6 million loan from the Mercantile Trust Company of San Francisco, of which $2.5 million was earmarked for improvements. The road did not pay off. In April 1904 Martin and associates sold all 60,000 shares of North Pacific Coast stock to the Southern Pacific for $800,000.

During these years Martin also pushed for development of the California Midland, a proposed third-rail system from Marysville to Auburn and Nevada City, California. The 1906 San Francisco earthquake precluded this railroad from ever becoming a reality.

Martin, a self-made man with "an inexhaustible energy, an indomitable will to succeed, an alert and facile mind, and a powerful physique," was at his prime during the late 1800s and early 1900s, as evidenced by the following account of his role in founding and guiding the Pacific Gas and Electric Company through its tumultuous early years:

Among Martin's acquaintances was an electrician who held a letter from the Stanley Electrical Manufacturing Company of Pittsfield, Massachusetts, authorizing him to sell its products on a commission basis. Martin apparently discussed with him the merits of electric power and Stanley equipment. Another of Martin's acquaintances, the manager of a Bay Area drugstore and owner of a mine in the Mother Lode country, was also interested in electric power. He in turn knew a young man, Eugene de Sabla, who with others was developing a powerhouse in Nevada County on the South Yuba River, above Grass Valley. Thinking to help Martin to a pipe contract, the friend arranged a luncheon meeting with de Sabla in San Francisco in 1894. Martin reportedly was late for the meeting, explaining when he arrived that the delay was occasioned by the birth that morning of his fifth child.

Charles M. Coleman, in his book *P. G. and E. of California*, reconstructs that meeting. The three men discussed power and pipe and electrical equipment. De Sabla told of studies of available generators, expressing his opinion that Stanley made the best generators for his Nevada County purposes. Martin seemed more interested in this phase of the discussion than in selling pipe. He and de Sabla did not meet again for two or three months, de Sabla assuming that Martin had forgotten their noontime discussion until one day he met Martin on Montgomery Street. "I'm ready now for your order," Martin said. "What order?" asked de Sabla. Then the story came out.

Intrigued by the talk of opportunities in electric power, Martin had gone to Pittsfield to meet William Stanley, the inventor and head of the manufacturing company. Although Martin had no training or experience in electrical construction, he was convincing enough to get the California agency for Stanley's products.

De Sabla did buy from Martin, commencing a long and mutually profitable association. The Nevada County project grew and prospered. Others soon followed: Sacramento Electric, Gas, and Railway; Yuba Electric Power; Butte County Power; California Central Gas and Electric. Martin sold equipment to these companies, but his enthusiasm gradually turned to utility company promotion. In just one five-month period he acquired 12 utilities from Chico to Colusa. Most of the holdings were eventually consolidated into two companies: California Gas and Electric, and San Francisco Gas and Electric. Then he and de Sabla created a new corporation, Pacific Gas and Electric, to amalgamate these two companies. That was in October 1905. The new corporation took charge January 2, 1906, bringing scores of utilities under one management.

Three months later came the San Francisco earthquake, forcing the new company to borrow $1.4 million over a nine-month period to rebuild its damaged facilities. This was in addition to nearly $1 million in bond interest due July 1, 1907. What followed next was an Eastern money crisis that sent financial shock waves through the nation, drying up sources of capital. One way out was bankruptcy, allowing the company to fall into receivership. Martin, de Sabla, and the other directors opposed this and pursued another plan reported in September 1907 by a Santa Cruz newspaper: "The assessment of $10 a share on the stock of the Pacific Gas and Electric Company, which became delinquent on August 31, has resulted in an unusual transaction in the securities of that company. The entire issue of common stock, amounting to $20 million, has been turned back into the treasury of the company, while the assessment on the preferred stock has been paid in full, amounting to a total increase in the company's resources of $1 million. The issue of 20 million of common stock has been held by the banking firm of Halsey and Company." The article went on to report unfounded rumors of an impending takeover of Pacific Gas and Electric by other interests, Martin and the bankers "maintaining a discreet silence."

By this maneuver Martin, de Sabla, and associates kept control of the giant utility, although at considerable personal expense. Martin had to come up with $200,000 to pay the assessment on his preferred stock. Pacific Gas and Electric weathered the storm, floated a bond issue, and was board-listed in 1910 by the New York Stock Exchange.

McGeoghegan, John T. d. San Jose December 16, 1906. Cashier and treasurer Garden City National Bank, San Jose, 1892.

McMillin, John Young. b. Indiana c. 1827. Member San Jose city council 1881. Listed occupation 1866 as lumberman.

McMurtry, William Sharp. b. Mercer County, Kentucky, August 24, 1818. d. Gilroy December 8, 1904. State senator 1863-64. Adventurer and entrepreneur. Attended Wabash College, University of Indiana, Miami University Medical College (Cincinnati), and Louisville Institute. Once physician in Indiana, Mississippi, and Louisiana. Gold and quartz miner Mother Lode country and Grass Valley, California, 1852-58. Veteran of two wars, serving with Texas Rangers under Col. Jack Hayes during Mexican-American War and with medical commission Army of the Potomac during Civil War. Came to Santa Clara County 1858 and located near Los Gatos, where he and J. Y. McMillin established first sawmill on Los Gatos Creek, above Lexington. President Los Gatos Manufacturing Company 1881.

Minor, Peter Overton. b. Virginia 1827. Pioneer San Jose member of state bar 1849. Built concrete structure west side of First Street down from Santa Clara Street. President Board of Trustees (equivalent to mayor) San Jose 1858. With Sam Bishop, Adolph Pfister, Jacob Rich, and others, invested 1885 in Paul O. Burns Wine Company, which later collapsed into bankruptcy.

Mintie, Alexander Erwin. b. Connecticut c. 1843. Listed occupation 1866 as orchardist.

Montgomery, T. S. Son of Rachel Rea (Mrs. George Montgomery) and cousin of James W. Rea, with whom he established San Jose real estate firm, T. S. Montgomery and Company, 7 Santa Clara Street. Called "one of San Jose's greatest benefactors." Director Garden City National Bank 1892. Exclusive agent Hanchett Residential Park 1907. Instrumental in developing South First Street business community, which for years was heart of San Jose central business district. Dick Barrett provides the following account:

"Years ago, on his 80th birthday, Montgomery told me, 'I looked east and west and saw San Jose running into the mountains. To the north it was blocked by the Bay. The only thing in the way to the south was Los Angeles.'

"So T. S. opted to look south. He built the Sainte Claire building at the southwest corner of First and San Carlos, and the Sainte Claire Hotel behind it. When Fox West Coast Theaters decided San Jose needed a 1920's cinema palace, it erected the Fox California south of the Sainte Claire building.

"The community's movers and shakers were firmly rooted in the South First Street business community—Charlie O'Brien, restaurateur and confectioner; Earle Bothwell and W. C. Lean, jewelers; J. S. Williams and Leon Jacobs, clothiers; W. L. Prussia and A. S. Appleton, women's wear; Frank C. Mitchell, Fred Oehler, and W. S. Clayton, bankers; Clarence Frazier (later of FMC) and John Giberson of Hale's; Fred Stern, leather goods; Henry Hirsch, W. L. Biebrach, Walter Trinkler, Curtis Lindsay, and in the background Charles Bigley, who has a garage across the street from City Hall, where he was said to wield considerable influence. The city was well and conservatively run under Manager C. B. Goodwin, and if Charlie rates some of the credit for that, God rest his soul."

According to Barrett, Montgomery provided an additional boost when he gave the city the site for the Civic Auditorium, across the street from the Sainte Claire Hotel, which got most of the resulting convention business. "The city received PWA funds and the downtown auditorium was built by Charlie Thomas, who told me long after that the contract price was $90,000 — hard to believe now."

Moody, David B. Son of founder, San Jose's first flour mill. With brothers Charles and Volney, operated San Jose City Mills, Third Street, producing wheat, flour, and macaroni. Acquired Central Milling Company of San Jose, originally built by Major McCoy, and expanded property to include mills in Victor, San Luis Obispo, Gilroy, and King City. Moody family sold the Central Milling Company during 1880s.

Moore, John Hendley. b. Missouri 1828. San Jose attorney 1850; founded law firm of Moore and Laine. State assemblyman 1867-68. One-time Santa Clara County District Attorney.

Morgareidge, Russell (Monty). b. Santa Cruz. Motorman Santa Cruz, Capitola and Watsonville electric railway 1903; credited with quick wit and skill in stopping car full of passengers when workman unexpectedly threw switch directing car onto side track. Worked briefly in construction Ocean Shore 1906, then for Peninsular as armature winder. Graduated to transportation department as conductor; often delivered spiel on Blossom Trolley Trips. Worked for Odgen, Logan, and Idaho and later as armature winder for Oakland, Antioch and Eastern. Employed San Francisco Terminal Railway about 1918 in Emoryville shops. In 1920 worked in S. P. West Alameda electric lines shop, in charge of dinkies.

Moulton, Stillman Augustus. b. Maine c. 1834. Listed occupation 1866 as fruit dryer.

Murphy, Bernard D. b. Quebec March 1, 1841. Came with family to California 1844 via Truckee River and Donner Lake, where father, Martin Murphy Jr., reportedly built cabins used by ill-fated Donner party in 1846. State assemblyman 1869-70. State senator two terms 1877-78, 1883-84. Mayor San Jose three terms 1873-77, 1880-81. President and trustee Commercial and Savings Bank 1881, serving as president about two decades. Trustee Agnews State Hospital 1889-93. Bank Commissioner 1890-92. Residing in San Francisco December 1911.

Newhall, Sylvester. b. Massachusetts c. 1827. Listed occupation 1866 as nurseryman.

Owen, James Jerome. d. San Francisco January 15, 1895. Long-time editor *San Jose Mercury.* Speaker pro-tem California State Assembly 1863-64. State library trustee 1882-85.

Parkinson, John Francis. b. Marshall County, West Virginia, December 2, 1864. d. September 2, 1956. Eldest son Dr. Benoni Parkinson, surgeon, Civil War veteran, and later physician, Washington County, Iowa. Lumberman, merchant, politician, and real estate developer. Owner J. F. Parkinson Hardware and Lumber Company destroyed by fire October 1915. Organizer of drive to incorporate Town of Palo Alto; first president Town Board of Trustees April 1906. First mayor Palo Alto 1906. With father and others, founded Bank of Palo Alto, later absorbed by American Trust Company. Also founded Palo Alto Savings, first savings and loan bank in community. Promoter Alba Park, early residential development near present Community Center. Incorporator Alta Mesa Memorial Park on southwest edge Palo Alto. With three others, bought several hundred acres of bayland 1907 in East Palo Alto area and founded two companies— Ravenswood Investment Company and Port Palo Alto Corporation—to promote industry and stimulate growth. Eventually he and his partners lost this land.

Parkinson, who attended the University of Michigan but was forced to drop out because of ill health, was a consummate planner and achiever. He worked briefly in Iowa as a banker and a lumberman. In 1888, driven by persisting poor health, he came to Santa Clara and took employment with a lumber yard. Soon he was foreman of a crew of more than 100, with income to match. He saw opportunity 1891 in new community of University Park (soon to be Palo Alto), invested his savings in a lumber yard there, and by year's end had a profitable and growing business. In later years, after selling lumber yard, he leased a sawmill in Sonoma County intent on expanding into home building. That was in the early 1920s. He saw a need and huge potential market for new housing, the key to which, he believed, was Federally supported financing. The slump after World War I caught up with him before he could fully develop his ideas, but he later presented them to his friend Herbert Hoover, then Secretary of Commerce. Hoover initiated a Federal home loan plan similar to Parkinson's during his presidency but was unable to complete it before his election defeat in 1932. President Franklin D. Roosevelt saw the plan to fruition.

Parkinson had a fine record of community service. In 1892 he gave University Park all the lumber for its first school. He ran for trustee of the first city school board in 1898, serving two terms. In 1903 he obtained a Carnegie Foundation grant for the city's first public library, at Hamilton and Bryant Streets.

Pfister, Adolph. b. Strasbourg 1821. Emigrated to New York 1846 and joined military regiment sent to California that year. San Jose mayor 1871. Established mercantile business, Pfister and Company, in San Jose and built brick structure 1858 on southeast corner First and Santa Clara Streets. Local agent for paper sales. Became partner in Saratoga paper mill (King, Meyer and Company) that began manufacturing rough brown wrapping paper September 1868. Acquired controlling interest and became president

of mill, which was destroyed by fire April 17, 1883. With Sam Bishop, P. O. Minor, Jacob Rich, and others, invested heavily 1885 in Paul O. Burns Wine Company, serving briefly as president.

Phelan, James Duval. b. San Francisco April 20, 1861; d. Saratoga (Montalvo), California, August 7, 1930. Graduate St. Ignatius College, San Francisco, 1881. Chairman Union Bank and Trust Company; director First National Bank and First Federal Trust Company, San Francisco. Mayor San Francisco; instrumental in bringing Hetch-Hetchy water to city. Regent University of California 1898-1914. U. S. Senator from California 1915-21. Following 1906 earthquake, President Theodore Roosevelt sent $10 million relief aid to Phelan personally rather than to San Francisco municipal government. Phelan died unmarried, willing Montalvo estate to San Francisco Art Association.

Quincey, Richard Henry. b. Canada c. 1849. Naturalized San Jose July 30, 1892.

Randol, James Butterworth. Superintendent Almaden Mines 1880. With A. J. Bowie and others, established Electric Improvement Company of San Francisco March 1887. Stockholder April 1892 in Central Avenue Railway Company, Oakland.

Rea, James William. b. Gilroy, California, August 23, 1854. Eldest son of Thomas Rea, farmer and dairyman who settled in Gilroy September 1853 and was town mayor, town councilman, one-term state assemblyman, and president Bank of Gilroy, which he helped found. Thomas Rea was an incorporator and director of the San Jose Brush Electric Light Company 1882. James Rea followed in father's footsteps. With cousin T. S. Montgomery, established San Jose real estate firm of Rea and Montgomery, later T. S. Montgomery and Company. Elected State Railroad Commissioner 1886, serving two terms (1866-94). Impeached by State Assembly for views on a horizontal reduction, the Senate refusing to concur. The Railroad Commission later adopted his views, which were sustained by the courts. Member and director, Santa Clara Valley Agricultural Society. With August J. Bowie, W. P. Dougherty, and others, founded Electric Improvement Company of San Jose October 1889, serving as vice president. Owned and operated Vendome Dairy north of San Jose.

"He is noted for his 'glad hand' and 'glad laugh,' which to the politician is the chief stock in trade," reported the *San Jose Pioneer* in September 1898. "About all the omissions and commissions of San Jose and Santa Clara County are laid at James' door. Some of them no doubt are his offsprings, yet the larger majority belong to his great army of friends, whose cross he is often called upon to bear."

Rhodes, Augustus Loring. b. Bridgewater, Oneida County, New York, May 21, 1821. d. October 23, 1918. Graduated Hamilton College, Clinton, New York, 1841. Practiced law in Indiana 1845. Captained train of 15 wagons to California 1854. Moved into home on The Alameda 1855; opened local law office. State senator two terms 1859-62. Justice California Supreme Court 1864-80. Judge Santa Clara County Superior Court 1899-1907. Regent State University 1880-88. Trustee State Normal School, San Jose, 1892-95.

Rich, Jacob. b. Poland October 15, 1826. Naturalized San Francisco September 20, 1859. d. San Jose January 6, 1901. Director San Jose Commercial Bank and San Jose Woolen Mills. With Sam Bishop, P. O. Minor, Adolph Pfister, and others, invested heavily 1885 in Paul O. Burns Wine Company, which fell into bankruptcy. Left estate valued at $2000 personal property, $7000 real property.

Rosenthal, Eugene Maximilian. b. California 1864. Life insurance agent.

Sauffrignon, Francois Jules. b. France 1823. Naturalized San Jose September 2, 1867.

Settle, Campbell Thompson. b. Indiana c. 1825. Listed occupation 1866 as fruit grower The Willows.

Shartzer, Hiram. Incorporator and director Saratoga and Pescadero Turnpike and Wagon Road Company 1866.

Shoup, Guy V. b. Bedford, Iowa, 1872. d. Mountain View, California, October 1965. Entered law practice San Bernardino, California, 1893. Joined Southern Pacific 1896 as claims department attorney, San Francisco. General solicitor United States Railroad Administration 1918. General solicitor Southern Pacific 1926; succeeded to direction S. P. Law Department 1927 on death of William F. Herrin. Retired from active S. P. service May 1, 1939, but continued until 1953 as a director of Southern Pacific and several affiliate companies. At time of death was a director of Wells Fargo Bank, San Francisco. With brother Paul (see below), formed Los Altos Land Company about 1915, which became First National Bank and, later, First Western Bank of Los Altos.

Shoup, Paul. b. San Bernardino, California, January 8, 1874. d. Los Angeles July 30, 1946. Newspaper carrier, later reporter *Los Angeles Express.* Worked briefly Santa Fe carshops, San Bernardino, then entered employ Southern Pacific 1891 as ticket clerk San Bernardino. Appointed district freight and passenger agent San Jose 1901. Assistant general manager, West Coast S. P. municipal and interurban electric lines, 1910. President Pacific Electric Railway 1912. Vice president in charge of Southern Pacific property interests 1918. Executive vice president 1925. Named director, member of executive committee, and president of Southern Pacific succeeding William Sproule 1929. In 1932 appointed S. P. vice chairman with headquarters at New York. Retired from active service June 1, 1938. For several years president and director Tidewater Associated Oil Company. President Pacific Oil Company December 1920. Director Anglo and London Paris National Bank of San Francisco and of California Development

Association. Trustee Stanford University 1923-46. Cofounder *Sunset Magazine*, originally an S. P. house organ.

Silent, Charles. b. Germany 1843; naturalized by naturalization of father, Ohio, 1854. With C. G. Harrison and others, incorporator San Lorenzo Flume and Lumber Company (1874), The Santa Cruz and Felton Rail Road Company (November 1874), and Pacific Avenue Street Railroad Company, Santa Cruz (April 5, 1876), serving as first president of Santa Cruz and Felton Rail Road and a director of all three companies. Also with Harrison and others, early investor Santa Cruz County Bank of Savings and Loan. Appointed Associate Justice Arizona Supreme Court February 1878. Target of lawsuit by Harrison in San Jose Superior Court December 1880 alleging misrepresentation of Harrison's Santa Cruz County investments. Went to Long Beach in mid-1880s to become land developer.

Southard, Albert B. (Abbie). b. Greencastle, Indiana c. 1859. d. San Francisco c. 1924. To San Francisco c. 1880. Organizer and first assistant superintendent, Richmond Methodist Episcopal Church (later Asbury Methodist Episcopal Church), San Francisco, April 1897. Younger brother of Frank Rose Southard, storekeeper and purchasing agent, Market Street Railway. Frank's son Earl Byron Southard, my wife's father, was also a storekeeper and purchasing agent, Market Street Railway and San Francisco Municipal Railway.

Spring, Thaddeus Warsaw. b. Buffalo, New York, June 17, 1829. d. San Jose August 13, 1890. Founded Spring's, Incorporated, San Jose clothing store, 1865. In 1868 reportedly had San Jose's third highest income: $32,679.

Swan, Rufus Chapman. b. New York State c. 1829. Gave occupation 1880 as clerk.

Tourney, George. Secretary German Savings and Loan Society, San Francisco, 1909.

Trimble, John. b. Missouri c. 1828. Gave occupation 1866 as farmer.

Van Schaick, Lewis Henry. b. Onondaga County, New York, 1835. At one time gave occupation as schoolmaster, Fremont Township.

Vestal, DeWitt Clinton. b. North Carolina c. 1836. Listed occupation 1866 as orchardist.

Whisman, John W. Came west with family 1847 by wagon train; generally credited with founding California's first stage line, San Francisco to San Jose, 1849. Ran old French omnibus hauled by half-wild mustangs. When winter rains made route impassible, he operated north from San Jose, meeting Bay steamers at Alviso embarcadero.

Selected Bibliography

Borden, Stanley T., "Sierra Lumber Company," *Western Railroader*, San Mateo, California, Vol. 31, No. 11, November 1968.

Bronson, William, *The Earth Shook; the Sky Burned*. Garden City, New York: Doubleday & Co., Inc., 1959.

Burrowes, Robert A., "Peerless Stages," *Motor Coach Age*, April 1971.

Cavette, Christopher J., private research, 1974, Palo Alto, California, Public Library.

Coleman, Charles M., *P. G. and E. of California*. New York: McGraw-Hill, 1952.

Cunningham, Florence R., *Saratoga's First Hundred Years*. Edited by Frances Fox. San Jose: Harlan-Young Press, 1967.

Dodge, John W. "Electric Railroading in Central California," *Pacific Railway Journal*, Vol. 1, No. 12, December 1956.

Field, Mary H., *An Arboreal Song of The Alameda*. San Jose: Ladies' Benevolent Society, 1878.

Foote, H. S., *Santa Clara County, California, Illustrated: Pen Pictures from the Garden of the World*. Chicago: Lewis Publishing Co., 1888.

Ford, Robert S., *Red Trains in the East Bay*. Glendale, California: Interurban Press, 1977.

Green, Larry, "San Francisco to San Jose and Back," *Rail Classics*, Vol. 9, No. 1, January 1980.

Gudde, Erwin G., *California Place Names*. Berkeley: University of California Press, 1969.

Hall, Frederic, "History of San Jose (1876)," *San Jose Pioneer*, 1877. (Courtesy Bancroft Library, University of California, Berkeley.)

Hall, Frederic, *The History of San Jose and Surroundings*. San Francisco: A. L. Bancroft & Co., 1871.

Harlan, George F., *San Francisco Bay Ferryboats*. Berkeley, California: Howell-North Books, 1967.

Heath, Ruth, "Fun Is Where You Find It," *The Trailblazer*, Quarterly Bulletin, California Pioneers of Santa Clara County, Vol. 11, No. 3, Summer 1971.

Historical Atlas Map of Santa Clara County. San Francisco: Thompson and West, 1876.

Kahn, Edgar M., *Cable Car Days in San Francisco*. Stanford, California: Stanford University Press, 1940.

Lewis, Oscar, *The Big Four*. New York: Alfred A. Knopf, 1938.

MacGregor, Bruce A., *South Pacific Coast*. Berkeley, California: Howell-North Books, 1968.

Mars, Amaury, *Reminiscenses of Santa Clara County and San Jose, Calif.* English edition translated from the French by Martha B. Straus, San Jose. Edited by H. L. Miller. San Francisco: The Mysell-Rollins Co, 1901.

McCaleb, Charles S., *Surf, Sand, and Streetcars: A Mobile History of Santa Cruz, California*. Glendale, California: Interurban Press, 1977.

McMurry, George H., and James, William F., *History of San Jose, California*. San Jose: A. H. Cawston, 1933.

Mitchell, David L., "Palo Alto Trolleys," *Pacific News*, March 1974.

Monro-Fraser, J. P., *History of Santa Clara County, California (Illustrated)*. San Francisco: Alley, Bowen, and Co., 1881.

Morse, Henry E., Jr., "San Jose Railroads," Booklet 373-E, *Western Railroader*.

"Peninsular Railway Co. Blossom Line," Booklet 348-E, *Western Railroader*.

Renovich, Steve, "Fresno Traction," *Western Railroader*, Vol. 23, No. 8, August 1960.

Santa Clara County, California (Illustrated). Chicago: Lewis Publishing Co., 1888.

"San Jose and Alum Rock Interurban," *Western Railroader*, Vol. 21, No. 3, January 1958.

Sawyer, Eugene T., *History of Santa Clara County*. Los Angeles: Historic Record Co., 1922.

Smallwood, Charles A., *The White Front Cars of San Francisco*. Glendale, California: Interurban Press, 1978.

Stindt, Fred A., "Peninsula Service: A Story of Southern Pacific Commuter Trains," *Western Railroader*, Vol. 20, No. 9, September 1957.

"Stockton Electric Railways," *Western Railroader*, Vol. 20, No. 6, June 1957.

Sunshine, Fruit and Flowers. Souvenir edition issued by *San Jose Mercury*, 1895 (A. C. Eaton) and 1896 (Smith Printing Co.)

Swett, Ira L., "Peninsular Issue," *Wheel Clicks*, Vol. 5, No. 1, July 1944.

Trimble, Paul C., *Interurban Railways of the Bay Area*. Fresno, California: Valley Publishers, 1977.

Rosters

SAN JOSE
SARATOGA
LOS GATOS

58

EQUIPMENT ROSTER: THE SAN JOSE RAILROADS

Sources: "Blue ribbon" committee; *The Western Railroader* (Booklet 373-E, Henry E. Morse, Jr., "San Jose Railroads," and Booklet 348-E, "Peninsular Railway Co. Blossom Line") private research of Vernon J. Sappers; local accounts; records of California State Railroad Commission.

PASSENGER EQUIPMENT

Nos.	Builder	Date	Length	Width	Height	Weight	Seats	Motors (hp)	Control	Brakes	Trucks	Cost	Type
1-3, 5-13	Sacramento Gas & Electric	1906	39'6"	7'10"	—	34,000	48	2-GE54(25)	GEK-10	Rope, hand	2-RDA	$3,700	Wood-body "old" California: six-window closed center section, longitudinal seating in open end sections.
2, 3, 31	American	1902	34'5"	7'4"	—	—	38	2-W58(35)	GEK-11	C-SA	2-B27G	$3,900	Wood-body California with steel frame: three compartments, straight bottom, transverse seating in ends, longitudinal seating in center. Steel sides on ends, wood sides in center. Two air-operated wire-mesh folding gates.
14, 15	Sacramento	1906	27'6"	7'10"	—	—	28	2-GE54(25)	GEK-10	Rope, hand	2-RDA	—	Wood-body "old" California: straight bottom, longitudinal seating in open end compartments, Clark fenders, two air-operated wire-mesh folding gates, two air-operated folding steps.
21	Sacramento	1906	39'6"	7'10"	—	34,000	48	2-GE54(25)	GEK-10	Rope, hand	2-RDA	—	Wood-body "old" California: six-window closed center section, longitudinal seating in open end sections, two air-operated wire-mesh folding gates, two double air-operated folding steps.
22, 23	American	1912	39'0"	7'11"	11'8"	—	40	2-GE203(50)	GEK-10	—	2-B27G	—	Wood-body California: full traverse seating, wire mesh to belt rail.
26-33													Wood-body California: one-compartment double-truck.
27-31	American	1919	27'10"	7'8"	9'10"	14,500	32	2-GE258C(25)	WK-100	W-SA	1-B78M1F	$6,300	Steel-body Birney Type F.
45-47			38'9"	8'0"			56			A	2-P	$500	Wood-body one-compartment trailer with open end platforms and transverse seating.
52, 55	Hammond	1889	42'10"	7'10"			40	2-GE201D(50)	GEK-36KAE	W-SA	2-B27GE1		Wood-body "long United Railways" double-truck California.
70-77	Jewett	1913	42'8"	8'0"									Wood-body: fully enclosed California: steel frame, transverse seating, wood or slatted pilot.
101, 102	Hammond	—	35'0"	6'11"			44	2-W58(35)	GEK-12 / GEK-10	Hand	2-P		Wood-body California: three compartments, straight bottom, full longitudinal seating in open ends.
105, 109, 112, 116	Hammond	1894-8	26'0"	7'2"			26	2-GE800(25) / 2-GE800(25) 2(25)	GEK-10	Hand	2-P		Probably wood-body California.
106, 108, 110 107, 113, 118	Hammond	1894-8	26'0"	7'2"			26	2-GE60(25) 2-W58(35)	GEK-10	Hand	2-P		Wood-body California: transverse seating in ends, longitudinal seating in center, wire-mesh folding gates, two hand-operated folding steps.
115			26'3"	7'3"			30	2-GE60(25)	GEK-10	Hand	1-B21E		Wood-body California: three compartments, straight bottom, longitudinal seating in center, transverse seating in open ends, hand-operated wire-mesh folding gates and folding steps.
120-126	American	1912	42'10"	8'0"		37,620	40	2-GE203(40)	GEK-36G	AC-A	2-B27G	$5,700	Wood-body California with steel frame: three compartments, full transverse seating, enclosed to belt rail by wire mesh. Originally had two swinging gates, two Brill folding gates.
127-130	Jewett	1913	42'10"	7'10"		38,800	40	2-GE201D(50)	GEK-36KEA	N-SA	2-B27G	$5,600	Wood-body California with continuous steel underframe: flush platform, straight bottom, transverse seating, steel sides on center, wire mesh on end compartments, wood pilots, lever-operated mesh exit gate, swing entrance gate.
131-136	Brill	1913	44'0"	8'2"	9'8"		51	2-GE201F(50)	GEK-36K	W-SA	2-B62E1	$5,100	Steel-body low-center-entrance Hedley-Doyle stepless "hobbleskirt."
137-158	St. Louis	1920	29'10"	7'8"	9'10"	16,500	34	2-W508A(28)	GEK-63	A	1-STL7		Steel-body Birney Type H.
159-163	American	1922	28'2"	7'8"	9'10"	15,500	34	2-GE264(25)		AC-SA	1-B79E1		Steel-body Birney Type J.
164-167	American	1910	38'8"	8'0"	11'5"		40	2-GE219A			2-B27GE1		Wood-body California with steel frame: full transverse seating, wire mesh to belt rail.

FREIGHT AND LINE EQUIPMENT

Nos.	Builder	Date	Length	Width	Height	Weight	Seats	Motors (hp)	Control	Brakes	Trucks	Cost	Type
2	Pacific Electric	1913	48'2"	8'10"	11'9"	87,000		4-GE222D(125)	GEM	W-EL14	2-SC80P		Wood-body express motor with steel frame (two steel bolsters).
10			34'6"	8'9"									Water car.
11	Peninsular	1914	40'6"	8'6"				2-GE87(60)	GEK-11	W-SA	2-B27E1		Motorized wood-body sprinkler with 4000-gallon steel tank.
13	Fitzgerald	1904	37'9"	8'7"	11'8"			3-WP30(15)	GEK-12	N-SA	RDA		Motorized wood-body sprinkler with 5000-gallon steel tank.
14	Holman	1894	26'0"	7'2"		38,000		4-W38B	WK-14	W-AMM	2-B27G	$1,500	Motorized wood-body line car with steel frame.
112	Holman	1905	41'5"	9'0"	12'3"	63,400		2-GE60(25)	GEK-10	Hand	2-P		Motorized wood-body sand car: two 1-yard sand boxes.
201	Kilburn-Jacobs		9'2"	6'4"				4-W38B	WK-14	Hand	2-B27GE3		Wood-body wrecker with steel frame.
													Eight unnumbered, unpowered single-truck side dump cars with steel frames, link-and-pin couplers.
302, 303													Flat cars.

Abbreviations:

Motors and control: GE = General Electric, W = Westinghouse.
Brakes: A = air, AC = Allis Chalmers, C = Christensen, N = National, SA = straight air, W = Westinghouse.
Trucks: B = Brill, P = Peckham, RDA = rebuilt diamond archbar, S = standard, STL = St. Louis.

Passenger Equipment Notes:

1-3, 5-13 Inherited from San Jose and Santa Clara County Railroad in 1911, these cars were part of 21-car order by Hanchett in 1906. Cost basis for car 6 was $3,700 and cars 9 and 10, $5,400. Cars 1, 2, 5, 7, 8, 11, and 13 scrapped about 1923 when 6, 9, 10, and 12 were converted for one-man operation as fully enclosed cars with new motors (total 100 hp), Westinghouse air brakes, Brill trucks, transverse seating, and whistle for interurban service. Car 6, the first to be rebuilt, had one marker light in center end; cars 9, 10, and 12 had two marker lights. These cars were scrapped and bodies sold about 1934. Car 3 was sold to Peninsular in 1920, converted for one-man operation, and renumbered 32. It came back to San Jose Railroads in 1930 as car 32, being scrapped prior to 1935.

2, 3, 31 Acquired from Los Angeles-Pacific in 1911 (former LAP 36, 38, and 39, respectively). Builder's order No. 407. Painted yellow. These cars retired 1923-24. Car 2 or 3 became diner on east side of El Camino Real (now State Highway 82) south of Mayfield. Car 31 became Espee Diner across from West Santa Clara Street carbarn, San Jose.

14,15 Also inherited from San Jose and Santa Clara County Railroad and part of Hanchett's 1906 21-car order, these cars

and 7'10" wide (compare data with 127-130, below), and 74-77, former Fresno Traction 41-44, 42'8" long and 8'0" wide. Cars 70, 71, and 73 scrapped about 1934, replaced with renumbered 164-class cars. Others scrapped 1938.

101, 102 Car 101 had Westinghouse motors and a K-12 controller. Car 102 had GE motors and a K-10 controller. Both cars were scrapped before 1926.

105, 107, 109, 112, 113, 116, 118 Believed to be ex-San Francisco and San Jose 28-37 class cars inherited from San Jose Railroad Company, acquired from United Railroads in 1905-06 and refitted for narrow gauge. Originally these were single-truck cars (Brill 21A, 21E trucks) with GE 25- and 28-hp motors and K-10 controllers. Records suggest that cars 107 and 118 were refitted for standard gauge, then returned to narrow gauge in 1914 and back to standard gauge in 1916. Cars 105, 109, 113, and 118—were converted for one-man operation in 1914. Car 112 was made into a sand car; car 116 was retired in 1913. The others—105, 107, 109, 113, and 118—were retired 1918-20. Cars 107, 113, and 118 were scrapped before 1926.

106 Destroyed by fire in 1916.

108, 110 Refitted for one-man operation 1914 but probably never converted to standard gauge. Car 110 scrapped by about 1916. Car 108 retired 1918-20.

115 Scrapped before 1926.

120-126 These cars, bought for San Jose Railroads by the Peninsular, had long, end platforms typical of Los Angeles PAYE cars but, according to Charles Smallwood, were patterned after rebuilt United Railroads 1375-1424 class. Builder's order number 920. They were later converted for one-man PAYE operation. Car 125 was scrapped 1938, the others about 1934. Car apparently were chopped down from original 39'6" length when rebuilt as one-compartment cars with transverse seating and Westinghouse air brakes. Car 14 sold to Peninsular in 1920. Car 15 scrapped before 1926.

21 Originally car 4, part of Hanchett's 1906 order; this car was rebuilt with new motors (total 100 hp), longitudinal seating, and Westinghouse air brakes. Scrapped before 1926.

22, 23 Acquired from Stockton Electric in 1937 and not renumbered for San Jose service. Builder's order No. 927.

26-33 Inherited from San Jose and Santa Clara Railroad in 1911, most of these narrow-gauge cars—used for Alum Rock Park service—were gone by 1914. Car 28, apparently purchased by Henry about 1898, was retired after 1914, as was car 33, which may have been an ex-Salinas car; an open-closed combination rebuilt with Brill 27G trucks from an old open-platform steam coach. Car 32, an ex-Salinas car, was sold to Peninsular and made into wrecker No. 5.

27-31 Acquired from Peninsular in 1934. Not repainted. Evidently saw limited service with San Jose Railroads and were scrapped in 1938.

45-47 Owned by Peninsular and carried on their records as Nos. 6-8. Lettered for SJRR. These trailers are believed to have come from Park and Ocean line, San Francisco, sold to Alum-Rock Railroad Company in early 1890s. Used in Alum Rock Park service. Given standard-gauge Peckham trucks in 1913 and retired before 1923. Scrapped 1925.

52, 55 Ex-Omnibus cable cars rebuilt 1898-1901 at 28th and Valencia carhouse, San Francisco. Believed to have been sold by United Railroads to San Jose Railroad Company 1905-06 and inherited from that company in 1909. Car 55 probably was standard-gauged and used on First Street lines. Car 52, once lettered "San Jose Traction," probably was not standard-gauged. Both cars retired after 1914.

70-77 Acquired from Peninsular in 1933, these cars comprised two classes; 70-73, former San Jose Railroads 127-130, 42'10" long

126 was replaced on the roster in 1934 by a renumbered 164-class car.

127-130 These cars, bought new for San Jose Railroads, were sold in 1927 to Peninsular, converted for one-man operation at 120 hp, and renumbered 70-73. Eventually they returned to San Jose Railroads as 70-73.

131-136 These cars also were bought new for the San Jose Railroads (builder's order number 18773). Car 135 scrapped after a wreck in San Jose. Others went in 1921 to Pacific Electric, which renumbered them 70-74.

137-158 Acquired in 1920 and originally 32-seaters, these cars were leased for $8,500/year (7½% of total purchase price) from S.P. equipment trust. Builder's order number 1243. Cars 137 and 141 went in 1936 to Sacramento Northern, which renumbered them 69 and 70. Cars 142-146 went to Stockton Electric in 1937; others were scrapped.

159-163 Acquired from San Diego Electric in 1925 (former SDE 326-329, 335). Builder's order number 1304.

164-167 Acquired from Fresno Traction in 1927-28 (former FT 25, 26, 32, and 34), these cars were rebuilt about 1932 into fully enclosed cars with transverse seating. Builder's order number 843. Renumbered in 1935 to 126, 70, 71, and 73. Scrapped 1938.

Freight and Line Equipment Notes:

2 Acquired from Peninsular 1934, scrapped 1938.
10 Sold to Peninsular 1910.
13 Scrapped by 1926.
14 Acquired from Peninsular 1934, scrapped 1938.
112 Converted from passenger car 112 (see above), sold to Peninsular 1922.

201 Acquired from Peninsular 1934, scrapped 1938.
302, 303 Sold about 1918.
Eight unnumbered dump cars scrapped before 1926.

Passengers from car 71 board Linda Vista-bound Birney 161 at the King Road transfer point in 1938.

Charles Smallwood Photo from James H. Harrison Collection

EQUIPMENT ROSTER: PENINSULAR

Sources: "Blue ribbon" committee; Ira L. Swett, "Peninsular Issue," *Wheel Clicks*, Vol. 5, No. 1, July 1944; Booklet 373-E, "San Jose Railroads"; private research of Vernon J. Sappers; local accounts; records of *The Western Railroader* (Booklet 348-E, "Peninsular Railway Co. Blossom Line," and Henry E. Morse, Jr.; California State Railroad Commission.

PASSENGER EQUIPMENT

Nos.	Builder	Date	Length	Width	Height	Weight	Seats	Motors (hp)	Control	Brakes	Trucks	Cost	Type
3	American	1902	34'5"	7'4"	—	—	38	2-W58(35)	GEK-11	C-SA	2-B27G	$3,900	Wood-body California with steel frame: three compartments, straight bottom, transverse seating in ends, longitudinal seating in center. Steel sides on ends, wood sides in center. Two air-operated wire-mesh folding gates.
13			30'4"	7'8"	10'6"	26,000	28	W56	WK-11	Hand	—	—	Wood-body city car.
14	Sacramento	1906	39'6"	7'10"	—	34,000	48	2-GE54(25)	GEK-10	Rope, hand	2-RDA	$3,700	Wood-body "old" California: six-window closed center section, longitudinal seating in open end sections.
15, 16	Holman	1905	34'2"	7'9"	10'8"	28,000	34	2-W56	WK-11	Rope	2-B27G	$3,900	Wood-body "old" California: four-window closed center section between two identical three-window open end sections.
17-20	St. Louis	1907	39'1"	8'1"	11'6"	33,640	40	2-GE80(40)	WK-11	W-A	2-B27G	$4,300	Wood-body California with two outside steel sills, whistles, large wood pilots.
22-26	Sacramento	1906	40'3"	8'7"	11'6"	38,000	40	2-GE54(25)	WK-10	Rope, hand	2-RDA	$3,000	Wood-body California.
27-31	American	1919	27'10"	7'8"	9'10"	14,500	32	2-GE258C(25)	WK-100	W-SA	1-B78M1F	$6,300	Steel-body Birney Type F.
32	Sacramento	1906	39'6"	7'10"	—	34,000	48	2-GE54(25)	GEK-10	WA	2-B27G	$2,500	Wood-body "old" California: six-window closed center section, longitudinal seating in open end sections.
50-61	American	1903	45'0"	8'3"	12'9"	55,000	52	4-W38B / 4-GE56	WK-14	W-AMM	2-B27MCB1	$6,400-7,700	Wood-body interurban with underframe of four steel I-beams, wooden cross-members, and two steel bolsters.
70-77	Jewett	1913	42'10"	7'10"	12'4"	—	40	2-GE201D(50)	GEK-36KEA	W-SA	2-B27GE1	—	Wood-body fully enclosed California: steel frame, transverse seating, wood or slatted pilot.
100-104	St. Louis	1909	43'1"	8'2"	—	59,600	48	W-306A	W264D2	W-AMM	2-A2 swing bolster	$8,600	Wood-body interurban with underframe of four steel I-beams, wooden cross-members, and two steel bolsters.
105-112	Jewett	1913	55'6"	9'4"	13'0"	85,200	64	W333	W272E	W-AMV	2-B27MCB3X	$13,000	Wood-body interurban with underframe of four steel I-beams, wooden cross-members, and two steel bolsters.
150	Hammond	1891	—	—	—	—	—	2-WALWP50(25)	K-2	—	2-M	—	Wood-body California: four-window closed center section.

FREIGHT AND LINE EQUIPMENT

Nos.	Builder	Date	Length	Width	Height	Weight	Seats	Motors (hp)	Control	Brakes	Trucks	Cost	Type
1	American	1903	43'0"	—	11'9"	48,000	—	4-GE87	WK-14	W-AMM	2-B27GE1	—	Wood-body baggage/express with two steel bolsters in underframe.
2	Pac. Electric	1913	48'2"	8'10"	12'8"	87,000	—	4-GE222D(125)	SCTAK	WEL14	2-SCROP	—	Wood-body express with steel frame (two steel bolsters).
4	Baldwin-Westinghouse	1912	34'0"	10'0"	11'10"	124,000	—	W308D3	WHL-D	WEL14	2-BALD rigid bolster	$19,170	60-ton steel-body box cab locomotive: tonnage rating 1400.
5	Peninsular	1912	38'0"	8'6"	12'1"	42,000	—	W38	WK-14	W-AMM	2-B27G	—	Wood-body double-truck one-compartment service motor.
9													Steel-body work motor.
10													Water car.
11													Weed sprayer.
12	Holman	1906	37'9"	8'7"	11'8"	38,000	—	2-W56	WK-14	W-AMM	2-B27G	—	Steel sprinkler.
14	Holman	1904	26'0"	7'2"	—	—	—	2-W38B	K-2	Hand	2-M	—	Motorized wood-body line car with steel frame.
101	Hammond	1891	—	—	—	—	—	—	GEK-10	WEL14	2-P	—	Wood-body California line car: four-window closed center section.
112	Hammond	1894-8	42'8"	9'3"	12'6"	68,000	—	2-WALWP50(25)	GEM	W-AMM	2-BALD78-25	—	Motorized wood-body sand car: two 1-yard sand boxes.
200	Holman	1906	41'5"	9'0"	12'3"	63,400	—	2-GE60(25)	WK-14	W-AMM	2-B27GE3	$520	Wood-body work motor.
201		1905	—	—	—	—	—	4-W56	WK-14	W-AMM		$700	Wood-body wrecker with steel frame.
300-307													Wooden flat car.
308	Peninsular	1918											Steel flat car.

Abbreviations:

Motors and control: GE = General Electric, WAL = Walker, W = Westinghouse.
Brakes: A = air, C = Christensen, N = National, SA = straight air, W = Westinghouse.
Trucks: BALD = Baldwin, B = Brill, M = McGuire, P = Peckham, RDA = rebuilt diamond archbar, S = standard.

Passenger Equipment Notes:

3 Acquired from Pacific Electric in 1923. Former Los Angeles–Pacific 32 and PE 110, similar to San Jose Railroads 2, 3, and 31. Builder's order No. 407.
13 Acquired from United Railroads in 1906 and rebuilt into double-truck car. Scrapped 1924.
14 Acquired in 1920 from San Jose Railroads. Former SJRR 14. Rebuilt after 1923 for one-man operation in Palo Alto.
15, 16 Acquired from San Jose–Los Gatos Interurban in 1905. Open sections enclosed when converted for one-man operation October 1916. Scrapped 1930.
17-20 Purchased in 1907. Converted for one-man operation October 1916–July 1918. Car 20 had open sections enclosed September 1922, others in August 1924. Car 20 wrecked 1926; others scrapped 1930.
22-26 Part of Hanchett's 1906 21-car order. Originally numbered 1-5 (not in order), with rope and hand brakes and rebuilt diamond archbar trucks. Car 5 wrecked in 1910; others were converted for one-man operation 1917 and probably renumbered as follows: 22 (old 5), 23 (old 2), 24 (old 4), 25 (old 1), and 26 (old 3). Air-operated gates and steps added 1919. Cars 23 and 24 scrapped 1926, others in 1930.
27-31 Acquired in 1919, these cars were leased from S.P. equipment trust for 6% per annum of total purchase price plus 3% annual depreciation on steel carbodies and 5% annual depreciation on electrical equipment. Builder's order number 1153C. Sold to San Jose Railroads in 1934.
32 Acquired from San Jose Railroads in 1920, this was former SJRR 3 rebuilt to resemble 22-class cars with Westinghouse air brakes and Brill trucks. Sold back to San Jose Railroads 1930 and scrapped before 1934.
50-61 As inherited from San Jose–Los Gatos Interurban in 1905, six of these cars—originally numbered 2, 4, 6, 8, 10, and 12—were powered and the other six—3, 5, 7, 9, 11, and 13—were unpowered. Builder's order numbers 483 (motor cars) and 483A (trailers). Rebuilt in 1910, at which time the trailers got GE motors and the cars were renumbered 50-61: 50, 52, 54, 56, 58, and 60 the former powered cars, 51, 53, 55, 57, 59, and 61 the former trailers. Cars 54, 57, and 58 got Brill trucks 1913 to replace original Peckhams, which were put on trailers 45-47. Class retired in 1928 when 70-class "comfort" cars were assigned to San Jose–Los Gatos run. Motors, controls, trucks, etc., removed from 50 and 51 in 1930 and installed in 60 and 61, at which time 60 got a GE motor and 52-61 were one-manned. All cars scrapped 1934. Car 52 became sewing room on ranch between Santa Clara and Cupertino, located by Charles Hopkins of San Jose, moved to California Railway Museum (Rio Vista Junction), rebuilt, dedicated for service 1976. Car 61, owned by Charles Smallwood, is now also at Rio Vista Junction.
70-77 These "comfort" cars, acquired in 1927 to replace 50-61 class, comprised two classes: 70-73, former San Jose Railroads 127-130 (42'10" long, 7'10" wide, Brill 27G trucks), and 74-77, former Fresno Traction 41-44 (42'8" long, 8'0" wide, Brill 27GE1 trucks). All rebuilt for one-man operation and sold to San Jose Railroads 1933.
102 Ex-San Francisco and San Mateo 15-27 class car inherited from San Jose–Los Gatos Interurban. Car observed in passenger service on Congress Springs line.
100-104 "Little Palys" bought in 1910. Builder's order number 850. Equipped with U.S.G. M-U Control. Open smoker end enclosed by Peninsular. Cars 102 and 103, sold to Fresno Traction in 1915, went to Pacific Electric 1918, renumbered 466 and 467. Cars 100, 101, and 104 sold to Pacific Electric 1921, renumbered 468-470. Car 467 was sold in 1934 and car 466 in 1935. Cars 468-470 scrapped 1934.
105-112 "Big Palys" acquired through S.P. equipment trust in 1913-14. Smoking section enclosed by Peninsular. Transferred to Pacific Electric 1934 and stored until 1937, when they went back to work as PE 1050-class cars.

Freight and Line Equipment Notes:

1 Inherited from San Jose–Los Gatos Interurban, this car was named "Rustler" when received from builder. Builder's order number 484. Retired 1926.
2 Acquired new from Pacific Electric in 1914. Sold to San Jose Railroads 1934 and scrapped 1938.
4 Acquired new from Westinghouse in 1913. Builder's order number 38299. Leased in 1921 to Pacific Electric, renumbered 1618. Later sold to Pacific Electric. Scrapped 1955.
5 Ex-Salinas car 32, acquired from San Jose Railroads and rebuilt as wrecker. Scrapped and burned about 1915. May have been called "Susie."
9 Scrapped after 1923.
10 Purchased from San Jose Railroads 1910. Gone by 1923.
— Unnumbered car called "Little Goat," body acquired from SJRR, rebuilt by PRy 1913.
11 Gone by 1923.
12 Scrapped 1934.
14 Inherited from San Jose–Los Gatos Interurban, this car got new Holman superstructure and Trenton tower 1911. Sold to San Jose Railroads 1934, scrapped 1938.
101 Ex-San Francisco and San Mateo 15-27 class car inherited from San Jose–Los Gatos Interurban, which acquired it from United Railroads. Sister to car 150. Outfitted with wooden tower and served as line car.
112 Acquired from San Jose Railroads 1922.
200 Acquired new. Nicknamed "The Goat." Rebuilt 1926 with steeple cab and with new heavy Baldwin trucks purchased, less wheels, from San Francisco and Sacramento Railway (Sacramento Northern). Scrapped 1934.
201 Acquired new in 1905, this former work motor was converted to a wrecker, sold to San Jose Railroads 1934, and scrapped 1938.
300-307 Purchased about 1920. Cars 304-307 scrapped in 1930, 300-303 in 1934.
308 Scrapped 1934.

Peninsular 107 in San Carlos Street opposite the San Jose carbarn. (J.C. Gordon photo from Lorin Silleman Collection)

The center section of Peninsular 107. (J.C. Gordon photo from Lorin Silleman Collection)

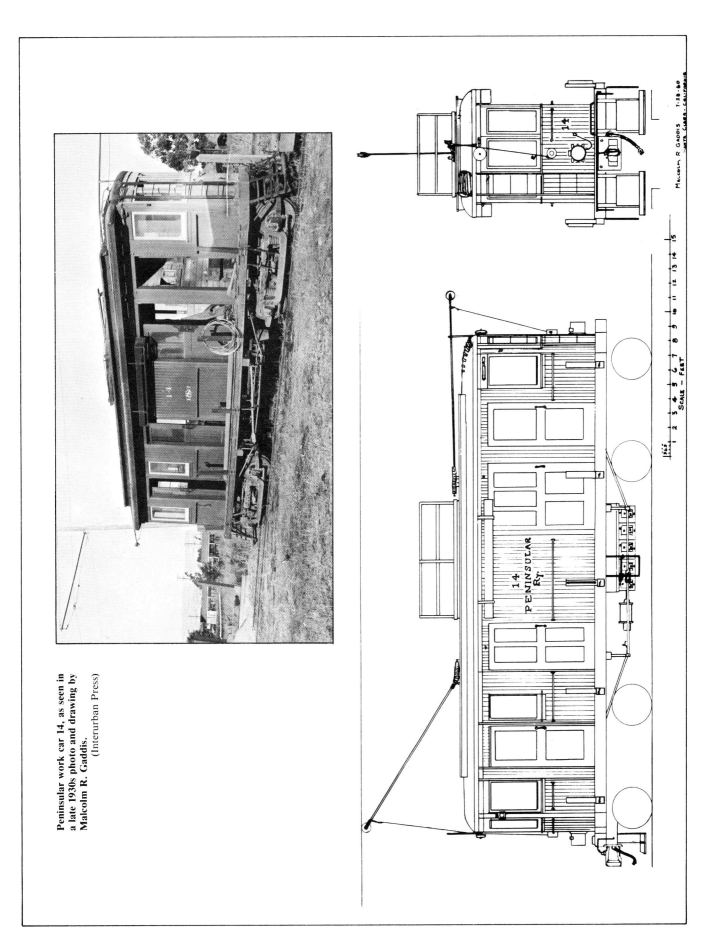

Peninsular work car 14, as seen in a late 1930s photo and drawing by Malcolm R. Gaddis.

(Interurban Press)

PENINSULAR RAILWAY COMPANY
CARS NUMBERED 50 TO 61 INCL.

SCALE

DRAWN BY 8-9-58
MALCOLM R. GADDIS

MECHANICAL DEPT. SOUTHERN PACIFIC CO.

BUILDER: AMERICAN CAR CO. 1903
SEATS: 52
WEIGHT: 55,000
LENGTH: 45-0
WIDTH: 8-5
HEIGHT: 12-5
MOTORS: WESTINGHOUSE 38 B
CONTROL: WESTINGHOUSE K-14
BRAKES: WESTINGHOUSE AM
TRUCKS: BRILL 27 MCB 1
DISMANTLED: 1934

This drawing, by Malcolm R. Gaddis, is representative of the Peninsular's 50-61 series.   (Interurban Press)

San Jose Railroads 123 at the Alameda carbarn, San Jose. (J.C. Gordon photo from Henry E. Morse Jr. Collection) **BELOW: Drawing is of SJRR 127-130 class after transfer to Pacific Electric Railway as part of 160-169 class.** (Interurban Press)

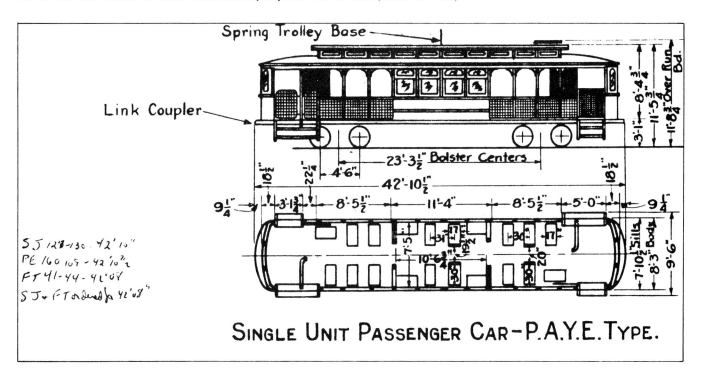

SINGLE UNIT PASSENGER CAR—P.A.Y.E. TYPE.

PARTIAL MOTOR COACH ROSTER: SAN JOSE RAILROADS

Source: James H. Graebner, San Jose, California

Year	Quantity	Builder	Model	Serial	Seats
1935	4	Yellow	717		30
	4	Twin Coach	25R		25
	4	Twin Coach	23R		23
1936	5	Twin Coach	23R		23
	2	Twin Coach			20
1938	9	Twin Coach	30R		31
	5	Twin Coach	23R		23

Notes:
Data from *Transit Journal* annual statistical numbers. Jack Perry comments that Twin was not known to be building 20-passenger coaches in 1936. Among coaches on October 1945 San Jose City Lines roster, claims Norman Holmes, were three Yellow 717s (2222-2224), 20 Twin 23Rs (2226-38, 2250-54, 2297, 2298), and 11 Twin 30Rs (2239-49), which probably included most of the above.

MOTOR COACH ROSTER: PENINSULAR RAILWAY

Source: Vernon J. Sappers, Oakland, California

Nos.	Year	Builder	Type	Serial	Seats
213-216	1924	Fageol	4 cyl		29
217-219	1930	ACF	6 cyl		21
3	1916	PERy	6-wheel		
8-11	1923	Reo	Wooden body		

Notes:
3 body built by Pacific Electric, engine by Fageol. Duplicate of bus built for Fresno Traction. Passenger compartment was actually a 2-wheel trailer. Scrapped 1923.
8 chassis by Reo, body by Eagle Body Works, San Jose.
213, 214, 217, 218, 219 sold 1934; 213, 214 to SJRR.

MOTOR COACH ROSTER: SAN JOSE CITY LINES

Source: Allen Copeland, El Cajon, California, and Eli Bail, San Jose, California

Nos.	Year	Builder	Model	Serial	Seats
3501-3508	1964	GMC	TDH-3501	163-170	35
6501-6510	1948	GMC	TDH-4507	2426-2435	45
6511, 6512	1959	GMC	TDH-4512	3249, 3263	45
6513-6517	1960	GMC	TDH-4517	389-393	45
6518-6522	1962	GMC	TDH-4517	1542-1546	45
6523-6527	1967	GMC	TDH-4519	1669, 1734-1737	45
6601-6605	1944	GMC	TG-3609	301-302, 305-303	36
6601-6605	1946	GMC	TD-3609	197-201	36
6606-6611	1946	GMC	TD-3609	095-100	36
6612	1946	GMC	TD-3609	124	36
6613-6620	1946	GMC	TD-3609	248-255	36
6621-6630	1947	GMC	TDH-3610	416-425	36
6637	1946	GMC	TD-3609	202	36
6641-6644	1951	GMC	TDH-3612	1038-1041	36

Notes:
First 6601-6605 to Glendale City Lines (9615-9619).
Second 6601-6605 from Glendale City Lines (9615-9619); ex-Glendale City Lines 1031, 1026-1029 (4616-4620).
6637 from Glendale City Lines (9620); ex-Glendale City Lines 1030 (4621).

MOTOR COACH ROSTER: ALMADEN STAGE LINES

Source: Norman W. Holmes, Portola, California

No.	Year	Builder	Model/Serial	Seats	Date	Original Owner
11	1941	Yellow	TG2706-023	29	10-51	Utah Light & Traction
12	1942	Chevrolet		11	5-52	U.S. Army
14	1945	GMC	TG3609-747	38	4-55	U.S. Navy
15	1945	Ford		29	8-55	Asbury Rapid Transit (Los Angeles)

Notes:
11 Six-cylinder GMC gasoline engine and three-speed transmission. Stockton City Lines an interim owner. Orig. Utah Light & Traction Co. 273. Eventually scrapped.
12 Used exclusively on Almaden line; eventually scrapped.
14 Bought from McCoy Charter Service, San Francisco. Gas engine, three-speed transmission. Was to have become Mayfair No. 64. Finally went to Golden Arrow Charter Service.
15 Single-door transit bus purchased from a Los Angeles dealer. Six-cylinder 8MB engine. Workhorse of Almaden fleet. Sold to Modesto Bus Lines.

MOTOR COACH ROSTER:
PALO ALTO CITY LINES AND PALO ALTO TRANSIT

Source: Jack Perry, Sunnyvale, California, and Eli Bail, San Jose, California

Nos.	Year	Builder	Type/Model	Co.	Remarks
99	1935	Flxible/Chev.	Conv./Airway	CL	Disp. c. 1945
101	1933?	White	Conventional	CL	Disp. c. 1942
102-107	1930?	Yellow Coach	Conv./Intercity/25-pass.	T	Bought 1934. Disp. 1938-41
102	1938	Flxible	Intercity/Clipper/25-pass.	T	
103-105	1941?	GMC	Conventional	CL	Disp. c. 1945
103	1941	Flxible	Intercity/Clipper/25-pass.	T	Ex-Moyers Stage 81; Bought 1946
106, 107	1938	Diamond T	Conv./25-pass. Gillig body	T	
108	1935	Diamond T	Conv./25-pass. Gillig body	T	Disp. 1946
109, 110	1938	Diamond T	Conv./37-pass. Gillig body	CL	Disp. 1948
112	1935	Flxible/Chev.	Conv./Airway	T	Bought 1941. Disp. c. 1950
114, 115	1932	Twin Coach	Transit/Model 19	CL	Ex-East Bay Transit 308, 310. Sold to Martin Transportation Co. 1945
213-216	1924	Fageol	Conv./Safety Coach	CL	Ex-Peninsular Ry. 213-216; 213, 214 sold 1938; 215 sold 1941
217-219	1930	ACF	Conv./Intercity	T	Ex-Peninsular Ry. Disp. c. 1934
217-239	1944-46	Ford	Transit/49-B, 59-B, 69-B	CL	Many second-hand
240-245	1941-42	Twin Coach	Transit/41 G	CL	Ex-Key Sys. 440s, 450s, and 460s bought 1948, sold 1950-54
246	1947	Martin	Transit	CL	Ex-Martin Transport 23 bought 1948, sold 1954
247	1945	Ford	Transit/59-B	CL	Bought 1951
248-250	1945-46	Ford	Transit/59-B, 69-B	CL	Ex-Key System
251-255	1946	Ford	Transit/69-B	CL	Second-hand

Notes:
115 enlarged to a 23-passenger coach by Palo Alto City Lines.
213-216 had gold-leaf lettering inside—PRy—denoting ownership by Peninsular Railway. 216 was used in active service until 1949 and then restored to operating condition for Palo Alto new bus ceremony December 2, 1963. This coach is still in existence.
Palo Alto City Lines buses were painted green and white; Palo Alto Transit buses were painted red and white. As of November 30, 1963—the final day of private operation for Peninsula Transit—only 15 Ford Transits were still licensed for operation; the remainder had been sold, scrapped, or cannibalized for parts. As of February 21, 1964, seven Ford Transits were licensed for operation.

MOTOR COACH ROSTER: MAYFAIR SUBURBAN LINES

Source: Norman W. Holmes, Portola, California

No.	Year	Builder	Model/Serial	Seats	Date	Original Owner
51	1943	Ford	29B/570313	27	8-17-53	Capital Transp.
52	1943	Ford	29B/570214	27	8-17-53	Capital Transp. 43
53	1942	Twin Coach	41G/39828	41	11-3-54	Key System, prob. 458
54	1942	Twin Coach	41G/39822	41	(Not used)	Key System, prob. 452
55	1942	Yellow	TD4505/208	41	9-1-55	Greyhound 1183
56	1942	Yellow	TD4505/236	45	5-15-56	S.F. Muni 316
57	1942	Yellow	TD4505/238	45	5-15-56	S.F. Muni 320
58	1942	Yellow	TD4505/228	45	6-15-58	S.F. Muni 314
59	1946	White	798/319541	44	10-30-60	S.F. Muni 0144
60	1945	GMC	TD3206/430	39	1-14-58	S.M.-Burlingame Transit 15
61	1942	Twin Coach	30G/105834	33		
62	1943	White	798/279960	46	9-1-58	Gray Line
63	1941	White	798/240229	45	1-20-58	Pacific Electric 2077
65	1942	Yellow	TD4505/216	41	9-15-59	Greyhound 1191
66	1948	White	798/344654	44	11-12-59	S.F. Muni
81	1948	GMC	PD4151/004	41	4-1-59	Greyhound 95

Notes:

51 Sold as parts source to Modesto Bus Lines.

52 Always ran as No. 43 (original Capital Transp. number).

53 Bought from D'Arrigo Brothers and finally sold to a Santa Clara church for use as a classroom. Its replacement motor was the International 450 from No. 54.

54 Bought from Eastshore Lines, used for parts, and eventually scrapped.

55 Used for charter service; eventually sold to a farm labor contractor.

56-58 Originally built for New York Third Avenue Railway, diverted to Market Street Railway by ODT. Used for charter service; finally scrapped. Nos. 56 and 57 purchased from San Francisco Municipal Railway and No. 58 from Eastshore Lines.

59 Used for charter service; eventually sold to a private individual.

60 Originally a 32-passenger coach lengthened by San Mateo–Burlingame Transit using GMC kit. Engine and transmission eventually installed in Almaden No. 14; body scrapped.

61 Bought from farm labor contractor. Given to Pacific Locomotive Association, Richmond, where it was vandalized and finally scrapped.

62 Bought mainly for parts from Pink Elephant Market, San Jose, which had used it and three others as rolling grocery stores. Eventually scrapped.

63 Purchased from a Lafayette, California, charter company. Replacement motor installed. Used for charter service; sold after Mayfair folded.

65 Sister to No. 55. Purchased from a mobile home dealer; previously used by a church. Sold to truck operator who wanted it for a storage shed.

66 Twelve-cylinder gasoline bus with automatic transmission. Eventually went to Golden Arrow Charter Service.

81 Bought through Chicago dealer, picked up in Detroit, used in both route and charter service. Not air conditioned. Went to Golden Arrow, whose owner had financed initial purchase.

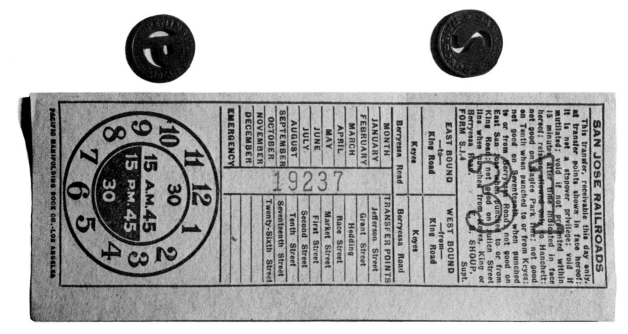

(Norman Holmes Collection)

NOVEMBER 1967 MOTOR COACH ROSTER: PENINSULA TRANSIT

Source: Jack Perry, Sunnyvale, California

Nos.	Year	Builder	Model	Serial	Remarks
216	1924	Fageol Safety Coach		104-65	Ex-Peninsular Ry 216
221	1945	Ford	59-B	99T-641053	
222	1945	Ford	59-B	997-641054	Not licensed
223	1944	Ford	49-B	99T-587605	
226	1946	Ford	69-B	99T-836243	Sold
227	1944	Ford	49-B		
230	1944	Ford	49-B	99T-587800	
231	1944	Ford	49-B	99T-587802	Sold
232	1944	Ford	49-B	99T-587799	
234	1946	Ford	69-B	99T-1027005	Sold
237	1946	Ford	69-B	99T-1069503	Sold
247	1944	Ford	49-B	99T-587590	
250	1945	Ford	59-B	99T-641548	Sold
251	1946	Ford	69-B	99T-1016207	
260-268	1963	GMC	TGH-3102	1536-1544	Owned by Palo Alto
269	1966	GMC	TGH-3501	087	Owned by Palo Alto
400, 401	1957	GMC	TGH-3101	643, 644	
5510, 5511	1940	Yellow Coach	TD-4502	223, 001	

Notes:
400 and 401 ex-Bay Rapid Transit 92 and 93.
5510 and 5511 ex-Sacramento Transit 5510 and 5511; 5511 was restored and renumbered 402.
Coaches 260, 261, 263-269, and 400 (renumbered 262) passed to County Transit January 1, 1973, where they operated until sold in July 1978.

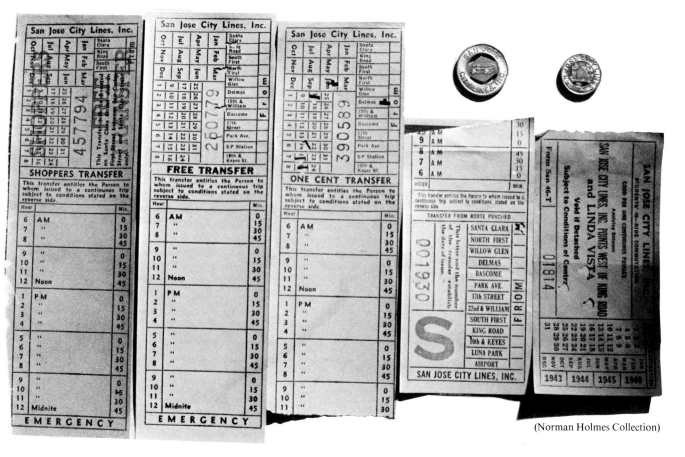

(Norman Holmes Collection)

APRIL 1971 MOTOR COACH ROSTER: PEERLESS STAGES

Source: Robert A. Burrowes, Eureka, California and Eli Bail, San Jose, California

Nos.	Year	Builder	Model	Serial	Seats
234, 235, 237	1948	GMC	PDA-4101	046, 047, 049	41
238, 239	1950	GMC	PDA-4101	333, 334	41
242, 243	1953	GMC	PD-4104	449, 450	41
244-246	1955	GMC	TDM-4512	124-126	47
247, 248	1957	GMC	TDM-4512	241, 242	47
249, 250	1957	GMC	PD-4104	2309, 2310	41
251	1941	Yellow	PDG-4101	169	41
252	1940	Yellow	PDG-4101	024	41
253, 254	1941	Yellow	PDG-4101	170, 167	41
257, 258	1959	GMC	PD-4104	4219, 4220	41
259	1942	Yellow	TD-4505	586	47
260	1945	GMC	TD-4506	234	45
261	1961	GMC	SDM-4501	053	45
262, 263	1961	GMC	PD-4106	432, 433	38
264-267	1945	GMC	TD-4506	130, 023, 032, 028	45
268, 269	1940	Yellow	PDG-4101	111, 006	41
270	1962	GMC	PD-4106	1217	41
273, 274	1966	GMC	PD-4107	494, 495	41
275, 276	1967	GMC	PD-4107	569, 570	41
277, 278	1969	GMC	PD-4903	294, 295	47
279		GMC	TD-4506		45
280	1942	Yellow	TD-4505	574	47
281	1945	GMC	TD-4506	226	45
282, 283	1950	GMC	PDA-4101	312, 316	41

Notes:
251-254 from Western Greyhound Lines 1958 (P814, P758, P815, P812).
264-267 from Los Angeles Metropolitan Transit District 1961 (2698, 2683, 2692, 2688).
279 from Berkeley Charter Lines.
280 from Franciscan Lines 1969 (425).
281, 283 from Eastshore Lines 1969 (405, 352).
282 from Southshore Lines 1969 (2001).

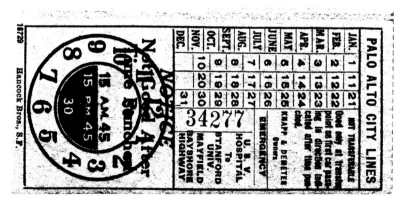

(Norman Holmes Collection)

MOTOR COACH ROSTER:
SANTA CLARA COUNTY TRANSIT DISTRICT

Source: Jack Perry, Sunnyvale, California

Nos.	Year	Builder	Model	Serial	Remarks
40, 41	1977	GMC	Rally Wagon		Never used in transit service
42-51	1978	Plymouth	Voyager Custom		Propane; transferred to other uses 1979
59	1942	Yellow Coach	TD-4505	586	Sold September 1973
60	1945	GMC	TD-4506	234	Sold September 1973
65-67	1945	GMC	TD-4506	023, 032, 028	Sold January 1978
80	1942	Yellow Coach	TD-4505	574	Sold September 1973
81, 85	1945	GMC	TD-4506	226, 223	Sold September 1973
200-208	1977	Mercedes-Benz	0390D	All in 309382-10 series	Bought November 1979
209, 210	1974	Mercedes-Benz	0309D	309382-10 -026801, -023593	Bought September 1980
260, 261	1963	GMC	TGH-3102	1536, 1537	Sold July 1978
262	1957	GMC	TGH-3102	643	Sold July 1978
263-268	1963	GMC	TGH-3102	1539-1544	Sold July 1978
269	1966	GMC	TGH-3501	087	Sold July 1978
400-533	1974	Twin Coach	TC-31B	25604-25737	About half scrapped, stored, or sold December 1978 to October 1979; rest 1981 (replaced by 4600s and 4800s)
534-537	1975	FMC	V-026	5-03-V-0784-0787	O.S. September 1978
600	1977	Gillig	PT477 35-96	EP-4601	Ford propane engine; renumbered from 601
602-681	1977-78	Gillig	PT477 35-96	E-4602-4681	Ford propane engines
682-733	1978	Gillig/Neoplan	PT477 35-96	E-8682-8733	Ford propane engines; front door lifts
1000-1065	1978	GMC	TH-8201	359-424	RTS-2 built for but never delivered to AC Transit
1100-1149	1979	GMC	T7H203	A001-A050	RTS-2 with rear door lifts
1202, 1207 1210, 1213 1215, 1309	1961-62	GMC	TDH-5301 2454, 2457 2459, 3131	2446, 2451	Leased from TBTGIC March 1978– March 1979 except 1213, bought at scrap value (see 6528)
1600-1818	1981	Grum'n-Flxible	53102-8-1	92902-93120	Flxible 870; front door lifts added after delivery to County Transit
1703, 1709 1712, 1717 1720, 1734 1735, 1774 1777, 1778 1788, 1799 1800, 1809 1814, 1815 1837, 1852	1947	GMC	TDH-4507 1476, 1495 1477, 1496 1470, 1516 1507, 1503 1501, 1513 1529, 1544 1543, 1552 1541, 1651	1488, 1469	Leased from AC Transit March– September 1973 (same fleet numbers); bought for $2000 each. 1777, 1778, 1800, 1837 sold January 1978; others July 1978
2103, 2111	1958	GMC	TDH-4801	530, 538, 542	Leased from AC Transit July 1979-February 1980; used only as training coaches
2313-2317 2319, 2326 2330-2332	1954	GMC	TDH-4801 092, 096-098	079-083, 085	Leased from Southern California Rapid Transit District (same fleet numbers) January-June 1978
2380-2389	1954	GMC	TDH-4801	146-155	Leased from Southern California Rapid Transit District (same fleet numbers) December 1977-July 1978
3501-3508	1965	GMC	TDH-3501	163-170	Sold July 1978
4501-4503	1958	GMC	TDH-5105	3538, 3535 3539	Leased from San Diego November 1977- November 1978
4541-4558	1956-58	GMC	TDH-4512	1259, 1260 1263, 1265 1266, 1269	Leased from Sacramento Rapid Transit April 1976-February 1980; 4551 returned Dec. 1977, others February 1980

Nos.	Year	Builder	Model	Serial	Remarks
				1271, 2135	
				2137, 2138	
				2837, 2809	
				1258, 1262	
				1268, 1272	
				1267, 2835	
4551	1951	GMC	TDH-5103	546	Bought from AIBE December 1977
4561-4564	1960	GMC	TDH-4517	334-337	Leased from Sacramento Rapid Transit July 1976. 4563 and 4564 exchanged for 4557 and 4558
4600-4655	1960-61	GMC	TDH-5302	172, 189, 202	Leased from NIMCO December 1978-December 1979, then bought and rebuilt
				205, 221, 211	
				227, 236, 238	
				256, 260, 268	
				264, 266, 272	
				273, 353, 357	
				396, 159, 151	
				153, 240, 262	
				167, 152, 145	
				174, 190, 168	
				194, 267, 206	
				203, 390, 163	
				228, 395, 148	
				252, 193, 394	
				388, 358, 389	
				355, 365, 391	
				184, 208, 262	
				269, 361, 379	
				384, 387	
4701	1960	GMC	TDH-4517	106	Leased September 1978
4702-4711	1961	GMC	TDH-5301	2197-2206	Leased September 1978
4712-4715	1965-6-8	GMC	TDH-5303	3116, 4060	Leased September 1978
				6042, 6043	
4716-4718	1969	GMC	TDH-5305A	421, 420, 419	Leased September 1978
4800-4881		GMC			Bought from NIMCO; deliveries started September 1980
4800	1960		TDH-5301	766	
4801	1962		TDH-5301	3409	
4804	1962		TDH-5302	547	
4806-4809	1962		TDH-5302	747, 549, 678	
				683	
4812-4816	1962		TDH-5302	719, 722, 538	
				735, 741	
4818	1962		TDH-5301	3375	
4823	1962		TDH-5301	3393	
4825-4830	1962		TDH-5301	3383, 3386	
				3390, 3052	
				3060, 3061	
4831	1961		TDH-5301	2443	
4833	1962		TDH-5302	540	
4838	1962		TDH-5302	740	
4840, 4841	1963		TDH-5304	181, 186	
4843	1963		TDH-5304	195	
4848-4850			TDH-5304	233, 238, 244	
4851-4855	1964		TDH-5304	541, 591, 598	
				601, 625	
4857-4861	1960		TDH-5302	158, ?, 240, 185	
				187	
4864-4866	1960		TDH-5302	201, 219, 231	
4868	1961		TDH-5302	371	
4870	1960		TDH-5302	237	
4874	1960		TDH-5302	246	
4876, 4877	1960		TDH-5302	253, 258	

Nos.	Year	Builder	Model	Serial	Remarks
4879-4881	1961		TDH-5302	354, 375, 382	
6501-6510	1948	GMC	TDH-4507	2426-2435	6505 sold September 1973; 6501, 6504 sold January 1978; others July 1978
6511, 6512	1959	GMC	TDH-4512	3149, 3263	OS February 1980
6513-6517	1960	GMC	TDH-4517	389-393	
6518-6522	1962	GMC	TDH-4517	1542-1546	
6523-6527	1967	GMC	TDH-4519	1669, 1734-1737	
6528	1961	GMC	TDH-5301	2457	Rebuilt from 1213; in service May 1980
6604	1946	GMC	TD-3609	200	Sold January 1978
6616-6619	1946	GMC	TD-3609	251-254	Sold January 1978
6621-6630	1947	GMC	TDH-3610	416-425	6621, 6622, 6624-6627 sold September 1973; others January 1978
6641-6644	1951	GMC	TDH-3612	1038-1041	Sold July 1978
VP20-VP39	1975	Plymouth	Voyager		All scrapped, sold, or OS by 1979
———	1977?	Dodge	Sportsman Maxivan		Leased from Pinetree Transportation November 1977-March 1978

Notes:

59 Ex-Peerless 259; single door.

60 Ex-Peerless 260; single door.

65-67 Ex-Peerless 265-267; two doors. 66 rebuilt late 1975.

80 Ex-Peerless 280; single door.

81, 85 Ex-Peerless 281, 285; single door.

200-202 Ex-City of Bettendorf, Iowa. 201 has center-door lift.

203-208 Ex-Dominic Motor Company, Charlottesville, Virginia. Rear door lifts installed by County Transit on 206, 207, 208.

209, 210 Ex-Western Company of North America (Colorado); bought from Dub Shaw Leasing, Fort Worth, Texas.

260, 261 Ex-Peninsula Transit 260, 261. Converted to propane.

262 Ex-Peninsula Transit 400. Substituted for original 262; converted to propane.

263-269 Ex-Peninsula Transit 263-269. Converted to propane.

400-533 Chrysler propane engines. 472 scrapped July 1976; 516 rebuilt with TE-1 lift 1976; 458 rebuilt with TE-2 lift 1977.

534-537 Center-door-lift "handy buses"; Chrysler propane engines.

1202, 1207, 1210, 1213, 1215, 1309 Former Indianapolis coaches (same fleet numbers).

2313, 2317, 2319, 2332, 2382, 2383, 2387 Coaches had "black window" paint scheme.

3501-3508 Ex-San Jose City Lines 3501-3508. 3503-3507 re-engined and converted to propane.

4541-4558 Former Sacramento Rapid Transit 102, 103, 106, 108, 109, 112, 116, 118, 119, 125, 130, 101, 111, 115, 110, 123.

4551 Former Gray Lines of Los Angeles 5106, former LATL 6415.

4561-4564 Former Sacramento Rapid Transit 132-135.

4501-4503 Former Bus That Goes in Circles, Inc. (San Diego) 1511, 5122?, 1512.

4600-4655 Ex-Transport of New Jersey (TNJ) P300s, P400s, R300s.

4701 Ex-Richmond, Virginia 356. 4701-4718 renumbered from 4601-4618 December 1979-January 1980.

4702-4711 Ex-Greyhound 9700-9709; hydraulic transmission.

4712-4718 Ex-Hawaiian Scenic Tours 705, 709, 712, 713, 718, 717, 716.

4800-4881 Ex-Houston Rapid Transit 200s; TNJ P300s, P400s, R300s; Washington Metropolitan Area Transit Authority 3300s, 6400s.

6501-6527 Ex-San Jose City Lines 6501-6527. Coach 6512 was last TDH-4512 ever built.

6604 Ex-San Jose City Lines 6604, former Glendale City Lines 9618.

6616-6619 Ex-San Jose City Lines 6616-6619.

6621-6630 Ex-San Jose City Lines 6621-6630.

6641-6644 Ex-San Jose City Lines 6641-6644.

Index

Gathered around the luncheon table for "blue ribbon" convocation, left to right, were Dave Nelson, Dave Mitchell, Francis Guido, Jim Gibson, Bill Wulf, Willys Peck, Paul Trimble, the author, Will Whittaker, Charles Smallwood, Jim Graebner, Lorin Silleman, Randolph Brandt, Vernon J. Sappers. Seated at this end of the table were Henry Morse (who had not arrived yet) and Donald McCaleb (who was taking the picture). The other photographer, right rear, is Jim Walker of Interurban Press.   (Don McCaleb)

Blue Ribbon Committee

Seventeen dyed-in-the-wool railfans, many of them published authors, met for luncheon in Oakland November 16, 1979, to swap stories, study photographs, and share information on the Peninsular and San Jose Railroads cars that went into preparing the equipment rosters for this book. Presented here are brief biographies and photographs of this "blue ribbon committee" that also included the author and Jim Walker of Interurban Press.

Brandt, Randolph (Rudy). b. San Francisco August 1914. Residing San Francisco. Motorman, Market Street Railway 1942, Pacific Electric Railway 1944, and San Francisco Municipal Railway 1945. Retired from Muni 1975. Member Bay Area Electric Railroad Association.

Gibson, James K. b. Cincinnati, Ohio, November 29, 1911. Residing San Francisco. Assistant Director, Financial Analysis, Revenue Requirements Division, California Public Utilities Commission. Formerly with Miami Beach Railway, Cincinnati Street Railway, New Orleans Public Service, and American Transit Association. Member Electric Railroaders Association, Central Electric Railfan Association, and Motor Bus Society.

Graebner, James H. b. New Castle, Pennsylvania, August 5, 1940. Residing San Jose. Director Santa Clara County Transit District. Employee Pullman-Standard 1962-66, Westinghouse Air Brake 1966-68, W. C. Gilman and Co. 1968-71, and Denver, Colorado, Regional Transportation District 1971-75. General Manager, Rhode Island Public Transit Authority, 1975-78. Member Bay Area Electric Railroad Association, Seashore, and Central Electric Railfan Association.

Guido, Francis A. b. San Francisco December 8, 1920. Residing San Mateo, California. Graduated Stanford University 1942 and Stanford Law School 1945. Driver, San Mateo-Burlingame Transit, while in law school. Attorney in private practice, San Mateo, since 1946. Editor-publisher *The Western Railroader* since 1937. Director, Pacific Coast Chapter, R&LHS. Member Bay Area Electric Railroad Association, Northern California Railroad Club, California Nevada Railroad Historical Association, Pacific Locomotive, Southern California Chapter R&LHS, Pacific Railroad Society, and Central Coast Chapter, NRHS.

McCaleb, Donald C. b. Newport, Rhode Island, September 9, 1952. Residing Fremont, California. Graduated Chico State University 1974. Employee Westinghouse Credit Corporation, Burlingame, California. Former employee Dun and Bradstreet, San Jose. Now developing early history of Oakland-Alameda transit lines.

Mitchell, David L. b. Oakland, California, May 5, 1931. Residing Sunnyvale, California. Employee Varian Associates, Palo Alto. Interested in traction history, especially East Bay and South Bay. Member Bay Area Electric Railroad Association.

Morse, Henry E., Jr. b. San Francisco May 4, 1926. Residing Lakeport, California. Graduated Stanford University 1949 and Stanford Law School 1955. Justice court and judge, Lake County, mainly on assignment as municipal court judge in Southern California. Reared in San Jose-Santa Clara area "before subdivisions took over the orchards."

Nelson, David H. b. December 2, 1952. Residing Fremont, California. Employee Hewlett-Packard. Interested in historical research.

Peck, Willys I. b. Oakland, California, August 21, 1923. Residing Saratoga, California. Copy editor *San Jose Mercury*, self-employed attorney. Since 1963, president Saratoga Historical Foundation. Founding member Santa Clara County Historical Heritage Commission 1973-76.

Sappers, Vernon J. b. Oakland, California, August 15, 1917. Residing Oakland. Social worker, City of Oakland. Founding member Bay Area Electric Railroad Association. Charter member, California Nevada Railroad Historical Society. Descendant of three-generation railroad family representing Southern Pacific, Northwestern Pacific, Key Route, North Shore Railroad, and Oakland, Antioch, and Eastern Railway.

Smallwood, Charles. b. San Francisco October 10, 1912. Residing San Francisco. Former shop mechanic and shop foreman, Market Street Railway and San Francisco Municipal Railway. Member Electric Railroaders Association and Bay Area Electric Railroad Association.

Silleman, Lorin. b. San Francisco October 18, 1902. Residing San Francisco. Former carman, Market Street Railway, San Francisco Municipal Railway, and Pacific Electric Railway. Antique store operator, San Francisco, 1962-78.

Trimble, Paul C. b. San Francisco June 9, 1940. Residing Novato, California. Employed 21 years with San Francisco newspapers as journeyman pressman. Author *Interurban Railways of the Bay Area.* Taught course on history of Bay Area electric railways, winter quarter 1980, De Anza Junior College.

Whittaker, Wilbur C. b. Palo Alto, California, January 1, 1908. Residing Mill Valley, California. Employed 37 years by Southern Pacific. Especially interested in photographs of steam and juice. Member NorCal and Bay Area Electric Railroad Association.

Wulf, William Arie. b. San Jose January 12, 1939. Residing Los Gatos, California. Employed 19 years by Radiology Department, Santa Clara Valley Medical Center, San Jose. Los Gatos Historian. Member Saratoga Historical Foundation.